Fairness in Educational Assessment and Measurement

The importance of fairness, validity, and accessibility in assessment is 𝓏 than ever as testing expands to include more diverse populations, more complex purposes, and more sophisticated technologies. This book offers a detailed account of fairness in assessment, and illustrates the interplay between assessment and broader changes in education. In 16 chapters written by leading experts, this volume explores the philosophical, technical, and practical questions surrounding fair measurement.

Fairness in Educational Assessment and Measurement addresses issues pertaining to the construction, administration, and scoring of tests, the comparison of performance across test takers, grade levels and tests, and the uses of educational test scores. Perfect for researchers and professionals in test development, design, and administration, *Fairness in Educational Assessment and Measurement* presents a diverse array of perspectives on this topic of enduring interest.

The *NCME Applications of Educational Measurement and Assessment* series includes edited volumes designed to inform research-based applications of educational measurement and assessment. Edited by leading experts, these books are comprehensive and practical resources on the latest developments in the field.

The NCME series editorial board is comprised of Michael J. Kolen, Chair; Robert L. Brennan; Wayne Camara; Edward H. Haertel; Suzanne Lane; and Rebecca Zwick.

Neil J. Dorans is in the Center for Statistical and Psychometric Theory and Practice in the Research & Development Division at Educational Testing Service, where he has worked since 1979. Recipient of the NCME Career Award in 2010, he has been concerned with fairness for test takers for decades, developing procedures for the quantitative assessment of fairness at both the item and score levels.

Linda L. Cook, President of the NCME in 2011–2012, was employed at Educational Testing Service in Princeton, New Jersey, from 1978 until she retired in 2010. While at ETS, she served as Vice President of the Assessment Division and Executive Director of the SAT testing program. Improving the fairness of inferences made from assessments remains a major professional focus for her, particularly in the area of accessibility.

The NCME Applications of Educational Measurement and Assessment Book Series

Editorial Board:

Michael J. Kolen, University of Iowa, Editor
Robert L. Brennan, University of Iowa
Wayne Camara, ACT
Edward H. Haertel, Stanford University
Suzanne Lane, University of Pittsburgh
Rebecca Zwick, Educational Testing Service

Technology and Testing
Improving Educational and Psychological Measurement
Edited by Fritz Drasgow

Meeting the Challenges to Measurement in an Era of Accountability
Edited by Henry Braun

Fairness in Educational Assessment and Measurement
Edited by Neil J. Dorans and Linda L. Cook

Forthcoming:

Testing the Professions
Credentialing Policies and Practice
Edited by Susan Davis-Becker and Chad W. Buckendahl

Validation of Score Meaning in the Next Generation of Assessments
Edited by Kadriye Ercikan and James W. Pellegrino

Fairness in Educational Assessment and Measurement

Edited by
Neil J. Dorans and
Linda L. Cook

Routledge
Taylor & Francis Group

NEW YORK AND LONDON

First published 2016
by Routledge
711 Third Avenue, New York, NY 10017

and by Routledge
2 Park Square, Milton Park, Abingdon, Oxon, OX14 4RN

Routledge is an imprint of the Taylor & Francis Group, an informa business

Library of Congress Cataloging in Publication Data
A catalog record for this book has been requested

ISBN: 978-1-138-02618-6 (hbk)
ISBN: 978-1-138-02619-3 (pbk)
ISBN: 978-1-315-77452-7 (ebk)

Typeset in Minion Pro
by Florence Production Ltd, Stoodleigh, Devon, UK

Printed and bound in the United States of America by Publishers Graphics,
LLC on sustainably sourced paper.

To Alicia and Daniel

Contents

Illustrations

Figures

Tables

Foreword

It's not fair! How many times have we heard (or said) these three words? During my recent experience as co-chair of the committee to revise the AERA/APA/NCME Standards for Educational and Psychological Testing, I heard this or related expressions many times. As Dorans and Cook point out, in the Introduction to this volume, it is often easier to identify something that is unfair than it is to define what we mean by fairness. The goal of this volume is to provide information about fairness as it pertains to educational assessment and measurement. Even in the narrower perspective of educational assessment, there are many important topics and issues that relate to fairness.

First, fairness issues relate to how the assessment is designed, administered, and scored. In addition, fairness issues are connected to how the test scores are interpreted. All of these considerations are directly related to the validity of score interpretations. If the test does not measure what it is intended to measure (by way of content coverage or content balance as articulated in the test blueprint), then its scores will not provide a fair and appropriate representation of the intended construct. If the test is created appropriately, but the administration is flawed, then again, the scores from the test will not appropriately measure what the test taker knows and is able to do.

Careful attention to test design and development, followed by sound test administration procedures, will not ensure valid test scores if the scoring itself is flawed. It is essential that appropriate and psychometrically sound scoring procedures are in place to produce scores that will support the intended score interpretations. Finally, even when all of these prior steps are carried out in a fair and appropriate manner, valid interpretations of test scores are limited to the intended interpretations and uses of the scores. These topics form the basis for the first section of the volume devoted to *Ensuring Fairness in Test Design, Construction, Administration, and Scoring*.

Second, once the test is constructed using fairness principles, other threats to valid score interpretations and use relate to the use of educational assessments to make comparisons of test results under a variety of measurement conditions. Frequently, assessment results obtained across different tests and different modes of administration are compared. An important question is: does it matter whether the test is administered on paper or delivered on a computer? Or, does the type of computer or device impact the scores of the test taker? If so, then the mode of test delivery could possibly advantage or disadvantage some test takers and will become a fairness issue.

In educational settings, it is often desirable to compare performance of students across grades. If the testing system is not designed to support such interpretations, will fair score interpretations result? How can tests be designed and delivered for special populations, especially those with significant cognitive impairments for whom the intended construct is difficult to assess? In our ever-increasing global environment, what issues need to be considered in order to support fair assessment of individuals with diverse language backgrounds or administered in different languages? These are the topics that are the focus of the second section of the volume, titled *Assessing the Fairness of Comparisons under Divergent Measurement Conditions.*

The final section of the volume, *Perspectives on Fair Assessment,* contains a chapter on fairness in the use of derived scores, a chapter on legal considerations for test fairness, and a chapter on philosophical perspectives of fairness in educational assessment. These three chapters lead the reader to broaden his or her perspective on fairness in educational assessment by considering the many uses, and implications of the uses, of educational test scores.

The authors who have contributed to *Fairness in Educational Assessment and Measurement* are well-respected professionals in the field of educational measurement. In addition to these highly-qualified authors of the individual chapters, each major section of the volume ends with a commentary by another highly-respected professional in the field. The commentaries following each section present the commentator's thoughts about the overall theme of the section and also provide a critical perspective on the individual contributions to the section.

This volume on *Fairness in Educational Assessment and Measurement,* sponsored by the National Council on Measurement in Education (NCME), provides a thorough and comprehensive treatment of critical issues related to the topic. This volume presents educational measurement professionals with details about features of educational testing that support fair assessment practices and provide test users and policymakers with needed information about how testing practices can lead to fair and appropriate test score interpretations for their intended uses.

One of the NCME series on measurement in education, this volume is a valuable resource that will provide guidance to all those who are interested in the development of fair and valid interpretations of educational test scores.

Barbara Plake
1992 NCME President
2007 NCME Career Contributions Award Recipient

Acknowledgments

This volume benefitted greatly from the financial support of the Educational Testing Service (ETS), and the expertise of ETS staff. Support was provided in several ways, including the establishment of a volume-specific site for Scholar One that was dedicated to this volume and set up by Kimberly Fryer. That site was managed by Elizabeth Brophy, who took care of virtually all of the administrative matters associated with this volume.

Reviews play a major role in the production of a volume such as this one. In addition to the editors who reviewed every chapter at least once, experts willingly provided feedback to authors and improved chapters resulted.

For the chapters in the section entitled *Ensuring Fairness in Test Design, Construction, Administration and Scoring*, expert reviews from outside ETS were provided by Allan Cohen of the University of Georgia, Kadriye Ercikan of the University of British Columbia, John Fremer of Caveon Test Security, David Frisbee of the University of Iowa, Anne Corrine Huggins-Manley of the University of Florida, and Nancy Petersen of ACT. In addition, expert reviews were provided by the following ETS staff members: Yi Du, Mary Pitoniak, Daniel Lapinski, and Gautam Puhan.

For the chapters in the section entitled *Assessing the Fairness of Comparisons under Divergent Measurement Conditions*, expert reviews from outside ETS were provided by Derek Briggs of the University of Colorado, Kadriye Ercikan of the University of British Columbia, Michael Kolen of the University of Iowa, Mary Pommerich of the Defense Manpower Data Center, Richard Sawyer of ACT, Willy Solano-Flores of the University of Colorado, and Martha Thurlow of the University of Minnesota. In addition, expert reviews were provided by the following ETS staff members: Heather Buzick, Daniel McCaffrey, Jonathon Weeks, and Mikyung Wolf.

For the chapters in the section entitled *Perspectives on Fair Assessment*, expert reviews from outside ETS were provided by Robert Brennan of the University of Iowa, Wayne Camara of ACT, William Mehrens of Michigan State University, Michelle Moses of the University of Colorado, and Barbara Plake of the University of Nebraska. In addition, expert reviews were provided by the following ETS staff members: Shelby Haberman, Eric Hansen, Stephen Lazer, J. R. Lockwood, Michael Kane, Robert Mislevy, Michael Zieky, and Rebecca Zwick.

Reviews for the first and last chapters were made by ETS staff members: Shelby Haberman, William Monaghan, Gautam Puhan, Cathy Wendler, and Rebecca Zwick.

In addition, the editors acknowledge contributions by Gerunda Hughes of Howard University, Suzanne Lane of the University of Pittsburgh, Kyndra Middleton of Howard University, Paul Sackett of the University of Minnesota, and Elizabeth Stone of ETS.

Contributors

Susan M. Case, Director of Testing Emeritus, National Conference of Bar Examiners, 302 South Bedford Street, Madison, WI 53703-3622

Katherine E. Castellano, Educational Testing Service, 90 New Montgomery Street, Suite 1500, San Francisco, CA 94105

Linda L. Cook, Educational Testing Service, 660 Rosedale Road, Princeton, NJ 08541

Neil J. Dorans, Educational Testing Service, 660 Rosedale Road, Princeton, NJ 08541

Edward Haertel, Professor, Emeritus Stanford University, School of Education, 485 Lasuen Mall, Stanford, CA 94305

Andrew Ho, Harvard Graduate School of Education, 455 Gutman Library, 6 Appian Way, Cambridge, MA 02138

Michael J. Kolen, University of Iowa, 224B1 Linquist Center, Iowa City, IA 52242

Jinghua Liu, Secondary School Admission Test Board, 862 County Rd 518, Skillman, NJ 08543

Randall D. Penfield, University of North Carolina, Greensboro, 1000 Spring Garden Street, Greensboro, North Carolina 27402

S. E. Phillips, Mesa, AZ 85205

Barbara Plake, Professor Emeritus, University of Nebraska—Lincoln, PO Box 4658, Buena Vista, CO 81211

Mary Pommerich, Defense Manpower Data Center, 400 Gigling Road, Seaside CA 93955

Sonya Powers, Pearson, 400 Center Ridge Drive, Austin, TX 78753

Joseph A. Rios, Educational Testing Service, 660 Rosedale Road, Princeton, NJ 08541

Sandip Sinharay, Pacific Metrics Corporation, 1 Lower Ragsdale Dr #150, Monterey, CA 93940

Stephen G. Sireci, University of Massachusetts, 156 Hills South, Amherst, MA 01003

Elizabeth A. Stone, Educational Testing Service, 660 Rosedale Road, Princeton, NJ 08541

David Thissen, L. L. Thurstone Psychometric Laboratory, CB #3270, Davie Hall, University of North Carolina, Chapel Hill, NC 27599-3270

James A. Wollack, University of Wisconsin, Madison, 1025 West Johns Street, Madison, WI 53706

Frank C. Worrell, Cognition and Development, Graduate School of Education, University of California, Berkeley, 4511 Tolman Hall, Berkeley, CA 94720-1670

Michael J. Zieky, Educational Testing Service, 660 Rosedale Road, Princeton, NJ 08541

Rebecca Zwick, Educational Testing Service and University of California, Santa Barbara, 2709 Macadamia Lane, Santa Barbara CA 93108

1 Introduction

Neil J. Dorans and Linda L. Cook[1]

Introduction

Fairness, a concept familiar to most readers, can mean different things to different people. The concept of fairness has a long history, with a definition that has evolved over time. Legal prescriptions and proscriptions of fairness have also changed with time. When Justice Potter Stewart first joined the Supreme Court in 1958, he said, "fairness is what justice really is" (National Affairs: The Young Justice, 1958). Potter linked fairness with justice. But what is fairness? It is probably easier to detect unfairness when we see it than it is to define fairness.

From an historical perspective using a 21st century vantage point, several practices that were accepted during the early part of the 20th century would be judged unfair by present standards. At the start of the 20th century, colonialism, was rampant, a byproduct of the imperialism of the late 19th century. In addition, at the start of the 20th century, racism was legally sanctioned in many parts of the United States,[2] and women were not allowed to vote in national elections or hold elective national office. The end of World War II and the decades immediately following it saw the beginning of extensive decolonization, the passage of the United Nations Declaration of Human Rights, and the codification of laws and practices in the United States that led to equal rights and equal protection for U.S. citizens.

Fairness touches many aspects of human existence. Young children recognize fair and unfair play. Laws and regulations exist to ensure fair play in sports, fair trade in economics, fair allocation of resources, fair access to education, housing, and employment.

This volume examines fairness in the context of educational assessment and measurement. Our focus is primarily on educational assessment in the United States, and it is written from that perspective. We begin by journeying back in time to the first third of the 20th century.

A Testing Example from the Early 20th Century

Eugenics was a term attributed to the British polymath Sir Francis Galton, who, among other things, made important contributions to psychometrics and statistics. Galton (1883), who introduced the concepts of standard deviation and correlation to the field of statistics, concluded in *Inquiries into Human Faculty and Its Development* that superior social position was due to a superior genetic makeup, essentially a causal inference based on analyses of observational data from a variety of biographical sources.

The social movement of eugenics played a significant role in the history and culture of early 20th century United States and other countries. Eugenics was widely accepted.

It was supported by the influential and respected, including British statesman Winston Churchill, President Theodore Roosevelt, Margaret Sanger, proponent of birth control rights for women, and playwright George Bernard Shaw, among many others (Kelves, 1985). Applied eugenic practices included genetic screening, forced birth control, compulsory sterilization, forced abortions, marriage restrictions, and segregation. The most infamous example of applied eugenics was engineered by Adolf Hitler, who cited eugenic theories as a justification for Aryan superiority and the genocide of those he considered to be defectives and racially inferior.

Toward the end of World War I, tests were developed to systematically and objectively evaluate those recruited by the U.S. military. These tests were devised by the Committee on the Classification of Personnel in the Army, established in 1917. Its membership included the psychologists and early psychometricians E. L. Thorndike, Lewis Terman, Robert Yerkes, L. L. Thurstone, and Truman Kelley. By the end of 1918, the Army had tested over 1.7 million men using the "Alpha" and "Beta" Army tests.

The Army Alpha test measured verbal ability, numerical ability, ability to follow directions, and knowledge of information, and was administered in English. Soldiers who were illiterate or who were not sufficiently proficient in English would take the Army Beta test. It was more complex to administer and score than the Army Alpha test. The Army Beta test used demonstration charts and pantomime to convey instructions to the persons being tested. The performance tasks on the Army Beta test used geometrical designs, mutilated or incomplete pictures, e.g. a table with a leg missing, a baby carriage with no handle, and other types of test questions that required different principles in its construction and response evaluation than those used on the Army Alpha test. Consequently, scores on the two tests did not measure the same thing and fair comparisons of the scores could not be made. For sample items from both tests, see http://official-asvab.com/armysamples_coun.htm. Yoakum and Yerkes (1920) gave a detailed description of both instruments.

Carl Brigham (1923) wrote a book based on the Army Alpha and Beta test data, *A Study of American Intelligence*. Several of the tables in the book report results based on a "combination scale" on which Alpha and Beta scores and Stanford Binet scores were all expressed. Based on these results, he concluded that Blacks, Jews, Mediterraneans, and Alpines were inherently intellectually inferior to Nordics.[3]

Table 33 of Brigham (1923) contains estimates of the proportions of the three types of white "blood" in each European country. According to Table 35 of Brigham (1923), from 1840 to 1890, immigrants of Nordic blood accounted for at least 40% of the immigrants to the United States. Between 1890 and 1920, the Alpine race supplanted the Nordic race. For those in the eugenics movement who were concerned about dilution of the gene pool, the shift away from Nordics to other groups was a cause for alarm.

By today's standards, Brigham's book would be considered racist. In the 1920s, it was widely, though not universally, accepted as an accurate representation (Cole and Zieky, 2001). During that time, Congress passed the Immigration Act of 1924, a federal law that limited the annual number of immigrants who could be admitted from any country to 2% of the number of people from that country who were already living in the United States in 1890. The law restricted the flow of Southern and Eastern Europeans and prohibited the immigration of Middle Easterners, East Asians, and Indians. The purpose of the law was to preserve the homogeneity of the American people.

Brigham went on to develop the Scholastic Aptitude Test (SAT) for the College Board in 1926. Based on his analyses of early SAT data, he concluded that test scores may not be a function of unitary dimensions, and that they were influenced by cultural factors that were not rooted in genetics, such as familiarity with the language of the test. These analyses are summarized in the book *A Study of Error* (Brigham, 1932).

Prior to publication of that book, Brigham (1930) wrote an article in *Psychological Review* in which he recanted his earlier work. The abstract of that article states:

> In the light of recent investigations showing that test scores may not represent unitary things, the author criticizes attempts to establish racial differences and national differences with existing tests, in which mixture of verbal, quantitative, and spatial intelligence factors and dependence on vernacular destroy the significance of the scores. The author includes his own comparative racial study in this criticism.
>
> (p. 158)

One technical concern related to Brigham's research was the comparability of scores achieved on the Alpha and Beta versions of the Army test. A special sample of military personnel was tested with both, and these data were used to put the Alpha and Beta on a common seven-point scale (A, B, C+, C, C–, D, D–). Because these two tests were quite different in terms of format and questions asked, and measured different constructs, scores from these tests could not be treated as if they were interchangeable. When interpreting the results of his research, Brigham (1923) had treated scale alignments of the Army Alpha and Beta tests as if they produced interchangeable scores. By 1930, he realized that was a mistake. He doubted whether the subcomponents of the Alpha test measured a unitary construct and acknowledged the effects of culture, particularly knowledge of the language of the test.

The Emergence of the Civil Rights Movement after World War II

World War II changed much in American society, including race relations and the role of women in the workforce. During World War II, President Franklin Roosevelt issued an executive order in June 1941 in response to complaints about discrimination at home against Black Americans, who constituted about 10% of the population. This order directed that Black workers be accepted into job-training programs in defense plants, and forbade discrimination by defense contractors. Still, the military remained segregated until July 1948 when President Harry Truman issued an executive order ordering full integration of the armed services. Full integration was not achieved until the end of the Korean War.

Integration also occurred in the national pastime, baseball, after World War II. On April 15, 1947, Jackie Robinson, a college graduate and military veteran who had been groomed by Brooklyn Dodgers general manager Branch Rickey to break the color line that kept gifted Black athletes from pursuing their living in baseball's major leagues, broke that barrier. Robinson encountered widespread racism, including legally sanctioned segregation in the South, and vicious abuse including death threats simply because of his race. Robinson maintained his composure and succeeded in breaking the color line, a major symbolic step away from segregation.

During World War II, Robinson was arrested for failing to go to the back of an unsegregated Army bus, as was required. He was court-martialed and eventually acquitted. The mistreatment he experienced prepared him for the abuse that he would experience integrating baseball.

A quiet seamstress, Rosa Parks, refused to go to the back of a bus in Montgomery, Alabama, in 1955. Her stoic defiance of the law landed her in jail and is considered a pivotal moment in American history. In the first of his trilogy, *America in the King Years*, Taylor Branch (1988) reports that the Montgomery boycott, organized by Martin Luther King in response to Rosa Parks' arrest, marked Martin Luther King's emergence as a leader of the Civil Rights movement. The nonviolent protest practiced by King and his associates often met with resistance, and in some cases deadly force. Despite the blood that was shed by some of its members, the Civil Rights movement persisted and served as a catalyst for change in America in the 1960s. In 1964, King received the Nobel Peace Prize in recognition of his leadership. Those interested in the Civil Rights movement in the 1950s and 1960s should consult the three-volume work by Branch (1988, 1998, 2006).

The Zenith of the Civil Rights Movement and its Aftermath

The Civil Rights movement reached its peak in the mid-1960s, with the passage of the Civil Rights Act of 1965, the Voting Rights Act of 1966, and the Civil Rights Act of 1968, which was passed shortly after King's assassination in Memphis, Tennessee. As documented in the fourth volume of Robert Caro's *The Years of Lyndon Johnson* (Caro, 2012), President Lyndon Johnson's commitment to civil rights, his empathy for the poor, and his political acumen helped convert the momentum created by the Civil Rights movement into law.

While these laws made discrimination on the basis of color, creed, and gender illegal and removed barriers to voting and access to housing, they did not address the long-standing historical consequences of legal discrimination and slavery. In 1961, President John Kennedy issued an executive order mandating that projects financed with federal funds take what was called affirmative action to ensure that hiring and employment practices are free of racial bias. Affirmative action was synonymous with anti-discrimination. The meaning of affirmative action changed with executive orders issued in 1965 by President Johnson that attempted to redress the consequences of past discrimination. These efforts were later expanded by President Richard Nixon, during his first term as president, with the Philadelphia Plan, which required government contractors to hire minorities.

These attempts to remedy past discrimination met with much opposition, as noted by Hartigan and Wigdor (1989), who summarize the arguments for and against the practice of preferential treatment circa 1985. That volume examines a since-abandoned experimental practice by the U.S. Employment Service of the Department of Labor that represented an extreme form of affirmative action, namely the use of within-group percentiles by race as measures of proficiency on the General Aptitude Test Battery. This practice, which began during the early years of President Ronald Reagan's administration, was halted at the request of the U.S. Justice Department in 1986 on the grounds that it was an unlawful violation of an applicant's right to be free from racial discrimination, a right guaranteed under the Civil Rights Act of 1965.

Within-group norming is still used today, albeit the norming is not conducted by racial group. In 1997, the state of Texas, after other forms of affirmative action were successfully challenged, passed a rule that guaranteed admissions, to any public university, to students who had a high school GPA in the top 10% of their high school graduating class. To date, this rule has not been successfully challenged. As discussed in the Zwick and Dorans chapter in this volume, the National Merit Scholarship Program uses within-group norming by state to identify semifinalists for their scholarship competition.

To summarize, in the 1920s, there was a widespread use of intelligence tests that were developed during World War I. Many users of these tests believed that the test results were valid and buttressed eugenic claims, as illustrated in Chapters 4 and 5 of Kelves (1985). By the early 1980s, concerns about the legacy of over two centuries of racial discrimination had led to within-group norming. This use of test scores in itself violated a law that grew out the Civil Rights movement of the mid-20th century.

The Civil Rights movement was in the vanguard of other rights movements, such as women's rights, the rights of Spanish-speaking and Asian minorities, and the rights of individuals with disabilities. In time, test takers as a group were given the right to see their scored exams and question the answer key. These other rights movements followed the path that was forged by the travail of trailblazers of the Civil Rights movement.

As indicated in this chapter, the definition of fairness varies over time. Segregation gave way to integration, and affirmative action was instituted to address the consequences of that formal discrimination, only to be challenged as discriminatory itself. We have also shown how shifts in attitudes about testing reflect shifts in how society perceives difference in test scores, their antecedents, and the consequence of their use.

This brief selective summary of the interplay between testing and society has implications for the testing of today and tomorrow.[4] Comparisons are often made of test takers who take tests under different conditions (perhaps even different languages). There are social and political movements today that cite test scores to promote their cause and that enjoy the support of many prominent people. For example, test scores on measures of educational achievement are used to assess a teacher's effectiveness. A eugenicist from 100 years ago would probably scoff at this idea, stating that the students' performance is more likely to be a function of their genes than the effectiveness of the teacher. Test scores are cited by some as justifications for the superiority or inferiority of certain groups. Test scores are viewed by others as reflections of sources of societal injustices.

This Volume

Fairness is a major concern for society. As noted in the opening paragraph, it is probably easier to detect unfairness than it is to define fairness. The preceding material on the Civil Rights movement contained multiple examples of unfairness. This book focuses on a restricted aspect of fairness, namely as it pertains to education assessment and measurement. Some chapters try to identify practices and policies that lead to fair measurement and assessment. Other chapters describe procedures for detecting unfairness. As in the case of scientific theories, it is easier to devise procedures for detecting unfairness than it is to ensure that the decisions made using test scores are fair.

This volume has three major parts. Each part contains multiple chapters authored by experts, and concludes with a commentary by an expert who critiques and synthesizes the chapters in the section. The three sections are: Ensuring Fairness in Test Design, Construction, Administration and Scoring; Assessing the Fairness of Comparisons under Divergent Measurement Conditions; and Perspectives on Fair Assessment. The final chapter in the book is written by the editors. It discusses societal changes that have occurred over the last half-century that may affect how the nature of fairness assessment in the future.

Notes

1. The views expressed are those of the authors and not necessarily those of the Educational Testing Service.
2. Jim Crow laws, which were enacted in many southern states in the late 1800s, mandated the segregation of public schools, public places, and public transportation, and the segregation of restrooms, restaurants, and drinking fountains.
3. Ripley (1899), an American economist, divided Europeans into three main subcategories: Teutonic or Nordic Alpine and Mediterranean. According to Ripley, the "Teutonic race" resided in Scandinavia, north Germany, the Baltic states and East Prussia, north Poland, north Russia, Britain, Ireland, and parts of Central Europe. The Alpine race was predominant in Central/Southern/Eastern Europe and parts of Western/Central Asia. The Mediterranean race was said to be prevalent in Southern Europe (including Southern France), Latin America, parts of Eastern Europe (including Romania), North Africa, the Horn of Africa, Western Asia, Central Asia and South Asia, and in certain parts of the British Isles and Germany.
4. This brief review of the 20th century is far from exhaustive. For a more extensive consideration of this interplay between testing and society, consult Camilli (2006).

References

Branch, T. (1988). *Parting the waters: America in the King years 1954–1963*. New York: Simon & Schuster.

Branch, T. (1998). *Pillar of fire: America in the King years 1963–1965*. New York: Simon & Schuster.

Branch, T. (2006). *At Canaan's edge: America in the King years 1965–1968*. New York: Simon & Schuster.

Brigham, C. C. (1923). *A study of American intelligence*. Princeton, NJ: Princeton University Press.

Brigham, C. C. (1930). Intelligence tests of immigrant groups. *Psychological Review, 37*, 158–165.

Brigham, C. C. (1932). *A study of error: A summary and evaluation of methods used in six years of study of the Scholastic Aptitude Test of the College Entrance Examination Board*. New York: College Entrance Examination Board.

Camilli, G. (2006). Test fairness. In R. L. Brennan (Ed.), *Educational measurement* (4th ed., pp. 221–256). Westport, CT: American Council on Education/Praeger.

Caro, R. A. (2012). *The passage of power: The years of Lyndon Johnson*. New York: Alfred A. Knopf.

Cole, N. S., & Zieky, M. J. (2001). The new faces of fairness. *Journal of Educational Measurement, 38*, 369–382.

Galton, F. (1883). *Inquiries into human faculty and its development*. London: J. M. Dent.

Hartigan, J. A., & Wigdor, A. K. (Eds.) (1989). *Fairness in employment testing: Validity generalization, minority issues, and the General Aptitude Test Battery*. Washington, DC: National Academy Press.

Kelves, D. J. (1985). *In the name of eugenics: Genetics and the uses of human heredity*. Berkeley, CA: University of California Press.

National Affairs: The Young Justice. (1958, October 20). *Time*, p. 24.

Ripley, W. Z. (1899). *The races of Europe: A sociological study*. New York: D. Appleton.

Yoakum, C. S., & Yerkes, R. M. (1920). *Army mental tests*. New York: Henry Holt.

Part I

Ensuring Fairness in Test Design, Construction, Administration, and Scoring

Part 1 of the book contains chapters that examine existing strategies for designing, developing, and administering fair assessments. It also includes chapters that describe methods for detecting unfairness issues in scoring assessments and in the fair use of scores. These unfairness detection methods are designed to be used where the conditions of measurement permit direct comparisons of test takers.

In "Fairness in Test Design and Development," Zieky treats fairness as an aspect of validity in which an attempt is made to prevent sources of construct-irrelevant variance from contributing to variation in test scores. He details the procedures used and decisions to be made during test design, item writing, test assembly, and test review. Included is a summary of fairness review guidelines. He also describes the rules used in item analysis, test analysis, and scoring that help ensure fairness for various groups of test takers.

Wollack and Case, in their chapter "Maintaining Fairness through Test Administration," describe administrative practices that have evolved to foster fairness and ultimately score validity before, during, and after the administration of a test. Pre-administration considerations include establishing a comfortable and secure testing environment, fair and efficient check-in procedures, and proper test preparation advice. During the administration, important factors include proctoring, and ensuring security during testing and during breaks. Post-administration activities include securing testing materials and orderly dismissal of test takers.

Penfield, in "Fairness in Test Scoring," focuses on the issue of fairness in the context of tests that include traditional multiple-choice questions and questions that require human rater scoring or automated machine (computer) scoring. The chapter provides an overview on how to evaluate fairness in test scoring. The first part of the chapter is concerned with the evaluation of differential item functioning (DIF) for objectively scored multiple-choice items. The second part focuses on evaluating fairness for constructed-response items that are scored by humans. The third part suggests ways to gather evidence pertaining to the fairness of automated algorithms for scoring constructed responses.

In the chapter "Fairness in Score Interpretation," Liu and Dorans examine the fairness of test score interpretation from three perspectives: the degree to which scores on different versions of the same test are related in the same way across subpopulations, the degree to which test scores that purport to measure the same thing do in fact measure the same thing in the same way across subpopulations, and the invariance of the prediction of external criteria from test scores. The chapter discusses score equity assessment that uses the subpopulation invariance requirement of equating to assess whether equating relationships among multiple measures hold up across subpopulations. Other topics discussed in the chapter are factorial invariance, which refers to the degree to which the factorial composition of a test is the same across different subpopulations, and differential prediction, which refers to differences in predicted scores for different subpopulations.

The critique and synthesis by Sinharay concludes this section on fairness considerations related to test scoring, score interpretation, and score use.

2 Fairness in Test Design and Development

Michael J. Zieky[1]

The purpose of this chapter is to describe how to design and develop fair tests. Because the focus of the chapter is on fairness concerns, readers who are unfamiliar with the general rudiments of test design and development would benefit from the overviews of the process in such sources as Downing (2006), Kingston, Scheuring, and Kramer (2013), or Schmeiser and Welch (2006).

Overview

The chapter begins with a brief discussion of some of the meanings of fairness in testing and recommends that test designers and developers use a definition of fairness linked to validity. Next, the chapter examines the sources of score variance and how they affect fairness. The chapter makes the point that construct-relevant sources of score variance allow valid and fair inferences about test takers. Construct-irrelevant sources of score variance lead to unfair inferences if the irrelevant variance is associated with group membership.

The chapter then discusses how to help ensure fairness in the major phases of the assessment development process, including:

- designing tests;
- writing and reviewing items (with a discussion of fairness guidelines);
- assembling and reviewing tests;
- developing scoring rules; and
- analyzing items and tests.

In the discussion of each phase, the chapter describes the steps that should be taken to decrease the likelihood that test scores will be affected by construct-irrelevant sources of score variance associated with unfair group differences.

Meanings of Fairness

There are many definitions of fairness in testing, but there is no universally accepted definition (American Educational Research Association, American Psychological Association, & National Council on Measurement in Education, 2014, p. 49). Some of the few areas of agreement and some of the many areas of disagreement about fairness in testing are described below, and the view of fairness of most use to test developers is explained. (For a discussion of the many different ways in which fairness has been viewed, see Zwick and Dorans, this volume, Chapter 14.)

Some Useful Vocabulary

The discussion of fairness in this chapter requires knowledge of the terms *validity*, *construct*, and *score variance*.

- *Validity* is the most comprehensive and important indicator of test quality. Messick (1989, p. 13) defined validity as "an integrated evaluative judgment of the degree to which empirical evidence and theoretical rationales support the *adequacy* and *appropriateness* of *inferences* and *actions* based on test scores" (emphasis in original). Kane (2013) focused his discussion of validity on the extent to which the claims made about test takers on the basis of their scores are plausible and backed by logical and empirical evidence. (For more information about validity, see Kane, 2006; Sireci & Sukin, 2013.)
- A *construct* is the set of related knowledge, skills, or other attributes (KSAs) that a test is intended to measure. Examples of constructs are agility, the manual skills required in entry-level dentistry, anxiety, the knowledge taught in typical high school chemistry classes, intelligence, introversion, logical reasoning, quantitative ability, and reading comprehension. Any KSAs that are part of the construct to be measured are referred to as *construct-relevant*. Any KSAs that are not part of the construct are referred to as *construct-irrelevant*. For example, verbal ability is construct-irrelevant in a mathematics test, but construct-relevant in a reading test.
- *Score variance* is a term for the differences among a set of scores. If all test takers receive identical scores, the variance is zero. The further away the scores are from the mean score, the greater the variance will be. (Knowledge of the statistical meaning of variance is not required for this chapter.) A source or cause of score variance is anything that affects differences among scores, such as a characteristic of the test taker (e.g., good or poor reading comprehension), an aspect of the test (e.g., use of constructed-response items or multiple-choice items), or a factor in the environment (e.g., a quiet or a noisy testing site). A source of score variance may be either construct-relevant or construct-irrelevant.

Impartiality

There is agreement that fairness requires treating all test takers respectfully and impartially throughout the testing process. (See Wollack & Case, this volume, Chapter 3, for a discussion of the administrative aspects of fairness in testing.) All test takers should be given an equal chance for a validly interpreted test score, without regard to group membership. Providing such a chance sometimes requires providing accommodations to "level the playing field" for test takers with construct-irrelevant characteristics that could distort their test results. For example, if vision is construct-irrelevant, test takers who are blind should have access to an appropriate accommodation (e.g., voiced or Brailled testing materials). (See Cook and Stone, this volume, Chapter 9, for a discussion of accommodations for test takers with disabilities and test takers who are English language learners.[2])

Group Score Differences

Many members of the general public believe that if a test is harder for members of group X than for members of group Y, the test is unfair for members of group X. Psycho-metricians, however, do not accept that definition. Score differences among groups of test takers should not be overlooked, but the differences are not proof that the test is unfair. As Cole and Zieky have noted, "If the members of the measurement community currently agree on any aspect of fairness, it is that score differences alone are not proof of bias" (2001, p. 375).

Differences in Prediction and Selection

Psychometricians have published various definitions of fairness based on the results of using tests to predict performance or on the outcomes of using test scores to make admissions or hiring decisions. (For examples of such definitions of fairness, see, e.g., Cleary, 1968; Cole, 1973; Darlington, 1971; Linn, 1973; Liu & Dorans, this volume, Chapter 5; Petersen & Novick, 1976; Thorndike, 1971.) Some of the definitions are mutually contradictory. For example, Cleary (1968) accepts a test as fair if it neither under-predicts nor over-predicts the criterion for any of the groups being compared. According to Darlington (1971), however, fairness may involve over-prediction of criterion scores for members of underrepresented groups to increase the selection of members of such groups. In any case, the definitions of fairness based on prediction or selection are useless for informing the process of test design and development because they apply only to completed tests for which data on predicted criteria or on the outcomes of selection have already been collected.

Fairness Based on Validity

As stated in the *ETS Standards for Quality and Fairness* (Education Testing Service, 2014, p. 19), "The most useful definition of fairness for test developers is the extent to which the inferences made on the basis of test scores are valid for different groups of test takers." Shepard (1987, p. 179) defined bias as "invalidity." Because validity is so closely associated with fairness, an increase in one will result in an increase in the other, and a decrease in one will result in a decrease in the other.

Groups of Concern for Fairness

Though theoretically ideal to do so, it is literally impossible to consider fairness separately for every group of test takers during the test design and development process. Therefore, test developers concerned with fairness have generally focused on the groups that have been, or are currently, the targets of discrimination. In the United States, that includes groups such as women; people who are physically or mentally disabled; people who are Asian, Black, Hispanic, or Native American; people who are gay or lesbian; people who are poor; and people who are English language learners. Test developers in other countries are likely to have differences in the groups of concern for fairness. For example, test developers in Chile are not likely to consider people who speak Spanish rather than English a group of particular concern for fairness.

Score Variance

The sources of the variance in scores determine whether or not the scores support valid and fair inferences, actions, and claims. It has long been known that score variance can be partitioned and classified in various ways (Cronbach, 1949). With respect to fairness, it is possible to partition the total score variance into the variance that leads to appropriate inferences about test takers (henceforth, construct-relevant or valid variance) and the variance that leads to inappropriate inferences about test takers (henceforth, construct-irrelevant or invalid variance). Investigating the sources of score variance helps test designers and developers decide on the actions to take to improve the fairness of tests because a source of invalid variance that affects some group(s) more than others is a cause of unfairness.

Lasting and General Sources

Score variance has many sources. Some sources of score variance are characteristic of test takers for significant periods of time and will influence all forms of a test that they take during that time. Such sources include the test taker's:

- construct-relevant KSAs;
- construct-irrelevant KSAs nevertheless required to answer items correctly;
- experience with and comfort in taking tests;
- physical abilities to perceive the test items and to register responses to the items;
- typical processing and response speeds;
- ability to concentrate for the amount of time required to complete the test; and
- general attitudes, feelings, beliefs, motivation, and interests.

Temporary and Specific Sources

Some sources of score variance are specific to a particular test administration date or site, or to a particular test form such as the test taker's:

- comfort with the conditions at the test administration site;
- reactions to disruptions during the test administration;
- familiarity with the types of items (e.g., sentence completion, vocabulary in context) used in the administered form of the test;
- prior knowledge of specific stimuli or specific items in the administered form of the test;
- anxiety, fatigue, frustration, anger, injury, upset, or illness at time of testing;
- temporary failure to recall a fact or a step in a procedure;
- careless errors in responding to an item;
- luck in getting a lenient or severe marker for a constructed-response item; and
- luck in guessing correctly or incorrectly on a multiple-choice item.

Valid Variance, Random Variance, and Unfair Variance

It is crucial for test developers and designers to remain aware of the relationships among sources of score variance, validity, and fairness:

- The only sources of score variance that contribute positively to validity and fairness are differences in the construct-relevant KSAs of the test takers.
- All other sources of score variance diminish validity, and may or may not diminish fairness.
- Construct-irrelevant sources of score variance associated with group membership diminish validity and also diminish fairness.

- Random sources of score variance (e.g., luck in guessing an answer) diminish validity, but do not diminish fairness because the effects of random variation are necessarily evenly distributed across groups.

(For a discussion of sources of construct-irrelevant variance, see Haladyna & Downing, 2004.)

The relationships among sources of variance, fairness, and validity are summarized in Table 2.1.

Table 2.1 Relationships among Sources of Variance, Fairness, and Validity

	Unfair	*Fair*
Valid		Construct-relevant variance
Invalid	Construct-irrelevant variance related to group membership	Randomly distributed construct-irrelevant variance

As shown in Table 2.1, sources of construct-relevant variance are both valid and fair. An invalid source of score variance may or may not be a source of unfairness depending on whether it is randomly distributed across groups, or if it is correlated with group membership. For example, some score variance in a constructed-response test scored by human beings is caused by the severity or lenience of the scorer of a test taker's response. Good test scoring practices (briefly explained in a later section of this chapter) can reduce the invalid variance, but are not likely to reduce it to zero. As long as the severity of scorers is randomly distributed with respect to groups of test takers, the invalid variance caused by differences in the severity of scorers is fair. If, however, one group of test takers is more likely to be scored severely than is another group of test takers, the source of invalid variance is also a source of unfair variance.

Goal of Test Designers and Developers

The primary goal of test designers and developers can be thought of as increasing the proportion of desired, construct-relevant (valid and fair) score variance and decreasing the proportion of undesired, construct-irrelevant (invalid and potentially unfair) score variance. Note that increasing construct-relevant variance may sometimes increase the mean score differences between groups. Score differences are, however, not an indicator of unfairness. When construct-irrelevant score variance cannot be reduced to insignificant amounts, fairness requires ensuring, to the extent possible, that the effects of the invalid variance are randomly distributed among groups. The following discussions of the major steps in the test design and development process describe how to help ensure that undesired sources of score variance are minimized and are not unfairly associated with group membership.

Fairness in Test Design

Every test is a compromise among competing demands. For example, the test length selected by test designers is the result of the need to balance two desirable goals: the greater reliability and enhanced content coverage of longer tests, and the lower costs and reduced administration time of shorter tests. Choices made at the test design stage can influence how various sources of score variance will affect test scores. Test designers strive to maximize the proportion of the score variance that leads to valid inferences about test takers. Within that goal, it is important that fairness concerns be among the demands attended to by test designers as they decide on the "best" compromises. For example, if English language skills are not part of the KSAs to be measured, the decisions about the appropriate balance between free-response and selected response items should take into account the increased difficulty of free-response items for English language learners and for test takers with language-related disabilities.

Choices among Valid Content

Valid variance is necessarily fair, but different content may be equally valid and yet have dissimilar effects on group differences (Willingham & Cole, 1997). Every test is only a sample from some universe of content to be measured. Except in trivial instances (e.g., decoding initial consonants), it is impossible to list all members of the universe and systematically or randomly sample the content to be included in a particular form of a test. Therefore, the exact content to be measured is almost always a matter of judgment. Knowledge of resulting group score differences should enter into judgments about the content to be selected, if validity can be maintained.

For example, there has long been evidence that female test takers tend to be less facile at spatial visualization than are male test takers (Voyer, Voyer, & Bryden, 1995). If items without a large spatial visualization component are judged to meet the purpose of the test as well as items with such a component, then items that depend greatly on spatial skills should be minimized in the test design.

Evidence-Centered Design

Evidence-centered design (ECD) is a family of modern test development practices based on evidentiary reasoning. ECD includes procedures that help test designers decide what to measure and how best to measure it. ECD also includes procedures that help test developers link the claims to be made about test takers to the evidence revealed by their performances on tasks in a test. An important means of increasing the validity and fairness of a test is the meticulous avoidance of construct-irrelevant variance. Doing so requires a clear definition of the construct and a clear definition of the intended population of test takers, both of which ECD helps to provide. ECD helps test designers avoid invalid and unfair sources of variance because ECD "ensures that the way in which evidence is gathered and interpreted bears on the underlying knowledge and purposes the assessment is intended to address" (Mislevy, Steinberg, & Almond, 1999, p. 1). Because ECD helps to ensure the validity of the inferences made about test takers, it necessarily helps to ensure fairness. (For more information about ECD, see Mislevy, Almond, & Lukas, 2003; Mislevy & Riconscente, 2005.)

Universal Design

Concerns about test takers with disabilities should also affect the decisions made by test designers. Universal design (UD) helps focus test designers' efforts on fairness for people with disabilities and results in better tests for all test takers (National Center on Educational Outcomes, 2002; Thompson, Johnstone, & Thurlow, 2002). One of the goals of test designers should be to measure the construct-relevant KSAs and not the irrelevant effects of a test taker's disability. The principles of UD help test designers meet that goal. It is necessary to be very clear about all of the KSAs required to take the test in its general form and all of the KSAs the test is intended to measure. KSAs required to take the test that are not the intended targets of measurement are potential sources of construct-irrelevant, invalid variance. For example, if the ability to read a small font is required to take the test, but is not construct-relevant, then the small font is a potential source of invalid variance. If the invalid variance has unequal effects on the scores of people with visual disabilities, it is unfair and should be eliminated to the extent possible by using an easily legible font.

UD seeks to remove the irrelevant sources of variance that inordinately affect people with disabilities by requiring that, for example:

- directions for taking the test are clear and concise;
- test book pages or computer displays are easily legible;
- maps, diagrams, or other visual materials are amenable to verbal descriptions or tactile representations;
- items are amenable to accommodations such as large type or increased contrast;
- language in items is no more difficult than necessary; and
- people with disabilities are included in the pretest population.

Furthermore, unnecessary aspects of items that may be a barrier to people with disabilities should be eliminated. For example, a mathematics item may require a graph, but it may not be necessary for the graph to have multiple lines distinguished by differences in color that are difficult for people with color-blindness to discern. (See Cook and Stone, this volume, Chapter 9, for more information on fairness for special populations of test takers.)

Fairness for English Language Learners

English language learners (ELLs) (or learners of the language of any test in which the language is not construct-relevant) are not to be confused with test takers with disabilities, but some of the actions taken in the service of UD (e.g., clear and concise directions) will benefit test takers who are ELLs as well. Fairness for ELLs requires the determination of whether English is merely an incidental means of conveying test content and directions or whether knowledge of English is construct-relevant. If the use of English is merely incidental, then simplified language, glossaries, and even translations are useful strategies for reducing irrelevant and unfair variance. If, however, English is a construct-relevant source of variance, then care must be taken to avoid reducing valid variance by the use of such strategies. Even in seemingly English-incidental tests such as mathematics, English may be construct-relevant if, for example, the claim about students is that they will succeed in the next level mathematics course in an institution in which the language of instruction is English. (For more information about testing ELLs, see Pitoniak et al., 2009.)

Fairness Advisory Committee

It can be very helpful to have an advisory committee with a focus on fairness involved in test design and in later stages of the test development process. Though they are not likely to characterize their task in this way, the goal of the committee members is to point out construct-irrelevant sources of variance that may be associated with group membership. Test designers have to satisfy multiple requirements simultaneously. The use of a fairness advisory committee will help to ensure that fairness concerns are appropriately taken into account as decisions are made about the content to be tested, the types of items to use, the timing of the test, the administration and response modes, and so forth.

Item Writing and Fairness Guidelines

It is essential that test developers clearly define what they mean by fairness in item content and train item writers to generate items that meet the definition, before item writing begins. Item writing is costly and time-consuming. It is counterproductive to write items only to have them discarded because they have been judged to be unfair later in the process.

Many test development organizations, publishers, and government agencies in the United States have developed sets of rules for the generation of fair publications, including tests. Titles generally include some combination of the words "Bias," "Fairness," and "Sensitivity" with the words "Guidelines" or "Review." For example, the American Psychological Association (2010, p. 71.) has "General Guidelines for Reducing Bias." Data Recognition Corporation (2003) has *Fairness in Testing: Guidelines for Training Bias, Fairness and Sensitivity Issues*. Educational Testing Service (2015) has *ETS Guidelines for Fair Tests and Communications*. The Smarter Balanced Assessment Consortium (2012) has *Bias and Sensitivity Guidelines*.

Similarities among Guidelines

In addition to similarities in titles, the various documents tend to be extremely similar in the topics they address and in the general thrust of their comments. The documents vary most in level of detail, but actual disagreements are rare and tend to be in minor details such as whether or not to use a hyphen in "African American." In fact, the documents overlap not only in the concepts covered, but also in the wording used to express the concepts (Ravitch, 2003).

The rules for fairness described below are a summarized selection of the most important content from the *ETS Guidelines for Fair Tests and Communications* (Educational Testing Service, 2015, henceforth, the *GFTC*). The *GFTC* is employed in this chapter as the exemplar for compilations of rules for achieving item fairness because the document is representative of many other available versions of fairness guidelines. It has been in widespread use with many highly visible tests designed for a wide range of test takers since 1980, and has been periodically revised and expanded to comply with changing views of fairness. Please see the *GFTC* for a more complete exposition of rules for fairness in items and tests than is possible to include in this chapter. The document is available at no charge from www.ets.org.

The rules for fairness in the *GFTC* are designed for use in the United States. The general principles for fairness (e.g., Do not unnecessarily offend test takers.) apply everywhere. Many of the specific rules, however, would have to be revised for use in different countries. For example, what is considered offensive in Pakistan is not necessarily offensive in Japan. (See Educational Testing Service, 2009a, for strategies for revising the *GFTC* for use in other countries.)

Purpose and Use of Guidelines

The primary purpose of applying rules for fairness is to avoid the use of items or stimuli that may cause construct-irrelevant, unfair score variance. The rules are used by the item writers and test assemblers who create the testing materials and by reviewers who strive to ensure that the item writers and test assemblers produced materials in compliance with the rules for fairness. Another important purpose for using guidelines is to help people to agree on what is meant by fairness in test content and thereby reduce subjective, often idiosyncratic, decisions about fairness by reviewers. The goal of using guidelines is to measure the intended construct without group-related, construct-irrelevant barriers such as:

- cognitive barriers caused by the measurement of irrelevant knowledge;
- affective barriers caused by the unnecessary elicitation of strong emotions; or
- physical barriers caused by the extraneous sensory and mobility requirements of the testing situation.

Any content required for valid measurement is considered fair, even if it would be prohibited by the guidelines if it were construct-irrelevant. For example, the topic of the contamination of food with intestinal bacteria would be considered too disgusting and offensive for inclusion in a reading comprehension test. The topic might be required and, therefore, acceptable (construct-relevant and fair) in a test for restaurant inspectors, however. The fact that any materials required for validity are allowed in tests refutes the claims of some critics (see, e.g., Ravitch, 2003) that fairness review is a form of censorship.

Following are detailed rules designed to remove potential sources of group-related, construct-irrelevant variance. People may disagree about some of the individual rules (e.g., Is social dancing a topic to be avoided?), but the goal of measuring the intended construct equally well for all relevant groups of test takers is straightforward and sensible.

Cognitive Sources of Construct-Irrelevant Variance

Cognitive sources of construct-irrelevant variance diminish fairness when both of the following are true:

- Knowledge or skill not required for valid measurement is necessary to respond correctly to an item.
- Groups differ in possession of that knowledge or skill.

Many items outside of pure mathematics require that some construct-irrelevant content or context be used. For example, reading comprehension passages have to be about some content, even though the construct is reading comprehension in general, not comprehension of the particular content of a given reading passage. If the construct-irrelevant content causes differences between groups, the content is a cognitive source of unfair score variance.

Similarly, practical problems in mathematics have to be placed in some context. The particular context of the problem (e.g., dividing a pizza equally among some children in an item measuring knowledge of fractions) is construct-irrelevant. If solving the problem in a particular context requires construct-irrelevant knowledge that differs between groups, the context is a cognitive source of unfair score variance.

For occupational licensing tests, any contexts likely to be encountered during entry-level work on the job are acceptable. For most tests, however, it is difficult to distinguish between the construct-irrelevant knowledge expected of all test takers that is "fair game" for use in tests, and the construct-irrelevant knowledge that will unfairly disadvantage some group(s) of test takers. For example, does a reading passage about life on a farm unfairly disadvantage test takers who live in cities? Does a mathematics problem about a subway schedule disadvantage test takers who live in rural areas? Is it fair to have a reading passage about a footrace if some test takers with disabilities are unable to participate in such races?

It is likely to be impossible to find materials with which all test takers are equally familiar. For K-12 academic tests, one reasonable approach is to learn about typical school curricula because the school environments of test takers in the United States tend to differ less than their home environments. For example, by third grade, students have very likely been exposed to the concept of boats while the students are in school, even if they have never been on a boat. The problem of finding acceptable construct-irrelevant contextual material is more difficult if students from many countries will be among the test takers. A partial solution is to avoid construct-irrelevant content that is unique to the United States. For example, avoid the use of American coins in a mathematics problem unless knowledge of the coins is part of the construct.

With respect to the contents of reading comprehension passages, a common and very important reason to read is to learn new concepts. It is, therefore, appropriate to include novel concepts in reading comprehension passages as long as the information required to answer the items correctly is included in the passage. The same rationale can be applied to test takers with disabilities. For example, a test taker may be unable to participate in a physical activity, but it is acceptable to include the activity in a reading passage as long as the information required to answer the item is likely to have been taught in school or is included in the passage. For some sensory disabilities, a concept is acceptable only with the additional condition that it need not be obtained through personal experience. For example, a test taker in tenth grade who is deaf may be expected to know what a siren is, but it is not fair to expect the test taker to know what a siren sounds like.

Unnecessarily Difficult Language

A clear example of a cognitive source of construct-irrelevant variance is the use of unnecessarily difficult language in test directions, items, or stimuli when language is not the focus of measurement. The groups most likely to be affected are ELLs and people with language-related disabilities. The rules for writing clearly, concisely, and at the appropriate level of difficulty are beyond the scope of this chapter, but many reference works are available, such as American Psychological Association (2010), Educational Testing Service (2009b), and University of Chicago Press (2003). In applying this guideline, it is important to distinguish between construct-irrelevant language and language that is part of the construct being tested. While construct-irrelevant difficult language should be avoided, construct-relevant language may be as difficult as is required for valid measurement.

Construct-Irrelevant Specialized Knowledge

In addition to avoiding unnecessarily difficult language, it is necessary to avoid requiring construct-irrelevant, unevenly distributed information to respond correctly to an item.

Specialized aspects of certain topics are likely to be cognitive sources of construct-irrelevant variance (see, e.g., O'Neill & McPeek, 1993).

Any aspect of the topics is perfectly acceptable when it is construct-relevant, and the more common and familiar aspects of the topics are acceptable even when they are construct-irrelevant. Even for adult test takers, however, the specialized, less familiar aspects of the following topics should be avoided when they are construct-irrelevant:

- agriculture (e.g., *plow* is acceptable, *thresher* is not);
- finance (e.g., *bank* is acceptable, *credit default swap* is not);
- law (e.g., *jury* is acceptable, *subpoena* is not);
- machinery (e.g., *spring* is acceptable, *cam* is not);
- military topics (e.g., *rifle* is acceptable, *RPG* is not);
- politics (e.g., *vote* is acceptable, *filibuster* is not);
- religion (e.g., *prayer* is acceptable, *chasuble* is not);
- science (e.g., *cell* is acceptable, *vacuole* is not);
- sports (e.g., *ball*—the spherical object—is acceptable, *ball*—the umpire's call—is not);
- technology (e.g., *computer* is acceptable, *JPEG* is not);
- tools (e.g., *hammer* is acceptable, *chuck* is not); and
- vocabulary limited to a region of the county (e.g., *bag* is acceptable, *poke* is not).

If tests will be taken by people unfamiliar with U.S. culture, then do not require construct-irrelevant knowledge of U.S. culture to answer items. For example, not all test takers outside of the United States will know how Halloween is celebrated in the United States.

Affective Sources of Construct-Irrelevant Variance

Construct-irrelevant test material that is likely to anger, annoy, distract, offend, insult, or upset members of some group(s) of test takers is likely to be an unfair affective source of construct-irrelevant variance. Such material should be avoided. It is also useful to avoid construct-irrelevant material that is widely believed to be unfair or inappropriate, whether it is or not, because such material will cause test takers, score users, educators, policymakers, and others to mistrust the results of the test.

The dividing line between acceptable material and material that is an unacceptable affective source of construct-irrelevant variance is vague and ill-defined. It depends greatly on the age and sophistication of the test takers. Clearly, the strictest interpretation of the rules is needed for primary and elementary school students, while a more liberal interpretation of the guideline is acceptable for high school students and an even more liberal interpretation is acceptable for adults. The dividing line also depends on local customs and values. What is acceptable in one school district, state, or country may be unacceptable elsewhere. Because the guideline applies only to unnecessary, construct-irrelevant material, there is no loss of validity in avoiding material that is potentially unacceptable in the most sensitive location in which the test will be used.

Topics That Are Best Avoided

Some topics have become so upsetting or controversial and inflammatory that it is best to avoid them in test materials unless they are required for valid measurement:

- abortion;
- abuse of people (particularly children) or animals;
- atrocities;
- contraception;
- deportation of immigrants;
- ethnic conflicts (current or recent);
- euthanasia;
- experimentation that is dangerous or painful;
- genocide;
- gun control;
- killing animals for sport;
- occult topics such as ghosts, witches, Satanism, or vampires;
- political disputes (current or recent);
- prayer in schools;
- profanity;
- rape;
- sexual subject matter;
- suffering (graphic or extreme);
- suicide;
- terrorism; and
- torture.

The list of topics to be avoided is not complete because a well-publicized, shocking event (e.g., the attacks on September 11, 2001) can raise sufficiently negative emotions that it is best to avoid associated locations, situations, people, etc. on tests. Despite its occurrence on the list above, any topic that is required to meet the purpose of the test is construct-relevant and is, therefore, fair and acceptable. For example, ethnic conflicts and religious disputes would be included in current events tests and suicide would be included in tests for mental health workers.

Topics Requiring Care

There are other topics that require particular care to avoid potential affective sources of construct-irrelevant variance. Again, any content is acceptable if it is required for valid measurement, but even in those circumstances the topic should be presented in ways that reduce the likelihood of eliciting strong, negative emotions in test takers:

- Advocacy. Test materials should not advocate for one side in disputed issues unless required for valid measurement, as in measuring a test taker's ability to evaluate an argument. When advocacy is required for measurement purposes, fairness requires the use of the least controversial issue that allows valid measurement.
- Death, disease, disasters. Except when necessary, avoid a focus on horrific details. Graphic detail may be required, however, in a test for medical personnel, for example.
- Evolution. When required for valid measurement, as in a biology test, any aspect of evolution is acceptable. When not required by the construct, it is best to avoid a focus on evolution in test materials, particularly anything touching on the evolution of human beings, such as similarities between human beings and other primates.
- Personal questions. Unless it is important for valid measurement, do not ask test takers overly personal questions about themselves or family members regarding

private issues such as criminal behavior, political activities, religious beliefs, or sexual practices.

- Religion. Religion was previously cited as a likely cognitive source of construct-irrelevant variance. It is also a common affective source of construct-irrelevant variance. Some test takers may be strongly emotionally attached to one of the positions in a religious dispute and may be upset by any perceived acceptance of the opposite position. Anything even slightly negative or even slightly positive about religion in general or about a specific religion is likely to anger some group of test takers. Fairness requires being as objective, as factual, and as neutral as possible if religion must be included on a test.

- Slavery. Any construct-relevant aspect of slavery is acceptable, as in an American history test. Slavery may be mentioned but should not be the primary focus of construct-irrelevant test materials. For example, a reading passage about Phillis Wheatley may mention that she was a slave but should focus on her work as a poet rather than on her life as a slave.

Terminology for Groups

Using an inappropriate label for a group can cause construct-irrelevant, group-related variance. In general, the labels that group members prefer for themselves are most appropriate. Care is necessary, however, because group members do not always agree on the preferred term, and preferences change over time. When possible, group names are to be used as adjectives rather than as nouns. For example, "Black people" is preferable to "Blacks." Insulting names for groups in test materials should be avoided unless required for valid measurement. For example, test takers may be asked to evaluate historical materials that contain terms currently considered insulting.

Acceptable and unacceptable terms for groups are listed below in Table 2.2.

Gender Issues

Except in literary or historical materials required for valid measurement, men and women should be referred to in comparable ways. For example, if women are referred to by their first names, men should be referred to the same way. If women are referred to by family roles (e.g., wife), men should be referred to in a parallel way (e.g., husband). If women are referred to by physical attributes, men should be referred to the same way. Professions such as "teacher" or "nurse" include both males and females. For example, "nurses and their spouses" is acceptable, but "nurses and their husbands" is not unless the reference is to a particular group of nurses with husbands. Do not assume that spouses are necessarily of opposite genders. Phrases such as "man-sized job" and "scream like a girl" reinforce stereotypes and should not appear in test materials, except in literary or historical materials.

Gender-specific labels for various roles are not appropriate. Gender-neutral terms are preferable, as shown in Table 2.3.

The assumption that there are only two genders is not correct. Some particular group may consist only of males and females, but it is wrong to assume that males plus females include all human beings all of the time. There are people who identify themselves as neither male nor female, as both male and female, or as male or female at different times. This has implications for testing. For example, the question "If there are 9 male students and 11 female students in a class, how many students are in the class?" cannot be answered as written without assuming that there are only two genders.

Table 2.2 Acceptable and Unacceptable Terms for Groups

Acceptable	Unacceptable
African American (no hyphen), Black (uppercase B).	Negro, Colored (except in literary or historical materials or in names of organizations).
Asian American (no hyphen). More specific terms such as "Chinese American" are preferable when it is possible to be specific.	Oriental to describe human beings (except in historical or literary materials or in names of organizations).
Bisexual, gay, lesbian, transgendered. Sexual orientation.	Homosexual (except in scientific contexts), Queer (except in reference to academic theories or studies). Sexual preference.
Hispanic American, Latino or Latina American. More specific terms such as "Cuban American" are preferable when it is possible to be specific.	While Chicano or Chicana American is accepted by some groups, it is rejected by others. Therefore, it is preferable to use one of the more accepted terms.
Deaf or hard of hearing. Blind, visually impaired. Put the person first and the disability second as in "person who is blind."	Deaf and dumb. Hearing impaired. The deaf, the blind, etc. (except in historical or literary materials or the names of institutions).
Intellectual disability. Cognitive disability.	Retarded.
Neutral terms (has cancer, is paralyzed).	Excessively negative or excessively positive terms (stricken with cancer, is physically challenged).
American Indian, Native American. Names of specific nations or peoples (e.g., Mohegan, Lakota).	Squaw, Buck, Brave (as noun).
Names of specific nations or peoples such as Aleut, Inuit.	Eskimo.
Refer to people by specific age ranges, e.g., "People aged 65 and above."	Elderly, seniors.
White, European American (to be parallel with African American, Asian American, etc.). Caucasian is still acceptable, but is becoming less commonly used.	

Table 2.3 Gender-Specific and Gender-Neutral Terms

Acceptable	Unacceptable, Except in Historical or Literary Material
Chair, leader	Chairman
Firefighter	Fireman
Human beings, people	Man, mankind
Mail carrier	Mailman
Sales representative	Salesman
Insurance agent	Insurance man
Supervisor	Foreman
Workers, personnel, labor	Manpower

Additional Requirements for Children

Children are considered particularly vulnerable to affective sources of variance. Therefore, many jurisdictions have imposed additional constraints for tests given to schoolchildren. The additional requirements focus on topics that might be particularly upsetting for children, or that might serve as models for inappropriate behavior in children, or that might offend the moral standards that some groups in the jurisdiction expect of children.

If topics such as the following are construct relevant and cannot be avoided, use the least upsetting, the least offensive, and the least controversial representation that will meet the requirements of valid measurement. It is, however, best to avoid the following topics in tests for children:

- animals, things or situations likely to frighten children (e.g., spiders, snakes, house fires, abductions);
- body image problems (e.g., anorexia, disfigurement, obesity);
- cynicism about values believed to be important by groups within the jurisdiction (e.g., democracy, faith, honesty, hard work, patriotism);
- family problems (e.g., domestic violence, divorce, eviction from home, parent's loss of job, sibling rivalry);
- inappropriate behavior (e.g., cheating, cutting school, doing dangerous things, fighting, gambling, lying, running away from home, stealing);
- local controversies (e.g., in some jurisdictions environmental conflicts, such as coal miners against environmentalists, are highly controversial);
- sexuality and associated topics (e.g., dating, pregnancy, social dancing [in some jurisdictions]); and
- unhealthy activities (e.g., alcohol use, drug abuse, excessive junk food, tobacco use).

There can be a lag (sometimes a year or more) between the time test items are written and the time the tests are administered. Biographical material about famous living individuals (e.g., sports stars, entertainers) can cause problems because the individuals may engage in highly publicized, inappropriate behaviors, such as drug abuse or domestic violence. If they do so after the test has been assembled but before the test is administered, the material about them may need to be removed from the test. Late changes to test content are both expensive and prone to error so it is safest to avoid the construct-irrelevant inclusion of famous living individuals in test materials.

Physical Sources of Construct-Irrelevant Variance

Some physical barriers in test items are required by the tested construct. For example, an aspiring music teacher must be able to hear and correct a student's errors, even though the need to hear music is a barrier for test takers who are deaf. Such necessary and construct-relevant barriers should be retained. An indicator that a physical barrier is required is that no accommodation for a construct-related disability is possible that allows measurement of the intended construct.

Some physical barriers in test items are very helpful in measuring the intended construct, even though they are not required. For example, a test for aspiring teachers may use videos to present realistic classroom situations. The visual stimuli are a barrier for test takers who are blind, but the advantages of using such stimuli justify their use for sighted test takers. Of course, appropriate accommodations are required for test takers who are blind.

Finally, there are physical barriers that are neither required for valid measurement nor offer any major advantages over less problematic alternatives. Such barriers are to be avoided because they are a needless physical source of construct-irrelevant variance. Examples are:

- fonts that are unnecessarily small;
- novel fonts meant to be decorative or innovative rather than clear;
- novel response formats such as dragging and dropping words in a table when the same construct could be measured by simpler items;
- poor contrast between figure and ground;
- special symbols that could have been avoided;
- text printed vertically or on a slant;
- three-dimensional renditions used when the information could be presented in two dimensions; and
- visual material used solely to make tests more interesting.

General Principles

No list of rules can cover every possible situation and there will probably be disagreements about some of the rules. Furthermore, rules are likely to become obsolete. For example, the use of "man" to refer to all human beings was a common and accepted practice not very long ago. Therefore, when there are doubts about the fairness of an item, it is useful to refer to some general principles for fairness that are universal and constant:

- Include whatever is necessary for valid measurement.
- Show respect for all test takers.
- Give different groups of test takers an equal chance for a validly interpreted score.
- Avoid construct-irrelevant material that may lead people to believe that the test is unfair or inappropriate.

Training Item Writers and Reviewers

The mere existence of rules for fairness in items is insufficient. Item writers and fairness reviewers must learn to apply the guidelines appropriately. Effective training requires several stages, and it is advantageous to train item writers and reviewers together because every item writer is a potential reviewer, even though some reviewers may not be item writers. The first task in the training is a discussion of the meanings of the rules for fairness with clear examples of violations. The second stage of training involves discussions of borderline materials that some people believe are acceptable and other people believe are out of compliance with the guidelines. Consensus may or may not be reached. This process may identify rules that are ambiguous or controversial and in need of augmentation or revision. After item writers and reviewers have had the opportunity to apply the rules for fairness for several months, it is helpful to have them gather periodically in the ongoing third stage of training to discuss their experiences, to agree on solutions to common problems, to resolve misunderstandings, and so forth. Because views of fairness change (e.g., *Negro* was once the accepted term for a Black person), whatever rules have been adopted should be reviewed and updated as necessary.

Item Reviews

Even though item writers have been trained to follow the fairness guidelines that have been adopted, it is necessary to have the items reviewed for fairness. There will certainly be some disagreements between item writers and fairness reviewers. To avoid problems, it is necessary to have documented procedures for the reviews such as the following:

- Item "owners" (not necessarily the item writer, but the person in charge of the item) should not be able to choose the reviewers of their items. Assignment of reviewers should be done by a third party. Ideally, the reviewer should have no vested interest in the survival of the items, nor be supervised by the owner.
- The reviewer's task is to evaluate the compliance of the item with the fairness guidelines and to challenge an item that violates a guideline. It is not acceptable for the reviewer simply to say an item is unfair. The reviewer must cite the guideline(s) that the item violates and explain why the item is in violation. If there is a revision that will make the item acceptable, the reviewer should suggest it.
- The owner of the item may agree or disagree with the fairness reviewer. If the owner and reviewer agree, the owner revises or deletes the item. Revised items are re-reviewed.
- If they disagree, the owner and reviewer discuss their differences. If agreement is not reached, some resolution mechanism is invoked. For example, a small group of experienced fairness reviewers could evaluate the item and reach a decision, or a very experienced fairness reviewer could be appointed as the final arbiter.

Fairness in Test Assembly and Review

Assembly

The assembly of a test is based on detailed blueprints (test specifications) that define all of the important characteristics the assembled test is supposed to have (e.g., the numbers and types of items to be used in the test, the mix of KSAs to be measured in the test, the desired statistical characteristics of the test, and the required representation of different groups of people.) The primary task of the test assembler is to meet the test specifications to the extent possible given the available pool of items. Often, compromises have to be made because the pool of items is insufficient to meet all of the constraints in the test specifications at the same time. Validity should be the primary driver of the decisions that are made during test assembly. As long as validity can be maintained, however, fairness concerns should be addressed during test assembly.

By selecting an item from the pool, the assembler is confirming the item writer's and the fairness reviewer's judgments that the item is in compliance with the fairness guidelines. In addition, the test assembler is responsible for the fairness of the mix of items in the tests. This includes representing diversity and avoiding stereotypes.

Any test that mentions or shows people should, to the extent possible, reflect the diversity of the test-taking population. The goal of representing diversity is to avoid making test takers feel excluded and alienated, which could be an affective source of construct-irrelevant score variance. Therefore, items that mention people should include both men and women, members of demographic groups represented among the test takers, and people with disabilities.

The extent to which representation is possible depends on the type of test. In some pure mathematics tests, for example, no people are mentioned at all. In some other tests, such as military history, almost all of the people mentioned will be males because almost all of the leaders in historical conflicts were males. In other types of tests, such as literature and sociology, a greater percentage of the items are about people and more groups can be represented. In any case, it is usually impossible to represent all of the different groups in the test-taking population in any single test form. In a continuing testing program, representation can be approached across forms.

In addition to representing various groups, the test assembler should avoid reinforcing demeaning stereotypes. It is acceptable to include traditional group behaviors in test materials as long as those behaviors are balanced by nontraditional activities. For example, depicting a woman caring for children is acceptable as long as women are also depicted in some nontraditional activity. Showing only traditional activities in a test form reinforces stereotypes.

Review

Just as items are reviewed for fairness even though item writers have been trained to apply the fairness guidelines, tests should be reviewed for fairness even though test assemblers strive to follow the guidelines. In addition to checking each item for compliance with the guidelines in operation, test fairness reviewers try to ensure that the test form as a whole does not reinforce stereotypes and that the test form represents diversity appropriately. The reviewer should also try to ensure that the directions for taking the test are easy to read for the intended population of test takers, are complete, and are unambiguous. Procedures for selecting test fairness reviewers and procedures for resolving disputes between test assemblers and test fairness reviewers should be similar to the procedures described above for item fairness reviewers.

Fairness in Scoring by Human Scorers

Scoring machines are not affected by any personal characteristics of the test takers. Human scorers, however, may be affected by such characteristics. Therefore, if possible, the scorers of responses should not know any of the personal characteristics of the test takers. If video responses or observations of test takers are used, scorers should be trained to ignore the construct-irrelevant personal characteristics of test takers. For example, if accents are construct-irrelevant, examples of test takers with accents should appear in the training, and scorers should be told that such construct-irrelevant characteristics should not affect scores. Training scorers on the meanings of rubrics for assigning scores is crucial. The characteristics of the response that should affect the scores, and those aspects of the response that should be ignored are to be stressed in training. For example, if the construct is subject-matter knowledge rather than writing skill, scorers should be told to ignore errors in grammar.

When possible, more than one independent scorer should evaluate each response. Significant discrepancies between the scores assigned by different scorers should be adjudicated by using a third scorer. If some scorers seem to consistently favor or disfavor members of certain groups, the apparent problem should be discussed privately with the scorer. If the problem continues, the scorer should be retrained. If the retraining is ineffective, the scorer should be disqualified. (See Penfield, this volume, Chapter 4, for more information on fairness in scoring practices, and Pitoniak et al., 2009, for fairness in scoring as it relates to ELLs.)

Fairness in Item and Test Analysis

If sample sizes are sufficient, it can be instructive to perform separate item analyses for different groups of test takers. For example, are Black test takers attracted to different distracters in multiple-choice items than are White test takers? The problem with such analyses is that construct-relevant (fair) differences between groups are confounded with construct-irrelevant (unfair) differences. Therefore, a special type of item analysis, called differential item functioning (DIF), which was designed to help investigate fairness issues, should be used.

Differential Item Functioning

DIF is found when people in different groups perform differently on an item, even though the people have been matched on some relevant criterion. The matching is almost always based on test scores. For example, men with scores of X are matched with women who received scores of X. Men with scores of X-1 are matched with women who received scores of X-1, and so forth. Though they are not identical, the men and women who received the same scores on a test are probably reasonably well matched in terms of the KSAs that the test is measuring.

The differences between the matched groups in performance on the item are aggregated across score levels. The greater the differences, the greater the absolute value of DIF becomes. It has become the convention to assign negative values of DIF to items in which the "focal group" (e.g., Asian American, Black, Female, Hispanic, or Native American test takers) finds the item more difficult than the matched "reference group" (e.g., White or male test takers). (For information on the statistical aspects of DIF, see Dorans, 1989; Dorans & Holland, 1993; Penfield, this volume, Chapter 4.)

Inspections of patterns of DIF can lead to fairer tests. For example, in some focal group of test takers, multiple-choice items with options printed side by side in a horizontal line may tend to be more difficult than similar items with options printed in a column (O'Neill & McPeek, 1993). Because there is no construct-relevant reason to favor items with a horizontal layout, the horizontal layout may be an unfair source of construct-irrelevant variance.

DIF is a signal that the item may be unfair, but DIF is not proof that the item is unfair. The group differences may be construct-relevant. For example, vocabulary items containing words with Latin roots may be easier for Hispanic test takers than for a matched group of non-Hispanic test takers (Schmitt, Holland, & Dorans, 1993). That does not mean it is unfair to include English words with Latin roots on a test. Also, the same item may show DIF in one context, but not in another. For example, an algebra item may show DIF in a math test that contains few algebra items, but not show DIF in a math test that contains many algebra items, simply because the latter test will have better matched the groups on knowledge of algebra.

Procedures for the use of DIF, such as those described below, help to ensure the appropriate use of DIF (Zieky, 1993, 2011):

- Divide items into categories based on the absolute value of DIF: (A) insignificant or small, (B) moderate, (C) large. The largest absolute value of DIF for any group determines the category of the item.
- When DIF data are available for items in a pool, assemble the test with Group A items to the extent possible.

- If necessary to meet specifications, use Group B items.
- Do not use Group C items unless required to meet specifications and an independent panel has said the item is fair.
- If an operational test must be assembled without DIF data, calculate DIF after test administration, but before the scores are released.
- Have an independent panel review any items in Group C. Retain the item for scoring only if the panel certifies the fairness of the item.

Test Analysis

A review of the characteristics of an entire test for different groups can be informative about fairness, but not all differences between groups are easily interpreted. Some group differences will likely be found in a fair test, particularly if the groups differ in variances of scores as well as in means of scores.

Differences in Difficulty

As noted previously, differences in mean difficulty between groups do not indicate that the test is unfair for the lower-scoring group. The difference is, however, a sign that careful attention is needed to help ensure that construct-irrelevant sources of score variance contributing to the difference have been eliminated to the extent possible.

If the mean scores differ, an inspection of the distributions of item difficulties across groups will necessarily show some differences. It can, however, be informative to look for patterns or consistencies among the items with the largest differences and among the items with the smallest differences. Do items from a particular segment of the domain, or items of a particular type, tend to cluster at either extreme? How do items with the smallest differences differ from items with the largest differences? Items with large differences between groups are not necessarily unfair unless construct-irrelevant components can be identified. In fact, items with the highest item-test correlations will tend to show the largest differences in difficulty, if there are real and construct-relevant differences between groups.

Differences in Speededness

Unless the test is intended to measure rate of response, not completing the test is a source of construct-irrelevant variance. If some groups are less likely to complete the test than are other groups, it is possible that the timing of the test is a source of unfairness. The reasonableness of the time limit should be investigated.

Differences in Reliability and in Other Correlations

Looking at differences among the reliabilities of a test for different groups can be misleading because reliability is greatly affected by the group's score variance. On a test of any given quality, the calculated reliability will be higher for a group with higher score variance than for a group with lower score variance. The fact that groups differ in score variance does not make the test unfair. It is more instructive to compare the standard errors of measurement across groups because those data are less affected by differences in score variance.

As is the case with reliability (which can be thought of as the correlation of a test with itself), correlations of parts of the test with each other, or of the test scores with a criterion depend greatly on the score variance of the group. All other things being equal, groups with higher score variance will show higher correlations than will groups with lower score variance. Therefore, differences in the correlations of scores with external variables do not necessarily mean that a test is unfair. Differences in correlations among parts of the test for different groups of test takers are worth investigating, however. For example, a relatively high correlation between performance on word problems in mathematics and performance on reading comprehension items for a group could signal that verbal skills are affecting mathematics scores for that group.

In the case of predictive evidence of validity, comparing correlations is insufficient. According to Cleary (1968), who proposed one of the first definitions of fairness in assessment that was widely accepted by psychometricians, the slopes and intercepts of the test-criterion regression lines should be investigated. Cleary considered a test used for prediction to be fair if the same regression line fits the groups being compared (see Liu and Dorans, this volume, Chapter 5).

Conclusion

Fairness in testing is not a matter of niceness, of sensitivity, or of political correctness. It is a matter of validity. A fair test is one that is valid for different groups of test takers. Of the many sources of score variance, only construct-relevant sources of variance enhance validity. All other sources of variance weaken validity. If construct-irrelevant sources of variance are correlated with group membership, they also weaken fairness.

Therefore, fairness in assessment is achieved by maximizing the proportion of the score variance that is construct-relevant, and minimizing the proportion of the score variance that is construct-irrelevant and associated with group membership. That is easy to say and hard to do. It requires careful attention during test design, item writing, test assembly, scoring, and analysis.

No matter how carefully those tasks are accomplished, fair and valid tests are likely to have group score differences. Tests are constantly being attacked as unfair because of group score differences, but those differences exist because social, economic, and educational resources are far from equally distributed across groups in the United States (Barton, 2003). There is no way to prove that a test is fair, but more care is taken to help ensure the fairness of professionally developed tests than is taken with school grades, teacher's recommendations, supervisor's ratings, or other methods commonly used to evaluate human beings in academic or occupational settings. Without tests, group differences in KSAs would still exist, but it would be easier to ignore them and impossible to track progress toward the elimination of the differences. (For additional discussions of fairness in testing, see Camilli, 2006; Cole & Moss, 1989; Zieky, 2006, 2013; and, of course, the other chapters in this volume.)

Notes

1. The views expressed are those of the author and not necessarily those of the Educational Testing Service.
2. References in this chapter to "English language learners" apply generally to learners of the language of the test, as long as the language itself is not the focus of measurement.

References

American Educational Research Association, American Psychological Association, & National Council on Measurement in Education. (2014). *Standards for educational and psychological testing.* Washington, DC: American Educational Research Association.

American Psychological Association. (2010). *Publication manual of the American Psychological Association.* Washington, DC: American Psychological Association.

Barton, P. (2003). *Parsing the achievement gap.* Princeton, NJ: Educational Testing Service.

Camilli, G. (2006). Test fairness. In R. L. Brennan (Ed.), *Educational measurement* (4th ed., pp. 221–256). Westport, CT: America Council on Education/Praeger.

Cleary, T. A. (1968). Test bias: Prediction of grades of Negro and White students in integrated colleges. *Journal of Educational Measurement, 5,* 115–124.

Cole, N. S. (1973). Bias in selection. *Journal of Educational Measurement, 10,* 237–255.

Cole, N. S., & Moss, P. (1989). Bias in test use. In R. Linn (Ed.), *Educational measurement* (3rd ed., pp. 201–220). New York: Macmillan.

Cole, N. S., & Zieky, M. J. (2001). The new faces of fairness. *Journal of Educational Measurement, 38,* 369–382.

Cronbach, L. J. (1949). *Essentials of psychological testing.* New York: Harper & Row.

Darlington, R. B. (1971). Another look at "culture fairness." *Journal of Educational Measurement, 8,* 71–82.

Data Recognition Corporation. (2003). *Fairness in testing: Guidelines for training bias, fairness, and sensitivity issues.* Maple Grove, MI: Data Recognition Corporation.

Downing, S. (2006). Twelve steps for effective test development. In. S. Downing & T. Haladyna (Eds.), *Handbook of Test Development* (pp. 3–26). Mahwah, NJ: Erlbaum.

Dorans, N. (1989). Two new approaches to assessing differential item functioning: Standardization and the Mantel-Haenszel method. *Applied Measurement in Education, 2,* 217–233.

Dorans, N., & Holland, P. (1993). DIF detection and description: Mantel-Haenszel and standardization. In P. Holland & H. Wainer (Eds.), *Differential item functioning* (pp. 35–66). Hillsdale, NJ: Erlbaum.

Educational Testing Service. (2009a). *ETS international principles for fairness review of assessments.* Princeton, NJ: Educational Testing Service. Retrieved from www.ets.org/s/about/pdf/fairness_review_international.pdf

Educational Testing Service. (2009b). *ETS guidelines for using accessible language in tests.* Princeton, NJ: Educational Testing Service.

Educational Testing Service. (2014). *ETS standards for quality and fairness.* Princeton, NJ: Educational Testing Service.

Educational Testing Service. (2015). *ETS guidelines for fair tests and communications.* Princeton, NJ: Educational Testing Service.

Haladyna, T., & Downing, S. (2004). Construct-irrelevant variance in high stakes testing. *Educational Measurement: Issues and Practice, 23*(1), 17–27.

Kane, M. T. (2006). Validation. In R. L. Brennan (Ed.), *Educational measurement* (4th ed., pp. 17–64). Westport, CT: America Council on Education/Praeger.

Kane, M. T. (2013). Validating the interpretation and uses of test scores. *Journal of Educational Measurement, 50,* 1–73.

Kingston, N., Scheuring, S., & Kramer, L. (2013). Test development strategies. In K. Geisinger (Ed.), *APA handbook of testing and assessment in psychology: Vol. 1. Test theory* and *Testing and assessment in industrial and organizational psychology* (pp.165–184). Washington, DC: American Psychological Association.

Linn, R. L. (1973). Fair test use in selection. *Review of Educational Research, 43,* 139–161.

Messick, S. (1989). Validity. In R. Linn (Ed.), *Educational measurement* (3rd ed., pp. 13–103). New York: Macmillan.

Mislevy, R. J., & Riconscente, M. M. (2005). *Evidence-centered design: Layers, structures, and terminology.* Menlo Park, CA: SRI International.

Mislevy, R. J., Steinberg, L. S., & Almond, R. G. (1999). *Evidence-centered assessment design*. Princeton, NJ: Educational Testing Service.

Mislevy, R. J., Almond, R. G., & Lukas, J. F. (2003). *A brief introduction to evidence centered design. (ETS Research Report RR-03-16)*. Princeton, NJ: Educational Testing Service.

National Center on Educational Outcomes. (2002). *Universally designed assessments: Better tests for everyone*. Minneapolis, MN: National Center on Educational Outcomes.

O'Neill, K. A., & McPeek, W. M. (1993). Item and test characteristics that are associated with differential item functioning. In P. Holland & H. Wainer (Eds.), *Differential item functioning* (pp. 255–276). Hillsdale, NJ: Erlbaum.

Petersen, N. S., & Novick, M. R. (1976). An evaluation of some models for culture fair selection. *Journal of Educational Measurement, 13*, 3–29.

Pitoniak, M. J., Young, J. W., Martiniello, M., King, T. C., Buteux, A., & Ginsburgh, M. (2009). *Guidelines for the assessment of English-language learners*. Princeton, NJ: Educational Testing Service. Retrieved from http://www.ets.org/s/about/pdf/ell_guidelines.pdf

Ravitch, D. (2003). *The language police: How pressure groups restrict what students learn*. New York: Knopf.

Schmeiser, C. B., & Welch, C. J. (2006). Test development. In R. L. Brennan (Ed.), *Educational measurement* (4th ed., pp. 307–353). Westport, CT: America Council on Education/Praeger.

Schmitt, A. P., Holland, P. W., & Dorans, N. J. (1993). Evaluating hypotheses about differential item functioning. In P. W. Holland & H. Wainer (Eds.), *Differential item functioning* (pp. 281–315). Hillsdale, NJ: Erlbaum Associates.

Shepard, L. A. (1987). The case for bias in tests of achievement and scholastic aptitude. In S. Modgil & C. Modgil (Eds.), *Arthur Jensen: Consensus and controversy* (pp. 210–226). London: Falmer Press.

Sireci, S. G., & Sukin, T. (2013). Test validity. In K. Geisinger (Ed.), *APA handbook of testing and assessment in psychology: Vol. 1. Test theory* and *Testing and assessment in industrial and organizational psychology* (pp. 61–84). Washington, DC: American Psychological Association.

Smarter Balanced Assessment Consortium. (2012). *Bias and sensitivity guidelines*. Olympia, WA: Smarter Balanced Assessment Consortium.

Thompson, S. J., Johnstone, C. J., & Thurlow, M. L. (2002). *Universal design applied to large scale assessments*. Minneapolis, MN: University of Minnesota, National Center on Educational Outcomes.

Thorndike, R. L. (1971). Concepts of culture fairness. *Journal of Educational Measurement, 8*, 63–70.

University of Chicago Press. (2003). *The Chicago manual of style*. Chicago, IL: University of Chicago Press.

Voyer, D., Voyer, S., & Bryden, P. (1995). Magnitude of sex differences in spatial abilities: A meta-analysis and consideration of critical variables. *Psychological Bulletin, 117*, 250–270.

Willingham, W. W., & Cole, N. S. (1997). *Gender and fair assessment*. Mahwah, NJ: Erlbaum.

Zieky, M. J. (1993). Practical questions in the use of DIF statistics in test development. In P. Holland & H. Wainer (Eds.), *Differential item functioning* (pp. 347–348). Hillsdale, NJ: Lawrence Erlbaum.

Zieky, M. J. (2006). Fairness review. In S. M. Downing & T. M. Haladyna (Eds.), *Handbook of test development* (pp. 359–376). Mahwah, NJ: Erlbaum.

Zieky, M. J. (2011). The origins of procedures for using differential item functioning statistics at Educational Testing Service. In N. Dorans & S. Sinharay (Eds.), *Looking back: Proceedings of a conference in honor of Paul W. Holland* (pp. 115–128). New York: Springer.

Zieky, M. J. (2013). Fairness review in assessments. In K. Geisinger (Ed.), *APA handbook of testing and assessment in psychology: Vol. 1. Test theory* and *Testing and assessment in industrial and organizational psychology* (pp. 293–302). Washington, DC: American Psychological Association.

3   Maintaining Fairness through Test Administration

James A. Wollack[1] *and Susan M. Case*[2]

When the lay public considers issues of fairness in testing, it is likely that its focus is predominantly on matters other than test administration: test content, test format, test use, test scoring, and test standards. The purpose of this chapter is not to disparage any of the above, as all are of critical importance in ensuring test fairness. However, this chapter will focus on test administration, and its significance in assuring that all examinees are assessed under the same conditions. In particular, we will focus on maintaining fairness throughout the administration of standardized achievement tests. Here, we use the term "achievement tests" to be inclusive of standardized tests for educational achievement and accountability, admissions, certification, and licensure, as well as content-based employment tests. We also briefly discuss classroom testing, treating it as a special case of standardized achievement testing in which some of the standardization and security policies are relaxed. Although many of the concepts discussed throughout are applicable to other genres of testing (e.g., psychological testing, performance testing, etc.), the discussion here does not attempt to capture all the important nuances and intricacies of those categories of testing.

The educational literature is replete with evidence that examinee behavior is influenced by a wide number of environmental and administration factors, such as lighting, temperature, noise, timing, item layout, proximity to other examinees, and testing medium, not to mention scoring considerations, such as penalties for guessing and ability to revisit questions during computer-based testing (Haladyna & Downing, 2004; McCallin, 2006). However, it should be noted that many examples of test administration incidents are not documented in the literature, but are gleaned from the personal experiences of the authors. Unless these factors are carefully controlled by the test developer so that, to as large an extent as possible, all examinees are administered tests in the same way and under the same circumstances, it is likely that the scores will mean different things for different examinees and some examinees will be advantaged over others, thereby limiting the utility of the scores. The process of unifying the various conditions under which examinations are administered and scored is one important aspect of standardization. Whenever an exam is administered for which the intent is to compare results from examinees that may have completed the test at different times or in different settings, standardization of test administration is essential. Absent standardization, even though the individual test questions themselves may be identical or randomly equivalent across examinees, individual differences between settings or between examinees will contribute numerous sources of error to the data, potentially biasing test scores. It is for this reason that McCallin (2006) argues that test administration is a key component in upholding the validity of test score interpretations.

Although standardization is a huge element of test fairness, it is but one consideration. Fair testing necessitates that administration conditions are comparable across examinees;

however, the administration conditions must also be designed to promote valid score inferences. One of the fundamental principles of fairness in testing is that each examinee's test score reflects the knowledge, skills, competencies, and abilities of that examinee, and that examinee alone. Therefore, the administration conditions must be set up so as to both prevent and deter answer copying/sharing, use of prohibited materials, item theft, and other forms of cheating on tests. Conditions must also be designed to be harmonious with any data analytic and investigative approaches that may be used by the testing company to detect cheating after the fact.

Similarly, test instructions must be written to be clear and precise so that the testing company, test administrators, proctors, and examinees are united in a common understanding (and implementation) of the administration procedures. The instructions should begin by defining the exact purposes of the assessment and include a listing of the administration rules that must be followed to achieve that aim (Clemans, 1971). These rules include scripted language to be read by administrators at specified times, explicit instructions for examinees about permitted and prohibited materials and behaviors, directions about exam handling, room setup, rules for proctoring, how to respond to a host of unusual situations, and how to report irregularities. Collectively, these rules should be included in an administrator's manual and associated materials (e.g., proctor manual, test accommodations manual, etc.), which is made available to the administrators several months prior to exam delivery so that they may familiarize themselves with protocol and hire and train proctors and other staff accordingly.

One of the most significant changes in the newly revised *Standards for Educational and Psychological Testing* (American Educational Research Association, American Psychological Association, & National Council on Measurement in Education, 2014) is the treatment of fairness (Plake & Wise, 2014). The revised *Standards* elevate fairness to a foundational issue in testing, and the fairness theme runs throughout the standards and commentaries within each of the chapters. In light of the increased emphasis on fairness, it should not be surprising that test administration receives considerably more attention in the revised *Standards* than it did in previous editions. The Standards are clear that "[t]hose responsible for testing should adhere to standardized test administration, scoring, and security protocols so that test scores will reflect the construct(s) being assessed and will not be unduly influenced by idiosyncrasies in the testing process" (p. 65); however, the Standards broaden the responsibilities of test administrators to ensure that test administration procedures and processes are "fair to all examinees" (p. 83) and that all examinees receive "comparable treatment" (Standard 3.4, p. 65).

It is important to understand that being considerate of examinees and fair to examinees are not necessarily equivalent concepts. *Fair* relates to equal treatment of all examinees, remaining consistent with the law and program policies, and maintaining the integrity of test scores. Therefore, while individual programs may consider, for example, admitting examinees who fail to provide adequate documentation or allowing examinees to continue testing after being observed using their cell phones during a break (asking proctors to file an irregularity report and attempting to reconcile the details after the fact), it is our opinion that it would be equally fair to disallow such individuals to test, provided that approach is taken uniformly across all test administrations for that program. Therefore, our focus in writing this chapter will be on maintaining standardization, protecting the integrity of the test scores, and ensuring the comparable treatment of all examinees. Organizationally, we will address the administration concerns prior to, during, and following the examination so as to best ensure that examinees are treated fairly throughout the entire testing process and the validity of the intended test score interpretations is preserved.

Maintaining Fairness Prior to the Exam

From a test administration perspective, the time during which an examinee sits for the exam itself is fairly short. Similarly, the post-test administration effort, while important, tends to be quite brief. Overwhelmingly, the most time-consuming and arguably the most important administration tasks occur before the exam is administered. Obviously, it is during this pre-administration time that the administrator's manual is developed, but this is also the time for preparing the room and examinees for the test and for training the testing staff. In this section, we will discuss the physical considerations for exam day, the check-in process, and the importance of being faithful to your stated policies. Although proctor training must occur prior to the exam, the topic of proctoring will be discussed in the next section on maintaining fairness during the exam.

Test Site Considerations

An important element in fairness is that the testing environment should be conducive to the examinees demonstrating their best work. As a result, it is important to minimize distractions and the extent to which construct-irrelevant factors play a role. With that in mind, the testing environment should be as comfortable as possible. The testing room should be well-lit throughout. Rooms should be selected that allow for both air conditioning and heat, so that the room temperature is not at the mercy of Mother Nature. Testing facilities should have as few windows as possible, because rooms with windows tend to be noisier (especially if a window should be open) and less standardized with respect to light, pose greater opportunities for distraction, and present greater opportunities for examinees to communicate with individuals outside the testing facility. Rooms should be as quiet as possible. If testing staff learn of an event overlapping a scheduled test administration that is likely to be noisy and cause examinees to become distracted (e.g., building or road construction, nearby sporting events, etc.), the site coordinator should attempt to identify an alternate site that will be more ideally suited for testing.

It is also important to consider the seat and desk configuration in a testing space. For a paper-based exam, seating examinees at tables or counters with freely moving and adjustable chairs provides maximum flexibility with respect to construct irrelevant variables such as an examinee's handedness, height, and weight, thereby allowing all examinees to be comfortable. When using a lecture style room with fixed seating and individual seat desks, it is important to make sure that the seat desks are large enough for the examinees' test materials. In a classroom testing environment, where students are often seated at movable desks, desks should be spread out as much as much as possible to add greater space between desks—both side-to-side and front-to-back— while still leaving room at the front and back for the test administrators. Desks should be aligned so that each desk is directly behind the one in front of it. This will make it harder for students to copy off the person in the row ahead, and will make it easier for the proctor to identify any students who shift their desks to achieve a more advantageous viewing angle.

Check every testing room and the seating configuration with an eye to potential cheating. Ensure that the proctors have clear vision to each examinee; avoid rooms with pillars and other obstructions that affect the line of sight. All examinees should be facing the same direction, and with enough space between them so that neighboring examinees cannot see one another's work. To the extent possible, avoid any testing room with tiered seating; examinees can see the work of other examinees many rows in front of them. If tiered seating rooms cannot be avoided, every other row should be left vacant and examinees should be seated every other seat. For flat floor sites, if more than one examinee is seated at a single table, most testing programs suggest using tables that are at least 8 feet wide, as 6 foot tables do not allow sufficient space between examinees. Prior to test administration, to explore possible security vulnerabilities, evaluate the adequacy of the site using mock test materials and staff of a similar age to the examinees (younger examinees often have better eyesight than older staff!). Regardless of the configuration, ensure that examinees are far enough apart that they cannot look at each other's papers.

For computer-based exams, examinees should be seated at workstations with adjustable chairs, thereby allowing examinees greater control over their comfort level. Workstations should be arranged to facilitate proctor site lines so that examinees may be carefully and inconspicuously monitored by proctors. Workstations should be sufficiently well spaced to allow examinees to enter and exit their workstations and to allow proctors/administrators to move about the room as needed without disturbing other examinees. Partitions should be used between workstations unless the physical arrangement of computers prevents examinees from seeing other testers' monitors. Also, video cameras should be positioned to capture the entire examinee (face, hands, and body) and the keyboard. These video materials should be checked in advance to ensure that they are of sufficient quality to be useful.

It is the responsibility of the test site to ensure that the computer facilities meet the program specifications with regard to both the equipment and the examinee seat requirements. Computer equipment that does not meet the minimum requirements could result in graphics being displayed incorrectly, slow item loading times, poor Internet connectivity, or unreliable or reduced functionality, any one of which is likely to increase the amount of construct-irrelevant variance in an examinee's score. Pilot testing of sample test material should be undertaken to ensure that all systems are compatible, particularly if there have been any recent software or hardware updates.

Testing sites must also be selected and designed to be accessible by examinees with disabilities (Americans with Disabilities Act (ADA) of 1990). Depending on the nature of examinees' disabilities and accommodations, it is often necessary for them to have more space, fully adjustable chairs/tables, and assistive technology. For these reasons, examinees with disabilities are often tested in a separate, private or semiprivate space, removed from other examinees. Of course, these spaces need to be adequately proctored as well. Administration of exams for examinees with disabilities is of critical importance. Although there is much to be said on this subject, a detailed discussion of the Americans with Disabilities Act and its implications for maintaining fairness in test administration is beyond the scope of this chapter. The interested reader is referred to Cook and Stone (this volume, Chapter 9) and Thurlow, Thompson, and Lazarus (2006).

Testing facilities should be equipped with break areas and bathrooms that are large enough to accommodate the volume of test takers, in light of scheduled break times. Both should ideally be located within a restricted access part of the testing site to ensure that examinees are not interacting with individuals outside the testing center. Procedures should limit the number of examinees using each facility so there is no opportunity for examinees to interact with each other during testing time, or to switch seats upon returning to the testing site. Bathrooms are a common place for examinees to hide unauthorized testing materials to access during the test. Therefore, bathrooms should always be carefully inspected (including waste receptacles, toilet paper rolls, paper towel dispensers, toilet tanks, and ceiling tiles) prior to testing for signs of tampering or unauthorized resources. If break or restroom areas are located outside the testing facility and are also accessible to the public, both should be monitored by testing personnel whenever they are in use.

While many of the check-in and security protocols are more rigorous for standardized testing than for classroom testing, the notion of treating examinees fairly and providing them with equal opportunities to demonstrate their standing on the measured construct remains. While teachers often do not need to concern themselves with standardization across classes, ensuring a quiet, comfortable testing environment remains critical. Yet this can be a challenge, especially in older, overcrowded schools. One advantage the schools have that many standardized testing programs do not is the opportunity to easily reschedule testing. If the room conditions on the day of an exam are particularly ill-suited for testing (e.g., it is 100 degrees outside and the room has no air conditioning), unless the conditions are unlikely to improve any time soon, the teacher would be wise to consider postponing the exam to give examinees a better opportunity to focus on their work and receive a score representative of their skill level.

Storage of Test Material

A huge security issue involved with testing facilities is that test administrators receive testing-related materials in advance of the exam. Many of these materials are secure (e.g., test booklets, answer sheets, passwords, etc.) and the integrity of test scores would be jeopardized if they were accessed by examinees before or after the exam. Consequently, secure testing materials should be received as close to the test date (or opening of the testing window) as possible, without risking not having the materials on time. All such materials must be kept in a private, dedicated, locked, access-controlled room. Access to the room should be limited to a small number of individuals, each of whom has received security training and has signed a legal agreement with the test provider preventing disclosure. Entry into the test storage area and chain of custody of materials should be logged.

Here again, it is important to emphasize that most of these procedures to prevent unauthorized access prior to a test are equally applicable for classroom testing situations. Often, one of the simplest ways for students to cheat is to steal a copy of the test from an unsuspecting teacher. Teachers should never leave copies of exams in places where students have easy access. Exams should remain in locked cabinets or in the teacher's possession at all times prior to the exam. If copies of the exam are on the classroom computer, that computer should be locked and/or the relevant files should be password-protected.

Check-In Process and Staffing the Exam

The check-in process is the primary means by which we ensure that tests are delivered only to individuals who are authorized to sit for the exam. For purposes of this chapter, we distinguish between two types of unauthorized examinees. *Proxy test takers* are impersonators or individuals who assume the identity of an authorized examinee for purposes of taking a test. *Ineligible candidates* are individuals who may represent as themselves, but do not meet the eligibility requirements. Detecting proxy test takers during the exam can be quite challenging and is nearly impossible following the exam. Ineligible candidates are relatively easy to identify following the exam. However, most of the reasons that an ineligible candidate would want to take an exam relate to serious test security issues (e.g., item memorization or theft of an exam book), so every effort should be made to identify such examinees prior to testing and prevent them from sitting for the exam. Although the check-in process can often be cumbersome, especially for a paper-and-pencil test where many hundreds of examinees may be testing at the same time, it is critically important that it be handled well.

For paper-based programs, all examinees are usually checked in prior the start of the exam. However, for many computer-based programs, testing is continuous and examinees from different programs may be testing simultaneously. Therefore, the check-in area should be located outside the testing room so that newly arriving examinees can be checked in and have their questions answered without disturbing those in the middle of their testing sessions.

To ensure an efficient and thorough check-in and test administration process, it is important that ample, well-trained administration staff be on-site. All staff should be properly trained and vetted prior to test day. The test administrator should verify that the testing staff do not have a personal relationship with any of the examinees. This includes conducting background checks to identify and avoid potential security concerns or conflicts of interest, as well as obtaining signed nondisclosure agreements from all personnel with access to secure testing materials. Collect contact information from each potential proctor to facilitate communication, especially during last-minute emergencies regarding any changes in venue, timing, or even cancellation (e.g., weather emergency or power outage).

It is poor practice for individuals involved in test preparation to also be involved in test delivery (of those same tests), because such a conflict of interest increases the likelihood of proctor misconduct. The one exception to this rule might be classroom testing, where instructors are the test publishers, but are not stakeholders in the traditional sense. However, with K-12 accountability testing, students' test scores are used to determine whether the students were adequately trained. Hence, although it is very common for teachers to administer tests to their own students, schools should make every effort to shuffle school personnel on testing days so that teachers are not administering tests to their own students.

A protocol must be developed for every situation that can be imagined that threatens the standardization protocol. Each proctor needs to be able to call for help and reach the chief proctor as needed. If a proctor must leave the assigned station, someone else must be available to step in. Staff must be available for medical emergencies as well as for a security breach situation. And of course, if someone gets pulled away, there need to be other proctors available to step in.

The number of staff assisting with check-in and proctoring should be proportional to the number of examinees testing. Staffing guidelines will often be addressed in the administrator's manual and may vary depending on the complexity of the program, but the test site should be staffed with enough people to comfortably complete the check-in for all examinees and get all examinees seated in the testing room within a reasonable amount of time, and to monitor examinees as the exam is administered. It is important to have enough staff available for any unexpected issues that arise, such as dealing with potentially unauthorized examinees, without delaying the start of the exam. Acceptable proctor-to-examinee ratios vary program by program, but it has been recommended that paper-based administrations should have a chief proctor or site supervisor plus at least one additional proctor for every 25 examinees, (Association of Test Publishers/ National College Testing Association, 2015; Scicchitano & Meade, 2013). While no similar ratio for computer-based testing exists at present, it is commonly held that proctor-examinee ratios should be smaller for computer-based tests, and smaller still for exams that are remotely proctored (i.e., when proctors are not on-site with examinees, but monitor the administration through live video streaming) (Association of Test Publishers/National College Testing Association, 2015). Additional proctors may be required for separate testing rooms and to monitor bathrooms and break areas. Some programs also hire police and EMTs to assist as needed.

One of the primary goals of the check-in process is to make certain that the test is administered only to authorized individuals. To verify the authenticity and legitimacy of the examinees, each examinee should be asked to present at least one form of government-issued picture identification and documentation from the testing company authorizing them to test at that time and location (e.g., an admission ticket), and should be asked to sign their names on the roster. Testing personnel must carefully inspect the photo identification, comparing the written information with that on the admission ticket, the signature with the one provided on the roster, and the likeness of the photo and the individual appearing to test. If signature or photos were collected during the registration process or from prior testing experiences, it is important to compare against that information as well. Should any name or address discrepancies arise, administrators should follow the program protocol, as outlined in the administrator's manual.

In the event that a test administrator suspects the examinee appearing to test may be a proxy tester, a second administrator, preferably the site supervisor, should be consulted. If the testing personnel remain unable to confidently authenticate the examinee, either because of poor photo quality, dramatic changes in physical appearance relative to photo (e.g., aging, weight loss/gain, facial hair), or seemingly a different individual than in the picture, unless the guidelines for the specific program allow testing (and reporting on an irregularity report), the individual should not be allowed to test at that time.

With devices designed to collect biometric data becoming much smaller, less expensive, and more reliable, an increasing number of testing programs also collect biometric information from examinees. Biometric data are ideally suited for establishing that the examinee who registered and was authorized to test is the same examinee appearing to test. This process is most effective if biometric data are also captured during the registration process and test-day biometrics are cross-checked against the registration data prior to examinees being admitted.

In admitting and checking in examinees, testing personnel must be cognizant and respectful of attire or devices for religious, medical, or disability-related purposes. The National College Testing Association has developed an excellent, publicly available webinar that both introduces the types of clothing or devices that one might encounter, and how to protect the security of the test while honoring examinees' religious and legal rights (Mitchell, Ben-Dov, Mirdamadi, Duffy, & Keyser, 2013).

Several religions require men and women to wear head coverings in public. Such coverings should be visually inspected by testing personnel, but unless there is observational evidence to suggest an actual test security violation (e.g., concealed communication devices, notes, etc.), such clothing should not be hand inspected nor removed for inspection, and examinees may proceed to wear them during the examination. In the event that they do need to be removed for inspection purposes, it is important that the examinee remove them, and that the inspection be done in a private room and by a staff member of the same sex as the examinee. Under no circumstances should examinees be allowed to wear face veils during either the identification check or testing, and the headgear should be pulled to the hairline and situated to expose as much of the face as possible. For tests requiring that the examinee be photographed during check-in, all examinees who will wear headgear during the exam must be photographed in the headgear. Examinees not wanting to be photographed should not be permitted to test unless they possess approved documentation from the testing company exempting them from this requirement (Mitchell et al., 2013).

Similarly, testing staff should visually inspect medical or assistive technologies (e.g., cochlear implants/hearing aids, insulin pumps, prosthesis) for evidence of test security violations. If staff are uncertain about the legitimacy of a device, they may ask examinees if it is needed for a medical condition and to explain the purpose it fulfills. They may also photograph the device and submit it to the testing program for potential follow-up. Devices with Internet, recording, or image capture capabilities should not be permitted during testing. If staff believe the device in question may be used to capture and/or transmit testing information during the exam, they should contact the testing agency prior to admitting the examinee (Mitchell et al., 2013).

Another important function of the check-in process is to limit the materials brought into the testing room to only those authorized by the testing entity. This is not only to prevent examinees from illegally accessing information during the test, but also to preclude them from removing secure testing information from the site. Examinees should be given access to a secure locker for their excess belongings. If no lockers are available, examinees should be advised to leave belongings elsewhere. For a paper-based exam, it may be permissible to leave belongings in a bag, provided that bag is inspected during check-in and remains sealed and on the floor throughout the exam. Examinees should be informed that testing staff will report to the testing company any incidents in which prohibited materials are discovered after being admitted, and that any such materials will be assumed to be intended for fraudulent purposes, even if such behavior is not directly observed. Examinees should be asked to turn their pockets inside out to show that they are empty, prior to being admitted to the testing room.

Protocols must outline what is and is not permitted in the exam room. For paper-based exams, examinees are generally permitted to bring number two pencils, but use of other materials such as pens, erasers, highlighters, earplugs, and calculators vary by program. For computer-based tests and even some paper-based tests, examinees are often not allowed to bring anything of their own into the testing environment, except their photo ID and admission ticket. Some programs provide a whiteboard and dry erase markers for use during the test. If scratch paper is allowed, such paper should be issued by the test administrator, numbered and labeled for identification purposes, and collected and accounted for at the end of the exam. Examinees should not be allowed to bring into the testing room bags/backpacks/purses, clothing that interferes with testing personnel's ability to proctor (e.g., sunglasses, hoodies, hats), or food/drink, etc. Devices used for communication or data storage (e.g., phones, pagers, headsets, voice recorders) and prohibited resource material should not be allowed in the testing facility so as to prevent examinees from accessing them during breaks. In the event that an examinee does bring a phone, it should be turned off before storing it in the locker. Examinees should be told that if testing staff learn of a device that is turned on (as could happen if a phone rings from inside someone's locker during the exam), it will be reported to the testing company and the examinee's test scores may be canceled.

The check-in stations should be at the entrance gate to the exam room for a paper-based exam, and as mentioned earlier, should be outside the testing room for a computer-based exam. Examinees should be checked in one at a time, after which they should immediately be directed to take their assigned seats. No one should be permitted access to the exam room without first passing through check-in, and any checked-in examinees who leave the exam room must both formally check out and pass through check-in again, prior to re-entry. If, prior to the administration, there is concern for the safety of proctors and examinees, off-duty police or security personnel may be hired.

For programs that allow examinees to switch test sites or test sections, in the event that a test site is over capacity, examinees should be admitted in priority order. Top priority should be given to those examinees for whom the information on their admission ticket matches exactly the test site and test sections they wish to take. Students registered for the correct site but wishing to change or add test sections should be admitted next, and the lowest priority should be given to individuals who are registered for a different test site.

It is important that examinees not be permitted to select their own seats, as this may thwart opportunities for examinees to collaborate or to situate themselves near pre-planted materials or with good sight lines to examinees of their choosing. This is true even for computer-based testing programs, where examinees in a testing site are often starting at different times or completing different exams. If a seating chart is not supplied by the test publisher, the test administrator should randomly (i.e., not alphabetically or in order of registering for the test) assign examinees to seats and develop a seating chart that he or she can submit when materials are returned. The seating chart should indicate which examinees are seated in each seat, as well as the location of any doors, pillars/obstructions, and other things of interest in the room. An accurate, complete, carefully drawn seating chart provides a critically important piece of information in misconduct investigations (Harris & Schoenig, 2013).

Once examinees are seated for a paper-based exam, examination materials should be distributed. For a paper-based test, it is customary that the program provides detailed directions on how exams are to be distributed. Exams should always be distributed to examinees individually from the top of the pile to preserve the randomization and serialization of test forms. This ensures that alternate forms are spiraled throughout the room in an optimal and standardized way, thereby preventing some examinees from accidentally having the same test form as a neighboring examinee and providing another means to verify an examinee's test form in the event of a misconduct investigation. It is imperative that extra test booklets not be left unattended at a front desk or on an examinee desk at any point during the test administration.

For a computer-based exam, administrators should help examinees to access the specific exam for which they are authorized, should ask the examinee to enter his or her assigned login credentials, and should input the administrator login credentials to launch the exam. Testing personnel should never give the administrator login or password to a testing examinee and should not allow examinees to share passwords with one another.

Managing Examinee Expectations

It is well recognized that examinees are entitled to receive information from the testing company detailing the purpose of the exam, the constructs being measured, and the specific content being assessed. It is common to share with examinees a test blueprint, a description of the various item types (including directions for each section), sample questions/practice exam, and a study guide. By having this information up front, examinees can take the steps necessary to prepare themselves for doing their best.

Although it is less often discussed, examinees are also entitled to receive information detailing the administration conditions for the test. Basic administration information, such as eligibility criteria, timing, item review opportunities, prohibited attire/materials, specialized scoring instructions (such as corrections for guessing, score expiration dates, etc.), mechanics of score reporting, delivery medium, testing dates/windows/locations, retest rules, etc. should be posted on the test's website and freely and widely shared with potential examinees.

For computer-based exams, one must also be concerned about examinees' familiarity with both the hardware and software required for the exam. Examinees taking computer-based exams should have an opportunity to try out the test delivery software in advance of the exam. Any functionality that will exist during the live exam, such as item navigation, online calculators, font enlargement, requesting scheduled or unscheduled breaks, and submitting answers, should be available for practice. Also, it is important that schools delivering computer-based exams provide all students with opportunities to familiarize themselves with the basics of operating a computer, so as to ensure that test scores are not contaminated by one's computer proficiency. This is particularly important with innovative item types (many of which will be utilized by the Smarter Balanced and PARCC consortia) that require users to do more than simply select a multiple-choice option (Parshall, Spray, Kalohn, & Davey, 2002; Perlman, Berger, & Tyler, 1993).

At the point that an examinee first registers for an exam and indicates his or her intention to sit for the exam, the testing program should require the individual to sign an *Examinee Agreement*. The Examinee Agreement is a legal document that informs the examinee of the terms and conditions under which the exam is to be taken, and the policies and procedures that will be used by the testing company in the face of a potential security breach. This document should describe in detail the program's misconduct process, including the types of activities/behaviors that are prohibited (before, during, and after the exam), the process by which it will be determined whether the program should take action against the examinee, possible sanctions (including score cancelation, restrictions on future testing opportunities, and legal action) should examinees engage in fraudulent activity, and the appeals process. All examinees should be required to sign the Examinee Agreement prior to being authorized to test. It is increasingly common for testing programs to remind examinees of the terms of the Examinee Agreement immediately before (and sometimes immediately following) the exam so as to ensure that examinees clearly and unambiguously understand their responsibilities and the consequences for violating them. Some programs require that examinees sign an abbreviated agreement highlighted on the front cover of the test book, or to indicate agreement on the first screen in a computer-based exam.

Sanctioning examinees is a very serious step and often results in litigation. The U.S. Courts have generally ruled in favor of testing companies provided they can demonstrate: (a) that the examinees were thoroughly informed of the program's policies and procedures surrounding issues that compromise test score integrity; and (b) that the program's policies and procedures were followed in good faith (Semko & Hunt, 2013). Consequently, it is critically important that when incidents arise, everyone representing the testing company (which includes test administrators and proctors) adhere strictly to company policy, as stated in the Examinee Agreement. Harris and Schoenig (2013) provide an excellent overview of the fairness considerations facing testing companies throughout an entire misconduct investigation. It should be obvious that avoiding issues through careful proctoring is more cost-efficient than relying on legal measures after test administration.

Maintaining Fairness during the Exam

The administration of a high-stakes exam is unquestionably a stressful environment for everyone involved. Examinees' anxiety results from the fact that exams often serve as gatekeepers for examinees to achieve their professional goals. But the stress is compounded by the sensitivity of dealing with potential security issues, the lack of confidentiality and privacy associated with multiple examinees testing simultaneously, and the time constraints under which exams are administered. Hence, critical decisions must be made very quickly. For this reason, testing staff must be thoroughly trained. Too often, this training focuses only on routine issues, such as how to get the exam started and proctoring throughout the exam. Obviously, these skills will serve them well the majority of the time. However, unless testing staff are also well trained to deal with the exceptions, the pressures of the moment are likely to result in those situations being mishandled and the fairness of the exam becoming compromised.

Basic Administration

The idea behind standardization is that exam administrations should be as similar as possible for all examinees, no matter the location or individuals involved. This is generally easier to do in computer-based testing because such tests are more self-contained than are paper-based tests. That is, with computer-based tests, no materials need to be distributed or collected, examinees are often responsible for reading their own instructions, software manages the timing and access to different sections, examinees submit their own exams, etc. Paper-based testing requires that these same processes be managed by test administrators, so careful rules must be established so that all examinees are treated equitably, regardless of where they test and who administers the exam.

For a group-administered paper-and-pencil test, the testing room door should be closed promptly at the scheduled start time. An examinee may continue to be seated up until the exam itself begins, provided it can be done without interruption to other examinees and enough time remains for the individual to receive the instructions and ask questions. Exam directions should be read verbatim, as described in the administrator's manual. Administrators should not paraphrase or abbreviate the instructions. If there are questions relating to the directions, the relevant sections may be reread, but directions should not be interpreted for examinees. This latter point is true whether the exam is paper-and-pencil or computer-administered.

If an exam consists of separate sections and the administrator's manual specifies a required order of administration, the sections must be administered in that order. The proctors should ensure that examinees do not begin any separately timed section of the test until after directions have been read and the administrator has indicated that they may begin that section. When time expires, administrators should instruct all examinees that the exam is over and that they must stop working immediately. Examinees who continue to mark bubbles should be reminded to put down their pencils. If they continue to work beyond the time limit, it should be reported in an irregularity report.

Testing personnel should never provide feedback on specific test questions, such as interpreting the question, helping eliminate alternatives, or suggesting that examinees check their work. During the exam, proctors are not allowed to point out to examinees that they skipped questions or to encourage them to guess, even if the test instructions encourage guessing. This point applies to all testing programs, but is particularly relevant for school-based accountability testing where the test administrator often: (a) is an educator involved in the delivery of the curriculum (i.e., is an individual who is likely to know the answers); and (b) has a conflict of interest in that he or she is one of the primary stakeholders of the exam results. Furthermore, research suggests that educators do not have a clear understanding of the types of help, either prior to a test or during a test, that are acceptable and the types that are prohibited because they give those students an unfair advantage over others who do not receive those same aids (Amrein-Beardsley, Berliner, & Rideau, 2010). The interested reader is referred to NCME (2012) for more information on best test preparation and administration practices for K-12 accountability exams.

If examinees have a problem with a specific test question, they should be encouraged to file a report at the conclusion of the exam. If an examinee informs the proctor that he or she made a mistake on the answer sheet by filling bubbles in the wrong section of the answer sheet, inadvertently skipped a test question, or otherwise filled bubbles in the wrong place, the proctor should follow the procedures that are in place (e.g., collecting the existing answer sheet and issuing a new answer sheet for the remainder of the test). The proctor should complete an incident report fully explaining what occurred so that the testing agency can follow the procedures in place for scoring the test.

In classroom testing situations (not including accountability testing, which should strictly adhere to the standardization guidelines), it is understood that teachers: (a) are less rigorous with regard to the crafting of test directions and test items; and (b) are the authoritative source with respect to the construct definition and the intended interpretation of items. Hence, it may be necessary and appropriate for them to allow individual students to ask questions of clarification during the exam. However, instructors must be very careful that their responses only serve to clarify what the question is asking, but do not offer information that can be used by the student to answer the question. In addition, if an instructor is amenable to answering clarifying questions during the exam, an important fairness consideration is that all students have equal access to the instructor during the exam. This is particularly relevant for students with disabilities. Often, the nature of an accommodation makes it difficult or impossible to provide it during the regular class period (e.g., extended time, distraction-reduced space, etc.). Especially considering that examinees with disabilities may be at increased risk for having clarifying questions, they should not be required to vacate their right to access a teacher during an exam in order to receive their accommodations. Similarly, students who were absent during an exam and require a makeup should be allowed an opportunity to ask questions. If it is not possible for the instructor to supervise the entire exam, thereby allowing just-in-time feedback, at a minimum, a plan should be put in place for the instructor to check in with the student once or twice during the exam.

Monitoring Examinees for Possible Cheating

For most testing programs, the vast majority of examinees will not attempt to cheat during the test. Although examinees should be presumed honest until evidence suggests otherwise, the job of the proctor is to view everything out of the ordinary with some suspicion.

Proctoring is the first line of defense against the use of prohibited resources, heat-of-the-moment cheating, such as answer copying, and many forms of item/test theft. Proctoring involves actively monitoring examinees throughout the test administration for purposes of ensuring compliance with program policies and standardization procedures, and preventing, detecting, and documenting potential security violations. Active monitoring is much more than simply doing the rounds and waiting for an alarm to sound when an examinee attempts to cheat. Today's test cheaters are an extraordinarily clever and technologically savvy bunch, in some cases brazenly hiding their cheating gear in plain sight, yet in ways that are virtually undetectable. Video cameras, Internet browsers, and Bluetooth headsets may be disguised as jewelry, woven into clothing, or worn as glasses. Frequently, the actual devices themselves will either not be visible to proctors or they will be so cleverly disguised that recognition is very challenging (Wollack, 2014). Consequently, detecting when they are being used requires the ability to recognize significant departures from expected examinee behavior.

Typical examinee behavior involves focused attention on the computer screen or test booklet and answer sheet. Examinees should be sitting in a comfortable position, either for reading a computer screen or for marking an answer sheet. Except for the occasional stretch, cough, itch, or yawn, examinees should be expected to sit fairly still.

Consequently, proctors should be on the lookout for deviations from this pattern. Because examinees should be focused on their exam/answer sheet or computer screen/keyboard/mouse, those frequently attending to extraneous stimuli should be monitored closely, especially if their attention is repeatedly drawn to the same extraneous stimulus. Examples of especially suspicious activities include examinees looking at parts of their bodies (or clothing), other examinees (or their papers), or an object on their desk. It is also suspicious for examinees to be staring at proctors or unusually attentive to the location of various proctors about the room.

Examinees should be sitting still and not fidgeting or sitting in awkward positions. Both could suggest that the examinee is trying to subtly and discretely access unauthorized resources (including a neighbor's exam) or hide any such resources he or she may have. Examinees covering their eyes, ears, or mouths for extended periods should be watched closely for indications that they are sending or receiving information during the test. Examinees sitting very close to their keyboards or exams or who are bent down over their desks may well be attempting to conceal something. This is especially true in a computer-based testing environment, where video cameras are often placed overhead and directed down onto examinees' computers. Examinees with unauthorized materials will often attempt to use their bodies to shield the cameras from getting a good view.

Another example of unusual behavior is examinees who spend an inordinate amount of time engaged in non-test-taking behaviors, examples of which are taking repeated breaks or approaching proctors to ask questions or complain about different issues. Examinees taking breaks may use that opportunity to access information or contact individuals outside the testing room. They may also use it as an opportunity to change places with a proxy examinee. Examinees who interact frequently with proctors may be using that as an excuse to interact with another testing examinee or to look at answers from several other examinees as they walk by. Also, proctors must be on alert for the possibility that the interaction is an attempt to divert their attention from another examinee (a co-conspirator) who is engaged in fraudulent behavior.

In the face of suspicious activity, the proctor should not give the examinee the benefit of the doubt, but should take some action. Within the context of a remote proctoring situation, where the proctor may unobtrusively interact with the examinee without disturbing others, it is common practice to intervene immediately with a quick reminder to the examinee about appropriate exam behavior. Alternatively, the proctor may ask the examinee to shift positions or move the camera to improve the viewing angle. In a more traditional exam environment, it is important to corroborate previous observations and form a professional opinion about whether the observed behavior constitutes a security risk. The easiest way to do this is to observe the behavior over an extended period to see if it persists. To the extent possible, behavior should also be observed from multiple vantage points. This is particularly helpful if one believes that the examinee may be concealing something. If the anomalous behavior continues, the proctor should ask a second proctor to monitor the examinee, as well. If two experienced proctors concur that the behavior is suspicious and constitutes a potential security violation, it is a safe bet that the testing program is going to regard it as worthy of further investigation.

In some cases, it may be that the best way to view a suspicious behavior is on video camera. Video cameras have the advantages of providing viewing angles that are often not available to proctors, enabling covert and inconspicuous monitoring, and allowing post hoc review of the exact behaviors that struck proctors as potentially suspicious. Proctoring through video camera is usually an option for computer-based testing, because most computer-based testing programs require that the exams be video recorded. Videotaping of paper-and-pencil administrations is less common because examinees often test in large groups; however, video cameras can still be quite useful provided they are of sufficiently high resolution and have pan and zoom functionality.

In other cases, the best way to view the suspicious behavior is during a walk-through. Walk-throughs allow the proctors to get close to testing examinees to more closely inspect their workstations. In computer-based testing, where proctors are usually stationed in an adjoining room and viewing through an observation window, walk-throughs should be conducted approximately once every 10–15 minutes (Association of Test Publishers/ National College Testing Association, 2015; Scicchitano & Meade, 2013). However, examinees, especially those who are engaged in fraudulent behaviors that could be observed by a proctor, are often keenly aware of proctors' locations, so may well not repeat the behavior when a proctor is approaching. Consequently, the primary role of the proctor at the front of the room or the one who passes by examinees during the test is to serve as a deterrent, a constant reminder to the examinees that they are being actively monitored. It is often the proctors in the back of the room who cannot be easily accounted for by examinees, who are best able to observe examinees cheating. When testing personnel believe that an examinee is cheating, it may be useful to work with other proctors to set up a trap, wherein one proctor close to and in plain view of the examinee situates him or herself with his or her back to the examinee, creating a false sense of security for the examinee. Meanwhile, one or two proctors from behind with different viewing angles monitor the examinee's behavior.

After proctors become sufficiently confident that the examinee is engaged in unusual behavior, the challenge is to determine how best to respond. Some programs recommend intervening immediately to confiscate materials, remind examinees to keep their eyes on their own exams, or to reseat one or both examinees. Others propose intervening, but waiting to do so at a scheduled break when it would be less disruptive to all examinees. Others still ask that testing personnel simply continue to monitor the activities. The administrator's manuals should be very clear with regard to how testing staff should address these situations. Testing personnel should always follow the protocol specified for each program to ensure that all examinees suspected of engaging in a particular form of misconduct are treated equally. However, regardless of the steps specified by the testing program, it is a good idea to document exactly what was observed, by whom, and when. These incident reports should be detailed and contain as many facts as possible, noting, for example, the time of observation, notes of the item numbers the examinee is working on, and anything else the proctor believes is relevant. Proctor reports will often serve as the trigger for, and potentially the center of, a more thorough investigation, so should give as complete a picture of the circumstances as possible. Proctor training should focus on good and bad examples of incident reports.

Generally speaking, best practice is to allow behaviors to continue provided they are not disruptive to other examinees and do not involve possible capture or transmission of test content. Most programs do not intervene when it is believed that examinees are working together or that one examinee may be copying from another. Examinees copying from one another will produce an unusual number of answer matches that can be detected through statistical analysis after the exam; interrupting the behavior may mute the magnitude of the effect, thereby making statistical corroboration more challenging.

When it is believed that the person may be using written materials expressly prohibited by the program, most programs ask that the examinee be approached privately during a break and asked to turn pockets inside out. It if is believed that the material is hidden elsewhere in an examinee's clothing, you may ask the examinee to remove and submit outerwear for inspection. Any materials that are found should be confiscated and submitted to the testing company along with an irregularity report.

Possession of electronic devices must be handled differently because many can be used to both capture and transmit test content during the exam. Not only may stolen test questions cost the testing program tens if not hundreds of thousands of dollars to replace, but they also have high potential to produce spuriously inflated scores for many future examinees. If a proctor sees a device on an examinee's person, but does not believe that the device is being used (e.g., a cell phone in a pocket), at the program's discretion, the proctor may wait until a break to approach the examinee. However, if the examinee is observed accessing the device during the test, the proctor should immediately approach the examinee and confiscate the device. The proctor should ask the examinee to consent to an inspection of the phone. During the inspection, the proctor should look for evidence of phone, text, or email messages sent or received during the exam, as well as any pictures of testing content that may have been taken. Following the incident, a detailed report of what transpired should be filed with the testing company (Carson, 2011). In the event that testing staff are dealing with a security incident for which the administrator's manual does not provide sufficient guidance, the test administrator should contact the testing program immediately (during the exam administration) for further instructions. If at any point an examinee becomes aggressive and the testing personnel feel that anyone's personal safety is in jeopardy, they should immediately call the police. Similarly, the test administrator should contact the police if the testing personnel are confident that an examinee is possessing prohibited items that were used to capture test content (e.g., a cell phone), but he or she refuses to turn over the items or allow a suspicious item or article of clothing to be inspected (Schoenig, 2014). Every effort must be made to ensure that the examinee does not leave the test site with stolen test content.

Scheduled and Unscheduled Breaks

Most standardized exams that are longer than a couple of hours build in scheduled breaks for examinees to allow them to re-energize and increase the likelihood that their test performance reflects their best efforts.

Breaks are intended for examinees to use the bathrooms, eat/drink, take medicine, rest, and get their minds ready for the next section of the test. However, test administrators (and testing programs) should realize that breaks also provide an opportunity for potential misconduct. Breaks provide greater opportunities for examinees to communicate with each other or with individuals outside the testing environment. Breaks provide examinees with opportunities to access their belongings, possibly including prohibited items. Breaks also provide an opportunity for examinees to change places with each other. And breaks may even provide opportunities for unauthorized individuals (e.g., an educator) to access others' exams and tamper with their answers.

The severity of these different types of concerns varies depending on the break policy of the program. The most secure break policies allow breaks only in between sections, so that examinees may not return to the same set of items after break. This type of a policy would also safeguard against potential test tampering by an educator. Other programs, however, allow examinees to take breaks at their leisure, but provide a fixed amount of break time, after which any additional breaks will count against their actual testing time. Most programs inform examinees that unusually long or frequent breaks may result in the filing of an irregularity report.

Because breaks present increased security risks, they must be carefully administered by testing personnel. Prior to a break, examinees must either turn in their exam materials to the test administrator or log out of their workstations (or set them to the break screen). Many programs ask examinees to present photo ID, sign out in a logbook, and/or submit to biometric testing prior to being allowed to leave on break. Examinees should not be allowed to leave the immediate vicinity of the testing room during break and should be monitored closely to ensure that they do not access cell phones, study materials, or discuss test content with other examinees during this time. Proctors should also pay close attention to the examinees as they check out to go on break, in case an examinee decides to switch places with another similar-looking individual. When biometrics are not used, the testing program is reliant on the proctor's attentiveness to prevent a proxy examinee from testing in the stead of an authorized examinee. Ideally, the check-in/check-out area should be monitored by video so that the legitimacy of changes in examinee attire/appearance during breaks may be verified.

At the end of breaks, examinees must repeat the check-in process, and should be advised of such prior to taking breaks, and encouraged to budget their time accordingly. To re-enter the testing room, examinees should be reminded to return any disallowed items still in their possession to their lockers and asked to turn their pockets inside out. Examinees should also re-authenticate, including signing the examinee log, showing picture ID, and submitting to any biometric testing required by the program. Programs that routinely use metal-detection wands upon check-in will likely repeat that procedure for examinees returning from breaks. The same level of attention that went into initially authenticating examinees and verifying that prohibited materials were not brought into the testing room should be repeated every time upon re-entry.

These authors strongly discourage allowing breaks during classroom testing. A school is not a sufficiently controlled assessment environment and too few testing staff are available to monitor break behavior. Therefore, it is impossible to safeguard against a student using the break to visit their locker to look up information in their textbook or on their cell phone. Students should be notified the day before the exam that no breaks will be allowed and encouraged to use the restroom during the change of classes. In the event that they forget or were unable, they should be given an opportunity to go at the very beginning of class before receiving a copy of the exam. It should be understood that any time they spend on break will count against their total testing time.

Dealing with Emergencies and Unforeseen Situations

By definition, unforeseen situations happen rarely, but when they do, it is important that testing personnel be prepared and understand how to proceed. As with handling suspected cheating, guidelines for handling these situations should be addressed in the administrator's manual. Best practice suggests that when dealing with an emergency situation, such as a fire alarm or bomb threat, the top priority is the lives and safety of the examinees and testing personnel. Securing testing materials is important, but not at the risk of anyone's life. If time does not allow for test booklets to be collected or for workstations to be locked, ask that examinees simply leave their materials in place, remind them that they are not to discuss the test with other examinees, and escort them out of the building. In dealing with an evacuation situation for which it is practical to collect test materials (e.g., an extended power outage, a tornado warning, etc.), examinees should be instructed to lock their workstations or place their testing materials inside their test booklets and hand them to a proctor as they exit the building.

Testing personnel should monitor the exits to ensure that examinees are not removing any testing materials from the room. The testing room should be locked after the last person has left.

Unusual distractions, such as high construction noise, a flickering light, a disruptive examinee, or a temperamental computer, may also present problems for some examinees. If it is possible to adequately address the concern by reseating affected examinees (possibly in another room, if adequate staff are available), waiting a short while until the distraction passes, or offering the examinees earplugs (if allowed), that option should be explored first. In the event that the distraction persists and the examinees are either unable to complete the test or unable to do their best work, the administrator should collect the names and examinee numbers, if available, for all affected examinees and submit the list to the testing program, along with an irregularity report that documents the event and when it occurred.

In responding to unusual situations, the principle of maintaining standardization should be kept in mind. It arises in situations where an emergency affects only some of the examinees, and in these situations, some procedures are better than others. For example, if there is a power outage, and those seated near the windows can continue to see well enough to work, it is better to direct all examinees to stop working and close their test books in order to treat everyone in the same way. On the other hand, in a large testing center where a disruption occurs because of the illness of a single examinee, it simply might not be practical to halt the exam for everyone. In this situation, the problem should be handled as quickly and expeditiously as possible and an incident report should be written to document what occurred. Of course, the seating plan will document where examinees are seated relative to where the incident occurred.

Maintaining Fairness Following the Exam

Compared to the responsibilities prior to and during the test, the administration responsibilities at the end of the test are relatively straightforward. Still, ends of tests can be rather chaotic, with examinees racing to get out of the testing facility.

But important work remains for the test administrators, who must collect and account for all test materials and prepare them to be returned to the testing vendor for scoring and reporting.

Check-Out Procedures

For most individually administered tests, examinees may leave as soon as they are finished testing. For group-administered tests, procedures vary. Some allow test takers to leave when they complete the exam, perhaps until the last 10 or 15 minutes of testing time. Others require that all individuals must remain in their seats until time has expired. In all cases, however, examinees must be formally checked out by testing staff.

For paper-based exams that allow examinees to leave when they are finished, as examinees leave, they turn in their exam materials, which are placed in numerical order. Examinees remaining at the end of the exam should remain in their seats until materials are collected from each individual. Most programs require that exams be collected individually from the examinees to avoid having their exams handled by other test takers. Examinees should leave the testing room single file through a single exit, with proctors stationed on either side of the exit to make sure that examinees are not removing any test materials from the room.

For a computer-based exam, the process is much simpler. Test administrators should make sure that before examinees leave their workstations, they submit their scores and log out of the system. For programs for which examinees automatically receive test scores upon submission, the proctors should not help examinees to interpret those scores. Administrators should collect all whiteboards, and should collect and count any scratch paper that may have been issued. When all materials are accounted for, the examinees may leave the testing facility.

Irregularity Reports

Proctors need to complete an irregularity report for every unexpected incident, especially those where the security of the test may have been compromised. It is not necessary for the proctor to have proof that the test was compromised in order to file a report, just a strong professional judgment that it was at risk of being compromised. It is the responsibility of the testing program to follow up on all such incident reports and to make a determination of which reports warrant further action.

An incident or irregularity report must be as detailed as possible with respect to the specific behavior and the circumstances under which it occurred. What exactly was observed? Where was the examinee seated? What other individuals may have been involved, either actively (as co-conspirators) or passively (as potential source examinees)? At what time did the event occur and for how long did it continue? Who observed the behavior and from what vantage point? If the proctor interacted with the examinee as a result of the incident, that encounter must also be described fully. What was said? When did it happen? Were any prohibited materials actually found and taken? Although most programs perform some data forensics following the exam to identify cheating, many programs will not pursue alleged misconduct unless suspicious behavior was observed during the exam. Therefore, it is very important that proctor reports be a thorough and accurate accounting of the anomalous activity during an exam. How to complete an appropriate irregularity report should be a focus of proctor training.

Irregularity reports, however, are not only used to report potential security violations. Other deviations from the standardized conditions should be reported also. This includes examinees who get sick, examinees who are disruptive, power outages, network failures that caused disruption during testing or the inability to complete the test or submit scores, defective test materials, timing errors, misplaced answers, and emergency situations such as a fire alarm or bomb threat. The testing program will then use the information in the irregularity report to determine, for example, whether affected examinees should have their tests scored or be given a free retest.

Returning Materials

For paper-based programs, following the administration, testing materials must be packaged for shipping to the designated scanning/scoring vendor. Prior to assembling, answer sheets and test booklets should be checked against master rosters to ensure that both were collected for each examinee. Take special care not to miss test materials in alternate testing rooms used for examinees being tested under special accommodations.

If the program utilizes a testing window rather than fixed-date testing, as do most accountability testing programs, all materials should be returned to the secured storage area for test materials. Because storing completed answer sheets on premises constitutes a significant security risk, if it is not possible to return completed materials daily, as exams are completed, the likelihood of tampering with answer sheets can be reduced by packaging completed sheets in stamped security envelopes or boxed in ways that tampering would be evident (e.g., requiring cutting across a seal).

Testing materials should always be returned as quickly as is feasible. If it is practical to bring them to the shipping facility the same day as the test, that is ideal, provided the tests will then be shipped that same day. If the packages arrive at the shipping facility too late to send that same day, it is preferable to keep them in a locked, secured area within the testing facility until the next day when shipping is available.

Very often, the scanning/scoring vendor is different than the testing company from whom tests were sent to the testing site; therefore, it is important to use supplied shipping labels so tests are sent to the correct place. It is also important to use only approved shipping vendors to ensure that appropriate security and tracking procedures are in place.

Conclusion

The intersection of test administration and fairness is given much attention in the *Standards for Educational and Psychological Testing* (AERA et al., 2014). Chapter 6 of the Standards is specifically focused on test administration (among other topics), and highlights the importance of following standardization procedures (Standard 6.1), maintaining a comfortable environment with minimal distractions (Standard 6.4), eliminating opportunities for examinees to cheat (Standard 6.6), protecting the security of testing materials (Standard 6.7), and documenting departures from standardization procedures (Standard 6.3). Furthermore, Chapter 4 ("Test Design and Development"), Chapter 7 ("Supporting Documentation for Tests"), Chapter 8 ("The Rights and Responsibilities of Test Takers"), Chapter 10 ("Psychological Testing and Assessment"), and Chapter 12 ("Educational Testing and Assessment") all include specific standards that relate to test administration and its role in the testing process.

Chapter 3 of the Standards (AERA et al., 2014) discusses the issue of fairness in testing. While most of the 20 Standards identified in this chapter relate to aspects of test construction, building a validity argument, offering accommodations to remove construct-irrelevant variance, test score interpretation, appropriate score use, or instrument selection, it is clear that fairness extends also to the test administration phase of testing. Standard 3.4 makes this explicit in saying that "test takers should receive comparable treatment during the test administration and scoring process" (p. 65). Also, the prologue for Chapter 3 expands on this notion to discuss the importance of standardization of both tests and administration conditions, to ensure that the contexts in which examinees attempt to demonstrate their mastery of the measured constructs are comparable. Failure to consider and level the playing field across the full range of administration conditions, according to the Standards, could "inadvertently influence the performance of some test takers relative to others" (p. 51), thereby compromising the validity of the test score interpretations for all examinees.

At the same time, it is important for all involved in testing to recognize that while the purpose of standardization is to level the playing field for all examinees, there are special cases in which deviating from the standardization procedures for specific examinees may actually enhance the meaningfulness or interpretability of those individuals' test scores (AERA et al., 2014). The most typical examples in which this might be true are students with disabilities (including temporary disabilities which may not be covered by the ADA [1990]) and English language learners; however, in unique circumstances, other factors, such as an examinee's cultural background, socioeconomic status, or age, may necessitate some departure from the standardization procedures (p. 51). Still, except in classroom testing situations where the teacher is both the test developer and test administrator, the test administrator is obligated to follow the program's guidelines regarding accommodation or modification (keeping in mind that in the case of accountability testing, the test publisher often relegates that responsibility back to the schools).

Despite the increased emphasis on administration in the revised *Standards* (AERA et al., 2014), the topic of day-of-test administration garnered relatively little attention. However, it is important to recall that the short window in which the examinees are actually engaged with the test itself must also be very carefully controlled and examinees must be placed into a situation that allows the test to do what it was developed to do.

Test administration is a much more sophisticated process than just reading scripts and watching examinees take tests. It is a vital element of the testing process and valid score inferences depend on testing programs knowing that tests were administered to authorized examinees only and in environments that are comparable, disallow use of prohibited resources, and afford all examinees an opportunity to accurately demonstrate their talents.

Notes

1. The views expressed are those of the author and not necessarily those of the University of Wisconsin-Madison.
2. The views expressed are those of the author and not necessarily those of the National Conference of Bar Examiners.

References

American Educational Research Association, American Psychological Association, & National Council on Measurement in Education. (2014). *Standards for educational and psychological testing.* Washington, DC: American Educational Research Association.

Americans with Disabilities Act of 1990, 42 U.S.C.A § 12101 *et seq.* (West 1993).

Amrein-Beardsley, A., Berliner, D. C., & Rideau, S. (2010). Cheating in the first, second, and third degree: Educators' responses to high-stakes testing. *Educational Policy Analysis Archives, 18*(14) Retrieved from http://epaa.asu.edu/ojs/article/view/714/841

Association of Test Publishers/National College Testing Association. (2015) *Proctoring Best Practices.* Retrieved from www.createspace.com/5657838

Carson, J. (2011). *What to do when cheating is suspected on the Bar Exam.* Presentation at the annual meeting of the National Conference of Bar Examiners, San Francisco, CA, April.

Clemans, W. V. (1971). Test administration. In. R. L. Thorndike (Ed.), *Educational measurement* (2nd ed., pp. 188–201). Washington, DC: American Council on Education.

Haladyna, T. M., & Downing, S. M. (2004). Construct-irrelevant variance in high-stakes testing. *Educational Measurement: Issues and Practice, 23*(1), 17–27.

Harris, D. J., & Schoenig, R. R. W. (2013). Conducting investigations of misconduct. In J. A. Wollack & J. J. Fremer (Eds.), *Handbook of test security* (pp. 201–219). New York: Routledge.

McCallin, R. C. (2006). Test administration. In S. M. Downing & T. M. Haladyna (Eds.), *Handbook of test development* (pp. 625–652). Mahwah, NJ: Lawrence Erlbaum Associates.

Mitchell, A., Ben-Dov, N., Mirdamadi, Y., Duffy, T., & Keyser, P. (2013). *Test security: Informed and respectful.* National College Testing Association webinar, October 21. Retrieved from www.ncta-testing.org

National Council on Measurement in Education. (2012). *Testing and data integrity in the administration of statewide student assessment programs.* Madison, WI: NCME.

Parshall, C. G., Spray, J. A., Kalohn, J. C., & Davey, T. (2002). *Practical considerations in computer-based testing.* New York: Springer-Verlag.

Perlman, M., Berger, K., & Tyler, L. (1993). *An application of multimedia software to standardized testing in music (Research Rep. No. 93–96).* Princeton, NJ: Educational Testing Service.

Plake, B. S., & Wise, L. L. (2014). Highlights on major changes in the revised Standards for Educational and Psychological Testing. *NCME Newsletter, 22*(2), 5–8.

Schoenig, R. (2014). *Ten years of test security: The road traveled, the road ahead.* Presentation at the annual conference of the National College Testing Association, Denver, CO, September.

Scicchitano, A. R., & Meade, R. D. (2013). Physical security at test centers and the testing company. In J. A. Wollack & J. J. Fremer (Eds.), *Handbook of test security* (pp. 237–258). New York: Routledge.

Semko, J. A., & Hunt, R. (2013). Legal matters in test security. In J. A. Wollack & J. J. Fremer (Eds.), *Handbook of test security* (pp. 237–258). New York: Routledge.

Thurlow, M. L., Thompson, S. J., & Lazarus, S. S. (2006). Considerations for the administration of tests to special needs students: Accommodations, modifications, and more. In S. M. Downing & T. M. Haladyna (Eds.), *Handbook of test development* (pp. 653–673). Mahwah, NJ: Lawrence Erlbaum Associates.

Wollack, J. A. (2014). *Responding to cheating: Where we've been, where we're headed.* Presentation at the annual meeting of the National Council on Measurement in Education, Philadelphia, PA, April.

4 Fairness in Test Scoring

Randall D. Penfield[1]

Introduction

To introduce the topic of this chapter, let us consider a test developed with the goal of measuring writing proficiency. Ultimately, the test will be used to produce test scores reflecting each examinee's level of writing proficiency, and to do so the test must elicit examinee responses to generate evidence of writing proficiency. To this end, the test developer is faced with a decision concerning the type of items or tasks to be used to elicit examinee responses. The test developer may opt to use multiple-choice (MC) items. Although cost-effective and efficient, MC items are indirect measures of writing proficiency and may not yield inferences about an examinee's writing skills that rise to the same level of validity as those offered by more authentic writing tasks. To overcome limitations of MC items, the test developer may choose to employ constructed-response (CR) items consisting of a series of prompts used to elicit written responses from examinees, and have human-raters score the written responses using scoring rubrics. The resulting test may be comprised entirely of CR items or a combination of CR and MC items. While the CR item format offers a much more authentic assessment context, human-rater scoring suffers from several drawbacks, including inconsistency (e.g., due to rater severity/leniency, fatigue, etc.) and a high expense due to the time and resources required to train raters and conduct the scoring process (see Zhang, 2013). The test developer can avoid the drawbacks of human-rater scoring by using CR items that are scored by a computer-automated scoring engine (referred to as automated scoring hereafter), which applies a set of predefined decision rules to assign a score to a CR item based on particular features of the examinee's response. Automated scoring has the advantageous properties of being perfectly consistent across examinees and being highly efficient from a resource perspective, but these scores may yield biased estimates of scores assigned by human raters.

Regardless of the approach used to elicit and score examinee responses, a test score reflecting writing proficiency must be computed for each examinee. The test score is generated by aggregating available evidence of writing proficiency garnered from the scored elements of the examinee's response to the items of the test, what is referred to as the *evidence accumulation process* (Mislevy & Haertel, 2006). The nature of scored elements used in the evidence accumulation process varies depending on the type of item used to elicit responses (MC vs. CR) and the approach used to score the responses (human rater vs. automated). If the test of writing proficiency is comprised entirely of MC items, then each item is associated with a single dichotomously scored element (correct or incorrect), and the scored elements used in the evidence accumulation process comprise the resulting pattern of dichotomously scored responses. If the test of writing proficiency includes CR items that are scored by multiple human raters, then each rater's score of an examinee's response to each CR item serves as a scored element in the evidence accumulation process. In this context, evidence of writing proficiency is accumulated across the multiple raters' scores of the examinee's response to each CR item as well as across the CR items of the test. If our test of writing proficiency involves automated scoring based on a series of features of the examinee's response, then each scored feature used in assigning the automated score to a CR item serves as a scored element, and the evidence accumulation process occurs across the scored features of each CR item as well as across the CR items of the test. Lastly, it is possible for the test to include a combination of MC items and CR items scored by either human raters or an automated scoring engine, and the resulting scored elements used in the evidence accumulation process correspond to the scored elements associated with each item format.

The example of the test of writing proficiency described above sets the stage for the specific topic of fairness addressed in this chapter; namely, fairness in test scoring. Because the test score is based on an accumulation of evidence across the scored elements of the examinee's response, an argument for fairness of test scores can be developed from the evaluation of construct-irrelevant factors associated with the individual scored elements used in generating the test score; evidence that each scored element is free of construct-irrelevant factors provides a compelling argument that the resulting test score is free of construct-irrelevant factors. But, how should the test developer evaluate the presence of construct-irrelevant factors of each scored element used in arriving at the test score? The answer to this question resides in two issues associated with the scored elements of an examinee's response to the items of a test. The first issue concerns whether each scored element holds the same meaning with respect to the proficiency measured by the test regardless of the examinee's standing on key background variables such as race, ethnicity, gender, linguistic background, and disability status. This issue is addressed using the frameworks of differential item functioning, differential step functioning, and differential feature functioning as described throughout this chapter. A second issue pertains to the consistency of multiple independent scorings of each examinee's response, and whether the consistency of the assigned scores is sufficiently high for all examinees, regardless of the examinee's standing on key background variables.

The goal of this chapter is to provide an accessible overview of methods used to evaluate potential violations of fairness associated with the individual scored elements used in generating test scores. To this end, this chapter organizes the description of relevant methods according to the three types of item scores introduced in the example of the test of writing proficiency described in the beginning of the chapter: (a) automated scores of MC items; (b) human-rater scores of CR items; and (c) automated scores of CR items.

Multiple-Choice Items

Responses to MC items are scored dichotomously as correct ($Y = 1$) or incorrect ($Y = 0$), and these scored responses serve as the scored elements in the evidence accumulation process used to generate the test score. Machine scoring of MC items is perfectly consistent, and thus the issue of score consistency is of little concern to fairness of test scores generated from MC items. Rather, the primary consideration for fairness in the scored responses to MC items is whether the scored outcome of an MC item holds the same meaning with respect to the proficiency being measured by the test across examinee subgroups. This consideration is evaluated using the framework of differential item functioning (DIF).

The Concept of DIF for MC Items

In the creation of any test, the test developer aspires to create items for which examinee responses are determined by the proficiency intended to be measured by the test and not construct-irrelevant factors. If the correct response to an item is dependent not only on the intended proficiency, but also on a construct-irrelevant factor, then examinees with the same level of the proficiency may obtain different scores on the item depending on their respective level of the construct-irrelevant factor. This leads to the undesirable situation of the scored response generating different evidence of examinee proficiency depending on the examinee's standing on the construct-irrelevant factor. For example, if a correct response to an MC item intending to measure knowledge of proper grammar usage in a written passage is determined by not only knowledge of the relevant grammar, but also knowledge of the content of the passage (the construct-irrelevant factor), then the meaning of a correct response with respect to knowledge of proper grammar may differ across examinees having different levels of familiarity with the passage content; for examinees lacking familiarity with the passage content, an incorrect response may not be reflective of a lack of knowledge of proper grammar.

One way to evaluate whether the response to an MC item is dependent upon one or more construct-irrelevant factors is to compare the chance of success on the item for examinees having the same level of proficiency, but belonging to different subgroups that vary with respect to their standing on the relevant construct-irrelevant factor (e.g., subgroups defined by examinee background variables such as gender, race, ethnicity, linguistic and cultural backgrounds, disability status, or socioeconomic status). If examinees having the same proficiency, but belonging to different subgroups, have a different chance of success on the item, then there is evidence that success on the item is dependent upon construct-irrelevant factors that are inducing a disadvantage for one of the subgroups. The presence of such subgroup differences indicates that the item is functioning differently for different subgroups, and DIF is said to exist.

A visual representation of DIF for an MC item is shown in Figure 4.1a. This figure portrays the proportion of examinees having a correct response for two examinee subgroups at each level of total test score, which is a proxy for proficiency. By convention, the two subgroups shown in Figure 4.1a are referred to as the reference subgroup (solid line, $n = 500$) and focal subgroup (dashed line, $n = 500$). In this figure, we see a consistent between-subgroup difference in rate of success at each level of total test score, thus reflecting the presence of DIF; examinees in the reference subgroup tend to have a higher rate of success than focal subgroup examinees with the same test score.

The use of DIF evaluations in test development has served a foundational role in establishing psychometrically defensible claims that test scores are free of bias (Angoff, 1993; Phillips & Camara, 2006; Zieky, 2011), and it remains a key approach used to identify items containing content that limits the opportunity for particular examinee subgroups to demonstrate their standing on the proficiency being measured (AERA, APA, & NCME, 2014; O'Neill & McPeek, 1993). Numerous DIF evaluation methods are available, and a detailed description of all such methods is beyond the scope of this chapter. In this section, I provide an overview of DIF methodology pertaining to MC items. Because MC items are usually scored dichotomously, this overview is also relevant for dichotomously scored responses to CR items. Readers seeking additional descriptions of DIF methods for MC items are referred to Camilli (2006), Clauser and Mazor (1998), Holland and Wainer (1993), Mapuranga, Dorans, and Middleton (2008), Osterlind and Everson (2009), and Penfield and Camilli (2007).

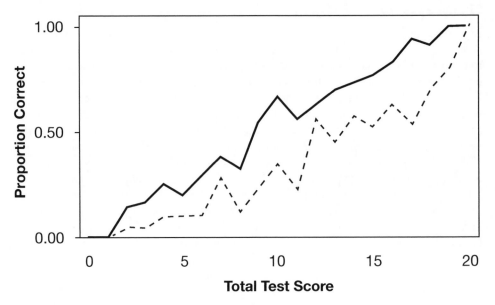

Figure 4.1a DIF in a Dichotomously Scored Item

Considerations for Conducting DIF Analyses for MC Items

A critical component to implementing DIF analyses yielding accurate and useful results for informing decisions of fairness is ensuring that the data hold necessary properties required for the methodology being implemented. These properties pertain to the quantity and quality of data used in the statistical estimation of DIF effects, and also the manner in which the DIF effects are interpreted to inform the potential of bias. A summary of these properties is presented below.

Stratifying Variable

Many DIF methodologies are based on first stratifying examinees according to an observed measure of proficiency, and then directly evaluating between-subgroup differences in item performance within each stratum of proficiency. A commonly adopted stratifying variable is the summated test score, which is the approach depicted in Figure 4.1a. However, other approaches for defining the stratifying variable are available, and the form of the stratifying variable adopted for a DIF analysis will depend on the specific context of the test under investigation. For simplicity, the variable used to stratify examinees on proficiency will be denoted here by S. Regardless of the approach used to define S, it is important that S holds the following properties to ensure that it generates a valid matching of examinees on proficiency. First, S must have a high degree of reliability to ensure proper matching of examinees, and the reliability of S should be reported with the results of the DIF analysis. Second, S must have an appropriately high number of strata to allow effective differentiation of examinees having different levels of proficiency.

Sample Size

DIF analyses are based on evaluating between-subgroup differences in item performance at each level of S, and thus sample sizes must be large enough to ensure that within each subgroup there are enough examinees to accommodate this comparison. In many instances, subgroups comprise less-represented examinee populations, creating an obstacle for achieving the needed sample size. DIF methodologies vary with respect to sample size requirements, and thus no single sample size guideline exists. However, even for the least sample-size-intensive DIF methods, a minimum of several hundred examinees per subgroup typically is required to attain an appropriate degree of stability.

Impact

Impact refers to the between-subgroup difference in mean proficiency. A large degree of impact can lead to bias in DIF effect estimation, and this bias increases as the reliability of S decreases. As a result, it is important to evaluate the mean proficiency (e.g., mean value of S) for each subgroup, and document the observed impact when reporting the results of DIF analyses. The smaller the average impact on S, the more likely it is that alternative DIF methods will agree with each other.

Evaluating DIF Effects

In evaluating DIF effects, it is important to consider the magnitude of the DIF effect size in coordination with a statistical significance test of the absence of DIF. While all investigations of DIF should consider both of these evaluative approaches, the magnitude of the DIF effect plays an especially important role in classifying the severity of the DIF effect because it is the magnitude of the DIF effect that informs the extent to which the observed effect presents a meaningful threat to fairness. As a result, all evaluations of DIF should include a statistical test of DIF as well as a measure of the DIF effect magnitude that is easily interpretable according to well-understood criteria.

Interpreting the Cause of DIF

If a substantial DIF effect is observed, it is important to review the item content to identify the factor responsible for the DIF effect. It is only when the causal factor has been identified and deemed to be construct-irrelevant that the DIF effect reflects a bias in the assessment (for a broader discussion, see Angoff, 1993; Penfield and Camilli, 2007). Ideally, hypotheses about the sources of DIF will be assessed via experiments such as that described in Schmitt, Holland, and Dorans (1993).

DIF Methods for MC Items

Perhaps the most intuitive approach to evaluating DIF in an MC item is to consider the between-subgroup difference in the observed proportion of responses to the item that are correct at each stratum of S, and then aggregate these stratum-level differences across all strata of S. This is the approach taken by the standardized p-difference index (*SPD*) (Dorans & Kulick, 1986):

$$SPD = \frac{\sum_s W_s \left(\hat{P}_{RS} - \hat{P}_{FS} \right)}{\sum_s W_s} \qquad (1)$$

where $\hat{P}_{RS} - \hat{P}_{FS}$ represents the difference in proportion correct between the reference subgroup (R) and the focal subgroup (F) at stratum S. The weight assigned to each stratum, W_S, is typically the number of focal subgroup members in the stratum. The value of SPD provides an index of the magnitude of the DIF effect; $|SPD| < .05$ reflects a negligible DIF effect, items with $0.05 \leq |SPD| \leq 0.10$ should be inspected to ensure possible construct-irrelevant factors are not overlooked, and items with $|SPD| > 0.10$ should receive careful examination for the presence of construct-irrelevant factors (Dorans & Holland, 1993, pp. 49–50). The value of SPD for the data illustrated in Figure 4.1a is $SPD = 0.21$, reflecting an item that should be carefully reviewed to identify potential construct-irrelevant factors.

An alternative approach for evaluating DIF in an MC item is based on the concept of the *odds ratio*. Rather than quantifying the between-subgroup difference in item success at each stratum of S using the observed proportion correct (i.e., $\hat{P}_{RS} - \hat{P}_{FS}$ in Equation 1), the odd ratio approach quantifies the between-subgroup difference in item success at each stratum of S using the ratio of the odds of correct response of the reference subgroup over that of the focal subgroup. The odds ratio observed at stratum S can be computed using the simplified form of:

$$O_S = \frac{A_S D_S}{B_S C_S},$$
(2)

where A_S and B_S represent the frequency of correct and incorrect responses for reference subgroup members at S, respectively, and C_S and D_S represent the frequency of correct and incorrect responses for focal subgroup members at S, respectively. The outcome $O_S = 1$ reflects no between-subgroup difference in item success, the outcome $O_S > 1$ reflects a relatively higher success for the reference subgroup, and the outcome $O_S < 1$ reflects a relatively higher success for the focal subgroup.

An index of DIF can be obtained using a weighted average of the obtained values of O_S across all strata of S. This is the approach taken by Mantel and Haenszel's (1959) common log-odds ratio estimator, which computes a weighted average of the O_S values transformed to the logit scale using:

$$\hat{\lambda}_{MH} = \ln \left[\frac{\sum_S W_S O_S}{\sum_S W_S} \right],$$
(3)

where the weight assigned at a given level of S is $W_S = B_S C_S / (A_S + B_S + C_S + D_S)$. Values of $\hat{\lambda}_{MH}$ are symmetric about zero, such that $\hat{\lambda}_{MH} = 0$ reflects no DIF, $\hat{\lambda}_{MH} > 0$ reflects DIF favoring the reference subgroup, and $\hat{\lambda}_{MH} < 0$ reflects DIF favoring the focal subgroup. The null hypothesis of no DIF can be tested using either a z-test or a chi-square test of conditional independence (Dorans & Holland, 1993; Penfield & Camilli, 2007). Applying $\hat{\lambda}_{MH}$ to the data shown in Figure 4.1a, we find $\hat{\lambda}_{MH} = 1.09$ with an estimated standard error of 0.15, and the null hypothesis of no DIF is rejected.

The evaluation of DIF using statistical tests of significance is highly dependent on sample size; with a large enough sample size, even near-zero DIF effects are likely to be statistically significant despite minimal practical implication. As a result, interpretations of DIF should give ample consideration to the magnitude of the DIF effect (e.g., as estimated by $\hat{\lambda}_{MH}$). The question to be asked, then, is how should $\hat{\lambda}_{MH}$ be interpreted with respect to DIF magnitude? There is no universally accepted set of values of $\hat{\lambda}_{MH}$ that delineate small, moderate, and large values of DIF effect, and the severity assigned to a particular magnitude of $\hat{\lambda}_{MH}$ will depend on the specific context of the assessment. I offer here a heuristic that may prove useful in interpreting the magnitude of the DIF effect: $|\hat{\lambda}_{MH}| < 0.3$ reflects a small DIF effect, $0.3 \geq |\hat{\lambda}_{MH}| < 0.6$ reflects a moderate DIF effect, and $|\hat{\lambda}_{MH}| \geq 0.6$ reflects a large DIF effect. Using this heuristic, the magnitude of the DIF effect depicted in the data of Figure 4.1a ($\hat{\lambda}_{MH} = 1.09$) is interpreted as being large.

The value of $\hat{\lambda}_{MH}$ also plays an instrumental role in an ETS test assembly decision rule designed to guard against the presence of potentially biased items. In their seminal application of the Mantel-Haenszel procedure to the evaluation of DIF, Holland and Thayer (1988) proposed the transformation of $\hat{\lambda}_{MH}$ from a logit scale to the more meaningful delta scale using *MH D-DIF* = $-2.35 \times \hat{\lambda}_{MH}$. Using the *MH D-DIF* transformation, items are classified into one of three categories (labeled A, B, and C) according to the following rules: Category A if either *MH D-DIF* is not significantly different from zero or $|MH\ D\text{-}DIF| < 1.0$; Category C if $|MH\ D\text{-}DIF|$ is significantly greater than 1.0 and $|MH\ D\text{-}DIF| \geq 1.5$; and Category B otherwise (Zieky, 1993). Items classified as Category C are flagged for removal from the item pool, items classified as Category B are flagged for potential revision or removal, and items classified as Category A are retained in the item pool. Applying this classification scheme to the data shown in Figure 4.1a leads to $|MH\ D\text{-}DIF| = 2.56$, which is significantly greater than 1.0, and thus the item is classified as Category C and would be flagged for removal from the item bank.

Test developers employing an item response theory (IRT) framework (de Ayala, 2009) can evaluate DIF directly through between-subgroup differences in the IRT model parameters for each item. Most commonly, DIF is evaluated with respect to between-subgroup differences in the item difficulty parameter and/or the item discrimination parameter. The magnitude of DIF can be quantified by the size of the between-subgroup differences. A statistical test of the equality of item parameters for examinee subgroups can be accomplished through either a chi-square test or a likelihood ratio test, as described by Penfield and Camilli (2007) and Thissen, Steinberg, and Wainer (1993). While IRT approaches have the advantage of providing a model-based method for evaluating DIF, they come with several notable drawbacks. First, the interpretation of the magnitude of the DIF effect in an IRT context is dependent on the scale of measurement used for the IRT calibration, making decisions of DIF effect magnitude ambiguous. Second, sample size requirements for implementing IRT models can be relatively large, which poses a particular obstacle to evaluating DIF with examinee subgroups that do not have large sizes (e.g., race/ethnicity, exceptionality status, accommodation status). Third, IRT approaches require good fit to the IRT model being used for the analysis.

Which DIF approach is most appropriate will depend on the specific context of the assessment. *SPD* and $\hat{\lambda}_{MH}$ have several notable advantages: (a) lack of any requirement of fit to a particular IRT model; (b) independence of the DIF effect magnitude from the scale used to measure proficiency; (c) relatively simple estimation procedures; and (d) applicability with relatively small sample sizes compared to those required by some IRT models. A potential limitation of both *SPD* and $\hat{\lambda}_{MH}$ is their insensitivity to changes in the sign of the between-subgroup difference in performance across level of *S*; both can yield a negligible DIF effect estimate despite large between-subgroup differences that favor different subgroups at different levels of *S*. This restricts the interpretation of *SPD* and $\hat{\lambda}_{MH}$ to reflect the overall advantage of the reference subgroup over that of the focal subgroup across the proficiency continuum.

Human Scored Constructed Responses

When human raters are used to score examinee responses to CR items, the potential for rater inconsistency often necessitates having two or more raters score each response to arrive at an adequately reliable and valid interpretation of examinee performance. Ideally, each examinee response is associated with multiple scores, and each score is a unique scored element used in the evidence accumulation process to arrive at the examinee's test score. In this context, the corresponding evidence accumulation process has two levels: (a) item-level accumulation; and (b) test-level accumulation. The item-level accumulation involves aggregating the multiple rater scores of an examinee's response to a given item into a single overall item score. Examples of item-level accumulation include summing or averaging the rater scores assigned to an examinee's response. Of critical importance in this stage of evidence accumulation is that the rater scores be based on the same decision rules and not be impacted by construct-irrelevant factors, which can be evaluated through the consistency of the rater scores. The test-level accumulation involves aggregating across the overall item scores (obtained from the item-level accumulation phase) to arrive at the test score. Examples of test-level accumulation include computing the summated test score or obtaining an IRT-based estimate of proficiency. As was the case for tests comprised of MC items, a critical concern in the test-level evidence accumulation process is that the overall item scores hold the same meaning with respect to level of proficiency regardless of subgroup membership, which is evaluated using DIF.

This section describes methods used to evaluate rater consistency and DIF in the context of human-rater scoring of CR items. Because CR items are commonly scored according to rubric specifications having more than two score levels, the scored outcomes are typically polytomous in nature. As a result, this section describes relevant procedures and methods in the context of polytomously scored responses. However, all methods described here can be specialized to the case of dichotomously scored responses.

Rater Consistency

Human-rater scores are based on judgment guided by a series of established scoring decision rules. When the scoring rules are relatively complex, as would be the case in scoring an essay or a complex performance task, the human judgment underlying the scoring process may lead to inconsistency in rater scores. Rater inconsistency has myriad causes, including context effects, rater fatigue, halo effects, rater attention to irrelevant features, and rater leniency/severity (see Bridgeman, 2013; Lane & Stone, 2006; Ramineni, Trapani, Williamson, Davey, & Bridgeman, 2012; Wolfe, 2004). Regardless of the cause, a sizable inconsistency between raters' scores can impact the quality of the estimate of proficiency, and thus steps must be taken to ensure that potentially impactful inconsistencies are identified and addressed. To guard against the adverse effects of rater inconsistency when scoring CR items, the final score assigned to an examinee's response can be based on an aggregate of two or more independent scorings (Young, So, & Ockey, 2013).

Evaluating rater consistency should be conducted at the level of each examinee and the level of particular groups of examinees. Examinee-level consistency addresses whether the raters' scores of a particular examinee's response are adequately consistent. If the scores assigned to a particular examinee's response are not adequately consistent, then there is evidence that the raters employed different decision rules, which may reflect the presence of construct-irrelevant factors in the scores assigned by one or more of the raters. Group-level consistency addresses whether rater consistency holds for one or more groups of examinees. A lack of adequate rater consistency for an examinee group indicates the presence of a systematic impact of construct-irrelevant factors on the scoring of the entire group. Not only is it important to evaluate rater consistency for the entire examinee group, but it is also important to demonstrate adequate rater consistency for particular examinee subgroups defined by key background variables such as gender, race/ethnicity, language background, and the like. Methods for evaluating examinee-level consistency and group-level consistency are described below.

Examinee-Level Consistency

To describe the process of evaluating examinee-level consistency, let us consider the situation in which an examinee's response to a CR item is scored by two human raters, where the resulting scores are denoted by Y_1 and Y_2. The difference between the two scores assigned to the same examinee response is symbolized here by $\Delta = Y_1 - Y_2$. The outcome of $\Delta = 0$ corresponds to perfect rater agreement for that particular scored response, providing evidence that the raters are using the same decision rules free of influences of construct-irrelevant factors. In contrast, the outcome of $\Delta \neq 0$ indicates a lack of agreement between the two raters, suggesting the possibility of construct-irrelevant factors in Y_1 and/or Y_2. As Δ increases in magnitude, there is increasing evidence that construct-irrelevant factors impacted the scoring of the examinee's response.

Given the complex judgments required of human raters in scoring CR items, non-systematic differences between Y_1 and Y_2 are expected to arise, reflecting expected measurement error in the scoring process. As a result, some level of deviation of Δ from zero is typically permissible. However, there reaches a point at which the magnitude of Δ is so large that it suggests the presence of systematic differences in the scoring process used to generate Y_1 and Y_2. It follows that a threshold must be established specifying the largest permissible magnitude of Δ. This threshold is referred to as the *adjudication threshold*. Any instance of Δ exceeding the adjudication threshold triggers additional action to ensure that the final score assigned to the examinee is robust to the impacts of rater inconsistency. The approach described above for the situation of two human-rater scores (Y_1 and Y_2) can be extended to other contexts involving more than two scores, in which case Δ would be computed for each pair of scores and compared to the adjudication threshold in the same fashion described above.

The value set as the adjudication threshold will be dependent on the specific context of the assessment and the particular scale of Y. When the scale of Y consists of a moderate number of integer score levels (e.g., five score levels of $Y = 0, 1, 2, 3, 4$), then a commonly employed adjudication threshold is 1, such that any instance of $\Delta > 1$ will trigger additional action to resolve the discrepancy between Y_1 and Y_2 (Williamson, Xi, & Breyer, 2012). When the scale of Y has a high number or score levels, or includes decimals (e.g., 0.5 increments), then an adjudication threshold will need to be established that considers the specific properties of the scale of Y. Regardless of the particular scale of Y, the adjudication threshold should be clearly documented by the test developer.

A value of Δ exceeding the adjudication threshold triggers a resolution process, which typically involves obtaining an additional human-rater score. The specific approach for resolving the discrepant scores using the additional rating may vary depending on the context of the assessment. In general, however, the most reliable approach to obtain the overall item score is to use an aggregate of all available ratings.

Group-Level Consistency

While evaluating the examinee-level consistency is a critical component of ensuring fairness in the scores assigned to individual examinees, it is also important to demonstrate adequate rater consistency for the scores assigned to responses of each CR item across examinee groups. This applies both to the total examinee group and also each examinee subgroup defined by key background variables.

Several approaches can be used to evaluate rater consistency for an examinee group. One approach is to apply the Pearson product-moment correlation coefficient (r) to the situation of double-scored responses. The value of r estimates the linear relationship between Y_1 and Y_2, and the criterion of $r = .70$ is commonly adopted as the lower bound of acceptability in high-stakes assessment contexts (Williamson et al., 2012). In practice, it is recommended that r be computed for: (a) either the total examinee group, or a sample that is representative of the total examinee group, to ensure that adequate consistency exists across the overall examinee population; and (b) each relevant examinee subgroup.

A second approach, which directly addresses the agreement of Y_1 and Y_2, is the quadratic-weighted kappa index (k_w) (Fleiss & Cohen, 1973). The value of k_w ranges from 0 to 1, such that $k_w = 1$ represents perfect agreement and $k_w = 0$ represents independence of Y_1 and Y_2. The advantage of k_w over r is that k_w reflects the actual agreement of Y_1 and Y_2, rather than just the linear relationship between Y_1 and Y_2. To calculate k_w, let us denote the possible values of Y_1 by i and the possible values of Y_2 by j, such that i and j can assume integer values 0, 1, 2, . . ., m. Then, we can consider each possible combination of $Y_1 = i$ and $Y_2 = j$ and denote the frequency that a given combination is observed in the sample by O_{ij}. We can also consider the number of occurrences of a particular combination $Y_1 = i$ and $Y_2 = j$ that would be expected if Y_1 and Y_2 were independent (i.e., no relationship between Y_1 and Y_2), and denote this expected number of occurrences by E_{ij}, whereby E_{ij} = (frequency of $Y_1 = i$) × (frequency of $Y_2 = j$) / n, where n is the total group size. Using this notation, k_w is given by:[2]

$$k_W = 1 - \frac{\sum_{i=0}^{m} \sum_{j=0}^{m} (i-j)^2 O_{ij}}{\sum_{i=0}^{m} \sum_{j=0}^{m} (i-j)^2 E_{ij}} . \tag{4}$$

The name of quadratic-weighed kappa stems from the use of the squared difference between i and j as the weight applied to each value of O_{ij} and E_{ij} in Equation 4. Notice that the term $(i - j)$ shown in Equation 4 corresponds to Δ, and thus as the observed values of Δ approach zero, k_w will approach 1. The lower bound of acceptability of k_w in high-stakes assessment contexts is commonly set to .70 (Williamson et al., 2012). As described above for r, it is recommended that k_w be computed for a sample that is representative of the total examinee group as well as for relevant examinee subgroups.

Two Definitions of DIF for Polytomously Scored Items

The item-level phase of evidence accumulation across multiple ratings of an examinee's response to CR items results in a single overall score for each item. Armed with the overall item score, it is germane to evaluate DIF for each item. Recall that scores to CR items are commonly polytomous, with potential outcomes denoted here by the ordered values $Y = 0, 1, . . ., m$. Due to the multiple score levels of polytomously scored items, there are two different definitions of DIF that are adopted in practice, referred to here as *net* DIF and *global* DIF (Penfield, 2010). Net DIF pertains to the between-subgroup differences in success on the item aggregated across all levels of Y. The condition of no net DIF holds if individuals having the same level of proficiency, but belonging to different subgroups, have the same expected score (i.e., mean score) on Y. An example of net DIF is presented in Figure 4.1b, which plots the mean of a polytomously scored item at each stratum of S for a reference subgroup (solid line, $n = 1,500$) and a focal subgroup (dashed line, $n = 1,500$). We see that at many levels of S, the mean score on Y is slightly higher for the reference subgroup than for the focal subgroup, reflecting a net DIF effect.

In contrast to net DIF, which aggregates between-subgroup differences across all levels of Y to arrive at an overall "net" effect, global DIF addresses whether between-subgroup differences exist in the chance of successfully advancing to each possible level of Y. A useful framework for evaluating global DIF is that of differential step functioning (DSF) (Penfield, 2007a; Penfield, Gattamorta, & Childs, 2009). To describe DSF, let us conceptualize the levels of Y as being the result of a series of transitions, or steps, to successively higher score levels. For example, a polytomously scored item having four score levels ($Y = 0, 1, 2, 3$) will have three steps: the first step corresponds to the transition from $Y = 0$ to $Y \geq 1$, the second step corresponds to the transition from $Y < 2$ to $Y \geq 2$, and the third step corresponds to the transition from $Y < 3$ to $Y = 3$. A between-subgroup difference in the chance of success on a particular step, after conditioning on proficiency, reflects the presence of a DSF effect for that step. If DSF exists for any one of the steps underlying Y, then global DIF is said to exist for that item. An example of DSF and global DIF is shown in Figure 4.1c for the same data upon which Figure 4.1b is based. Figure 4.1c presents the proportion of reference (solid line) and focal (dashed line) subgroup examinees successfully transitioning at each of the three steps underlying Y. The first two steps demonstrate no notable DSF effect. The third step, however, has a large DSF effect favoring the reference subgroup indicating a problem with the transition to the highest score category of Y. The comparison

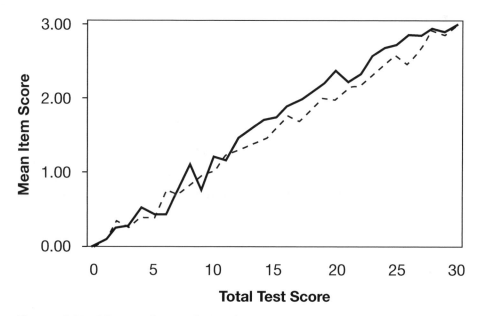

Figure 4.1b Net DIF in a Polytomously Scored Item

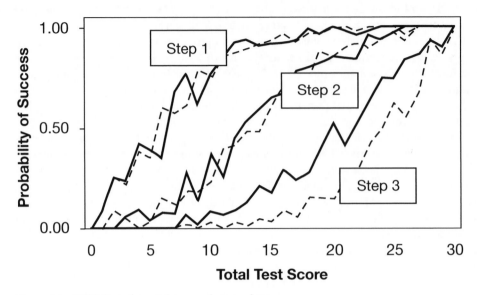

Figure 4.1c DSF Effects for a Polytomously Scored Item

of Figures 4.1b and 4.1c provides a useful comparison of net and global DIF; we see that the net DIF effect shown in Figure 4.1b is a result of a large DSF effect associated with the third step, thus reflecting the presence of a construct-irrelevant factor associated with achieving the score level $Y = 3$.

An important distinction between net DIF and global DIF is that it is possible to have negligible net DIF despite sizable between-subgroup differences associated with the chance of successfully achieving one or more levels of Y. In this manner, the absence of global DIF is a more rigorous standard of fairness to meet than the absence of net DIF. A second distinction between net DIF and global DIF is that the study of global DIF can provide a more detailed understanding of which score levels are responsible for a DIF effect. For example, Figure 4.1b presents an example of net DIF favoring the reference subgroup, but based on this information alone we cannot determine which levels of Y are implicated in this DIF effect. Was the relative advantage for the reference subgroup occurring for all levels of Y, or just an isolated level? The evaluation of global DIF can inform which score levels are responsible for a particular DIF effect, as demonstrated by the sizable DSF effect of the third step shown in Figure 4.1c.

Whether it is appropriate to collect net DIF or global DIF evidence of fairness will depend on the context of the assessment under investigation and the importance placed on ensuring the absence of differential difficulty across all steps underlying Y. A hybrid approach also may be valuable in some contexts, whereby net DIF is selected as the standard of fairness to be adopted, and any substantial net DIF effects are accompanied by a DSF analysis to inform which score levels are responsible for the net DIF.

Considerations for Conducting DIF Analyses for CR Items

As was the case for DIF analyses of MC items, there are several important considerations for conducting DIF analyses for CR items. All of the considerations for conducting DIF analyses described for MC items apply to the evaluation of DIF for CR items. In addition, several other considerations are relevant for CR items.

Stratifying Variable

When the stratifying variable (S) is based on CR items, several issues are important to consider. First, if S is based on overall item scores assigned by human raters, the reliability of S will be dependent on the degree of rater consistency. As a result, it is important to evaluate consistency of rater scores (i.e., evaluated using r and k_w as described previously in this chapter) and to ensure that the consistency is adequate. Second, in the case of mixed-format tests containing MC and CR items, the method used to generate S should be given careful consideration due to the potential multidimensionality that exists between these two item formats. For example, S can be computed as the summated score of only the MC items, the summated score of only the CR items, the summated score across MC and CR items, or using the bivariate distribution of summated scores for MC and CR items individually (Moses, Liu, Tan, Deng, & Dorans, 2013). Although there is no single approach for computing S that is universally most appropriate, using S computed as the summated score across all MC and CR items may lead to the most stable DIF results (Moses et al., 2013) and thus serves as a prudent strategy for practitioners. In all cases, a rationale should be provided supporting the approach taken to generate the most appropriate stratifying variable within the particular context of the assessment.

Sample Size

Sample size requirements will vary depending on the methodology used to evaluate DIF in CR items. As was the case for MC items, sample size requirements will be higher for IRT-based methods than for observed score methods (e.g., SMD and odds ratio methods). Furthermore, if the DIF analysis involves the evaluation of global DIF, then it is important to have a sufficient sample size to ensure responses across all levels of Y within most strata of S so that each DSF effect associated with Y can be estimated with adequate stability. This may necessitate larger sample sizes than what would be required for an evaluation of net DIF.

Evaluating Net DIF in Polytomously Scored Items

Among the most straightforward approaches for evaluating net DIF is the standardized mean difference index (SMD) (Dorans & Schmitt, 1991), which considers the between-subgroup differences in the mean of Y at each level of S ($\bar{Y}_{RS} - \bar{Y}_{FS}$), and then aggregates across all levels of S to arrive at a final estimate of the net DIF effect. The specific equation used for SMD is identical to that of the SPD index shown in Equation 1, with the exception that $\bar{Y}_{RS} - \bar{Y}_{FS}$ is substituted for $\hat{P}_{RS} - \hat{P}_{FS}$. Formulas for an estimated standard error of SMD and associated test statistic are provided by Zwick and Thayer (1996). Classifying the SMD effect size is complicated because its value is dependent on the scale of Y. One approach for controlling for the scale of Y in interpreting the magnitude of SMD is to consider the ratio of SMD over the standard deviation of Y, and then to classify the net DIF effect as negligible if the absolute value of the ratio is less than 0.17, and large if the absolute value of the ratio reaches 0.25 (see Zwick, Ye, & Isham, 2014). Applying SMD to the data shown in Figure 4.1b yields $SMD = 0.14$ and the ratio of $SMD/s(Y) = 0.15$, which reflects a negligible net DIF effect. It should be noted that the approach of using $SMD/s(Y)$ has the disadvantage of yielding an interpretation of the DIF effect magnitude that is dependent on the standard deviation of Y, such that items with a larger standard deviation will have a smaller DIF effect despite having a larger effect on between-subgroup differences on the total test score. As a result, the use of the aforementioned approach for classifying the magnitude of SMD should be used with caution.

An alternative approach for evaluating net DIF is to treat each step underlying Y as a dichotomous event having outcomes of success and non-success (much like a dichotomous item), obtain the odds ratio associated with the between-subgroup difference in success at each step for each level of S, and then obtain a weighted average of all such odds ratios across all steps and all levels of S using a formula that is similar to Equation 3 for $\hat{\lambda}_{MH}$. The resulting index of net DIF is the Liu-Agresti cumulative common log-odds ratio (Liu & Agresti, 1996; Penfield & Algina, 2003), denoted by $\hat{\lambda}_{LA}$. Details of an associated test of the null hypothesis of no net DIF are provided by Penfield and Algina (2003). The primary advantage of $\hat{\lambda}_{LA}$ is that it yields a log-odds ratio index that can be interpreted in an equivalent manner as $\hat{\lambda}_{MH}$ used for MC items, regardless of the number of score levels of Y (Penfield, 2007b). The heuristic described previously for interpreting the magnitude of $\hat{\lambda}_{MH}$ as small, moderate, or large may be applied equally to $\hat{\lambda}_{LA}$, such that the DIF effect of polytomously scored items is small for $|\hat{\lambda}_{LA}| < 0.3$, moderate for $0.3 \geq |\hat{\lambda}_{LA}| < 0.6$, and large for $|\hat{\lambda}_{LA}| \geq 0.6$. For the example shown in Figure 4.1b, $\hat{\lambda}_{LA} = 0.41$, which would be classified as a moderate DIF effect magnitude.

Net DIF can also be evaluated within an IRT framework. Widely adopted polytomous IRT models assign a difficulty parameter to each step underlying the scored outcome variable Y (Penfield, 2014). Net DIF can be evaluated through aggregating the between-subgroup differences in the difficulty parameter across all steps, and if the aggregated between-subgroup difference in difficulty is zero, then no net DIF exists. Approaches to conducting the aggregation consider the sum of the between-subgroup differences in the difficulty parameter across all steps (Cohen, Kim, & Baker, 1993; Penfield, 2010) or the average between-subgroup difference in the difficulty of the steps, which is the approach taken by the Winsteps program (Linacre, 2014).

Which net DIF approach is best? There is no single answer to this question. If the assessment is being calibrated in an IRT framework, then it may be desirable to conduct relevant DIF analyses under the same IRT framework. However, as was the case for evaluating DIF in MC items, IRT approaches for evaluating net DIF have several obstacles, including requiring relatively large sample sizes, requiring good fit to the IRT model being employed, and the ambiguity in interpreting the magnitude of the obtained net DIF effect. In contrast, the SMD and $\hat{\lambda}_{LA}$ approaches to evaluating net DIF have the potential advantages of having less reliance on large subgroup sizes and providing an easily interpretable DIF effect size.

Evaluating Global DIF in Polytomously Scored Items

Although the formal distinction between net and global DIF is a relatively new advancement in measurement, several methods have been described for evaluating global DIF. One method is the generalized Mantel-Haenszel statistic (GMH) (Somes, 1986), which has been applied to the evaluation of DIF in polytomous items by Zwick, Donoghue, and Grima (1993). The GMH statistic offers a chi-square test of the null hypothesis of no global DIF. However, it does not provide a measure of global DIF effect magnitude and offers no information concerning which score levels are implicated in the global DIF effect. As a result, the *GMH* statistic may be of limited practical use in evaluating the overall severity and causes of the global DIF effect.

An alternative approach for evaluating global DIF has been described by Penfield (2010), whereby the DSF effect of each step underlying Y is estimated individually, and then the conclusion of global DIF is based on the pattern of DSF effects across the steps. Because each step corresponds to a dichotomous event of success or non-success at that step, each step can be treated as a dichotomous item and an odds ratio estimate of the DSF effect for each step can be obtained by applying $\hat{\lambda}_{MH}$ to each step (see Penfield, 2007a, 2010 for details). The magnitude of $\hat{\lambda}_{MH}$ for each step can be interpreted according to the guidelines described previously for $\hat{\lambda}_{MH}$ in the context of MC items. For example, a polytomous item having three steps will have a separate DSF effect estimate for each step, denoted by $\hat{\lambda}_{MH1}$, $\hat{\lambda}_{MH2}$, and $\hat{\lambda}_{MH3}$. Inferences of global DIF are based on the profile of $\hat{\lambda}_{MH1}$, $\hat{\lambda}_{MH2}$, and $\hat{\lambda}_{MH3}$. The null hypothesis of no global DIF is rejected if any one of the three DSF effect estimates is significantly different from zero (Penfield, 2010). Applying this approach to the data used in Figure 4.1c, we have $\hat{\lambda}_{MH1} = 0.00$ ($p > .05$), $\hat{\lambda}_{MH2} = 0.09$ ($p > .05$), and $\hat{\lambda}_{MH3} = 1.28$ ($p < .01$). This profile indicates a large and statistically significant DSF effect for the third step, and we conclude that global DIF exists and is associated with a construct-irrelevant factor associated with the transition to $Y = 3$.

The evaluation of global DIF in polytomously scored items can also be conducted through consideration of the between-subgroup differences in the step-level difficulty parameters underlying the IRT model (see Penfield, 2014). A statistical test of the null hypothesis of no between-subgroup difference in step-level difficulty parameter across all steps underlying Y can be conducted using a likelihood ratio test (Kim & Cohen, 1998). The particular pattern of the between-subgroup differences in step-level difficulty parameters can provide valuable information concerning the cause of the DIF in the item, but the interpretation of the between-subgroup differences in the step-level difficulty parameters will be tied to the scale associated with the IRT analysis, which presents the same ambiguity of interpretation of DIF effects that has been discussed in relation to IRT approaches for evaluating DIF in MC items. As a result, evaluating global DIF through the pattern of odds ratio DSF effect estimates may hold greater practical utility in applied testing contexts.

Automated Scored Constructed Responses

Let us now turn our attention to the context of the automated scoring of complex performance tasks. Automated scores are generated by a computer algorithm involving a series of decision rules based on features of the examinee's response. In many instances, the automated scoring algorithm is intended to mirror the scoring processes followed by trained human raters (Williamson, Bejar, & Hone, 1999), and thus the features used by the scoring algorithm are aligned with those features used by human raters in assigning scores. In this context, each feature of the examinee's response involved in assigning an automated score serves as a scored element used in arriving at the examinee's test score.

As was the case for human-rater scored CR items, the evidence accumulation process of automated scoring of CR items consists of two levels: an item-level accumulation and a test-level accumulation. The item-level accumulation involves the aggregation of evidence across the scored features of the examinee's response for a CR item to arrive at an overall item score. In the context of automated scoring, the item-level evidence accumulation process corresponds to the automated scoring algorithm used to assign the overall item score. An example of item-level accumulation is the use of a linear regression model to assign an automated score for a written essay response, whereby the model generates a predicted human-rater score from a series of features of the examinee response (e.g., grammatical structure, word usage, lexile complexity of words used, writing mechanics). An important consideration for the item-level accumulation process of automated scoring is whether each scored feature of the examinee's response is free of construct-irrelevant factors, which is evaluated using the framework of *differential feature functioning*. The test-level evidence accumulation process mirrors that described previously for tests comprised of MC items and human-rater scored CR items, and involves the aggregation of overall item scores (obtained from the item-level accumulation phase) to arrive at the test score. This level of evidence accumulation has two concerns for fairness that are similar to those addressed for human-rater scores of CR items: (a) that the item-level automated scores are consistent with scores assigned by trained human raters, and that this consistency is held equally for relevant examinee subgroups; and (b) that the item-level scores hold the same meaning with respect to the level of proficiency measured by the test regardless of subgroup membership, as evaluated using DIF. This section describes methods used to evaluate these aspects of fairness in automated scoring.

Differential Feature Functioning

As described above, the automated scoring of a CR item often involves multiple scored features of the examinee's response. These scored features serve as the scored elements implemented in the item-level evidence accumulation process (i.e., the automated scoring algorithm) that generates the overall item score. Because each scored feature of the examinee response is used in the item-level evidence accumulation process, it is important that each scored feature holds the same meaning with respect to the proficiency measured by the item across examinee subgroups. If success on a particular feature is determined by a construct-irrelevant factor, then the meaning of the scored feature with respect to the intended proficiency may depend on the examinee's standing on the construct-irrelevant factor. As an example, consider the automated scoring of a writing task, for which one of the features used by the scoring algorithm is the number of words contained in the examinee's response. If different regions (e.g., England, United States, Canada, etc.) tend to construct written English using differential economy of words, then the number of words may not be equivalently related to writing proficiency for all examinees; a particular word count may be associated with high writing proficiency for one region but not for another region. In this instance, economy of word usage in written English is a construct-irrelevant factor that can lead to a disadvantage in the automated scoring for particular subgroups of examinees.

The presence of construct-irrelevant factors associated with individual features of the examinee's response used in automated scoring can be evaluated by extending the framework of DIF to the context of individual features, which is referred to here as differential feature functioning (DFF). In this context, DFF is evaluated by comparing the level of success on a given feature for examinees having the same overall item score, but belonging to different subgroups. If a between-subgroup difference in success on the feature exists (conditional on the overall item score), then DFF is said to exist. For clarity, note that the stratifying variable (S) in the evaluation of DFF is the overall item score (i.e., the score on the item associated with the feature being evaluated), rather than a test-level score. Because S is defined as the overall item score, the evaluation of DFF should be reserved for instances where there are multiple features used in generating the automated score.

In many instances, features of the examinee response are scored according to ordinal categories, in which case DFF can be evaluated using the DIF methodology described previously in this chapter. Features scored dichotomously (e.g., success vs. failure, yes vs. no, etc.) can be evaluated for DFF by applying the DIF methodology described for MC items. Features scored polytomously (e.g., not present, partially present, completely present) can be evaluated for DFF using DIF methodologies associated with net or global DIF described for human-rater scored CR items. In other instances, however, features are more continuous in nature (e.g., number of words in a writing passage). In these instances, the evaluation of DFF would be most practically evaluated using the *SMD* index of net DIF.

Differential Item Functioning

A fundamental component of evaluating whether the test-level evidence accumulation process leads to test scores having the same meaning for different examinee subgroups is demonstrating that each item score used in the test-level accumulation process is free of construct-irrelevant factors. As was the case for MC items and human-rater scored CR items, the presence of construct-irrelevant factors in the automated item score can be identified through an analysis of DIF. The evaluation of DIF for automated scored items follows the same procedures as outlined previously in this chapter. DIF in dichotomous automated scored items is evaluated using identical methodology, considerations, and interpretations as described for MC items. Similarly, DIF in polytomous automated scored items is evaluated using identical methodology, considerations, and interpretations as described for human-rater scored CR items.

When a substantial DIF effect is observed for an automated scored item, it may prove fruitful to conduct a DFF analysis for the item to shed light on which feature(s) of the scored responses are responsible for the DIF effect. In this way, evaluations of DFF can be used in conjunction with other forms of evidence of fairness to develop a comprehensive understanding of the potential effects that construct-irrelevant factors are having on the resulting test scores.

Consistency of Automated and Human-Rater Scores

In addition to the analysis of DIF, another important consideration for evaluating fairness is whether the automated item scores used in the test-level evidence accumulation process are consistent with corresponding human-rater scores, and whether this consistency holds equally across examinee subgroups. Methods for evaluating whether automated scores are consistent with corresponding human-rater scores are described below.

Difference Methods

Let us consider a situation for which a particular CR item is assigned an automated score (denoted by Y_A) and a human-rater score (denoted by Y_H) for each examinee in the sample. The difference between Y_A and Y_H for a given examinee is symbolized here by $\Delta = Y_A - Y_H$. One approach for evaluating the consistency of Y_A and Y_H is to consider the mean value of Δ (denoted by $\bar{\Delta}$) for the total examinee group and also for each relevant examinee subgroup. One approach for interpreting the magnitude of $\bar{\Delta}$ is to consider the value of $\bar{\Delta}$ in relation to the scale of Y to determine whether the use of Y_A is expected to lead to a different raw score than the use of Y_H. Under this approach, a useful criterion is $|\bar{\Delta}| \geq 0.5$, as any item meeting this criterion is expected to yield an automated score that differs from that of a human-rater score by at least one point on the scale of Y.

An alternative approach for evaluating the magnitude of $\bar{\Delta}$ is to control for the scale of Y to account for differences in the scale of Y across different items (e.g., 0 to 2 for one item, but 0 to 5 for another item). This can be accomplished using the effect size index:

$$ES = \frac{\bar{\Delta}}{s(Y_H)} , \tag{5}$$

where $s(Y_H)$ represents the standard deviation of Y_H for the group in question. The value of ES reflects the mean difference between Y_A and Y_H in standard deviation units; a value of $ES = 0.2$ indicates that Y_A is, on average, 0.2 standard deviation units higher than Y_H. A threshold of $|ES| \geq 0.10$ is proposed here as a criterion for flagging values of $\bar{\Delta}$ as being unacceptably large. This criterion is consistent with criteria applied by previous research evaluating the consistency of automated and human scores (Ramineni et al., 2012).

While $\bar{\Delta}$ and ES inform whether the values of Δ tend to systematically differ from zero for a particular examinee group, it does not provide information about whether any observed difference of $\bar{\Delta}$ from zero is statistically significant. To accomplish this, a single-sample t-test can be applied, whereby the relevant t statistic is computed using:

$$t = \frac{\bar{\Delta}}{\left[\dfrac{s(\bar{\Delta})}{\sqrt{n}} \right]} , \tag{6}$$

where n is the number of examinees in the group of interest and $s(\Delta)$ is the standard deviation of the n values of Δ for the group. The value of t follows a t distribution with n-1 degrees of freedom. Any group for which $|ES| \geq 0.10$ and t is significant at $p < .05$ should be flagged for review of potential construct-irrelevant factors in the automated scoring algorithm. To ensure that Y_A does not manifest a systematic difference from Y_H for particular examinee subgroups, the evaluation of $\bar{\Delta}$ and/or ES in coordination with the t-test should be conducted for the overall examinee group as well as all relevant examinee subgroups.

An obstacle to the use of the t-test to evaluate differences between Y_A and Y_H is the relatively large sample size required to achieve a desirable level of power in detecting a mean value of Δ in the population that deviates from zero. Assuming a Type I error rate of .05 and a true population mean value of Δ equaling 0.10, the t-test will be powered at .8 or higher for sample sizes of approximately 800 or greater. Similarly, assuming a Type I error rate of .05 and a true population mean value of Δ equaling 0.20, the t-test will be powered at .8 for sample sizes of approximately 200. As a result, the t-test is expected to be effective in identifying true differences between Y_A and Y_H that are meaningfully large only when a large group size is available. Absent large group sizes, interpretations of the magnitude of the difference between Y_A and Y_H should place emphasis on the effect sizes of $\bar{\Delta}$ and ES.

Agreement Methods

Whereas the evaluation of $\bar{\Delta}$ informs the average difference between Y_A and Y_H for a given examinee group, it does not directly address how well automated scores agree with human-rater scores. The condition of $\bar{\Delta} = 0$ for a given examinee group does not imply a strong relationship or high level of agreement between Y_A and Y_H for that group; it is possible for $\bar{\Delta} = 0$ despite there being large deviations between Y_A and Y_H that sum to zero. As a result, a complement to the evaluation of $\bar{\Delta}$ is a quantification of the relationship between Y_A and Y_H. Two approaches that serve this purpose are the Pearson product-moment correlation (r) and the quadratic-weighted kappa (k_w), which were previously described in the context of human-rater consistency. Extending the calculation of r and k_w to the current context involves the use of Y_A and Y_H in place of Y_1 and Y_2, and the resulting values of r and k_w are interpreted using the same criteria for the consistency of human-rater scores (i.e., lower bounds of acceptability of .70). To ensure that there is adequate consistency of Y_A and Y_H across all relevant examinee groups, the values of r and k_w should be computed for the total examinee group as well as each examinee subgroup defined according to key background variables. Any group for which $r < .70$ or $k_w < .70$ should be flagged for additional consideration.

Concluding Remarks

This chapter has provided an overview of methods used to evaluate the presence of construct-irrelevant factors implicated in the scored elements of examinee responses used in the calculation of test scores. Ensuring that test scores are free of construct-irrelevant factors is conducted by evaluating the consistency of scored elements used in assigning overall item scores and evaluating the differential functioning (DIF, DSF, and DFF) of the scored elements involved in generating test scores. By its very nature, this chapter is not intended to provide a detailed description of available methods. Readers seeking more detailed accounts of methods used to evaluate score consistency, DIF, and DSF are referred to other relevant resources cited throughout the chapter. To the best of my knowledge, the concept of DFF has not previously been documented in a published resource, and thus no other resources are cited on this topic. Naturally, this suggests DFF as an area ripe for further investigation and use in practical testing contexts.

Notes

1. The views expressed are those of the author and not necessarily those of The University of North Carolina at Greensboro.
2. The form of the quadratic-weighted kappa (k_w) shown in Equation 4 is consistent with that cited in Fleiss and Cohen (1973). Other expressions for weighted kappa coefficients exist (e.g., Cohen, 1968), and these forms are algebraically equivalent to the form shown in Equation 4.

References

American Educational Research Association, American Psychological Association, & National Council on Measurement in Education. (2014). *Standards for educational and psychological testing*. Washington, DC: AERA.

Angoff, W. H. (1993). Perspectives on differential item functioning. In P. W. Holland & H. Wainer (Eds.), *Differential item functioning* (pp. 3–23). Hillsdale, NJ: Lawrence Erlbaum.

Bridgeman, B. (2013). Human ratings and automated essay evaluation. In M. D. Shermis & J. Burstein (Eds.), *Handbook of automated essay evaluation: Current applications and new directions* (pp. 221–232). New York: Routledge.

Camilli, G. (2006). Test fairness. In R. L. Brennan (Ed.), *Educational measurement* (4th ed., pp. 221–256). Westport, CT: American Council on Education/Praeger.

Clauser, B. E., & Mazor, K. M. (1998). Using statistical procedures to identify differentially functioning test items. *Educational Measurement: Issues and Practice, 17*(1), 31–44.

Cohen, J. (1968). Weighted kappa: Nominal scale agreement with provision for scaled disagreement of partial credit. *Psychological Bulletin, 70,* 213–220.

Cohen, A. S., Kim, S-H., & Baker, F. B. (1993). Detection of differential item functioning in the graded response model. *Applied Psychological Measurement, 17,* 335–350.

de Ayala, R. J. (2009). *The theory and practice of item response theory.* New York: Guilford Press.

Dorans, N. J., & Holland, P. W. (1993). DIF detection and description: Mantel-Haenszel and standardization. In P. W. Holland & H. Wainer (Eds.), *Differential item functioning* (pp. 35–66). Hillsdale, NJ: Lawrence Erlbaum.

Dorans, N. J., & Kulick, E. M. (1986). Demonstrating the utility of the standardization approach to assessing unexpected differential item performance on the Scholastic Aptitude Test. *Journal of Educational Measurement, 23,* 355–386.

Dorans, N. J., & Schmitt, A. P. (1991). *Constructed response and differential item functioning: A pragmatic approach* (ETS Research Rep. No. 91-47). Princeton, NJ: Educational Testing Service.

Fleiss, J. L., & Cohen, J. (1973). The equivalence of weighted kappa and the intraclass correlation coefficient as measures of reliability. *Educational and Psychological Measurement, 33,* 613–619.

Holland, P. W., & Thayer, D. T. (1988). Differential item performance and the Mantel-Haenszel procedure. In H. Wainer & H. I. Braun (Eds.), *Test validity* (pp. 129–145). Hillsdale, NJ: Erlbaum.

Holland, P. W., & Wainer, H. (Eds.) (1993). *Differential item functioning.* Hillsdale, NJ: Erlbaum.

Kim, S.-H., & Cohen, A. S. (1998). Detection of differential item functioning under the graded response model with the likelihood ratio test. *Applied Psychological Measurement, 22,* 345–355.

Lane, S., & Stone, C. A. (2006). Performance assessment. In R. L. Brennan (Ed.), *Educational measurement* (4th ed., pp. 387–431). Westport, CT: American Council on Education/Praeger.

Linacre, J. M. (2014). *Winsteps(r) Rasch model computer programs.* Beaverton, OR: Winsteps.com.

Liu, I-M., & Agresti, A. (1996). Mantel-Haenszel-type inference for cumulative odds ratios with a stratified ordinal response. *Biometrics, 52,* 1223–1234.

Mantel, N., & Haenszel, W. (1959). Statistical aspects of the analysis of data from retrospective studies of disease. *Journal of the National Cancer Institute, 22,* 719–748.

Mapuranga, R., Dorans, N. J., & Middleton, K. (2008). *A review of recent developments in differential item functioning* (ETS Research Report No. RR-08-43). Princeton, NJ: Educational Testing Service.

Mislevy, R. J., & Haertel, G. D. (2006). Implications of evidence-centered design for educational testing. *Educational Measurement: Issues and Practice, 25*(4), 6–20.

Moses, T., Liu, J., Tan, A., Deng, W., & Dorans, N. J. (2013). *Constructed-response DIF evaluations for mixed-format tests* (ETS Research Report No. RR-13-33). Princeton, NJ: Educational Testing Service.

O'Neill, K. A., & McPeek, M. (1993). Item and test characteristics that are associated with differential item functioning. In P. W. Holland & H. Wainer (Eds.), *Differential item functioning* (pp. 255–276). Hillsdale, NJ: Lawrence Erlbaum.

Osterlind, S. J., & Everson, H. T. (2009). *Differential item functioning* (2nd ed.). Los Angeles, CA: Sage.

Penfield, R. D. (2007a). Assessing differential step functioning in polytomous items using a common odds ratio estimator. *Journal of Educational Measurement, 44,* 187–210.

Penfield, R. D. (2007b). An approach for categorizing DIF in polytomous items. *Applied Measurement in Education, 20,* 335–355.

Penfield, R. D. (2010). Distinguishing between net and global DIF in polytomous items. *Journal of Educational Measurement, 47,* 129–149.

Penfield, R. D. (2014). An NCME instructional module on polytomous item response theory models. *Educational Measurement: Issues and Practice, 33*(1), 36–48.

Penfield, R. D., & Algina, J. (2003). Applying the Liu-Agresti estimator of the cumulative common odds ratio to DIF detection in polytomous items. *Journal of Educational Measurement, 40,* 353–370.

Penfield, R. D., & Camilli, G. (2007). Differential item functioning and item bias. In S. Sinharay & C. R. Rao (Eds.), *Handbook of Statistics, Volume 26: Psychometrics* (pp. 125–167). New York: Elsevier.

Penfield, R. D., Gattamorta, K., & Childs, R. A. (2009). An NCME instructional module on using differential step functioning to refine the analysis of DIF in polytomous items. *Educational Measurement: Issues and Practice, 28*(1), 38–49.

Phillips, S. E., & Camara, W. J. (2006). Legal and ethical issues. In R. L. Brennan (Ed.), *Educational measurement* (4th ed., pp. 733–755). Westport, CT: American Council on Education/Praeger.

Ramineni, C., Trapani, C. S., Williamson, D. M., Davey, T., & Bridgeman, B. (2012). *Evaluation of the e-rater(r) scoring engine for the GRE(r) Issue and Argument prompts* (ETS Research Report No. RR-12-02). Princeton, NJ: Educational Testing Service.

Schmitt, A. P., Holland, P. W., & Dorans, N. J. (1993). Evaluating of hypotheses about differential item functioning. In P. W. Holland & H. Wainer (Eds.), *Differential item functioning* (pp. 281–315). Hillsdale, NJ: Erlbaum Associates.

Somes, G. W. (1986). The generalized Mantel-Haenszel statistic. *The American Statistician, 40,* 106–108.

Thissen, D., Steinberg, L., & Wainer, H. (1993). Detection of differential item functioning using the parameters of item response models. In P. W. Holland & H. Wainer (Eds.), *Differential item functioning* (pp. 67–113). Hillsdale, NJ: Lawrence Erlbaum.

Williamson, D. M., Bejar, I. I., & Hone, A. S. (1999). A mental model comparison of automated and human scoring. *Journal of Educational Measurement, 36,* 158–184.

Williamson, D. M., Xi, X., & Breyer, F. J. (2012). A framework for evaluation and use of automated scoring. *Educational Measurement: Issues and Practice, 31*(1), 2–13.

Wolfe, E. W. (2004). Identifying rater effects using latent trait models. *Psychology Science, 46,* 35–51.

Young, J. W., So, Y., & Ockey, G. J. (2013). *Guidelines for best test development practices to ensure validity and fairness for international English language proficiency assessments.* Princeton, NJ: Educational Testing Service.

Zhang, M. (2013). *Contrasting automated and human scoring of essays* (ETS R & D Connections, No. 21). Princeton, NJ: Educational Testing Service.

Zieky, M. (1993). Practical questions in the use of DIF statistics in item development. In P. W. Holland & H. Wainer (Eds.), *Differential item functioning* (pp. 337–347). Hillsdale, NJ: Lawrence Erlbaum.

Zieky, M. (2011). The origins of procedures for using differential item functioning statistics at Educational Testing Service. In N. J. Dorans & S. Sinharay (Eds.), *Looking back: Proceedings of a conference in honor of Paul W. Holland* (pp. 115–127). New York: Springer-Verlag.

Zwick, R., & Thayer, D. T. (1996). Evaluating the magnitude of differential item functioning in polytomous items. *Journal of Educational and Behavioral Statistics, 21,* 187–201.

Zwick, R., Donoghue, J. R., & Grima, A. (1993). Assessment of differential item functioning for performance tasks. *Journal of Educational Measurement, 30,* 233–251.

Zwick, R., Ye, L., & Isham, S. (2014, April). *Extending the empirical Bayes DIF procedure to polytomous items.* Paper presented at the annual meeting of the National Council on Measurement in Education, Philadelphia.

5 Fairness in Score Interpretation

Jinghua Liu[1] and Neil J. Dorans[2]

In the preceding chapter, Penfield described a variety of approaches to assessing the fairness of scoring responses to test questions. This chapter, "Fairness in Score Interpretation," focuses on the end product of the scoring process—the scores reported to the test takers. We assume that a total score has been produced. We consider three aspects of assessing the fairness of interpretations attached to that score. These three aspects are manifestations of a fundamental fairness question: Can scores from different versions of the same test be interpreted as and used as if they are interchangeable? One way to answer this question is to check whether the linking relationships among allegedly interchangeable scores are invariant across subpopulations of test takers (e.g., females and males). A second aspect to check is whether the test editions measure what they purport to measure in the same way across different groups. Finally, the third aspect to examine is whether the test scores serve their primary purpose in the same way across different subgroups. Technical terms that have been applied to the assessment of fairness in these three types of score interpretations are: (1) score equity assessment (Dorans, 2004; Dorans & Liu, 2009), which is used to assess linking invariance; (2) factorial invariance (Millsap and Meredith, 2007), which is used to examine measurement invariance; and (3) differential prediction (Petersen & Novick, 1976) to examine prediction invariance.

As noted by Dorans (2004), differential item functioning (DIF), score equity assessment (SEA), and differential prediction are three facets of fairness assessment that assess some type of subpopulation invariance. Differential item functioning asks whether an item is measuring what it purports to measure in much the same way across important subpopulations given the same level of proficiency. For many DIF methods, null DIF can be expressed as:

$$E\left(U|X,G=1\right)=E\left(U|X,G=2\right)=...E\left(U|X,G\right) \tag{1}$$

where U is the item score, often scored 0/1, X is the matching variable, typically total score for observed score DIF methods, G is the group membership, and E denotes the expectation operator.

Score equity assessment (SEA) examines whether the score-linking function in the total group is invariant across important subpopulations to assess the degree of score interchangeability. Equating functions, to the extent possible, should be subpopulation-invariant (Dorans & Holland, 2000; Holland & Dorans, 2006). That is, they should not be strongly influenced by the subpopulation of examinees on which they are computed:

$$L\left(Y \leftarrow X|X,G=1\right)=L\left(Y \leftarrow X|X,G=2\right)=...L\left(Y \leftarrow X|X,G=g\right) \tag{2}$$

where G is an index for subgroup, and $L(Y \leftarrow X | X, G=g)$ represents a linking function that maps scores from X to Y for subgroup g.

Differential prediction analyses examine whether the same prediction models hold across different groups. Petersen and Novick (1976) examined several fair selection models, including the Regression Model (Cleary, 1968), the Constant Ratio Model (Thorndike, 1971), the Conditional Probability Model (Cole, 1973), and the Constant Probability Model (Linn, 1973). In essence, the Regression Model, which is a differential prediction model, examines whether the regression of the criterion onto the predictor is invariant across subpopulations. That is:

$$R(Z|\mathbf{X},G=1) = R(Z|\mathbf{X},G=2) = \ldots R(Z|\mathbf{X},G=g) \tag{3}$$

where R is the symbol for the regression function used to predict Z, the criterion score, from $\mathbf{X}$, the matrix of the predictor scores. G is a variable indicating group membership.

Concerns about factorial invariance (FI) studies have been around since the early days of factor analysis. The factor model can be viewed as a regression model in which the dependent variables are observed scores on tests (or items) and the predictor variables are unobserved scores on underlying factors. Hence, one way of describing factorial invariance is as:

$$F(\mathbf{X}|\mathbf{T},G=1) = F(\mathbf{X}|\mathbf{T},G=2) = \ldots F(\mathbf{X}|\mathbf{T},G=g) \tag{4}$$

where F is the symbol for the function used to predict $\mathbf{X}$, observed test scores, from $\mathbf{T}$, the latent variables presumed to be measured by $\mathbf{X}$, and G is a variable indicating group membership. F is typically a linear factor analysis model for test scores, and a multivariate item response theory model for item scores.

An important thing to notice is that all these methods share a similar form, namely the invariance of a prediction, scaling, or measurement model over subpopulations. As noted earlier, DIF was described in the preceding chapter. Here, we focus on linking invariance, measurement invariance, and prediction invariance in that order. More time is devoted to linking invariance because, unlike measurement invariance and prediction invariance, it is easier to assess in practice.

Linking Invariance Assessed by Score Equity Assessment

Testing programs often produce multiple versions of the same test. Even with the most detailed test blueprint, variation in test difficulty is bound to occur. Test score linking is a statistical process that attempts to produce scores considered comparable enough across test forms to be used interchangeably. Score equating is the most rigorous form of score linking. There are five requirements that must be met to achieve equated scores (Dorans & Holland, 2000). Holland and Dorans (2006) reported these requirements:

(a) The equal construct requirement: The tests should measure the same constructs.
(b) The equal reliability requirement: The tests should have the same reliability.
(c) The symmetry requirement: The equating function for equating the scores of Y to those of X should be the inverse of the equating function for equating the scores of X to those of Y.

(d) The equity requirement: It should be a matter of indifference to an examinee to be tested by either one of two tests that have been equated.

(e) The population invariance requirement: The choice of (sub)population used to estimate the equating function between the scores of tests X and Y should not matter—that is, the equating function used to link the scores of X and Y should be population invariant.

Requirement (c) eliminates regression, which regresses scores to the mean, as an equating procedure. Requirement (d) suggests that once two test forms have been equated, it should not matter to a test taker which form of the test is administered in that his or her expected score should be the same on the two equated forms. The equity requirement, while of theoretical importance, is virtually impossible to observe in practice because individuals are differentially exposed to opportunities to learn specific test content. Most test takers would prefer a test composed of familiar content to one composed of unfamiliar content. Hence, the balancing of test content is essential to any effort to achieve the matter of indifference called for by requirement (d). Requirement (a) is difficult to assess because of data collection limitations, which will be discussed in the section on factorial invariance.

If the equal construct (a) and the equity requirement (d) hold, it follows that equal reliability (b) and the subpopulation invariance requirement (e) will hold. If equal reliability (b) does not hold, equity is violated. When tests X and Y measure different constructs, subpopulation invariance will not hold. This is most evident and easily understood in studies that have examined the differences of ACT-SAT concordances for males and females (e.g., Liu, Dorans, & Moses, 2010). The composite ACT score is one part math and three parts non-math, while the two-component SAT composite is equal parts math and non-math.

Requirement (b) is a falsifiable consequence of requirement (d). If equity holds in some population P, then the tests to be linked have to be equally reliable in any subpopulation of P. Requirement (e) is a falsifiable consequence of requirement (a). If the tests to be linked measure different constructs, then subpopulation invariance will not be achieved. If the observable consequences (b) and (e) fail to hold, then score interchangeability cannot be achieved. Ideally, scores from two tests that are equated should measure the same construct and be equally reliable in the target population that the test is designed for and in each subpopulation of that population.

Strict interchangeability of scores is an ideal, like Newton's laws of motion. Friction exists, though, and hence what is put in motion does not stay in motion. Likewise, the construction of essentially parallel test forms, while a goal, is rarely achieved. In addition, the specification of a target population is rarely achieved in practice. We return to the practical challenges that need to be addressed when checking for subpopulation sensitivity in the final section of this chapter.

Subgroup Equating

Score equating functions should be subpopulation-invariant. Dorans (2004) introduced the practice of assessing the invariance of subpopulations or SEA as a form of fairness analysis. SEA has been used to assess the subpopulation invariance of linking functions in several settings (Dorans & Liu, 2009; Liu, Cahn, & Dorans, 2006; Liu & Dorans, 2012; Liu & Walker, 2007).

Each equating between a new form X and an old form Y has two components: a raw-to-raw equating function and a raw-to-scale scaling function. The first step is to obtain a raw-to-raw equating function, $y = e(x)$, that transforms X-raw-score to Y-raw-score. This equating function can be obtained from any of a variety of equating methods, such as those described in Holland and Dorans (2006) and Kolen and Brennan (2014). The second step is to convert the equated raw score of X to the reporting scale of Y, through a scaling function $s(y)$ that maps the raw scores of Y to the scale. The first step of raw-to-raw equating function and the second step of raw-to-scale scaling function are combined to convert the raw scores of X onto the reporting scale of Y. The composite function, $s(x) = s(y) \circ e(x)$, is called the *score conversion function* for X (Holland & Dorans, 2006).

The subpopulation invariance usually refers to the raw-to-raw equating function. However, the reported or the scaled scores are the final scores that test users get, and most users are familiar with and can easily interpret scaled score values. Hence, subpopulation invariance is often evaluated in the scaled score units, which are the concatenated result of the raw-to-raw equating and the raw-to-scale scaling functions.

In a subpopulation linking invariance analysis, in addition to producing a linking function for the total group, linking functions are produced for each subpopulation of interest as well. The subgroup linking results are compared to the total group linking results at each score point, and the differences are evaluated. Let the total population P be composed of a set of subpopulations, P_g. Equating and scaling are usually conducted in the total group to produce a total group score conversion function $s_p(x)$. There are separate score conversion functions, $s_{P_g}(x)$ for each subpopulation.

Difference Plots of Conversions

A plot of the differences across score levels between the subgroup conversion and the total group conversion, $s_{P_g}(x) - s_p(x)$, is the most direct means of assessing population invariance for each subpopulation. At each score point level, the subgroup conversion can be compared to the total-group conversion.

Dorans and Holland (2000) suggested examining the subpopulation linking functions versus the total population linking function. Brennan (2007) argued that the differences of linking functions should be examined between pairs of subpopulations (e.g., males versus females). For treatments of the methods proposed by Brennan and his colleagues, see Huggins and Penfield (2012) and Kolen and Brennan (2014).

While the direct subgroup comparison avoids the overlap inherent in a subgroup to total comparison and follows the precedent set in DIF analyses of comparing focal and reference groups, it does not address the practical question of whether the total group linking is a satisfactory surrogate for the subgroup conversion. In practice, it is unlikely that one will apply the male-linking function to female examinees, or vice versa, or apply either subgroup-linking function to the total group.

Difference That Matters (DTM)

To evaluate the relative magnitude of a difference in score conversions, we use the difference that may cause practical consequences as a criterion, which we have called the *difference that matters* (DTM). Liu and Dorans (2013) recount the history of the DTM and some of the controversies surrounding its use. Eventually, the DTM evolved to be defined as half of a reported score unit, which can be viewed as an indifference threshold because any difference less than that would probably be reported as the same score. Any differences less than the DTM are considered not big enough to warrant concerns because they are less than half of a score reporting unit.

Percentage Indexes

Two percentage indices can be calculated: the percentage of raw scores for which the total and subpopulation raw-to-scale unrounded conversions differed by more than the DTM, and the percentage of examinees for which these unrounded conversions created scaled scores that differed by more than the DTM. These two indices provide straight-forward insights into lack of invariance as a percentage of score range and a percentage of test takers.

Equatability Indices

Dorans and Holland (2000) suggested using the standardized root mean square difference (RMSD) to quantify the differences between the subpopulation-linking functions and the total-population-linking functions at a given score value. They also suggested using the root expected mean square difference (REMSD) to summarize overall differences between the linking functions. These formulas are adapted to comparisons of raw-to-scale functions.

Root Mean Square Difference (RMSD)

At each raw score level x, the RMSD is defined as:

$$RMSD_{(x)} = \sqrt{\sum_g w_g \left[s_{P_g}(x) - s_P(x) \right]^2} \tag{5}$$

where

$$w_g = \frac{N_g}{N}$$

denotes the relative proportion of examinees from total population P that are in P_g so that

$$\sum_g w_g = 1.$$

This means that in addition to the groups of interest, analyses need to include an "Other" group, composed of any test taker not in one of the groups of interest. As indicated in Dorans and Liu (2009), the "Other" group might be negligible for some partitions of the total population, e.g., gender, and substantial for others such as ethnic and racial group partitions.

Root Expected Mean Square Difference (REMSD)

To obtain a single number summarizing the values of RMSD(x), Dorans and Holland (2000) introduced a summary measure by averaging over the distribution of X in P: the REMSD. The analogue for raw-to-scale scaling functions is:

$$REMSD = \sqrt{E_P \left\{ \sum_g w_g \left[s_{P_g}(x) - s_P(x) \right]^2 \right\}} = \sqrt{\sum_g w_g E_P \left\{ \left[s_{P_g}(x) - s_P(x) \right]^2 \right\}} , \qquad (6)$$

where $E_P \ldots$ denotes averaging over the distribution of raw scores on X in population P.

Root Expected Square Difference (RESD)

The value of REMSD could be misleadingly small in a situation where the dominant subpopulation (in terms of size) shows little linking dependency, whereas other smaller subpopulations suggest large subgroup-linking sensitivity (Yang, 2004). In order to evaluate how close the gth subpopulation's raw-to-scale function is to the full population raw-to-scale function, Yang (2004) and Dorans and Liu (2007) also computed the root expected square difference (RESD) statistic, which is:

$$RESD_{(g)} = \sqrt{E_P \sum_x f_{g(x)} \left[s_{P_g}(x) - s_P(x) \right]^2} . \qquad (7)$$

Let's briefly summarize the indexes discussed above. $RMSD_{(x)}$ provides an average across groups at each score level. The REMSD is the average of $RMSD_{(x)}$ across score levels. There is only one $RMSD_{(x)}$ across different partitions of P. In contrast, $RESD_{(g)}$ provides an average across score levels for each group. There is a $RESD_{(g)}$ for each subgroup.

Averages and Differences in Averages

In addition to these indices, the average scores that are obtained from use of the total group conversion, the average scores that would have been obtained from use of the subgroup conversion, as well as the difference in these average scores, can be calculated:

$$\text{Mean diff}_{(g)} = \sum_x f_{g(x)} \left[s_{P_g}(x) - s_P(x) \right] \qquad (8)$$

Mean diff weights by the relative frequency of new form raw scores, f_{gx}, in subpopulation g.

To illustrate the use of equatability indexes, we cite some of the findings from Dorans and Liu (2009). Figure 5.1 is what the authors call the "best case" among the set of SEA analyses they conducted. In this case, one SAT math form was equated to another SAT math form. The top panel in Figure 5.1 contains difference plots for the linking based on male-only and female-only conversions relative to the total group conversion. Both difference curves hug the no difference line, suggesting that each gender-specific conversion was very similar to the total group conversion. The lower panel contains the equatability indexes, RMSD and REMSD. The solid curve in the lower panel is the RMSD as a function of score level, the dashed horizontal line is the REMSD value, and the solid horizontal lines in both panels denote the DTM of 5. Both the RMSD curve and the RMSD line are very close to zero. Clearly, the subgroup conversions work in much the same way as the total group conversion.

Liu and Dorans (2013) describe conditions under which linking invariance is likely to hold. The test blueprint should be well specified from both the content and statistical

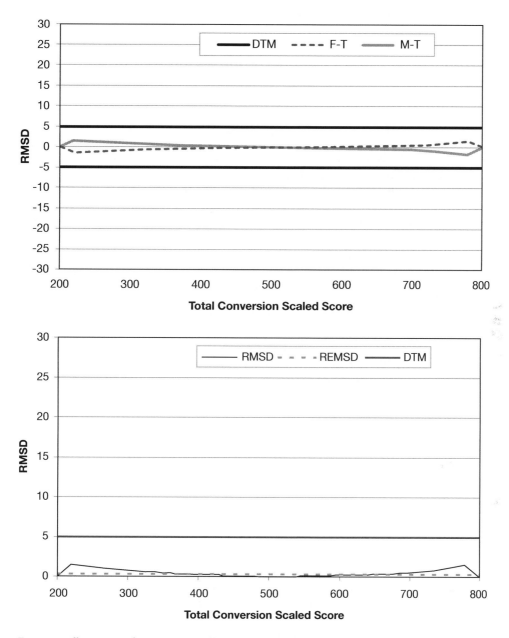

Figure 5.1 Illustration of Conversion Difference Curves, Root Mean Square Difference (RMSD), and Root Expected Mean Square Difference (REMSD) in a SEA Study

Note: DTM = difference that matters, F-T = female-total, M-T = male-total

perspectives. Vague specifications invite potential invariance problems. Having explicit test specifications is not enough. It is important to monitor how well the blueprints are followed during the test assembly. The different test editions should be administered under the same or similar conditions in terms of test delivery modes, test timing, and other testing conditions. The score equating design should be sound and data collection should involve large samples that are representative of the target population and subpopulations. If an equivalent groups equating design is employed, it is important to administer test forms to large equivalent groups of test takers. If anchor scores are used, they should be reliable and representative of scores on the tests to be equated. The two samples taking the new form and the old form should be similar enough to ensure sound equatings.

Using SEA as a Quality Control Check for Fairness

When a testing program builds multiple forms to a static set of specifications, the hope is that linkings between scores on these forms qualify as equatings. Dorans and Liu (2009) recommended use of SEA as a quality control check, much like DIF is used at the item level, to check whether in fact test assembly and equating practices are producing sufficiently interchangeable test scores. They argued that SEA analysis focuses directly on the end product of the test development and scoring process—the scores to be reported—and therefore should play a central role in ensuring the quality of test scores. For those interested in seeing how SEA works in practice, Dorans and Liu (2009) contains the results of a year's worth of SEA analyses on gender and ethnic or racial groups conducted on the SAT.

If SEA analysis indicates that the linkings over time are not invariant across subpopulations and the linking differences are large enough to have a practical impact on scores, then due diligence suggests further investigation. Liu and Dorans (2013) recommended that the test assembly, test administration, and statistical analysis processes should be scrutinized for possible explanations. They listed a number of questions that should be asked of the assembly, administration, and analysis processes. Among these were: Are the test blueprints adequately precise? Have there been changes in the measurement of the construct or the construct itself? Were there alterations in the test assembly process? Have test administration conditions changed? Have the equating processes been carried out properly? Has the composition of the test-taking population changed in non-trivial ways? For example, for a test given in English, has the test-taking population changed over time with respect to its composition of English native speakers and English as a Second Language speakers?

Measurement Invariance Assessed by Checking Factorial Invariance

Measurement invariance refers to the degree to which an instrument measures an entity in the same way across different subpopulations. It is closely related to the same construct requirement of score equating, as well as the equity requirement. As such, it is not as easy to assess as subpopulation invariance or equal reliability because it involves unobservable variables.

Measurement invariance presumes some type of measurement model, such as a factor model or an item response model. The same construct is one of the foundational score-equating requirements. Constructs are unobservable and measurement models typically relate an observable (test or item score) to a latent unobservable. Hence, measurement invariance, with its emphasis on latent constructs, seems to be appropriate for assessing the same construct requirement of score equating. Differential item functioning procedures that assume a measurement model are best thought of as measurement invariance procedures, while those that use only observed scores are best thought of as prediction-invariance models. Both types are discussed in Penfield (this volume, Chapter 4). Here, we only consider the measurement invariance approach referred to as factorial invariance (FI). These procedures assume that a linear factor analysis model adequately describes the relationships among test scores.

Millsap and Meredith (2007) reviewed factorial invariance from a variety of theoretical perspectives, and segmented the study of factorial invariance into three periods. The first period dealt with the impact of selection on factor structure in selected groups. The second period focused on strategies for detecting lack of invariance. The third period utilized confirmatory factor analysis techniques to study invariance across groups. Procedures developed in this period can be applied to the assessment of measurement invariance.

As stated earlier, factorial invariance[3] holds across subpopulations when the regression of observed scores ($\mathbf{X}$) onto latent variables ($\mathbf{T}$) holds across all g. That is:

$$F\left(\mathbf{X}|\mathbf{T},G=1\right)=F\left(\mathbf{X}|\mathbf{T},G=2\right)=...F\left(\mathbf{X}|\mathbf{T},G=g\right) \quad .$$

Typically, this regression is presumed to be linear:

$$\mathbf{x} = \mathbf{b}_x + \mathbf{A}_x\mathbf{t} + \mathbf{d}_x \tag{9}$$

where $\mathbf{x}$ is an n-by-1 vector of observed scores on tests that is expressed as a function of scores on m latent variables ($\mathbf{t}$), $\mathbf{A}_x$ is an n-by-m matrix of the regression weights for predicting $\mathbf{x}$ from $\mathbf{t}$, $\mathbf{b}_x$ contains the n intercepts, and $\mathbf{d}_x$ represents the unique portion (measurement error and specificity) in the test scores $\mathbf{x}$.

The following covariance structure can be derived from this model:

$$\mathbf{C}_{xx} = \mathbf{A}_x\mathbf{C}_{tt}\mathbf{A}_x' + \mathbf{D}_{xx} \tag{10}$$

where the n-by-n $\mathbf{C}_{xx}$ and the m-by-m $\mathbf{C}_{tt}$ are covariance matrices among the observed scores and the latent variables, respectively, and $\mathbf{D}_{xx}$ is a diagonal matrix of unique variances, $\mathbf{d}_{xx}$.

In addition, there is a mean structure represented by:

$$E(\mathbf{x}) = \mathbf{b}_x + \mathbf{A}_x E(\mathbf{t}) \tag{11}$$

where $E(\mathbf{x})$ is the n-by-1 vector of observed means, and $E(\mathbf{t})$ is the m-by-1 vector of latent variable means. Note the unique scores or errors of prediction are independent of each other and of the latent variables, $\mathbf{T}$.

The strictest form of factorial invariance is called *strict factorial invariance* (Meredith, 1993). Here, the regressions are invariant across subgroups. In particular, the slopes:

$$\mathbf{A}_{x1} = \mathbf{A}_{x2} = ... = \mathbf{A}_{xg} \tag{12}$$

and intercepts:

$$\mathbf{b}_{x1} = \mathbf{b}_{x2} = ... = \mathbf{b}_{xg} \tag{13}$$

are equal in all subgroups g. In addition, the unique variances are presumed to be the same across groups:

$$\mathbf{D}_{xx1} = \mathbf{D}_{xx2} = \ldots = \mathbf{D}_{xxg} \tag{14}$$

In practice, this strictest from of invariance is rarely met. What can be done when the inevitable occurs and strict factorial invariance is not achieved? Weaker forms of invariance are examined. In particular, a weaker form of factorial invariance called *strong factorial variance* (Meredith, 1993) is assumed to hold in which the tests have the same regressions on the underlying factors (slopes and intercept) across subpopulations, but the tests are measured with different error variances in the different subpopulations. Here, Equation 14 is relaxed but Equations 12 and 13 still hold. This is analogous to tests that measure the same constructs with variable precision.

Weak factorial invariance (Widaman & Reise, 1997) or *metric invariance* (Thurstone, 1947) allows the intercept to vary as well across groups. Here, Equation 12 is assumed to hold but both Equations 13 and 14 are relaxed.

The last type of factorial invariance is *configural invariance* (Thurstone, 1947). This approach presumes that the same simple structure (patterns of zeros and nonzeros) in $\mathbf{A}_x$ holds across all subgroups.

Table 5.1 summarizes the four types of invariance, pictorially, in terms of their restriction on the regression weight matrices ($\mathbf{A}_x$), the vectors of intercepts ($\mathbf{b}_x$), and the vectors that contain the diagonal elements of $\mathbf{D}$, namely the $\mathbf{d}_{xx}$. Note that for strict invariance, the subscript g is absent from all elements of these matrices. For strong invariance, the group subscript is introduced to the elements of the unique variances. For weak invariance, group dependency is allowed for the intercept vectors. For configural invariance, the only elements that are invariant across groups are the locations of zeros in the $\mathbf{A}$ matrix.

Differences in the strength of invariance are related to fairness issues about what the test scores measure. Strict factorial invariance holds if the parallel tests remain parallel across all subpopulations of interest (Rock, 1982). This is analogous to meeting both the population invariance and equity requirements of test score equating. Strong factorial invariance implies test scores that are predicted by the same constructs in the same way (common weight matrices), but with variable residual variances across subgroups. These differences in the variances of residuals are associated with differences in reliability of measurement or with differences in the variability in the reliable but specific variances of the test scores. These are what Lord and Novick (1968) called *tau-equivalent* scores. Though it is impossible to tease out these two influences, it seems plausible to presume that the source of the difference lies in the reliable specific variance, which might or might not be construct-irrelevant. Either way, there may be fairness concerns. Weak factorial invariance is associated with what Lord and Novick called *essentially tau-equivalent* scores. Configural invariance is weaker than weak invariance. If it is all that can be achieved, much work is needed before one should be comfortable inferring that the set of tests in $\mathbf{X}$ measure the same thing in the same way across subpopulations.

As noted by Dorans and Lawrence (1987, 1999), and verified by Dorans, Lin, Wang, and Yao (2014), the answer to questions about the dimensionality of test and item data depends on which question is asked of which data. Item-level analyses, either with MIRT models (Reckase, 2009) or with differential item functioning techniques (see Penfield, this volume, Chapter 4), do not answer questions about dimensionality at the test score level. Nor do the item parcel procedures advocated by Dorans and Lawrence, which focus on subtests. In fact, the assessment of measurement invariance across subgroups is difficult to examine at the test score level because it requires that test takers have scores from multiple test editions. Test takers who do take multiple versions of a test tend to

Table 5.1 Four Types of Factorial Invariance

---

1. Strict factorial invariance—A_x, b_x, and d_{xx} are invariant across subgroups

A_x	b_x	d_{xx}
$\begin{bmatrix} a_{11} & 0 \\ a_{21} & 0 \\ a_{31} & 0 \\ 0 & a_{42} \\ 0 & a_{52} \\ 0 & a_{62} \end{bmatrix}$	$\begin{bmatrix} b_1 \\ b_2 \\ b_3 \\ b_4 \\ b_5 \\ b_6 \end{bmatrix}$	$\begin{bmatrix} d_{11} \\ d_{22} \\ d_{33} \\ d_{44} \\ d_{55} \\ d_{66} \end{bmatrix}$

2. Strong factorial invariance—A_x and b_x are invariant across subgroups

A_x	b_x	d_{xx}
$\begin{bmatrix} a_{11} & 0 \\ a_{21} & 0 \\ a_{31} & 0 \\ 0 & a_{42} \\ 0 & a_{52} \\ 0 & a_{62} \end{bmatrix}$	$\begin{bmatrix} b_1 \\ b_2 \\ b_3 \\ b_4 \\ b_5 \\ b_6 \end{bmatrix}$	$\begin{bmatrix} d_{11g} \\ d_{22g} \\ d_{33g} \\ d_{44g} \\ d_{55g} \\ d_{66g} \end{bmatrix}$

3. Weak factorial invariance—A_x is invariant across subgroups

A_x	b_x	d_{xx}
$\begin{bmatrix} a_{11} & 0 \\ a_{21} & 0 \\ a_{31} & 0 \\ 0 & a_{42} \\ 0 & a_{52} \\ 0 & a_{62} \end{bmatrix}$	$\begin{bmatrix} b_{1g} \\ b_{2g} \\ b_{3g} \\ b_{4g} \\ b_{5g} \\ b_{6g} \end{bmatrix}$	$\begin{bmatrix} d_{11g} \\ d_{22g} \\ d_{33g} \\ d_{44g} \\ d_{55g} \\ d_{66g} \end{bmatrix}$

4. Configural invariance—locations of zero and nonzero elements in A_x are same across subgroups

A_x	b_x	d_{xx}
$\begin{bmatrix} a_{11g} & 0 \\ a_{21g} & 0 \\ a_{31g} & 0 \\ 0 & a_{42g} \\ 0 & a_{52g} \\ 0 & a_{62g} \end{bmatrix}$	$\begin{bmatrix} b_{1g} \\ b_{2g} \\ b_{3g} \\ b_{4g} \\ b_{5g} \\ b_{6g} \end{bmatrix}$	$\begin{bmatrix} d_{11g} \\ d_{22g} \\ d_{33g} \\ d_{44g} \\ d_{55g} \\ d_{66g} \end{bmatrix}$

take different sets of items. In addition, they tend to be a self-selected group. As a consequence, measurement invariance at the test score level may be difficult to assess in practice.

Prediction Invariance Assessed by Differential Prediction Analysis

For reasons cited in Dorans (2004), the 1970s witnessed the beginning of a series of differential validity and differential prediction studies. Differential validity refers to the differences in the correlation coefficient between predictors and criterion for different subgroups of test takers (e.g., males and females), whereas differential prediction refers to the differences in the regression lines using predictors to predict a criterion for different subgroups of test takers. Differential validity and differential prediction are related but not identical. Differential prediction analyses are preferred to differential validity studies because differences in predictor or criterion variability can produce differential validity even when the prediction model is fair (Linn, 1975).

Many of the methods proposed in the 1970s focused on fairness of selection across subgroups. Assuming that a cut score is used to select students, a simplification that rarely holds in admissions practice, there are four possible outcomes to consider, as illustrated in Table 5.2. An applicant is either accepted or rejected on the basis of a selection rule (based on test scores). An applicant would either succeed or fail on the outcome variable the selection rule is supposed to predict. As shown in Table 5.2, the four regions are:

- Region *I*: rejected but would have succeeded;
- Region **II**: accepted and succeeds;
- Region *III*: rejected and would have failed; and
- Region **IV**: accepted but fails.

Regions *I* and *III* can never be observed if the candidate is rejected; they can be observable if the "rejected" applicants are accepted. Regions **II** and **IV** can be observed. The following discussion of selection models will be based on these four regions.

In a review article, Petersen and Novick (1976) evaluated models for fair selection. Some models define fairness in terms of meeting some criterion of group equity. These included the Constant Ratio Model (Thorndike, 1971), the Equal Probability Model (Linn, 1973), and the Conditional Probability Model (Cole, 1973). All of these models collapse the variable used for selection (e.g. test score) into a binary variable, select vs. reject. In contrast, the Regression Model (Cleary, 1968) looked at success or failure in terms of all levels of the test score.

The Constant Ratio Model

Thorndike (1971) suggested that a selection is fair if the ratio of those accepted to those who reach the successful criterion performance is constant across subgroups. In other words, a selection is fair if the ratio of *(II + IV) / (I + II)* is constant across different subgroups. Note that while **II** and **IV** are observable, the proportion of those who are rejected but would have succeeded (*I*) is never observed. The Constant Ratio Model is not testable using empirical data.

Table 5.2 Selection: Four Possible Outcomes for Group Parity Models

		Predictor: Test Score	
		Rejected	*Accepted*
Criterion Performance	Succeed	*I*: Rejected but *would have* succeeded	**II**: Accepted and succeeds
	Fail	*III*: Rejected but *would have* failed	**IV**: Accepted but fails

Note: Bold font (**II** and **IV**) indicates an observed cell; italics (*I* and *III*) indicate an unobserved cell.

The Conditional Probability Model

Cole (1973) proposed a selection model considering only successful people as measured by criterion performance. That is, a selection is fair if people who could succeed have the same probability of being selected regardless of subgroup membership, or equivalently if the ratio of **II** / *(I* + **II***)* is constant across subgroups. Because this model is based on the conditional probability of being selected given satisfactory criterion performance, this model is referred to as the Conditional Probability Model. Like the model proposed by Thorndike, this model requires the missing data from Region *I*.

The Equal Probability Model

An alternative model states that a selection procedure is fair if all applicants who are selected have the same success rate, regardless of subgroup membership (Linn, 1973). In other words, the ratio of **II** / **(II + IV)** should be invariant across different subgroups. This model is referred to as the Equal Probability Model. This model is testable because both **II** and **IV** are observable.

Petersen and Novick demonstrated that the three group parity models, the Constant Ratio, the Equal Probability, and the Conditional Probability Models, are mutually contradictory. They lead to different cut scores except in the case where the correlation between the selection variable and the criterion variable is one. As noted, two models need missing data, namely the Constant Ratio and the Conditional Probability Models. In addition, Petersen and Novick (1976) noted that the Constant Ratio, the Equal Probability, and the Conditional Probability Models only focus on the positive aspects of the 2-by-2 table (success and selection). If one focused on the negative aspects (failure and rejection), then each cut score based on converses of each model (e.g., a converse Equal Probability Model would focus on probability of failure given rejection), would lead to cut scores that differed from the model that focuses on the positive aspect. Given these contradictions, the authors concluded that "the concepts of culture-fairness and group parity are neither useful nor tenable, and the models spawned from them should not enjoy institutional endorsement" (Petersen & Novick, 1976, p. 28).

Table 5.3 summarizes the three group parity models and their logical converses. The only one that could be computed in practice is the equal probability model.

The Regression Model

The group parity models contradicted each other and their converses in large part because they focused on the 2-by-2 decision table to define fair selection. As noted earlier the

Table 5.3 Group Parity Models and their Converses

	Models Focus on Selection and Success	*Converses Focus on Rejection and Failure*
Constant Ratio / Converse	**(II + IV)** / *(I* + **II***)*	*(I + III)* / *(III* + **IV***)*
Conditional Probability / Converse	**(II)** / *(I* + **II***)*	*(III)* / *(III* + **IV***)*
Equal Probability / Converse	**(II)** / **(II + IV)**	*(III)* / *(I + III)*

Note: Bold font (**II** and **IV**) indicates an observed cell; italics (*I* and *III*) indicate an unobserved cell.

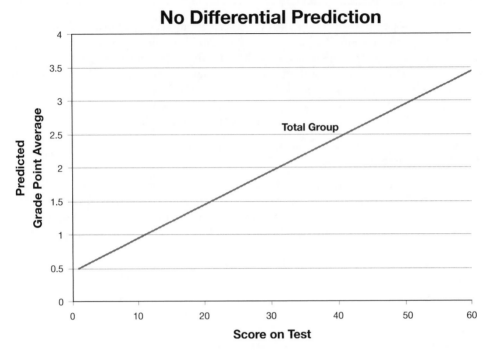

Figure 5.2 Illustration of the Regression Model: Regression Lines are Invariant across Subgroups

regression model proposed by Cleary was shown by Petersen and Novick to be logically consistent with its converse. The regression of a criterion score, namely its expected value given the predicted score was defined in Equation 3. For example, **X** may include test scores and high school grade point averages and *Y* might be a grade from a college course or averaged across several courses. We can use this regression to estimate future performance when we only have the scores on the selection test. If people's actual performance turns out to be higher than that predicted by the test scores, then the test is under-predicting; if people's actual performance is lower than the predicted score, then the test is over-predicting. Systematic under-prediction will disadvantage a subgroup of applicants, whereas systematic over-prediction will advantage them.

Cleary (1968) defined a test as being biased if the criterion score predicted from the common regression line is not consistent for members of subgroups. Figure 5.2 presents a hypothetical situation in which the regression lines for predicting grade point average from a test score (or a composite of predictors) are identical in both subgroups. In this case, the use of common regression based on total group is considered fair, according to Cleary's theory.

However, if the regression relationship differs across Group A and Group B, as illustrated in Figure 5.3, then the use of the common regression line will advantage some individuals but disadvantage others. For example, test takers in Group A will be under-predicted by 0.25 grade-point-average (GPA) units when the common regression line (the middle line) is used instead of the Group A regression line. On the other hand, test takers in Group B will be over-predicted by 0.25 GPA units when the common regression line is used instead of the lower Group B regression line. The selection will be considered unfair if the common regression is used, according to Cleary's definition. Fairness of predicted criterion scores could be achieved, though, if separate regression lines are used, but this would constitute differential treatment by subgroup, which might be viewed as unfair. The preferred approach would be to find other or additional predictors that exhibit little differential prediction, which is not an easy task to accomplish, as will be discussed in the following section.

The Regression Model is consistent with its converse in that it can deal with both outcomes of the selection process (success or failure). It is also very straightforward to calculate. It is the most widely used selection model, and it has been used in many empirical studies, such as those reported in Young (2001).

For fair prediction to hold, the particular regression model must be the appropriate model for that criterion. Otherwise, misspecification of the model can give the appearance of statistical bias. The particular regression model is appropriate if **X** contains all the predictors needed to predict Z and the functional form used to combine the predictors is the correct one. For example, grades in college are often predicted from high school grades and test scores, and in some cases, other variables. If high school grades or test scores are dropped as predictors, it is highly unlikely that the regression of college grades onto the remaining predictors will be invariant. In addition to identification of the proper predictors and functional form, the reliability of the criterion itself plays a role. As Linn and Werts (1971) demonstrated in a brief classic on test fairness, replacing a reliable predictor with a less reliable version can result in a lack of invariance of prediction equations in a setting where invariance existed with the more reliable predictor. Linn

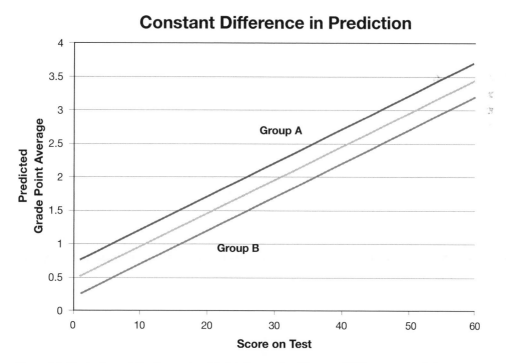

Figure 5.3 Illustration of the Regression Model: Regression Lines are Different across Subgroups

(1976), in his discussion of the Petersen and Novick analyses, noted that the quest to achieve fair prediction is hampered by the fact that the criterion in many studies may itself be unfairly measured.

Even when the correct equation is correctly specified in the full population, infallible predictors are used, and the criterion is measured well, invariance may not hold in subpopulations because of selection effects. Linn (1983) described this effect when he talked about predictive bias as an artifact of selection procedures. Linn used a simple case to illustrate his point. He posited that a single predictor X and linear model were needed to predict Y in the full population P. Samples drawn from P depend on a selection variable S that might depend on X in a linear way. Errors in the prediction of Y from X and S from X were also linearly related. Linn then showed that the sample $R(Y|X, G)$ equaled the population $R(Y|X)$ if the correlation between X and S were zero, or if errors in prediction of $Y|X$ and $U|X$ were uncorrelated. In other words, the slope of the relationship for predicting S from X must be zero or Y and S must be independent given X.

Achieving subpopulation invariance of regressions is difficult because of selection effects, misspecification errors, predictor reliability and criterion issues. Any attempt to assess whether a prediction equation is invariant across subpopulations such as males and females must keep these confounding influences in mind.

To complicate validity assessment even more, there are as many external criteria as there are uses of a score. Each use implies a criterion against which the test's effectiveness can be assessed. Haertel and Ho (this volume, Chapter 12) delve into other matters of score use, including what happens when scores are used for purposes other than what the test was designed to serve.

Discussion

In this chapter, we assume that a score has been produced and the fairness of score interpretations is of interest. We have not attempted to be exhaustive with respect to evaluating the pros and cons of different prediction methods, linking methods, or factor analysis methods. Our focus has been on the types of invariances that can and should be assessed.

The fairness of score interpretations across subpopulations was examined in three different ways. Score equity assessment focuses on linking invariance: Is the score linking relationship between tests that purport to measure the same thing defined in a population of test takers invariant across important subgroups, e.g., males and females? Measurement invariance, which was described in the context of factor analysis in this chapter, evaluates whether the prediction of observed test scores from unobservable latent variables is invariant across subgroups. In other words: Does the test measure whatever it measures in the same way across subgroups? Finally, differential prediction assesses the invariance of a particular score use: Is the prediction of a score on an external criterion from observed test scores and other observed variables invariant across subgroups?

As illustrated above, the notion of subpopulation invariance is central to all these analyses, as it is with DIF analysis. The three approaches described in this chapter, unlike DIF, examine invariance at the test score level. They differ among themselves with respect to whether invariance is related to internal validity or external validity. Measurement invariance of test scores assesses internal validity at the test score level. SEA also examines internal validity at the test score level. Differential prediction evaluates the external validity of a test score, often in conjunction with other predictors.

The measurement invariance assessed by factorial invariance at the test score level requires multiple editions of the test while the internal validity assessed by SEA focuses on the linking relationship between two versions of the same test. These different approaches cannot be substituted for one another. They are both important to assess.

The ease with which these different types of invariance can be assessed varies. Measurement invariance studies of test scores tend to avoid the nuisance variables associated with the binary nature of item scores. They require the use of a model relating test score data to the latent variables. As such, they are subject to misspecification errors that could result in a lack of invariance due to choice of model. Latent variables do not have an existence of their own. As noted by Thurstone (1947) and others, they depend on the observables, namely how they are constructed, the other items or tests with which they are administered, and the groups to whom they are administered.

Differential prediction analysis requires the collection of additional data (e.g., GPA) other than test scores, and is subject to the various problems described by Linn in the 1970s and 1980s. Achieving subpopulation invariance of regressions is difficult because of selection effects, misspecification errors, predictor reliability, and criterion issues. Any attempt to assess whether a prediction equation is invariant across subpopulations such as males and females must keep these confounding influences in mind.

Although differential prediction studies are fraught with potential problems, they are very important to attempt because they are directly germane to primary score usage, e.g., prediction of a criterion such as grades in college. Measurement invariance assessment, even with its dependency on choice of model and the differences associated with the level of analysis (item score vs. test score), should be investigated whenever possible. Results should not be over interpreted, however, as they depend on the particular items and tests administered; the constructs these methods reveal depend on how the sample of items and test takers were selected.

Score equity assessment is relatively easy to conduct. Score equity assessment, like DIF, is straightforward given the correct data collection design and sufficient data to conduct score linkings in subgroups. While a single group taking both tests is preferable, large equivalent groups taking either test is often adequate. It should become standard practice in the manner in which DIF has. Its results can provide clear indications for a testing program as to whether or not test score linkings are invariant across important subgroups, and whether or not these differences are large enough to have practical impact on the scores of test takers from different groups. The subgroups that can be studied depend on circumstances such as research interest, volume, and how the data are collected. The studied subgroups can be based on gender, geographic regions, English First Language and English Not First Language, ethnicity, and so on. We expect that most testing programs should be able to examine invariances across gender (Dorans & Liu, 2009).

A class of challenges to assessing subpopulation invariance pertains to the definition of the target population for a testing program, and a delineation of the important subpopulations. The target population is defined as the group for whom the test is designed. Members of the target population are a subset of the test-taking population, the people who actually take the test. Typically, the non-target portion of the test-taking population is small in nature. For example, college-bound juniors and seniors compose the SAT® target population. A small group of individuals in junior high school also take the test, although they are not part of the target population.

Testing programs that engage in due diligence will define their target populations. Given that the test-taking population will invariably include test takers who are not part of the target population, it is essential that steps be taken to ensure that these test takers do not adversely affect the integrity of psychometric analyses (Sinharay, Dorans, & Liang, 2011).

The non-target part of the population may include test takers who are not proficient enough in the language of the test. This is especially the case when insufficient language proficiency serves as a source of construct irrelevant variance, as is likely to be the case on tests that assess mathematical proficiency. Inclusion of these test takers in subpopulation invariance analyses, whether it is checking linking invariance, prediction invariance, or measurement invariance would allow insufficient language proficiency to complicate the analysis.

Integration has made certain subpopulation analyses harder to do. For example, intermarriage has become more commonplace in American society, which has led to more test takers of multiple races or ethnic background. This in turn has complicated invariance analyses. Studies based on gender are less likely to be affected by societal changes, but that may change in the future as well. Each testing program should examine its target population and enumerate important subgroups, such as males and females, for which enough data exist to conduct invariance analyses. Even though invariance analyses have become more difficult to conduct due to the heterogeneity of test taking populations, the need to ensure fair measurement and fair inferences remains salient.

In closing, fairness in score interpretation has multiple facets. Claims about fairness require validation: at the item level as well as at the score level; from the measurement perspective as well as from the score use perspective. To the extent applicable, testing professionals should perform due diligence to examine measurement invariance and differential predication analysis, albeit the invariances might be difficult to achieve in practice. Score equity assessment can be incorporated into testing programs to assess score interchangeability claims.

Notes

1. The views expressed are those of the author and not necessarily those of the Secondary School Admissions Test Board.
2. The views expressed are those of the author and not necessarily those of the Educational Testing Service.
3. This discussion of factorial invariance deals with factorial invariance of test scores, not item scores. Item score invariance is evaluated via DIF procedures or the invariance of parameters of item response models. The focus here is on test scores.

References

Brennan, R. L. (2007). Tests in transition: Synthesis and discussion. In N. J. Dorans, M. Pommerich, & P. W. Holland (Eds.), *Linking and aligning scores and scales* (pp. 161–175). New York: Springer-Verlag.

Cleary, T. A. (1968). Test bias: Prediction of grades of Negro and White students in integrated colleges. *Journal of Educational Measurement, 5*, 115–124.

Cole, N. S. (1973). Bias in selection. *Journal of Educational Measurement, 10*, 237–255.

Dorans, N. J. (2004). Using population invariance to assess test score equity. *Journal of Educational Measurement, 41*(1), 43–68.

Dorans, N. J., & Holland, P. W. (2000). Population invariance and the equatability of tests: Basic theory and the linear case. *Journal of Educational Measurement, 37*, 281–306.

Dorans, N. J., & Lawrence, I. M. (1987). *The internal construct validity of the SAT* (ETS Research Rep. No. RR-87-35). Princeton, NJ: ETS.

Dorans, N. J., & Lawrence, I. M. (1999). *The role of the unit of analysis in dimensionality assessment* (ETS Research Rep. No. RR-99-14). Princeton, NJ: ETS.

Dorans, N. J., & Liu, J. (2007, April). *Are reported scores the same when test content and conditions of measurement change?* Paper presented at the annual meeting of the National Council on Measurement in Education, Chicago, IL.

Dorans, N. J., & Liu, J. (2009). *Score equity assessment: Development of a prototype analysis using SAT mathematics test data across several administrations* (ETS Research Rep. No. RR-09-08). Princeton, NJ: ETS.

Dorans, N. J., Lin, P., Wang, W., & Yao, L. (2014). *The invariance of latent and observed linking functions in the presence of multiple latent test-taker dimensions* (ETS Research Report No. RR-14-41). Princeton, NJ: ETS.

Holland, P. W., & Dorans, N. J. (2006). Linking and equating. In R. L. Brennan (Ed.), *Educational measurement* (4th ed., pp. 187–220). Westport, CT: American Council on Education/Praeger.

Huggins, A. C., & Penfield, R. D. (2012). An NCME instructional module on population invariance in linking and equating. *Educational Measurement: Issues and Practice, 31*(1), 27–40.

Kolen, M. J., & Brennan, R. L. (2014). *Test equating, scaling, and linking: Methods and practices* (3rd ed.). New York: Springer-Verlag.

Linn, R. L. (1973). Fair test use in selection. *Review of Educational Research, 43*, 139–161.

Linn, R. L. (1975). Test bias and the prediction of grades in law school. *Journal of Legal Education, 27*, 293–323.

Linn, R. L. (1976). In search of fair selection procedures. *Journal of Educational Measurement, 13*, 53–58.

Linn, R. L. (1983). Predictive bias as an artifact of selection procedures. In H. Wainer & S. Messick (Eds.), *Principals of modern psychological measurement: A Festschrift for Frederic M. Lord* (pp. 27–40). Hillsdale, NJ: Lawrence Erlbaum Associates.

Linn, R. L., & Werts, C. E. (1971). Considerations for studies of test bias. *Journal of Educational Measurement, 8*, 1–4.

Liu, J., & Dorans, N. J. (2012). Assessing the practical equivalence of conversions when measurement conditions change. *Journal of Educational Measurement, 49*(1), 101–115.

Liu, J., & Dorans, N. J. (2013). Assessing a critical aspect of construct continuity when test specifications change or test forms deviate from specifications. *Educational Measurement: Issues and Practice, 32*(1), 15–22.

Liu, J., & Walker, M. E. (2007). Score linking issues related to test content changes. In N. J. Dorans, M. Pommerich, & P. Holland (Eds.), *Linking and aligning scores and scales* (pp. 109–134). New York: Springer-Verlag.

Liu, J., Cahn, M., & Dorans, N. J. (2006). An application of score equity assessment: Invariance of linking of new SAT to old SAT across gender groups. *Journal of Educational Measurement, 43*, 113–129.

Liu, J., Dorans, N. J., & Moses, T. P. (2010, May). *Evaluating the subpopulation sensitivity of the ACT-SAT concordances.* Paper presented in the coordinated session, Updating ACT/SAT concordances, at the 2010 annual meeting of the National Council on Measurement in Education, Denver, CO.

Lord, F. M., & Novick. M. R. (1968). *Statistical theories of mental test scores.* Reading, MA: Addison-Wesley.

Meredith, W. (1993). Measurement invariance, factor analysis, and factorial invariance. *Psychometrika, 58*, 525–543.

Millsap, R. E., & Meredith, W. (2007). Factorial invariance: Historical perspectives and new problems. In R. Cudeck & R. MacCallum (Eds.), *Factor analysis at 100: Historical developments and future directions* (pp. 131–152). Hillsdale, NJ: Lawrence Erlbaum.

Petersen, N. S., & Novick, M. R. (1976). An evaluation of some models of culture-fair selection. *Journal of Educational Measurement, 13*, 3–29.

Reckase, M. D. (2009). *Multidimensional item response theory.* New York: Springer.

Rock, D. R (1982). Equating using the confirmatory factor analysis model. In P. W. Holland & D. R. Rubin (Eds.), *Test equating* (pp. 247–257). New York: Academic Press.

Sinharay, S., Dorans, N. J., & Liang, L. (2011). First language of examinees and fairness assessment procedures. *Educational Measurement: Issues and Practice, 30,* 25–35.

Thorndike, R. L. (1971). Concepts of culture-fair selection. *Journal of Educational Measurement, 8,* 63–70.

Thurstone, L. L. (1947). *Multiple factor analysis.* Chicago, IL: University of Chicago Press.

Widaman, K. F., & Reise, S. P. (1997). Exploring the measurement invariance of psychological instruments: Applications in the substance use domain. In K. J. Bryant, M. Windle, & S. G. West (Eds.), *The science of prevention: Methodological advances from alcohol and substance abuse research* (pp. 281–324). Washington, DC: American Psychological Association.

Yang, W. (2004). Sensitivity of linkings between AP multiple-choice scores and composite scores to geographical region: An illustration of checking for population invariance. *Journal of Educational Measurement, 41*(1), 33–41.

Young, J. W. (2001). *Differential validity, differential prediction, and college admission testing: A comprehensive review and analysis* (College Board Research Rep. No. 2001-06). New York: The College Board.

6 Commentary on Ensuring Fairness in Test Design, Construction, Administration, and Scoring

Sandip Sinharay[1]

Introduction

Fairness is concerned with protecting test takers and test users in all aspects of testing. Fairness is a fundamental validity issue and requires attention throughout all stages of test development and use (American Educational Research Association, American Psychological Association, & National Council on Measurement in Education, 2014, p. 49). In the recently revised *Standards for Educational and Psychological Testing* (AERA et al., 2014), the third chapter is devoted solely to "fairness in testing." In that chapter, all the Standards except for Standard 3.0 (which is an overarching standard meant to convey the central intent or primary focus of the chapter) are separated into four thematic clusters. The first cluster is on test design, development, administration, and scoring procedures that minimize barriers to valid score interpretations for the widest possible range of individuals and relevant subgroups, and the second cluster is on validity of test score interpretations for intended uses for the intended examinee population. The four chapters, respectively, by Zieky, Wollack and Case, Penfield, and Liu and Dorans, are intended to address these two clusters of the fairness standards. The chapter by Zieky is on fairness in test design and development, the chapter by Wollack and Case is on fairness in test administration, and the remaining two chapters (by Penfield & Liu and Dorans) are on fairness in test scoring and interpretation.

The four chapters also address the requirement in the guidelines for quality control in scoring, test analysis, and reporting of test scores, published by the International Test Commission (2014, p. 196) that standardization and accuracy are essential in all stages of testing, beginning with test development and test administration, right through to scoring, test analysis, score interpretation, and score reporting.

In the next four sections, brief descriptions and comments are provided on each of the four chapters. The final section includes some additional comments.

The Chapter by Zieky on Fairness in Test Design and Development

A Brief Description of the Chapter

After providing an overview of the chapter, Zieky (this volume, Chapter 2) described the different meanings of "fairness" that are in existence. For example, the meaning could be any one among:

- treating all test takers respectfully and impartially throughout the testing process;
- no difference on average between groups of test takers (a meaning that the psychometricians do not accept, according to Zieky);
- no difference in prediction and selection of groups of test takers; and
- being valid for different groups of test takers in the intended population for the test (a meaning stated in the *ETS Guidelines for Fairness Review of Assessments*) (Educational Testing Service, 2009, p. 2).

Zieky recommended that test designers and developers use the last definition of fairness. Zieky then described two major sources of score variance:

- lasting and general sources such as construct-relevant knowledge, skills, or other attributes (KSAs), construct-irrelevant KSAs required to perform well in tests, experience with tests, and response speeds; and
- temporary, random, and specific sources such as comfort with the conditions at the test administration site, familiarity with the test items, prior knowledge of specific items, and luck in guessing an answer.

He then stated that:

- construct-relevant sources of score variance contribute positively to validity and fairness;
- all other sources of score variance diminish validity, and may or may not diminish fairness;
- construct-irrelevant sources of score variance associated with group membership diminish validity and also diminish fairness; and
- random sources of score variance (such as luck in guessing an answer) diminish validity but do not diminish fairness.

Zieky then reminded that the primary goal of the test designers and developers is to increase the proportion of desired, construct-relevant (valid and fair) score variance and to decrease the proportion of other kinds of score variance.

In the section on ensuring fairness during test design, Zieky stressed the importance of attending to fairness concerns while designing the test. He noted how evidence-centered design (e.g., Mislevy, Steinberg, & Almond, 1999) may be used as a tool that helps test designers avoid invalid and unfair sources of variance and also noted how application of universal design (e.g., Thompson, Johnstone, & Thurlow, 2002) might be used to ensure fairness for all test takers including those with disabilities who should receive special attention during the test design process. In tests given in English, Zieky recommended reducing irrelevant and unfair variance for English language learners (ELLs) using strategies such as simplified language when knowledge of English is construct-irrelevant. An advisory committee with a focus on fairness in test design and later stages of test development is also recommended.

In the section "Item Writing and Fairness Guidelines," Zieky recommended the item writers to follow a set of guidelines for the generation of fair tests and describes several existing guidelines. Zieky then described several guidelines for fairness that are a "summarized selection of the most important content from the *ETS Guidelines for Fair Tests and Communications* (Educational Testing Service, 2015)" and are designed to remove potential sources of group-related, construct-irrelevant variance. The guidelines relate to: (i) unnecessarily difficult language; (ii) construct-irrelevant specialized knowledge; (iii) construct-irrelevant test material that is likely to anger, annoy, offend, or upset members of some groups of test takers; (iv) topics that are best avoided (such as atrocities, ethnic conflicts, and suffering); (v) terminology for groups; (vi) gender issues; and (vii) children, etc. The general principles underlying these guidelines are to: (i) include whatever is necessary for valid measurement; (ii) show respect for all test takers; (iii) give different groups of test takers an equal chance for a validly interpreted score; and (iv) avoid construct-irrelevant material that may lead people to believe that the test is unfair or inappropriate.

Zieky then described how to ensure fairness in other major phases of the assessment development process including training item writers and reviewers, item reviews, test assembly and test review, scoring by human scorers, and item and test analysis. For each phase, he described the steps that should be taken to reduce the likelihood of construct-irrelevant sources of score variance.

Zieky concluded with the reminders that regardless of the extent of care about fairness, tests are likely to have group score differences and that there is no way to prove that a test is fair, but care should be taken to ensure the fairness of tests.

Comments

Zieky stated (this volume, Chapter 2) that for test developers and designers, the most useful definition of fairness is based on validity. However, I think that the definition of fairness based on validity is useful not only to test developers and designers, but to others (such as test users) as well. The *Standards for Educational and Psychological Testing* (AERA et al., 2014) describes several meanings of fairness, which are mostly in agreement with those of Zieky. While the Standards do not explicitly endorse a meaning in general, from the statement of the "overarching" Standard 3.0, it seems that by fairness, the Standards mean minimization of construct-irrelevant variance and promotion of valid score interpretations for the intended uses for all examinees in the extended population. It is interesting that while the 2014 version of the *ETS Standards for Quality and Fairness* (Educational Testing Service, 2014, p. 19) also mentions, like Zieky, that "The most useful definition of fairness for test developers is the extent to which the inferences made on the basis of test scores are valid for different groups of test takers," the previous version (Educational Testing Service, 2002) mentioned that "For the purposes of this chapter, fairness requires treating people with impartiality regardless of personal characteristics such as gender, race, ethnicity, or disability that are not relevant to their interaction with ETS.[2] With respect to assessments, fairness requires that construct-irrelevant personal characteristics of test takers have no appreciable effect on test results or their interpretation."

In his conclusion, Zieky stated that fairness in assessment is achieved by maximizing the proportion of the score variance that is construct-relevant, and minimizing the proportion of the score variance that is construct-irrelevant and associated with group membership. I think that this statement is a little incomplete because of the lack of a complete specification of the term "maximizing": maximizing over what and according to whom? While "maximizing" refers to the proportion of the score variance that is construct-relevant approaching very close to 1, a test-score user (such as a university admissions official) would probably prefer "very close to 1" to be something like 0.99 while the testing company might be able to achieve, for example, 0.90. I would prefer a statement such as "the fairness in an assessment is the extent to which the proportion of the score variance that is construct-relevant is close to 1." I also think that the other concluding statement of Zieky that "No matter how carefully those tasks are accomplished, fair and valid tests are likely to have group score differences" connotes that if the tasks are accomplished carefully, then the test would be fair and valid; I would prefer a statement such as "No matter how carefully those tasks are accomplished, there is no guarantee that the corresponding test would be fair and valid."[3] In fact, it is because of this precise reason that testing companies (such as ETS, where all the above-mentioned tasks are accomplished carefully most of the time) include procedures such as DIF analysis to search for evidence of unfairness[4] and that Liu and Dorans (this volume, Chapter 5) recommended the testing programs to use score equity assessment on a routine basis.

The Chapter by Wollack and Case on Fairness Regarding Test Administration

A Brief Description of the Chapter

Wollack and Case (this volume, Chapter 3) focused on test administration and its significance in assuring that all examinees are assessed under the same conditions in the context of standardized achievement tests, which include standardized tests for educational achievement and accountability, admissions, certification, and licensure, as well as content-based employment tests. They also briefly considered classroom testing. In the introduction of the chapter, they made the important points that: (i) one aspect of the "standardization" of standardized tests is the process of unifying the various conditions (such as lighting, temperature, and noise in the test administration site) under which examinations are administered and scored; (ii) test administration is a key component in upholding the validity of test score interpretations; (iii) administration conditions must be set up to prevent and deter all forms of cheating on tests; and (iv) test instructions, which should include a listing of the administration rules, must be clear and precise so that the testing company, test administrators, proctors, and examinees have a common understanding of the administration procedures, and mentioned the requirement in the *Standards for Educational and Psychological Testing* (AERA et al., 2014) that "those responsible for testing should adhere to standardized test administration, scoring, and security protocols so that test scores will reflect the constructs being assessed and will not be unduly influenced by idiosyncrasies in the testing process." Wollack and Case then listed in much detail several practical matters that should be attended to prior to, during, and following the examination so as to best ensure that examinees are treated fairly throughout the entire testing process and the validity of the intended test score interpretations is preserved.

The considerations prior to the examination include:

- the printing of the test administrator's manual;
- test site considerations to make the testing environment conducive to the examinees demonstrating their best work; examples of such consideration are:
  - testing room should be well lit;
  - rooms should allow for both air conditioning and heat;
  - rooms should be as quiet as possible;
  - testing rooms and seating configurations should not allow the examinees to see other examinees' work;

- for computer-based tests, the computer equipment should meet the minimum requirements with respect to factors such as functionality and internet connectivity;
- testing sites should be easily accessible by examinees with disabilities.

- considerations on storage of test material to prevent access of the materials by examinees before or after the examination;
- considerations on the check-in process and staffing to ensure that the tests are delivered only to the individuals who are authorized to take the examination and that the examinees cannot bring materials that would help them to perform any fraudulent activities;
- considerations on managing examinee expectations; examples of such considerations are:

  - examinees should receive information from the testing company on the purpose of the test, the constructs being measured, the content being assessed, sample questions, etc.;
  - examinees should receive information on the administration conditions for the test such as timing, prohibited attire/material, and delivery medium;
  - during registration, the examinees should be asked to sign an examinee agreement that should describe the test's misconduct process.

The considerations during the examination include:

- training of the proctors, especially on how to handle test security issues;
- considerations on basic administration such as:

  - instructions on the test should be read verbatim from the administrator's manual;
  - examinees should not begin a section until after they have been told that they can begin the section and should stop as soon as they are instructed to stop;
  - testing personnel should not provide feedback to the examinees on specific test questions.

- monitoring the examinees for possible cheating, including:

  - actively monitoring examinees throughout the test administration;
  - taking some action in the face of suspicious activity.

- considerations on scheduled and unscheduled breaks, including:

  - ensure that examinees do not switch places with another similar-looking individual;
  - ensure that after a break, the examinees do not work on items that they are not supposed to work on.
- considerations on emergencies and unforeseen situations.

Considerations after the examination include:

- considerations on check-out procedures;
- completion of irregularity reports for each unexpected incident, especially related to test security; and
- considerations on returning materials.

Wollack and Case concluded their chapter by reminding the readers that test administration is a vital element of the testing process and valid score inferences depend on ensuring that tests were administered to authorized examinees only and in environments that are comparable, so that all examinees have an opportunity to accurately demonstrate their talents.

Comments

The extensive set of recommendations in Wollack and Case describe steps that should be taken to ensure and maintain a fair testing environment. The list of considerations prior to testing on testing sites did not include at least the following two that I thought are important: (i) the testing site should be convenient with respect to transportation; and (ii) drinking water and food should be easily available at or close to the testing site. The chapter involved very little advice with respect to empirical analyses that could be used to address the effects of the inevitable situations where things don't go as planned. For example, the material on how to prevent fraudulent activities could have been augmented with material such as those covered in Kingston and Clark (2014) and McClintock (2015) on how one can investigate if examinees or the classroom teachers were involved in any fraudulent activities. In addition, some material could have been included on how the test administrators can assess whether the inadvertent exposure of an item or several items (e.g., Zhang, 2014) may have resulted in some examinees receiving an unfair advantage. Finally, analyses in Sinharay et al. (2014) and Sinharay, Wan, Choi, and Kim (2015) on how one can assess the effects on fairness if computer disruptions occurred is another example of empirical analyses that could augment the many preventive steps mentioned by Wollack and Case.

The Chapter by Penfield on Fairness in Test Scoring

A Brief Description of the Chapter

Penfield (this volume, Chapter 4) posited that an argument for fairness of test scores can be developed from the evaluation of construct-irrelevant factors associated with the individual scored responses used in generating the test score. This evaluation of construct-irrelevant factors can include at least two steps:

- evaluating if each scored element holds the same meaning with respect to the proficiency measured by the test regardless of the examinee's standing on key background variables such as gender, race, ethnicity, and disability status; differential item functioning (DIF), differential step functioning (DSF) and differential feature functioning can be used in this step; and
- evaluating if consistency of the multiple independent scores assigned to the same response is sufficiently high regardless of the examinee's background variables.

Penfield organized the relevant methods to evaluate potential violations of fairness associated with individual scored responses into three sections according to three types of item scores that are usually in existence in educational assessments: (i) automated scores of multiple-choice (MC) items; (ii) human rater scores of constructed response (CR) items; and (iii) automated scores of CR items.

In the section on automated scores of multiple-choice (MC) items, after defining the concept of DIF and providing a visual representation of DIF for such scores, Penfield listed the following issues that should be kept in mind while implementing DIF analysis: (i) the stratifying variable that forms the basis of matching in DIF analysis; (ii) the sample size requirements for DIF analysis; (iii) impact or group difference; (iv) consideration of the effect size of DIF along with statistical significance of DIF; and (v) the need to review the items to identify the factor responsible for the DIF. Penfield then described the following methods for assessing DIF for MC items: standardized p-difference method (Dorans & Kulick, 1986), the Mantel-Haenszel DIF method (e.g., Holland & Thayer, 1988), and mentioned the item-response-theory-based chi-square and likelihood ratio tests (Thissen, Steinberg, & Wainer, 1993).

In the section on human-scored CR items, Penfield first focused on rater consistency that can be examined at the level of the individual examinees or at the level of groups of examinees. Examination of consistency at the level of the individual examinees involves adjudication procedure in the case of too much discrepancy between multiple scores on the same response. Examination of consistency at the level of groups of examinees involves computation of rater consistency measures such as correlation coefficient and weighted kappa for a group of examinees. After the accumulation of multiple scores on each response to a single overall score, DIF analysis should be performed with the overall scores. For CR items, which are usually polytomous, one could think of net DIF and global DIF; net DIF addresses whether examinees with the same level of proficiency but belonging to different subgroups receive the same average score on the item, whereas global DIF addresses whether examinees with the same level of proficiency but belonging to different subgroups have the same chance of advancing to each possible level of scores on the item. Penfield then listed several issues that should be kept in mind while implementing DIF analysis for human-rated polytomous items. Methods for assessing net DIF, such as the standardized mean difference index (Dorans & Schmitt, 1991) and the Liu-Agresti cumulative common log-odds ratio method (e.g., Penfield & Algina, 2003) are discussed next. Methods for assessing global DIF, such as the generalized Mantel-Haenszel approach (Zwick, Donoghue, & Grima, 1993) and the differential step functioning approach (e.g., Penfield, 2007), are discussed next.

In the section on automated-scored CR items, for which an automated scoring algorithm assigns an overall item score based on several scored features on the item, Penfield suggested the use of *differential feature functioning* analysis to ensure that each scored feature of the examinee's response is free of construct-irrelevant factors. Differential feature functioning (DFF) is evaluated by comparing the level of success on a given feature for examinees with the same overall item score but belonging to different subgroups. Penfield then recommended DFF analysis for automated-scored CR items using the same methods used for MC items or human-scored CR items. Penfield then discussed two sets of methods for evaluating whether automated scores are consistent with the corresponding human scores: difference methods and agreement methods.

Penfield concluded with a recommendation for further research on differential feature functioning.

Comments

While there is an abundance of articles on DIF-related topics, those articles mostly do not include much discussion specific on automatically-scored CR items—so the readers should find those areas of Penfield's chapter quite useful.

The chapter would have been enhanced with discussions (or at least a mention) of:

- how the Golden Rule Insurance Company settlement impelled the development of the DIF procedures;
- the other existing DIF detection methods such as those based on logistic regression (e.g., Swaminathan & Rogers, 1990), the exact Mantel-Haenszel procedure (Parshall & Miller, 1995), the Bayesian DIF procedure (e.g., Zwick, Thayer, & Lewis, 1999), the IRT-based methods based on the area between item response functions (e.g., Raju, 1988), and the SIBTEST procedure (Shealy & Stout, 1993) and its extension to polytomous items (Chang, Mazzeo, & Roussos, 1996);
- the concept of uniform DIF and non-uniform DIF[5] (e.g., Swaminathan & Rogers, 1990);
- factors that have been found to have caused DIF (e.g., Schmitt, Curley, Bleistein, & Dorans, 1988; Schmitt, Holland, & Dorans, 1993); and
- the multidimensionality hypothesis of DIF (e.g., Ackerman, 1992; Hunter, 1975).

The Chapter by Liu and Dorans on Fairness in Test Score Interpretation

A Brief Description of the Chapter

While Penfield considered fairness of the individual scored responses (or item-level scores), Liu and Dorans (this volume, Chapter 5) assumed that the individual responses have already been accumulated to produce the scores of the examinees. They attempt to answer the overarching question, "Can scores from different versions of the same test be interpreted as and used as if they are interchangeable?" (p. 2) by focusing on the following three aspects of fairness of interpretations attached to those scores:

- whether the linking relationships among interchangeable scores are invariant across examinee subgroups (subpopulation invariance);
- whether the test editions measure what they purport to measure in the same way across different subgroups (measurement invariance); and
- whether the test scores serve their primary purpose in the same way across different subgroups (prediction invariance).

The three aspects are addressed by using, respectively, score equity assessment (e.g., Dorans, 2004), factorial invariance analysis (e.g., Meredith, 1993), and differential prediction analysis (Petersen & Novick, 1976).

In the section on assessment of subpopulation invariance by performing score equity assessment, Liu and Dorans stated the five requirements of equating from Holland and Dorans (2006). The fifth requirement of population invariance is examined by score equity assessment. Liu and Dorans then described the methods for performing a score equity assessment, or an assessment of whether the equating functions are subpopulation-invariant. Mathematically, a score equity assessment is performed by examining if the subgroup-specific equating function is different from the equating function for the other subgroups and that for all the examinees. Score equity assessment can be performed using a graphical plot. To interpret the differences between equating functions for different groups, a difference that is larger than the *difference that matters* (DTM) criterion (e.g., Liu & Dorans, 2013) can be considered to be too large. To augment the graphical plots, one can compute the percentage of raw scores for which the total and subgroup-specific raw-to-scale conversion differed by more than the DTM and the percentage of examinees for which these conversions created scaled scores that differed by more than the DTM. Score equity assessment can also be performed by computing several *equatability indices* such as root mean square difference, root expected mean square difference, root expected square difference, average scores, and differences in average scores. Liu and Dorans illustrated the indices using a real data example from Dorans and Liu (2009). Then, Liu and Dorans described conditions under which linking invariance is likely to hold and recommended the use of score equity assessment as a quality control check for ensuring fairness in operational assessments, in much the same way DIF analysis is used at the item level. If score equity analysis reveals a lack of subpopulation invariance, Liu and Dorans recommended further investigation of the test assembly, test administration, and statistical analysis procedures for possible explanations.

In the section on assessment of measurement invariance by checking factorial invariance, Liu and Dorans employed the common linear factor analysis model (where a score is expressed as the sum of a linear combination of several latent variables and an error term) to explain the concepts of strict factorial invariance, strong factorial invariance, weak factorial invariance, and configural invariance, four successively weaker versions of invariance. Liu and Dorans noted that measurement invariance is not as easy to assess as, for example, subpopulation invariance, because the former involves latent/unobservable variables.

In the section on assessment of prediction invariance by performing differential prediction analysis, Liu and Dorans discussed the following four major types of models that are typically used in differential prediction analysis: constant ratio model (Thorndike, 1971), equal probability model (Linn, 1973), conditional probability model (Cole, 1973), and the regression model (Cleary, 1968). Among these, the first three collapse the response variable (usually referred to as the "selection variable" in the context of such studies) to a binary variable (accept or reject).

Liu and Dorans concluded their chapter with the note that the concept of subpopulation invariance is central to the three types of analyses they focused on and they recommended that score equity assessment be incorporated into testing programs to assess fairness and that testing professionals should perform due diligence to examine measurement invariance and differential prediction analysis.

Comments

The chapter would have been more interesting with numerical examples, preferably from the same testing program. I would have liked examples of tests for which score equity assessment revealed a lack of population invariance, a subsequent scrutiny of the test assembly, test administration, and statistical analysis procedures revealed a problem, and fixing of the problem led to population invariance in the future. Such examples would convince testing programs to implement score equity assessment as a part of their routine statistical procedures. If such examples are lacking, then, there is probably room for further research in the same manner Schmitt et al. (1988) performed research on DIF. Clear recommendations on what subpopulations should be considered would have helped readers. It seems that Liu and Dorans referred to subpopulations based on gender, ethnicity, and race in the least. But what about subgroups based on language, disability status, and mode of administration (paper-and-pencil or computer)? Should one perform a score equity analysis based on those factors as well?[6]

Final Comments

The four chapters in this section, while addressing fairness in test design, construction, administration, and scoring, involve a variety of checks, some of which involve empirical data and some others that do not. While the checks and considerations (not involving empirical data) in the chapters by Zieky and Wollack and Case represent the best-case scenarios, there is always some room for some error to creep in during test design, construction, administration, and scoring. That is where the methods (involving empirical data) described in the chapters of Penfield (on fairness in test scoring) and Liu and Dorans (on fairness in score interpretation) are important as further checks on fairness. An interesting connection between the two latter chapters is that a lack of fairness in test scoring may amplify into a lack of fairness in score interpretation. Liu and Dorans (2013) recommended that if a lack of population invariance (that is, a form of lack of fairness in score interpretation) is found, one should examine DIF results; certain types of items favor or disfavor certain groups (that is, a form of lack of fairness in test scoring), even though the DIF for all items may be small, and Huggins (2014) used a simulation study to illustrate that when anchor item DIF varies across forms in a differential manner across subpopulations, population invariance of equating can be compromised.

The procedures described in these four chapters are readily applied to traditional testing scenarios where different versions of a test are developed from the same blueprint and administered with the intention of their scores being used interchangeably. The principles of fair design, construction, and administration are also pertinent to the areas of vertical scaling, test adaptation, and test accommodations, which are addressed in the next section of this book. The quantitative methods that assess fairness empirically may be appropriate, with appropriate caveats as noted by Thissen (this volume, Chapter 11), for these less straightforward fairness issues. Regardless of whether the procedures for ensuring and assessing fairness use empirical data or not, and whether they are completely or only partially appropriate in different settings, it is absolutely important for those in the measurement field to have a solid understanding of the material covered in these four chapters.

Notes

1. The views expressed are those of the author and not necessarily those of Pacific Metrics Corporation.
2. A meaning that is somewhat retained in the second sentence of the purpose ("ETS will treat people comparably and fairly regardless of differences in characteristics that are not relevant to the intended use of the product or service") of the 2014 ETS Standards.
3. Zieky admits a few lines later that "There is no way to prove that a test is fair."
4. Testing companies often find DIF on a few items (for examples of DIF found in operational tests, see, e.g., Schmitt, Curley, Bleistein, & Dorans, 1988).
5. In interpreting DIF in various instances, Penfield only considered what is referred to as the "uniform DIF."
6. There are separate chapters in this book that cover subpopulations based on language (Chapter 10), mode of administration (Chapter 7), and disability status (Chapter 9).

References

Ackerman, T. A. (1992). A didactic explanation of item bias, item impact, and item validity from a multidimensional perspective. *Journal of Educational Measurement, 29*, 67–91.

American Educational Research Association, American Psychological Association, & National Council on Measurement in Education. (2014). *Standards for educational and psychological testing*. Washington, DC: American Educational Research Association.

Chang, H. H., Mazzeo, J., & Roussos, L. (1996). Detecting DIF for polytomously scored items: An adaptation of the SIBTEST procedure. *Journal of Educational Measurement, 33,* 333–353.

Cleary, T. A. (1968). Test bias: Prediction of grades of Negro and White students in integrated colleges. *Journal of Educational Measurement, 5,* 115–124.

Cole, N. S. (1973). Bias in selection. *Journal of Educational Measurement, 10,* 237–255.

Dorans, N. J. (2004). Using population invariance to assess test score equity. *Journal of Educational Measurement, 41,* 43–68.

Dorans, N. J., & Kulick, E. (1986). Demonstrating the utility of the standardization approach to assessing unexpected differential item performance on the Scholastic Aptitude Test. *Journal of Educational Measurement, 23,* 355–368.

Dorans, N. J., & Liu, J. (2009). *Score equity assessment: Development of a prototype analysis using SAT mathematics test data across several administrations* (ETS Research Rep. No. RR-09-08). Princeton, NJ: ETS.

Dorans, N. J., & Schmitt, A. P. (1991). *Constructed response and differential item functioning: A pragmatic approach* (ETS Research Rep. No. 91-47). Princeton, NJ: Educational Testing Service.

Educational Testing Service. (2002). *ETS standards for quality and fairness.* Princeton, NJ: ETS.

Educational Testing Service. (2009). *ETS guidelines for fairness review of assessments.* Princeton, NJ: ETS. Retrieved from www.ets.org/Media/About_ETS/pdf/overview.pdf

Educational Testing Service. (2014). *ETS standards for quality and fairness.* Princeton, NJ: ETS. Retrieved from www.ets.org/s/about/pdf/standards.pdf

Holland, P. W., & Dorans, N. J. (2006). Linking and equating. In R. L. Brennan (Ed.), *Educational measurement* (4th ed., pp. 187–220). Westport, CT: American Council on Education/Praeger.

Holland, P. W., & Thayer, D. T. (1988). Differential item performance and the Mantel-Haenszel procedure. In H. Wainer & H. I. Braun (Eds.), *Test validity* (pp. 129–145). Hillsdale, NJ: Lawrence Erlbaum.

Huggins, A. C. (2014). The effect of differential item functioning in anchor items on population invariance of equating. *Educational and Psychological Measurement, 74,* 627–658.

Hunter, J. E. (1975, December). *A critical analysis of the use of item means and item-test correlations to determine the presence or absence of content bias in achievement test items.* Paper presented at the National Institute of Education Invitational Conference on Test Bias, Annapolis, MD.

International Test Commission (ITC). (2014). ITC guidelines on quality control in scoring, test analysis, and reporting of test scores. *International Journal of Testing, 14*(3), 195–217.

Kingston, N. M., & Clark, A. K. (2014). *Test fraud: Statistical detection and methodology.* New York: Springer.

Linn, R. L. (1973). Fair test use in selection. *Review of Educational Research, 43,* 139–161.

Liu, J., & Dorans, N. J. (2013). Assessing a critical aspect of construct continuity when test specifications change or test forms deviate from specifications. *Educational Measurement: Issues and Practice, 32*(1), 15–22.

McClintock, J. C. (2015). Erasure analyses: Reducing the number of false positives. *Applied Measurement in Education, 28,* 14–32.

Meredith, W. (1993). Measurement invariance, factor analysis, and factorial invariance. *Psychometrika, 58,* 525–543.

Mislevy, R. J., Steinberg, L. S., & Almond, R. G. (1999). *Evidence-centered assessment design.* Princeton, NJ: Educational Testing Service.

Parshall, C. G., & Miller, T. R. (1995). Exact versus asymptotic Mantel-Haenszel DIF statistics: A comparison of performance under small-sample conditions. *Journal of Educational Measurement, 32,* 302–316.

Penfield, R. D. (2007). Assessing differential step functioning in polytomous items using a common odds ratio estimator. *Journal of Educational Measurement, 44,* 187–210.

Penfield, R. D., & Algina, J. (2003). Applying the Liu-Agresti estimator of the cumulative common odds ratio to DIF detection in polytomous items. *Journal of Educational Measurement, 40,* 353–370.

Petersen, N. S., & Novick, M. R. (1976). An evaluation of some models of culture-fair selection. *Journal of Educational Measurement, 13*, 3–29.

Raju, N. S. (1988). The area between two item characteristic curves. *Psychometrika, 53*, 495–502.

Schmitt, A. P., Curley, W. E., Bleistein, C. A., & Dorans, N. J. (1988). Experimental evaluation of language and interest factors related to differential item functioning for Hispanic examinees on the SAT-Verbal. Paper presented at the annual meeting of the National Council on Measurement in Education, New Orleans.

Schmitt, A. P., Holland, P. W., & Dorans, N. J. (1993). Evaluating of hypotheses about differential item functioning. In P. W. Holland & H. Wainer (Eds.), *Differential item functioning* (pp. 281–315), Hillsdale, NJ: Erlbaum Associates.

Shealy, R., & Stout, W. (1993). A model-based standardization approach that separates true bias/DIF from group ability differences and detects test bias/DTF as well as item bias/DIF. *Psychometrika, 58*, 159–194.

Sinharay, S., Wan, P., Whitaker, M., Kim, D., Zhang, L., & Choi, S. W. (2014). Determining the overall impact of interruptions during online testing. *Journal of Educational Measurement, 51*, 419–440.

Sinharay, S., Wan, P., Choi, S. W., & Kim, D. (2015). Assessing individual-level impact of interruptions during online testing. *Journal of Educational Measurement, 52*, 80–105.

Swaminathan, H., & Rogers, H. J. (1990). Detecting differential item functioning using logistic regression procedures. *Journal of Educational Measurement, 27*, 361–369.

Thissen, D., Steinberg, L., & Wainer, H. (1993). Detection of differential item functioning using the parameters of item response models. In P. W. Holland & H. Wainer (Eds.), *Differential item functioning* (pp. 67–113). Hillsdale, NJ: Lawrence Erlbaum.

Thompson, S. J., Johnstone, C. J., & Thurlow, M. L. (2002). *Universal design applied to large scale assessments* (Synthesis Report 44). Minneapolis, MN: University of Minnesota, National Center on Educational Outcomes. Retrieved from http://education.umn.edu/NCEO/Online Pubs/Synthesis44.html

Thorndike, R. L. (1971). Concepts of culture-fair selection. *Journal of Educational Measurement, 8*, 63–70.

Zhang, J. (2014). A sequential procedure for detecting compromised items in the item pool of a CAT system. *Applied Psychological Measurement, 38*, 87–104.

Zwick, R., Donoghue, J. R., & Grima, A. (1993). Assessment of differential item functioning for performance tasks. *Journal of Educational Measurement, 30*, 233–251.

Zwick, R., Thayer, D. T., & Lewis, C. (1999). An empirical Bayes approach to Mantel-Haenszel DIF analysis. *Journal of Educational Measurement, 36*, 1–28.

Part II

Assessing the Fairness of Comparisons under Divergent Measurement Conditions

Part II of this book addresses how to assess the fairness of comparisons of test scores that are obtained via different assessments that are used for comparable purposes. Chapters in this part of the volume address issues for tests that differ primarily with respect to blueprint, those that differ with respect to how they are administered, those that differ with respect to target population, and those whose test takers speak different languages.

In her chapter, Pommerich examines "The Fairness of Comparing Test Scores across Different Tests or Modes of Administration." Scores across tests of similar content that are developed by competing test publishers in different ways for similar purposes are often compared. Users often compare scores across the same test that is given under different modes of administration. In addition, this chapter discusses the fairness of comparisons that result from the application of statistical methods to link scores across different tests or modes. Linking frameworks are reviewed, with a focus on the relevance of concordance and calibration to the scenarios of interest, and fairness issues pertaining to comparing linked scores under various conditions are elaborated upon.

Castellano and Kolen, in their chapter, address the fairness issues associated with "Comparing Tests across Grade Levels" to assess how well students are progressing over time. Three general approaches are considered: (1) changes in proficiency levels; (2) statistical models that include value-added models and student growth percentiles; and (3) vertical scales. Example testing programs are described that use each of these approaches. The focus of the chapter is on validation of each approach for students from various populations and students with special needs. The chapter concludes with a research agenda for fairness in comparing test scores across grade levels.

This part of the volume includes a chapter on fairness considerations for the design, development, and administration of tests given to members of relevant subgroups in the testing population, such as individuals with disabilities and individuals from diverse linguistic and cultural backgrounds. Stone and Cook, in "Testing Individuals in Special Populations," describe the fairness implications of changes in testing design, construction, and administration that are made to accommodate test takers with special needs. Two major classes of test takers are considered. There are those who require accommodation due to a disability, such as a visual impairment, that prevents them from taking tests under standard conditions. The other class includes individuals whose insufficient proficiency in the language of the test makes it difficult for them to demonstrate their level of competency in the skills or abilities measured by the test.

Sireci, Rios and Powers in the next chapter, "Comparing Scores from Tests Administered in Different Languages," examine the fairness of efforts to assess test takers who take tests in different languages. To create these tests, translations are often employed or versions of the tests are built in different languages to what are deemed to be the same set of specifications. These approaches require assumptions that entail validity issues regarding comparability of score interpretation across different language versions of an assessment. The chapter reviews these issues and research that has investigated: (a) linking different language versions of an assessment; (b) evaluating the psychometric properties of dual-language versions of an assessment; and (c) evaluating the psychometric properties of alternate-language versions of an assessment. Recommendations are provided for further research and practices that promote fairness in cross-lingual assessment.

In the last chapter of this section, Thissen critiques and synthesizes the three chapters dealing with assessing fairness in settings in which measurement conditions are divergent.

7 The Fairness of Comparing Test Scores across Different Tests or Modes of Administration

Mary Pommerich[1]

Introduction

There is often a desire among test users to compare scores across tests of similar content that are developed by competing test publishers for similar purposes. In cases where appropriate data are available, statistical methods can be applied to link scores across the different tests, facilitating the comparison of scores. College admissions is one realm where this practice occurs regularly. Given that different tests have different characteristics, the question arises as to whether it is fair to compare scores that have been linked across different tests. A different, yet related, concern arises when users wish to compare scores across the same test that is given under different modes of administration. Under this scenario, the test publisher might apply statistical methods to link scores across the different modes of administration, facilitating the comparison of scores. A testing program converting from paper-and-pencil to computer administration is one realm where this practice can occur. Given that the test differs in terms of how it is administered, the question arises as to whether it is fair to compare scores across the different modes of administration.

Fairness in testing has been addressed extensively in the measurement literature. However, the scope of the discussion typically focuses on a single test and does not include the contexts described here. Although practitioners have argued that it is the use of a test (or test scores) rather than the test itself that is fair (Camilli, 1993, 2006; Darlington, 1971; Thorndike, 1971), fair use of *linked* scores is usually not considered outside of the context of alternate forms of the same test.[2] Linked scores are scores that have been statistically linked so as to enable identification of *concordant* or *comparable* scores across tests or modes of interest. While sources of mode effects and the comparability of scores across administration modes are fairness concerns that have been investigated thoroughly in the measurement literature, comparability studies tend to focus on comparing scores across modes of administration rather than the *fairness* of comparing scores across modes of administration.[3] A subtle distinction perhaps, but important. Fairness may be implicitly assumed where score comparability is deemed to hold or scores have been linked across modes, but is that really the case? Considering score comparability from a fairness perspective may change how results are viewed. Likewise, while the limitations of linking scores across distinct tests have been addressed to some degree in the measurement literature (e.g., Dorans, Pommerich, & Holland, 2007; Feuer, Holland, Green, Bertenthal, & Hemphill, 1999; Pommerich & Dorans, 2004), the fairness of comparing scores that have been linked across different tests has not been a focus of the linkage literature.[4] This may be because fairness is a complex concept with social implications that make it difficult to address.

Although it may appear that comparing scores across different modes of administration and comparing scores across different tests are fundamentally different issues, there are some important commonalities to the two scenarios pertaining to score linking. First, the same statistical methods are often used across the two scenarios to link the scores to be compared. Second, linked scores may be substituted for actual scores on the test/mode not taken, and used to make decisions. Third, users may be inclined to treat linked scores as if they can be used interchangeably across tests/modes when such an interpretation may not be warranted. If this is the case, the use of linked scores can result in decisions that differentially impact individuals and/or groups. As Feuer et al. (1999) noted, test-based decisions involve error, and linkage can add to that error. Making decisions based on scores that have been linked across different administration modes or different tests creates possibilities for unfairness above and beyond that associated with making decisions based on scores from a single test or mode. Hence, it makes sense to discuss these two scenarios together.

This chapter focuses on two primary questions:

- Is it fair to compare scores that have been linked across different modes of administration?
- Is it fair to compare scores that have been linked across different tests?

First, a fairness overview is given and related to the context of interest. Next, a linking overview is given and likewise related to the context of interest. Specific fairness issues pertaining to comparing linked scores across different modes of administration and comparing linked scores across different tests are then elaborated upon.

Fairness Overview

In considering fairness issues associated with using linked scores, it appears essential to start with a working definition of fairness, to provide a setting for the discussion to follow. Defining fairness is a tricky problem, however, as there is no definition that is generally accepted by all (Cole & Zieky, 2001; Zieky, 2006). What constitutes fairness can be viewed as a social question (Willingham & Cole, 1997) with judgments of fairness driven by values that are likely to differ across people (Sawyer, Cole, & Cole, 1976). Darlington (1971) concluded that the term "fair" carries various connotations that generally conflict with each other and that no single test is likely to meet all the requirements needed for a fair test. The *Standards for Educational and Psychological Testing* similarly state that the term fairness has no single technical meaning and outline four general views of fairness: as equitable treatment in the testing process, as lack of bias, as access to the construct(s) measured, and as validity of individual test score interpretations for the intended uses (AERA et al., 2014).

In spite of the elusiveness of the concept of fairness, a couple of general fairness perspectives do stand out in the literature as being relevant to the current context. The first perspective suggests that fairness is a property of test use rather than the test itself (Camilli, 1993, 2006), and that a test may be fair for some uses but not others (Darlington, 1971; Thorndike, 1971). Although this perspective is not presented in terms of validity, test use is inherently associated with validity (Kane, 2013). The second perspective explicitly argues that the most meaningful definition of fairness is based on validity, because anything that lowers the validity of a test for a group reduces the fairness of the test (Zieky, 2006). More specifically, fairness is defined as *comparable validity* for individuals and groups at each assessment stage (Willingham & Cole, 1997; Xi, 2010). This perspective is related to the test use perspective in that, if score-based inferences are not equally valid for all relevant groups, decisions derived from those score inferences will not be fair (Langenfeld, 1997). Unfortunately, tying fairness to validity does not appear to provide a means for establishing a generally accepted definition of fairness— because validity is a matter of degree that may be interpreted differently based on personal values, fairness remains a matter of degree too (Cole & Zieky, 2001).

Different Modes Example

Both of the perspectives addressed above are relevant to the questions at hand. The issue lies with using linked scores in place of actual scores to make decisions about examinees. Consider the case where a test that has historically been administered via paper-and-pencil (P&P) has been converted to a computerized administration. This scenario is depicted in the left side of Figure 7.1. The test has likely been studied extensively with regard to validity for the P&P mode but not for the computer mode, and decision/selection criteria for test users will likely have been established based on the P&P test. Thus, fairness in terms of decision/selection outcomes will likely have been evaluated within the context of P&P administration. Green (1984, p. 77) stated the concern well for this type of scenario: "When a conventional test is transferred to the computer, it brings its validity with it. At least, we hope it does."

If scores from a computer administration have been linked to scores from a P&P administration to identify "comparable" or "concordant" score points across the two modes, decisions for examinees that take the test via computer will be based on concordant P&P scores rather than actual P&P scores. Note that comparable scores are not the same as interchangeable scores (to be addressed in more detail in the linking overview). Interchangeable scores are the ideal outcome of a linkage, while comparable scores imply a lower level of association (i.e., the linked scores can be compared across modes but not treated interchangeably). Interchangeable scores are expected when scores are equated across alternate forms of a test meeting certain prerequisites, but not necessarily when scores are linked across alternate modes of administration. Alternately, it might not be necessary to link scores across modes if evidence suggests they can be treated interchangeably without adjustment. Drasgow and Chuah (2005) advised that if a computerized administration does not yield scores that are equivalent to scores from a P&P administration, the test must be revalidated for the computer mode. Likewise, testing programs that choose not to revalidate should show strong evidence that scores are equivalent across modes.

The term *score equivalence* has been used to signify different things in the mode effects literature. The American Psychological Association (1986) stated that scores across modes of administration may be considered equivalent when score distributions are approximately the same across modes and individuals are rank ordered in approximately the same way. Elsewhere, the term score equivalence has been used to describe a situation where score distributions are approximately the same (e.g., Lottridge, Nicewander, Schulz, & Mitzel, 2008). In an attempt to clarify the terminology, the term *distributional equivalence* will be used here to describe the situation where score distributions are the same across two modes. It is generally expected that distributional equivalence should hold when comparing scores across modes (e.g., Kolen, 1999; Lottridge et al., 2008; Wang & Kolen, 2001).

Beyond distributional equivalence, researchers have suggested the need for *construct equivalence* across modes (e.g., Eignor, 2007; Kolen, 1999; Lottridge et al., 2008; Sawaki, 2001), such that the construct being measured across the two modes is equivalent. The presence of distributional equivalence and construct equivalence would be consistent with the APA (1986) definition of score equivalence (i.e., similar rank ordering of scores across modes is evidence of construct equivalence). However, the APA definition of score equivalence is less rigorous than that for the classical test theory definition of parallel tests, where equal correlations with criterion variables would also be needed for scores to be treated interchangeably across tests or modes (Bugbee, 1996). In the case of non-parallel tests, equal predictions of external criteria would not be attained because reliabilities are unequal (Neuman & Baydoun, 1998).

Hence, some researchers have suggested the need for *predictive equivalence* across modes (e.g., Bugbee, 1996; Neuman & Baydoun, 1998; Wolfe, Moreno, & Segall, 1997), such that external criteria are predicted equivalently, while others have suggested the need for *correlational equivalence* across modes (Bugbee, 1996; Kolen, 1999; Zitny, Halama, Jelinek, & Kveton, 2012), such that scores correlate equivalently with external criteria. The comparable validity perspective of fairness espoused by Cole and Zieky (2001) and Xi (2010) suggests that distributional equivalence, construct equivalence, and predictive equivalence[5] might all be needed to be truly fair when comparing scores across different modes of administration.

Different Tests Example

The case where scores have been linked across two distinct tests presents a similar concern to the different modes example, in that each test has likely been validated extensively for the particular uses that are specific to them (such as making selection decisions), but the use of linked scores as a substitute for actual scores has likely never been validated. Take the realm of college admissions. ACT and/or SAT scores are used by many post-secondary institutions in their admissions process. Although the market is changing, the ACT has generally been more popular in the central United States, while the SAT has been more popular along the east and west coasts. Hence, schools are likely to set their selection criteria on the basis of the test that is dominant in their region. Because many schools now accept ACT or SAT scores, there is a desire for a linkage between scores on the two tests to ensure that comparable decisions are made regardless of the type of test scores submitted. (Alternatively, schools may choose to evaluate validity, fairness, and selection criteria for each test and maintain separate systems.) An institution that relies on a linkage may develop its own, or use one that has been provided by the test developers (e.g. Dorans, Lyu, Pommerich, & Houston, 1997).

Consider the scenario where a school that has historically used SAT scores in the admissions process (i.e., evaluated validity and fairness and set selection criteria based on the SAT) now also accepts ACT scores and uses a linkage to facilitate the decision-making process. This scenario is depicted in the right side of Figure 7.1. In this case, ACT scores would be linked to SAT scores and individuals submitting ACT scores would be assigned concordant SAT scores, and decisions would be made based on the concordant SAT scores rather than actual SAT scores. In this scenario, distributional equivalence is likely to hold across the two tests, but construct equivalence and predictive equivalence might not. This raises questions about the inherent fairness of comparing scores that have been linked across different tests.

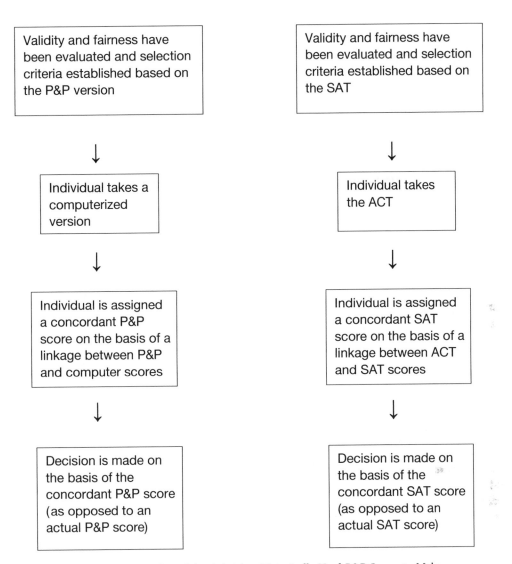

Figure 7.1 Linkage Scenarios for a School that has Historically Used P&P Scores to Make Decisions (Left) and for a School that has Historically Used SAT Scores to Make Decisions (Right)

Fairness to Individuals versus Fairness to Groups

In attempting to define fairness in the current context, it is important to make distinctions between fairness to individuals and fairness to groups because both outcomes might not be equally attainable. Thorndike (1971) demonstrated that there can be a trade-off between the two outcomes when making selection decisions (i.e., actions that are fair to individuals might be unfair to groups, and vice versa). Sawyer et al. (1976) framed this distinction in terms of maximization of success (based on individual parity) versus maximization of opportunity (based on group parity) and noted that the two concepts are often at odds, even though both are based on notions of individual merit. They also noted that concerns about fairness (at that time) tended to require that selection be based on the merits of individuals without regard to their group membership. Those concerns may have shifted over time, as more recently Cole and Zieky (2001) bemoaned the fact that the study of individual differences has been overshadowed by the study of group differences. They noted that there is more individual variation of scores within groups than variation between groups, and suggested that all concerns of fairness for groups be applied to the issue of individual differences.

More recently, Camilli (2006) considered the differences between individual and group interpretations of fairness and concluded that the question of whether individuals are disadvantaged is not the same as the question of whether a group is disadvantaged, because the group question makes the assumption that individuals within each group are similar for the purpose of comparison. A related issue had been raised earlier by Breland and Ironson (1976), namely that the classification of individuals into groups is not necessarily readily achieved. Thus, fairness to individuals and fairness to groups are somewhat contrasting outcomes that might need to be considered separately.

Summary

In light of the above discussion, it appears that fairness is a rather nebulous concept, and that establishing a working definition of fairness in the current context is not an easy task! It does seem clear, however, that there is a relationship between fairness, validity, and score comparability. The mode effects literature suggests three desirable properties of fairness that would ideally be established when comparing scores that have been linked across modes of administration or different tests:

1. distributional equivalence (e.g., the score distributions are the same for the linked scores);
2. construct equivalence (e.g., the tests or modes measure the same construct to the same degree);
3. predictive equivalence (e.g., the tests or modes have the same predictive relationship with a criterion measure).

The predictive equivalence requirement is particularly pertinent from a fairness perspective because historically, a regression model approach has been widely used to evaluate fairness in selection (Cleary, 1968; Petersen & Novick, 1976), essentially examining whether the regression of the criterion onto the predictor space is invariant across groups (Dorans, 2004b).

Relatedly, an empirical measure of construct equivalence is whether the linking relationship is invariant across groups (Dorans & Holland, 2000). When invariance does not hold for a linking, the question arises as to whether you would make the same decisions using a linkage based on the total group versus using group specific linkages. Note that this is a different sort of concern regarding fairness to groups than expressed in the fairness literature, which has focused on differences in proportions selected across groups (e.g., Hartigan & Wigdor, 1989). Misclassification of individuals is also a concern when using linked scores to make decisions.

Linking Overview

Before proceeding with a more detailed discussion of the two scenarios of interest, comparing scores that have been linked across different modes of administration and comparing scores that have been linked across different tests, it is helpful to provide some background on linking and define some of the relevant terms that are being used. Linking frameworks have been discussed in a variety of sources, including Flanagan (1951), Angoff (1971), Mislevy (1992), Linn (1993), Feuer et al. (1999), Dorans (2004a), and Kolen and Brennan (2014). Kolen (2004) compared and contrasted the various linking frameworks that have been defined. More recently, Holland (2007) and Holland and Dorans (2006) presented a linking framework that builds on the preceding frameworks; this chapter utilizes their framework and terminology.

For two forms (or modes of administration, or tests), a *link* between their scores is a transformation from a score on one to a score on the other. *Linking* is the means by which that transformation is obtained. Two categories of linking methods are germane in the current context: scale aligning and equating. *Scale aligning* has the goal of *comparable scores*, while *equating* has the more stringent goal of *interchangeable scores*: in the words of Dorans (2013), comparable scores are a necessary but not sufficient condition for producing interchangeable scores. Comparable scores have historically been defined as scores from tests with different psychological functions that are scaled to have the same distributions with respect to a particular group of examinees, with comparability assured only for that specific group taking the tests under specific conditions (Angoff, 1971).[6] Interchangeable scores are expected to have the same meaning across the two forms (or modes of administration, or tests), and so can be treated interchangeably. The *equipercentile function* is commonly employed in both scale aligning and equating. The equipercentile function links a score on Test X to the corresponding score on Test Y that has the same percentile in a target population. If the influence of the target population is small (i.e., the same results are likely to be obtained regardless of the population used to compute the linking function), the results are said to be *population invariant* (Dorans & Holland, 2000) and the linked scores are considered to be interchangeable. If there is a non-negligible influence for the target population, the linked scores are said to be comparable but not interchangeable.

A hallmark of equating is the rigorous requirements placed on forms/modes/tests to be linked. Dorans and Holland (2000) identified five requirements for a linking to be an equating: the tests should measure the same constructs (Equal Constructs Requirement) and have the same reliability (Equal Reliability Requirement), the function for linking the scores of Test Y to those of Test X should be the inverse of the function for linking the scores of Test X to those of Test Y (Symmetry Requirement), it should be a matter of indifference to an examinee to be tested by either one of the two tests that have been linked (Equity Requirement), and the choice of (sub)population used to estimate the linking function between the scores of Tests X and Y should not matter (Population Invariance Requirement). Additional requirements have been suggested by Kolen and Brennan (2014). The rigor of equating comes not from the statistical procedures applied to link the scores, but from the way the tests are constructed, namely to the same specifications (Mislevy, 1992), and from careful design of equating studies. This rigor is needed to ensure fair treatment of examinees, through the achievement of interchangeable scores.

Within the scale-aligning category of linking, there are two types of scaling that are pertinent to our fairness discussion: concordance and calibration. These and other types of scaling are delineated in Holland (2007) and Holland and Dorans (2006). The term *concordance* is assigned to a linking between forms/modes/tests that measure similar constructs at a similar level of reliability, while the term *calibration*[7] is assigned to a linking between forms/modes/tests that measure similar constructs but at a dissimilar level of reliability. Concordance also assumes similar difficulty and similar populations across the tests being linked. Dorans et al. (1997) labeled their linkage between ACT and SAT I scores as a concordance. Eignor (2007) labeled linkages between P&P and computer adaptive test (CAT) scores as a calibration because the Equity Requirement of equating is not met, but suggested that linkages between P&P and computer-based test (CBT) scores (i.e., scores from a linear administration of a P&P test on computer) could be labeled an equating. Eignor also noted that calibrated scores are often treated as though they are interchangeable and questioned the appropriateness of doing so, and that concorded scores cannot be treated as interchangeable. This is in contrast with equating, which is intended to produce interchangeable scores because of its stringent requirements. These distinctions will be discussed in more detail later.

Practitioners may have differing viewpoints on what label to apply to a linkage and its outcome. For example, based on considerations of population invariance, Dorans and Holland (2000) and Dorans (2004a) suggested that a linkage (concordance) between ACT and SAT I math scores might yield nearly interchangeable scores, even though a commonly stated equating requirement was not met (i.e., the tests are built to different specifications). Contrary to Eignor's (2007) viewpoint, Schaeffer, Steffen, Golub-Smith, Mills, and Durso (1995) reported that they expected that GRE CAT scores would be interchangeable with scores earned on the P&P and CBT versions. Hence, we shouldn't assume that scores are or are not interchangeable on the basis of whether or not a linkage scenario meets all of the requirements viewed as necessary to be considered an equating. Proper interpretation of a linkage outcome (i.e., whether the linked scores are best viewed as comparable versus interchangeable) can depend on a number of factors, including linking methodology, design of the linking study, characteristics of the groups and tests being linked, and how linkage results will be used. There are some tools that can be used to evaluate the feasibility of treating linked scores as interchangeable, to be discussed later. When linked scores are comparable (i.e., score distributions are aligned) but not interchangeable across different tests or modes of administration, there is a potential for unfairness to individuals or groups because assigned scores, score meanings, and decisions made from these scores could vary depending upon which test or mode is taken, or which group an examinee belongs to.

Fairness Properties Revisited

With this in mind, it is helpful to tie the discussion of comparable scores and inter-changeable scores back to the desirable fairness properties outlined earlier. Interchangeable scores as defined within an equating context (i.e., with regard to the equating requirements delineated by Dorans & Holland, 2000) appear to encompass the fairness properties of distributional equivalence, construct equivalence, and predictive equivalence, whereas comparable scores encompass distributional equivalence only. Hanson, Harris, Pommerich, Sconing, and Yi (2001) warned that it is possible to develop a link function that results in almost perfect comparability of distributions in one population, no matter how incomparable the two scores are for individuals. Eignor (2007) made a similar distinction between equivalent scores and scores that are equivalent in appearances only, noting that sets of scores that are identical in appearance share the same means, variances, and distributions of scores, but the scores themselves do not convey the same meaning. For these types of reasons, Lottridge et al. (2008) addressed the need to consider both distributional and construct equivalence when evaluating comparability across P&P and computerized tests. Dorans (2004b) suggested that three aspects of fairness should be addressed by testing programs: population invariance in linking functions, differential item functioning, and differential prediction. This supports the notion that distributional equivalence, construct equivalence, and predictive equivalence are all needed for optimal fairness when comparing scores that have been linked across different modes or tests.

More Fairness Considerations for Comparing Test Scores across Different Modes

Now that sufficient background information has been provided for the context of interest (fairness issues with regard to using linked scores), the issue of comparing scores across different modes of administration can be discussed in more detail. Fairness is a concern when there are two modes of administration that are in concurrent use, or when there is a single mode of administration in use (such as computer) but scores are compared with scores from a prior mode of administration (such as P&P). Within the realm of computer administration, distinctions also need to be made for the administration algorithm (linear versus adaptive), and the delivery method (Internet versus local). Using the acronyms introduced earlier, CBT corresponds to a linear administration while CAT corresponds to an adaptive administration. Under linear administration, a fixed-form test is administered in a non-adaptive manner. Under adaptive administration, the test is tailored to each examinee, with items selected to adapt to the examinee's estimated ability. Under Internet delivery, the test is delivered over the Internet. Under local delivery, the test is delivered over a local network or on a personal computer. Concerns specific to Internet delivery will be considered later.

Extensive research has been conducted comparing performance across computer and P&P modes of administration. Wang, Jiao, Young, Brooks, and Olson (2008) noted that there were over 300 mode of administration effects (mode effects) studies conducted in 25 years, spanning the realms of intelligence, aptitude, ability, vocational interest, personality, and achievement tests. That number is likely to have increased in the interim. It is not the intent of this chapter to summarize all of the mode effects literature; readers are referred to Blazer (2010), Lottridge et al. (2008), Texas Education Agency (2008), and Paek (2005) for some recent, thorough reviews of mode effects research and findings in the realm of educational testing. In addition, it is not the intent of this chapter to address how to evaluate score comparability across modes of administration; readers are referred to sources such as Kolen (1999), Wang and Kolen (2001), Eignor (2007), Lottridge et al. (2008), Texas Educational Agency (2008), Karkee, Kim, and Fatica (2010), Schroeders and Wilhelm (2011), Chua (2012), Randall, Sireci, Li, and Kaira (2012), and Mroch, Li, and Thompson (2015) for various discussions about how to collect data and evaluate score comparability.

Mode Effects Research

In general, the reviews of the mode effects literature suggest that scores tend to be comparable across P&P and computer administrations more often than not. Paek (2005) asserted that sufficient evidence exists to conclude that computer administration does not significantly affect student performance, with the exception of tests containing lengthy reading passages. Blazer (2010) noted that there are very few differences in test scores for multiple choice tests across computer and P&P administrations, but cautioned that examinees' demographic characteristics and computer skills, computer and test characteristics, item type, and content area could all affect comparability. The Texas

Education Agency (2008) raised the question of whether enough evidence has been collected to determine that mode effects studies are no longer needed, but concluded that states need to assess their own situation and weigh the costs and risks of conducting/ not conducting comparability studies. Recent meta-analyses of math tests (Wang, Jiao, Young, Brooks, & Olson, 2007) and reading tests (Wang et al., 2008) support the notion that comparability is more likely to be found than not, as did earlier meta-analyses (Bergstrom, 1992; Mead & Drasgow, 1993).

Although the overall trend may favor comparability, findings for specific tests may vary on an individual basis. Researchers have identified a number of concerns that need to be considered when comparing scores from P&P administration to computer administration. Kolen (1999) discussed a number of potential threats to score comparability across modes, including differences in test questions, differences in scoring, differences in operational testing conditions, differences in examinee groups, and violations of statistical assumptions for establishing comparability. Huff and Sireci (2001) elaborated on a number of potential threats to validity in computerized testing, including construct underrepresentation, construct-irrelevant variance, improper estimates of examinee scores, and unintended consequences. These concerns should not be ignored, as threats to score comparability and validity are also threats to fairness. Threats to score comparability could be addressed by linking scores across modes, but as discussed previously, that wouldn't necessarily ensure interchangeable scores.

In particular, differential access to computers is a notable fairness concern associated with mode of administration, related to socioeconomic status. If there is an advantage for taking a test on the computer rather than via P&P administration, then those examinees with less access to computers (and hence, potentially less familiarity with computers) could be disadvantaged. Concerns about a digital divide have been commonly raised, recently with regard to access to the Internet (Bartram, 2006). The U.S. Census Bureau (2014) reported that in 2012, 78.9% of all U.S. households had a computer at home, with 94.8% of those households using the computer to access the Internet, while overall, 74.8% of all U.S. households had Internet use at home. These computer/Internet usage statistics suggest that access issues are less of a concern now than in the past when computers and the Internet were more of a novelty, but that there still could be a digital divide that could threaten the fairness of comparing scores across modes of administration, especially for individuals with a lower socioeconomic status.

Linkage Issues

If a testing program conducts mode effects studies and finds that scores are not comparable across differing modes of administration, two approaches are commonly chosen. The first approach is to make iterative changes to the computer interface or administration in an attempt to eliminate mode effects. An iterative approach to computer interface development was demonstrated by Mazzeo, Druesne, Raffeld, Checketts, and Muhlstein (1991) and Pommerich (2004). The second approach is to link scores across the modes of administrations so that they can be compared. Eignor (2007) described in-depth ways one might design linking studies to relate scores across computer and P&P administrations, taking into consideration adaptive versus linear algorithms (i.e., CBT vs. CAT). Interchangeability of scores was a central concern in his discussion, particularly with regard to linkages between CAT and P&P scores. Rudner (2010) discussed a linkage study intended to equate CAT and P&P scores on the GMAT (i.e., yield interchangeable scores) and concluded that the CAT-based scaled scores were not truly equivalent to the P&P

scores even though the CAT scores were forced to the P&P scale. His experience demonstrates that merely conducting a linkage between scores across modes does not ensure that the desired outcome will be obtained and highlights the importance of evaluating the quality of a linkage, as recommended in Pommerich, Hanson, Harris, and Sconing (2004). When analyses suggest that linked scores are comparable but not interchangeable, then fairness is more likely to be a concern for reasons discussed earlier.

If a testing program chooses not to conduct mode effects studies or score linkages and compares scores across modes anyway, this would be similar to a *presumed linking* scenario, to borrow the terminology of Dorans and Middleton (2012). In a presumed linking scenario, comparisons of scores are made even though there is no evidence to support making them. There are some obvious fairness concerns in such a situation, as the degree of comparability in scores would be unknown, and individuals or groups could be negatively impacted by the fact that scores from one mode might not have the same value or meaning as scores from the other mode. In such a situation, Dorans and Middleton (2012) would recommend evaluating invariance relationships across the modes of administration to provide support for such a practice.

If mode effects studies are conducted and show evidence of no mode effects, testing programs may choose not to link scores across modes of administration. This is different from the presumed linking scenario, as there is evidence to support the decision not to link scores. Attention must still be paid, however, as to whether scores can be treated interchangeably across modes or not. Likewise, any time a linkage is conducted, there are fairness issues if comparable scores are treated as if they are interchangeable when they are not. If the name is any indication, comparability studies might be content to obtain comparable scores across linked modes, even though interchangeable scores would be fairer.

As discussed earlier, demonstrating distributional equivalence is sufficient evidence for comparable scores, but not necessarily for interchangeable scores. Lottridge et al. (2008) discussed the importance of evaluating construct equivalence in mode effects studies, how one might address comparability using a hypothesis-testing approach in a construct validation framework, and highlighted a number of mode effects studies that looked at various aspects of construct equivalence. Demonstrating construct equivalence as well as distributional equivalence of linked scores would be more in line with establishing interchangeable scores rather than merely comparable scores. On the other end of the spectrum, Winter (2010) asked the question of how comparable is comparable enough, and concluded that it depends on how the scores will be interpreted and used. She presented a continuum of score comparability that showed less score comparability required for pass/fail scores and achievement level scores than for scale scores and raw scores. Mroch et al. (2015) similarly suggested that score comparability is on a continuum between interchangeable and incomparable, where the required level of comparability is tied to how scores will be interpreted for a particular use. An evaluation of score comparability with regard to usage can be found in Kapoor and Welch (2011), who addressed the impact of mode of administration on proficiency classifications.

CAT Considerations

In considering the trend across mode effects studies favoring conclusions of comparability, there is one caveat that should probably be made. Namely, much of the research may have focused on CBT administration, which is a more straightforward (and more common) means of administration than CAT. Recall Eignor's (2007) suggestion that linkages between P&P and CBT scores could be labeled an equating, indicating an expectation of interchangeable scores across the two modes. In contrast, a number of researchers have expressed serious concerns about the interchangeability of CAT and P&P scores (Eignor, 2007; Kolen, 1999; Wang & Kolen, 2001; Wang & Shin, 2010). Other researchers have expressed related concerns pertaining to the impact of item calibration medium (P&P or computer) on CAT scores (Choi & Tinkler, 2002; Pommerich, 2007a).

The primary concern for comparing scores that have been linked across CAT and P&P administration modes focuses on the Equity Requirement of equating and the fact that it is not likely to hold, given that CAT differs substantially from P&P in terms of items administered, administration conditions, and scoring methods. In particular, the Equity Requirement will not hold if tests have different conditional standard errors of measurement across CAT and P&P administrations. Equipercentile methods can readily be applied to link scores across the administration modes; however, the scores can still differ in their conditional precision across modes. Hence, some would say that CAT scores cannot be treated interchangeably with P&P scores because they differ in their statistical specifications (e.g., Eignor, 2007). The same argument could be applied to linkages between CAT scores and scores from a linear CBT.

Kolen (1999) also warned that sufficient differences could exist between CAT and P&P tests, such that the construct measured could be affected and various subgroups might favor one mode over the other. If examinee preferences do exist across administration modes for an operational test, that would be a fairness concern. Because of the inherent differences between CAT and P&P administration, Wang and Kolen (2001) recommended that comparability be carefully established and evaluated. The thorough research and evaluation conducted by the ASVAB testing program prior to implementing CAT administration (Sands, Waters, & McBride, 1997) represents an example of the level of consideration that might be needed to alleviate fairness concerns, especially if CAT and P&P scores are to be used interchangeably.

Alternate Takes on Mode of Administration

There are a couple of variations on mode of administration that should be considered also with regard to score comparability. The first variation pertains to Internet delivery of computerized tests. The comparability between P&P and Internet administrations has not received a lot of attention in the realm of mode effects (Baumer, Roded, & Gafni, 2009; Naglieri et al., 2004). The second variation pertains to the use of unproctored Internet administration.

Internet Delivery

A notable concern associated with Internet delivery (also referred to as online testing) is that equipment and/or configurations can vary across administration locations, resulting in a loss of standardization (Bennett, 2003; Bridgeman, Lennon, & Jackenthal, 2003). Dorans (2012) raised fairness concerns associated with a loss of standardization in testing due to the increased use of technology. Naglieri et al. (2004) advised that the effects of mode of administration and the delivery method should both be studied to ensure the appropriate use of tests on the Internet. If a testing program utilizes Internet delivery of a computerized test in conjunction with local delivery or P&P administration, but doesn't study its impact (or link scores) across the different modes/delivery approaches, this invokes the fairness concerns discussed earlier for a presumed linking scenario.

Bennett (2003) highlighted a critical concern about Internet delivery of tests, discussing ways in which the Internet connection could cause item presentation to vary across equipment, focusing on possible sources of delays in the administration of items. Significant delays and/or problems in Internet delivery of several statewide assessments made the national news in the spring of 2013. In Minnesota, examinees experienced computer slowdowns, freezes, and other problems. In Indiana, some examinees were locked out of the testing website during their exams, while others were unable to log into their exams at all. In Kentucky, school districts reported slow and dropped Internet connections, resulting in the temporary suspension of online testing. In Oklahoma, servers crashed, preventing examinees from completing their tests. In prior years, similar problems were noted with online testing in Wyoming, Virginia, and Texas. Wyoming's experience caused the state to abandon online testing and revert back to P&P administration. Across all of these states, the frequency and magnitude of the problems observed suggested that the vendors providing Internet delivery were not prepared to handle the kinds of demands that statewide administration placed on the test delivery system.

Clearly, the types of problems that can occur with Internet delivery of statewide assessments are a major threat to validity and raise many fairness concerns. Validity questions include whether construct-irrelevant variance is introduced for examinees with disrupted sessions. Namely, is the test measuring the same construct across examinees that are and are not affected by Internet delivery problems? Fairness questions include whether all students are equitably treated in the testing process (AERA et al., 2014) and whether scores are interchangeable across disrupted and non-disrupted sessions. Analyses conducted by independent parties for Minnesota and Indiana in 2013 concluded that the Internet delivery problems did not affect performance. In Indiana, this conclusion was drawn on the basis of the fact that examinees that were interrupted had gains across years as high as examinees that were not disrupted (Stokes, 2013). While this may be true for the group of interrupted students as a whole, there are likely to have been individuals that did not experience gains across years as a result of the disruption. Given the high-stakes nature of the assessments, there was also likely a negative psychological impact experienced by examinees whose sessions were disrupted.

Unproctored Administration

A relatively new approach to test administration that has been broached primarily for use in employment testing is unproctored Internet administration (Tippins, 2009; Tippins et al., 2006). Under this approach, examinees first take an unproctored test via the Internet and then take a shorter, proctored test to verify that their unproctored scores represent their abilities. Such an approach would allow greater flexibility about where initial testing takes place and could reduce costs, but also introduces a number of fairness concerns. Clearly, cheating would be a key concern with unproctored administration. Cizek (1999) stated that nearly every research report on cheating has concluded that cheating is rampant. However, Drasgow, Nye, Guo, and Tay (2009) noted some recent studies that indicated that cheating on unproctored tests may not be as widespread as thought for some types of tests. Verification testing is intended to detect cheaters, but if large numbers of examinees do cheat on the unproctored version, validity of the unproctored form is threatened, and there might be little cost savings to using unproctored assessment. Loss of standardization due to the variation in equipment is also a potential concern in this scenario, as discussed earlier with regard to Internet delivery. Likewise, there would be concerns about the comparability of scores across unproctored and proctored settings. The concerns about a presumed linking scenario discussed previously would be relevant here too.

Future Considerations

In the future, we could see technology utilized in testing in ways that could result in an even greater loss of standardization. Pommerich (2012) noted that items and test characteristics can vary across examinees when CAT administration is used, equipment can vary across examinees when Internet delivery is used (i.e., if a testing program uses readily available equipment), and environment can vary across examinees when unproctored administration is used (i.e., if examinees test in their own home). It is possible that we could reach the point where no two examinees take a test under the same conditions. Given the prolific use of smartphones (and more recently, tablets), the profession will likely need to adapt to new ways of presenting and responding to tests that have not yet been extensively studied. Who knows what else the future may hold that could introduce even greater change into how people take tests—examinees taking tests while riding in self-driving cars or drones, using in-vehicle communication systems, perhaps? Dorans (2012) expressed a concern that the measurement profession has "lost sight of the essential need for controlled conditions of measurement" and gave examples associated with technology-driven assessment. His examples emphasize the importance of taking active steps to address the limitations of technology-based assessment and adapt our practices to compensate for them (Pommerich, 2012). Any changes to mode of administration should raise fairness concerns along the lines discussed in this chapter, until sufficient research has been conducted to alleviate them.

More Fairness Considerations for Comparing Test Scores across Different Tests

The issue of comparing scores across different tests is a more extreme scenario than comparing scores across different modes of administration for the same test. Under this scenario, scores from two distinct tests that are built to different specifications and administered to different populations are compared. It is more extreme than comparing scores across different modes of administration because the two tests are typically separate entities that are developed independently by different parties. These tests are likely not developed with any intention of linking scores across the two tests. Further, the linkages are typically conducted using a convenience sample of examinees that have taken both tests rather than based on a formal data collection design. If linked scores are used in place of actual scores to make decisions (Figure 7.1), this is a specialized type of test use that is probably not validated, and the test that is used to assign a concordant score is only indirectly being used for its intended purpose.

The discussion in this section focuses on a concordance situation, where the tests measure similar constructs, have similar levels of reliability and difficulty, and are administered to a similar population, and focuses on the equipercentile method as the means of linking scores. Concordances between scores from two college admissions exams, ACT and SAT, will be used as an example throughout the discussion to provide a familiar context from which to address fairness issues. The discussion here does not consider a presumed linking scenario

(Dorans & Middleton, 2012), as simple comparisons of ACT and SAT percentiles will lead to incorrect inferences about the relative performance of examinees on the ACT and SAT, due to population differences (Dorans & Petersen, 2010).

A limitation of concordances is that they don't typically result in scores that can be used interchangeably (with possible exceptions, such as noted by Dorans, 2004a and Dorans & Holland, 2000, discussed earlier). Unfortunately, evidence suggests that users are inclined to treat concordant ACT-SAT scores as if they are interchangeable or as predictions of scores on the test not taken. Thus, by virtue of making concordance results available, we create the potential for misuse and misinterpretation of those results, which raises concerns about fair treatment where concordant scores are used to assist in making selection decisions. Lindquist (1964) argued against creating ACT-SAT concordances because of concerns about misuse and misinterpretation; these concerns have not been alleviated over time. Pommerich et al. (2004) demonstrated that using equipercentile results for different purposes from which they are intended could give very misleading results for some examinees. They cautioned that if equipercentile-based concordant scores are used as a prediction of an individual's score (a misuse), the consequences should be considered, since the concordant scores will deviate to some degree from what the actual scores would be. Equipercentile-based linkages will be fair to the group used to conduct the linkage, in that equal percentages from the group will be selected using either test at concordant score points, but they will not necessarily be fair to individuals or specific subgroups, or to the larger population in which they will be applied (i.e., examinees taking the ACT or the SAT, but not both).

Brennan (2007) maintained that arguing against using comparable scores as if they were interchangeable might be a lost cause, but that cautioning users about potential errors in doing so is both necessary and possible. This is a call for disclosure that brings to mind Cole and Zieky's (2001) fairness recommendation that the measurement community take a greater leadership role in educating the public about potential misinterpretations of group differences (not pertaining to concordances) by addressing them directly in test materials and public discussions. They noted that the new faces of fairness require measurement professionals to react more directly and forcefully against instances of test misuse. The importance of disclosure or public education in a concordance scenario should not be underestimated. Pommerich (2007b) proposed five goals to strive for when conducting concordance. The goals, labeled the **FRANK** goals, are modified here to represent all linkage scenarios:

1. **F**lexibility in linking practices;
2. **R**esponsibility in creating and disseminating linkage results;
3. **A**wareness of the limitations of linkages;
4. **N**otification as to proper interpretation and use of results;
5. **K**nowledge of users and their practices.

In devising her **FRANK** acronym, Pommerich inadvertently channeled the thinking of Cronbach (1980), as cited in Linn (1984, p. 45), who stated that "the more we learn, and the franker we are with ourselves and our clientele, the more valid the use of tests will become." Full disclosure will allow test users to make informed choices about how to use concordance results and to better understand what impact their use may have on fairness.

On the other hand, Sawyer (2007) expressed a more realistic[8] viewpoint about the use of ACT-SAT concordances, stating that there is a sense among users that in the big scheme of things, ACT-SAT concordance tables are probably good enough for the uses they are put to. In some regards, he may be right, as concordant scores are not likely to be the only basis for an admissions decision. In addition, testing standards and guidelines indicate that some responsibility for proper interpretation and use of concordance results should lie with test users, not just test developers (AERA et al., 2014; Joint Committee on Testing Practices, 2004; NCME Ad Hoc Committee on the Development of a Code of Ethics, 1995). Feuer et al. (1999) stated that policymakers and educators must take responsibility for determining the degree to which they can tolerate imprecision in linking. This might be a bit of a catch-22, however, as many users might be unaware of the inherent problems with a linkage (i.e., lack of precision, lack of interchangeable scores) and fail to grasp the implications for decisions that are made on the basis of that linkage. Thus, the onus of disclosure and education appears to fall back onto the test developer or whoever conducts the linkage that is provided to users.

In Sawyer's (2007) perspective, a more pressing concern is that users might think that concordance between *any* two tests is unproblematic. Pommerich (2007b) noted that situations where concordance is not appropriate might be less apparent than situations where equating is not appropriate. Dorans (2004a) and Dorans and Walker (2007) proposed an index of reduction in uncertainty (RiU) to help decide whether to utilize concordance or prediction methods to link two sets of scores, and concluded that a correlation coefficient of 0.866 is needed between the scores on the two tests to reduce the uncertainty of knowing a person's score on one test by at least 50%, given the score on the other test. By this standard, concordance is not viewed as appropriate for tests where the correlation falls below 0.866. Fairness is already a concern for a concordance situation, and it becomes a greater concern when concordances are conducted between tests that do not correlate at that high level.

Assessing the Interchangeability of Linked Scores

Consistency rates (i.e. the percent of consistent classifications using concordant versus actual scores) provide evidence of the degree of misclassification that might be expected by using concordant scores in place of actual scores and serve as a means of approximating the departure from equity (Hanson et al., 2001). Pommerich et al. (2004) demonstrated how the disparity between actual and equipercentile concordant scores for examinees taking both the ACT and SAT I increased as the correlation between linked test scores decreased. They cautioned that although the equipercentile method will yield score points that result in the same percentages being selected on either test, the same individuals will not necessarily be selected. When two tests being linked are highly correlated, the consequences of using equipercentile results at an individual level should not be too severe. However, as the relationship between the two tests decreases and the consistency of classification based on concordant and actual scores lessens, it might be meaningless to use equipercentile concordances even at a group level, as intended (i.e., to set equivalent cutscores). Practically speaking, there may be little point to selecting equivalent proportions across the two groups if individuals would be classified differently by the two measures.

Population invariance of linking functions is another means by which to evaluate whether fairness is likely to be a concern for score linkages. When population invariance does not hold, linked scores are comparable but not interchangeable, and attempts to use scores interchangeably could result in unfair treatment of some examinees or groups. Recently, assessment of the invariance of linkings across important subpopulations[9] has received considerable attention in the measurement literature as a tool to assess the degree of interchangeability of scores (e.g., Dorans, 2004c; von Davier & Liu, 2008). Huggins and Penfield (2012) noted that the criteria of population invariance in linking functions (also referred to as score equity assessment) is becoming well-established as a necessary condition for fairness in tests that employ any form of linking. Score equity assessment was introduced and placed in a fairness context in Dorans (2004b) as a means to assess the fairness of a "test score exchange process" (Dorans & Liu, 2009). Violations of population invariance are a threat to test fairness because examinees from different groups that have the same score on one test will have different linked scores on the corresponding test, resulting in potential disadvantages for some group members (Huggins & Penfield, 2012). Dorans (2004b) recommended that score equity assessment be routinely addressed as a fairness consideration,[10] along with differential item functioning and differential prediction. The instability of linkages over time is another form of lack of invariance (Thissen, 2007) with implications for fairness too. If the test-taking populations change over time, a given concordance relationship may no longer hold. To ensure stability over time, linkages should be updated frequently.[11]

Recent applications of score equity assessment focused on score linkages across variations of the same test (e.g., Liu, Cahn, & Dorans, 2006; Liu & Dorans, 2013). The same approach can be applied to scores linked across different modes of administration for the same test or to scores linked across distinct tests. For example, Liu, Dorans, and Moses (2010) used score equity assessment to evaluate the population sensitivity of the most recent ACT-SAT concordances. The expectation that concordances are unlikely to be population invariant (Dorans & Petersen, 2010) was upheld for some groups/concordances that demonstrated a "substantial degree" of subgroup sensitivity. Other groups/concordances showed results that were essentially invariant. Likewise, Yin, Brennan, and Kolen (2004) evaluated invariance of concordances between ACT and Iowa Tests of Educational Development scores and found population invariance was upheld for some tests/linking methods, but not others. Dorans and Holland (2000) recommended creating different concordances for important subgroups when concordance results deviate considerably from invariance. However, the use of different concordances across different gender/ethnic groups, although intended to be fair, could be viewed as unfair by an undiscerning public, because it means that scores would be treated differently across groups (Dorans, 2004a). While the measurement community may not agree as to what can be done about lack of invariance in a concordance situation, we would all benefit from a public discussion (i.e., full disclosure) of the issues and the implications for common uses of the concordances.

Concluding Comments

Fairness proponents advocate promoting fairness at all stages of assessment from conception through score usage (Cole & Zieky, 2001; Downing & Haladyna, 1996; Kunnan, 2000; Willingham & Cole, 1997; Zieky, 2006). If linked scores are to be used to make decisions about examinees, then that type of usage should ideally be accounted for in fairness planning and evaluation. Xi (2010) demonstrated how a fairness argument might be built and substantiated in the context of a validity argument. Her fairness argument included a series of rebuttals that might "challenge the comparability of scores, score interpretations, score-based decisions and consequences for sub-groups" on the TOEFL iBT. She noted that to substantiate the argument, evidence has to be obtained that supports the comparability of the score-based interpretations and uses for relevant groups. It appears that the question of whether it is fair to compare scores that have been linked across different modes of administration could be readily incorporated into a fairness argument such as this for a specific test of interest.

Ideally, the question of whether it is fair to compare scores that have been linked across different tests would also be incorporated into a fairness argument (most likely pertaining to the utilization of test scores), but this is a more awkward proposition given that a test is usually developed and evaluated as an autonomous unit and fairness is usually addressed with regard to a single test. This brings us back to the question raised earlier of whose responsibility it is for the proper interpretation and use of linkage results, especially when the linkage involves two distinct tests. Although test users have a number of responsibilities pertaining to test score use (AERA et al., 2014; Joint Committee on Testing Practices, 2004; NCME Ad Hoc Committee on the Development of a Code of Ethics, 1995), it might seem logical to expect that if a test developer creates a linkage between scores on their test and an external test and disseminates that linkage to users, then the test developer should explicitly account for that type of usage in a fairness argument or framework. Conversely, if a user develops a linkage between two distinct tests independent of the test developers, then the responsibility of the fairness argument should, in theory, lie with the user. Unfortunately, test developers are not likely to develop a fairness argument for comparing scores that have been linked across different tests because it involves a test that falls outside of their scope of control and because aspects of the fairness argument (i.e., establishing predictive equivalence) would require the involvement of test users.

At the heart of the matter when using a score linkage to make decisions is the interchangeability of the linked scores (or lack of interchangeability of scores). In terms of the fairness properties outlined earlier, interchangeable scores imply distributional equivalence, construct equivalence, and predictive equivalence, while comparable scores imply distributional equivalence only. Fairness will always be threatened to some degree if analyses suggest linked scores are comparable but not interchangeable, but scores are used interchangeably anyway. However, in any linkage, even an equating, scores are not likely to be perfectly interchangeable. Liu and Walker (2007) maintained that the issue should be one of degree, namely whether requirements are met sufficiently such that scores can be treated as interchangeable, within a reasonable amount of error. Some tools were discussed earlier to evaluate whether scores can reasonably be treated as interchangeable.

If linking conditions are such that interchangeable or nearly interchangeable scores are not possible, it should be asked whether inappropriate or unfair decisions could be made or whether inappropriate or unfair conclusions could be drawn as a result. If the answer is yes, then the linkage might not be defensible. A conservative approach in such a case would be to maintain separate score scales for the two tests (or modes) in question, but that might not be palatable to policymakers. If it is necessary to report the linkage results, then it is of utmost importance to fully disclose all linkage details and educate users on proper and improper usage of the linked scores. Knowledge of user practices is helpful to the degree that consequences of misuse and/or misclassification can be taken into consideration when providing guidance. The amount of error in linked scores should be reported and explicitly discussed so that users can make an informed decision on whether and how to use the linkage results. In sum, test developers should be FRANK when conducting and reporting the results of a linkage, to better facilitate fair test score use.

If this chapter has made anything clear, it is that defining what is and what is not a fair use of linked test scores is likely to remain a somewhat arbitrary question that is specific to the test(s) at hand. The test characteristics, test administration/delivery conditions, testing population(s), examinee characteristics, linkage conditions, linkage quality, how the linked scores are used, and value judgments of test users will all play a role in determining fairness. As such, the answer to the questions of whether it is fair to compare scores that have been linked across different modes of administration and whether it is fair to compare scores that have been linked across different tests can probably be answered no more definitively than "it depends." What can be stated definitively, however, is that future fairness discussions and evaluations should be broadened to include the types of test score usage addressed here.

Notes

1. The views expressed are those of the author and not necessarily those of the Department of Defense or the United States Government.
2. The *Standards for Educational and Psychological Testing* (American Educational Research Association, American Psychological Association, & National Council on Measurement in Education, 2014) address broader types of linked scores in a chapter on scales, scores, norms, cut scores, and score linking, but not from a context of fairness. The chapter on fairness in testing raises the issue of score comparability pertaining to test accommodations, adaptations, and modifications, but makes no mention of the fairness of comparing test scores across different tests or modes of administration.
3. One exception is Willingham and Cole (1997), who addressed computer-based testing from a fairness perspective in their seminal book on gender fairness.
4. One exception is Dorans (2004a, 2012), who raised some specific fairness concerns associated with linkages between ACT and SAT scores.
5. Predictive equivalence is called for here instead of correlational equivalence, consistent with Dorans' (2004b) notion that differential prediction studies are preferential to differential validity (i.e. differential test/criterion correlation) studies.
6. Holland and Dorans (2006) stated a preference for the term "comparable scales" over "comparable scores" to make it clear that it is the score distributions that have been made comparable, not the scores (N. Dorans, personal communication, October 17, 2014). Because the focus here is on scores and score usage, the term comparable scores will be used rather than comparable scales.
7. The meaning assigned here to the term calibration is not to be confused with other meanings that have historically been applied, including vertical scaling and estimating item response theory item parameters to be on a common scale (Holland, 2007; Kolen & Brennan, 2014). In the latter case, a variation such as *scalibration* might be more appropriate in the context of linking, since a scaling component is often required to ensure that the calibrated parameters are on the desired scale.
8. Realistic in that institutions are not inclined to validate and use ACT and SAT scores separately, even when advised to do so if feasible (R. Sawyer, personal communication, August 4, 2014).
9. Concerns about the classification of individuals into groups (addressed earlier) are relevant here.
10. An SAS macro to compute systemized score equity assessment is presented in Moses, Liu, and Dorans (2010).
11 Linkages between ACT and SAT scores were conducted in 2010, 1997, 1991, and earlier. The current ACT-SAT concordances will need to be updated once again, following substantial changes to the SAT projected for 2016. The need for updated concordances highlights another problem with linkages between different tests; namely, every time a content or scoring change is made to one of the tests, the linkage needs to be updated. The upside, however, is that the instability of linkages over time is less likely to be a concern the more frequently a linkage is updated.

References

American Educational Research Association, American Psychological Association, & National Council on Measurement in Education (2014). *Standards for educational and psychological testing*. Washington, DC: American Educational Research Association.

American Psychological Association (1986). *Guidelines for computer-based tests and interpretations*. Washington, DC: American Psychological Association.

Angoff, W. H. (1971). Scales, norms, and equivalent scores. In R. L. Thorndike (Ed.), *Educational measurement* (2nd ed., pp. 508–600). Washington, DC: American Council on Education.

Bartram, D. (2006). Testing on the Internet: Issues, challenges and opportunities in the field of occupational assessment. In D. Bartram & R. K. Hambleton (Eds.), *Computer-based testing and the Internet: Issues and advances* (pp. 13–37). Hoboken, NJ: John Wiley & Sons.

Baumer, M., Roded, K., & Gafni, N. (2009). Assessing the equivalence of internet-based vs. paper-and-pencil psychometric tests. In D. J. Weiss (Ed.), *Proceedings of the 2009 GMAC conference on computerized adaptive testing*. Retrieved from www.psych.umn.edu/psylabs/CATCentral

Bennett, R.E. (2003). *Online assessment and the comparability of score meaning* (Research Memorandum RM-03-05). Princeton, NJ: Educational Testing Service.

Bergstrom, B. A. (1992, April). *Ability measure equivalence of computer adaptive and pencil and paper tests: A research synthesis*. Paper presented at the annual meeting of the American Educational Research Association, San Francisco, CA.

Blazer, C. (2010). *Computer-based assessments* (Information Capsule Vol. 0918). Miami, FL: Miami-Dade County Public Schools.

Breland, H. M., & Ironson, G. H. (1976). Defunis reconsidered: A comparative analysis of alternative admissions strategies. *Journal of Educational Measurement, 13*, 89–99.

Brennan, R. L. (2007). Tests in transition: Discussion and synthesis. In N. J. Dorans, M. Pommerich, & P. W. Holland (Eds.), *Linking and aligning scores and scales* (pp. 161–169). New York: Springer-Verlag.

Bridgeman, B., Lennon, M. L., & Jackenthal, A. (2003). Effects of screen size, screen resolution, and display rate on computer-based test performance. *Applied Measurement in Education, 16*, 191–205.

Bugbee, A. C. (1996). The equivalence of paper-and-pencil and computer-based testing. *Journal of Research on Computing in Education, 28*, 282–289.

Camilli, G. (1993). The case against item bias detection techniques based on external criteria: Do item bias procedures obscure test fairness issues? In P. W. Holland & H. Wainer (Eds.), *Differential item functioning* (pp. 397–417). Hillsdale, NJ: Lawrence Erlbaum.

Camilli, G. (2006). Test fairness. In R. L. Brennan (Ed.), *Educational measurement* (4th ed., pp. 221–256). Westport, CT: American Council on Education/Praeger.

Choi, S. W., & Tinkler, T. (2002, April). *Evaluating comparability of paper-and-pencil and computer-based assessment in a K-12 setting*. Paper presented at the annual meeting of the National Council on Measurement in Education, New Orleans, LA.

Chua, Y. P. (2012). Replacing paper-based testing with computer-based testing in assessment: Are we doing wrong? *Procedia: Social and Behavioral Sciences, 64*, 655–664.

Cizek, G. J. (1999). *Cheating on tests: How to do it, detect it, and prevent it*. Mahwah, NJ: Lawrence Erlbaum.

Cleary, T. A. (1968). Test bias: Prediction of grades of Negro and White students in integrated colleges. *Journal of Educational Measurement, 5*, 115–124.

Cole, N. S., & Zieky, M. J. (2001). The new faces of fairness. *Journal of Educational Measurement, 38*, 369–382.

Cronbach, L. J. (1980). Validity on parole: How can we go straight? In W. B.Schrader, (Ed.), *New directions for testing and measurement: Measuring achievement: Progress over a decade* (No. 5, pp. 99–108). San Francisco: Jossey-Bass.

Darlington, R. B. (1971). Another look at "cultural fairness." *Journal of Educational Measurement, 8*, 71–82.

Dorans, N. J. (2004a). Equating, concordance, and expectation. *Applied Psychological Measurement, 28*, 227–246.

Dorans, N. J. (2004b). Using population invariance to assess test score equity. *Journal of Educational Measurement, 41*, 43–68.

Dorans, N. J. (Ed.) (2004c). Assessing the population sensitivity of equating functions. [Special Issue]. *Journal of Educational Measurement, 41*(1).

Dorans, N. J. (2012). The contestant perspective on taking tests: Emanations from the statue within. *Educational Measurement: Issues and Practice, 31*(4), 20–37.

Dorans, N. J. (2013). On attempting to do what Lord said was impossible: Commentary on van der Linden's "Some conceptual issues in observed-score equating." *Journal of Educational Measurement, 50*, 304–314.

Dorans, N. J., & Holland, P. W. (2000). Population invariance and the equitability of tests: Basic theory and the linear case. *Journal of Educational Measurement, 37*, 281–306.

Dorans, N. J., & Liu, J. (2009). *Score equity assessment: Development of a prototype analysis using SAT mathematics test data across several administrations* (ETS Research Rep. No. RR-09-08). Princeton, NJ: Educational Testing Service.

Dorans, N. J., & Middleton, K. (2012). Addressing the extreme assumptions of presumed linkings. *Journal of Educational Measurement, 49*, 1–18.

Dorans, N. J., & Petersen, N. S. (2010, April–May). *Distinguishing concordances from equating.* Paper presented at the annual meeting of the National Council on Measurement in Education, Denver, CO.

Dorans, N. J., Pommerich, M., & Holland, P. W. (Eds.). (2007). *Linking and aligning scores and scales.* New York: Springer-Verlag.

Dorans, N. J., & Walker, M. E. (2007). Sizing up linkages. In N. J. Dorans, M. Pommerich, & P. W. Holland (Eds.), *Linking and aligning scores and scales* (pp. 179–198). New York: Springer-Verlag.

Dorans. N. J., Lyu, C. F., Pommerich, M., & Houston, W. M. (1997). Concordance between ACT assessment and recentered SAT I sum scores. *College and University, 73*(2), 24–34.

Downing, S. M., & Haladyna, T. M. (1996). A model for evaluating high-stakes testing programs: Why the fox should not guard the chicken coop. *Educational Measurement: Issues and Practice, 15*, 5–12.

Drasgow, F., & Chuah, S. C. (2005). Computer-based testing. In E. Diener & M. Eid (Eds.), *Multimethod measurement in psychology* (pp. 87–100). Washington, DC: American Psychological Association.

Drasgow, F., Nye, C. D., Guo, J., & Tay, L. (2009). Cheating on proctored tests: The other side of the unproctored debate. *Industrial and Organizational Psychology, 2*, 46–48.

Eignor, D. R. (2007). Linking scores derived under different modes of test administration. In N. J. Dorans, M. Pommerich, & P. W. Holland (Eds.), *Linking and aligning scores and scales* (pp. 135–159). New York: Springer.

Feuer, M. J., Holland, P. W., Green, B. F., Bertenthal, M. W., & Hemphill, F. C. (1999). *Uncommon measures: Equivalence and linkage among educational tests.* Washington, DC: National Academy Press.

Flanagan, J. C. (1951). Units, scores, and norms. In E. F. Lindquist (Ed.), *Educational measurement* (1st ed., pp. 695–763). Washington, DC: National Academy Press.

Green. B. F. (1984). Construct validity of computer-based tests. In H. Wainer & H. I. Braun (Eds.), *Test validity* (pp. 77–86). Hillsdale, NJ: Lawrence Erlbaum.

Hanson, B. A., Harris, D. J., Pommerich, M., Sconing, J. A., & Yi, Q. (2001). *Suggestions for the evaluation and use of concordance results* (ACT Research Report No. 2001-1). Iowa City, IA: ACT.

Hartigan, J. A., & Wigdor, A. K. (Eds.) (1989). *Fairness in employment testing: Validity generalization, minority issues, and the General Aptitude Battery.* Washington, DC: National Academy Press.

Holland, P. W. (2007). A framework and history for score linking. In N. J. Dorans, M. Pommerich, & P. W. Holland (Eds.), *Linking and aligning scores and scales* (pp. 5–30). New York: Springer.

Holland, P. W., & Dorans, N. J. (2006). Linking and equating. In R. L. Brennan (Ed.), *Educational measurement* (4th ed., pp. 187–220). Westport, CT: American Council on Education/Praeger.

Huff, K. L., & Sireci, S. G. (2001). Validity issues in computer-based testing. *Educational Measurement: Issues and Practice, 20*(3), 16–25.

Huggins, A. C., & Penfield, R. D. (2012). An NCME instructional module on population invariance in linking and equating. *Educational Measurement: Issues and Practice, 31*(1), 27–40.

Joint Committee on Testing Practices (2004). *Code of fair testing practices in education (revised)*. Washington, DC: Joint Committee on Testing Practices.

Kane, M. T. (2013). Validating the interpretations and uses of test scores. *Journal of Educational Measurement, 50*, 1–73.

Kapoor, S., & Welch, C. (2011, April). *Comparability of paper and computer administrations in terms of proficiency interpretations*. Paper presented at the annual meeting of the National Council on Measurement in Education, New Orleans, LA.

Karkee, T., Kim, D. I., & Fatica, K. (2010, April–May). *Comparability study of online and paper and pencil tests using modified internally and externally matched criteria*. Paper presented at the annual meeting of the American Educational Research Association, Denver, CO.

Kolen, M. J. (1999). Threats to score comparability with applications to performance assessments and computerized adaptive tests. *Educational Assessment, 6*, 73–96.

Kolen, M. J. (2004). Linking assessments: Concept and history. *Applied Psychological Measurement, 28*, 219–226.

Kolen, M. J., & Brennan, R. L. (2014). *Test equating, scaling, and linking: Methods and practices* (3rd ed.). New York: Springer.

Kunnan, A. J. (2000). Fairness and justice for all. In A. J. Kunnan (Ed.), *Fairness and validation in language assessment* (pp. 1–14). Cambridge: Cambridge University Press.

Langenfeld, T. E. (1997). Test fairness: Internal and external investigations of gender bias in mathematics testing. *Educational Measurement: Issues and Practices, 16*(1), 20–26.

Lindquist, E. F. (1964, February). *Equating scores on non-parallel tests*. Paper presented at the annual meeting of the American Educational Research Association, Chicago, IL.

Linn, R. L. (1984). Selection bias: Multiple meanings. *Journal of Educational Measurement, 21*, 33–47.

Linn, R. L. (1993). Linking results of distinct assessments. *Applied Measurement in Education, 6*, 83–102.

Liu, J., & Dorans, N. J. (2013). Assessing a critical aspect of content continuity when test specifications change or test forms deviate from specifications. *Educational Measurement: Issues and Practice, 32*(1), 15–22.

Liu, J., & Walker, M. E. (2007). Score linking issues related to test content changes. In N. J. Dorans, M. Pommerich, & P. W. Holland (Eds.), *Linking and aligning scores and scales* (pp. 109–134). New York: Springer-Verlag.

Liu, J., Cahn, M. F., & Dorans, N. J. (2006). An application of score equity assessment: Invariance of linkage of new SAT to old SAT across gender groups. *Journal of Educational Measurement, 43*, 113–129.

Liu, J., Dorans, N. J., & Moses, T. (2010, April–May). *Evaluating the subpopulation sensitivity of the ACT-SAT concordances*. Paper presented at the annual meeting of the National Council on Measurement in Education, Denver, CO.

Lottridge, S., Nicewander, A., Schulz, M., & Mitzel, H. (2008). *Comparability of paper-based and computer-based tests: A Review of the methodology*. Monterey, CA: Pacific Metrics Corporation.

Mazzeo, J., Druesne, B., Raffeld, P. C., Checketts, K. T., & Muhlstein, A. (1991). *Comparability of computer and paper-and-pencil scores for two CLEP general examinations* (College Board Rep. No. 91-5). New York: College Entrance Examination Board.

Mead, A. D., & Drasgow, F. (1993). Equivalence of computerized and paper-and-pencil cognitive ability tests: A meta-analysis. *Psychological Bulletin, 9*, 287–304.

Mislevy, R. J. (1992). *Linking educational assessments: Concepts, issues, methods, and prospects*. Princeton, NJ: ETS Policy Information Center.

Moses, T., Liu, J., & Dorans, N. (2010). Systemized SEA in SAS. *Applied Psychological Measurement, 24,* 552–553.

Mroch, A. A., Li, D., & Thompson, T. D. (2015, April). *A framework for evaluating score comparability.* Paper presented at the annual meeting of the National Council on Measurement in Education, Chicago, IL.

Naglieri, J. A., Drasgow, F., Schmit, M., Handler, L., Prifitera, A., Margolis, A., & Velasquez, R. (2004). Psychological testing on the Internet: New problems, old issues. *American Psychologist, 59,* 150–162.

NCME Ad Hoc Committee on the Development of a Code of Ethics. (1995). *Code of professional responsibilities in educational measurement.* Washington, DC: National Council on Measurement in Education.

Neuman, G., & Baydoun, R. B. (1998). Computerization of paper-and-pencil tests: When are they equivalent? *Applied Psychological Measurement, 22,* 71–83.

Paek, P. (2005). *Recent trends in comparability studies* (PEM Research Report No. 05-05). Iowa City, IA: Pearson Educational Measurement.

Petersen, N. S., & Novick, M. R. (1976). An evaluation of some models for culture-fair selection. *Journal of Educational Measurement, 13,* 3–29.

Pommerich, M. (2004). Developing computerized versions of paper-and-pencil tests: Mode effects for passage-based tests. *Journal of Technology, Learning, and Assessment, 2*(6). Retrieved from www.jtla.org

Pommerich, M. (2007a). The effect of using item parameters calibrated from paper administrations in computer adaptive test administrations. *Journal of Technology, Learning, and Assessment, 5*(7). Retrieved from www.jtla.org

Pommerich, M. (2007b). Concordance: The good, the bad, and the ugly. In N. J. Dorans, M. Pommerich, & P. W. Holland (Eds.), *Linking and aligning scores and scales* (pp. 199–216). New York: Springer-Verlag.

Pommerich, M. (2012). Comments on Neil Dorans's NCME career award address: The contestant perspective on taking tests: Emanations from the statue within. *Educational Measurement: Issues and Practice, 31*(4), 40–44.

Pommerich, M., & Dorans, N. J. (Eds.) (2004). Concordance. [Special Issue]. *Applied Psychological Measurement, 28*(4).

Pommerich, M., Hanson, B. A., Harris, D. J., & Sconing, J. A. (2004). Issues in conducting linkages between distinct tests. *Applied Psychological Measurement, 28,* 247–273.

Randall, J., Sireci, S., Li, X., & Kaira, L. (2012). Evaluating the comparability of paper- and computer-based science test across sex and SES subgroups. *Educational Measurement: Issues and Practice, 31*(4), 2–12.

Rudner, L. M. (2010). Implementing the Graduate Management Admission Test computerized adaptive test. In W. J. van der Linden (Ed.), *Elements of adaptive testing* (pp. 151–165). New York: Springer.

Sands, W. A., Waters, B. K., & McBride, J. R. (Eds.) (1997). *Computerized adaptive testing: From inquiry to operation.* Washington, DC: American Psychological Association.

Sawaki, Y. (2001). Comparability of conventional and computerized tests of reading in a second language. *Language Learning & Technology, 5,* 38–59.

Sawyer, R. (2007). Some further thoughts on concordance. In N. J. Dorans, M. Pommerich, & P. W. Holland (Eds.), *Linking and aligning scores and scales* (pp. 217–230). New York: Springer-Verlag.

Sawyer, R., Cole, N. S., & Cole, J. W. L. (1976). Utilities and the issue of fairness in a decision theoretic model for selection. *Journal of Educational Measurement, 13,* 59–76.

Schaeffer, G. A., Steffen, M., Golub-Smith, M. L., Mills, C. N., & Durso, R. (1995). *The introduction and comparability of the computer adaptive GRE General Test* (GRE Board Report No. 88-08aP). Princeton, NJ: Educational Testing Service.

Schroeders, U., & Wilhelm, O. (2011). Equivalence of reading and listening comprehension across test media. *Educational and Psychological Measurement, 71,* 849–869.

Stokes, K. (2013, July 29). Review: On average, online disruptions didn't hurt Indiana's ISTEP+ scores. *Indiana Public Media*. Retrieved from http://indianapublicmedia.org

Texas Education Agency (2008). *A review of literature on the comparability of scores obtained from examinees on computer-based and paper-based tests*. Texas Education Agency (TEA) Technical Report Series.

Thissen, D. (2007). Linking assessments based on aggregate reporting: Background and issues. In N. J. Dorans, M. Pommerich, & P. W. Holland (Eds.), *Linking and aligning scores and scales* (pp. 287–312). New York: Springer-Verlag.

Thorndike, R. L. (1971). Concepts of cultural fairness. *Journal of Educational Measurement, 8*, 63–70.

Tippins, N. T. (2009). Internet alternatives to traditional proctored testing: Where are we now? *Industrial and Organizational Psychology: Perspectives on Science and Practice, 2*, 2–10.

Tippins, N. T., Beaty, J., Drasgow, F., Gibson, W. M., Pearlman, K., Segall, D. O., & Shepard, W. (2006). Unproctored Internet testing in employment settings. *Personnel Psychology, 59*, 189–225.

U.S. Census Bureau. (2014). *Computer and Internet trends in America*. Retrieved from www.census.gov/hhes/computer/files/2012/Computer_Use_Infographic_FINAL.pdf

von Davier, A. A., & Liu, M. (2008). Population invariance. [Special Issue]. *Applied Psychological Measurement, 32*(1).

Wang, H, & Shin, C. D. (2010). *Comparability of computerized adaptive and paper-pencil tests*. Test, Measurement & Research Services Bulletin, Issue 13. Pearson Education.

Wang, S., Jiao, H., Young, M. J., Brooks, T. E., & Olson, J. (2007). A meta-analysis of testing mode effects in Grade K-12 mathematics tests. *Educational and Psychological Measurement, 67*, 219–238.

Wang, S., Jiao, H., Young, M. J., Brooks, T., & Olson, J. (2008). Comparability of computer-based and paper-and-pencil testing in K-12 reading assessments. *Educational and Psychological Measurement, 68*, 5–24.

Wang, T., & Kolen, M. J. (2001). Evaluating comparability in computerized adaptive testing: Issues, criteria and an example. *Journal of Educational Measurement, 38*, 19–49.

Willingham, W. W., & Cole, N. S. (1997). *Gender and fair assessment*. Mahwah, NJ: Lawrence Erlbaum.

Winter, P. C. (2010). Comparability and test variation. In P. C. Winter (Ed.), *Evaluating the comparability of scores from achievement test variations* (pp. 1–11). Washington, DC: Council of Chief State School Officers.

Wolfe, J. H., Moreno, K. E., & Segall, D. O. (1997). Evaluating the predictive validity of CAT-ASVAB. In W. A. Sands, B. K. Waters, & J. R. McBride (Eds.), *Computerized adaptive testing: From inquiry to operation* (pp. 175–179). Washington, DC: American Psychological Association.

Xi, X. (2010). How do we go about investigating test fairness? *Language Testing, 27*(2), 147–170.

Yin, P., Brennan, R. L., & Kolen, M. J. (2004). Concordance between ACT and ITED scores from different populations. *Applied Psychological Measurement, 28*, 274–289.

Zieky, M. (2006). Fairness reviews in assessment. In S. M. Downing & T. M. Haladyna (Eds.), *Handbook of test development* (pp. 359–376). Mahwah, NJ: Lawrence Erlbaum.

Zitny, P., Halama, P., Jelinek, M., & Kveton, P. (2012). Validity of cognitive ability tests: Comparison of computerized adaptive testing with paper and pencil and computer-based forms of administrations. *Studia Psychologica, 54*, 181–194.

8 Comparing Test Scores across Grade Levels

Katherine E. Castellano[1] *and*
Michael J. Kolen[2]

Introduction

Educational policies and initiatives, such as the Race to the Top Grant program (United States Department of Education, 2009) and the Elementary and Secondary Education Act (ESEA) Flexibility waivers (United States Department of Education, 2012), increasingly require comparisons of student test scores across grade levels to inform classifications of student progress, teacher/leader effectiveness, and school accountability. In response, state testing programs have developed sophisticated longitudinal student databases and chosen specific measures that use longitudinal student test score data for each of their intended uses. However, while a few studies and programs (e.g., Buzick & Laitusis, 2010; Colorado Department of Education, 2013b; Lakin & Young, 2013) have investigated some fairness considerations for particular subgroups, comprehensive collections of supportive evidence are rarely reported that validate the uses of the chosen measures or demonstrate that the measures can support their prescribed interpretations for all relevant student groups. For test scores from a given grade-level, content area assessment at a single point in time, there are established procedures for investigating fairness considerations, such as fairness reviews of the items, differential item functioning (DIF) studies, differential prediction, and assessment of a common factor structure across groups (e.g., Buzick, 2013). However, no clear procedures have been established for investigating fairness considerations for measures comparing test scores across multiple time points.

We argue that providing evidence of fairness for relevant subgroups for each grade-level, content area assessment of interest is not sufficient for establishing fairness for the same relevant subgroups when comparing test scores *across* those grade levels. Accordingly, Standard 3.15 in the *Standards for Educational and Psychological Testing* (the Standards) (American Educational Research Association, American Psychological Association, & National Council on Measurement in Education, 2014) also pertains to cross-grade comparisons: "Test developers and publishers who claim that a test can be used with examinees from specific subgroups are responsible for providing the necessary information to support appropriate test score interpretations for their intended uses for individuals from these subgroups" (p. 70).

In this case, we are not concerned with "a test," but several tests that are used in the cross-grade comparison measure of interest. As testing programs often report aggregated cross-grade comparison measures, such as mean Student Growth Percentiles by relevant subgroups, including gender and race/ethnicity, Standard 3.17 is also pertinent:

> When aggregate scores are publicly reported for relevant subgroups—for example, males and females, individuals of differing socioeconomic status, individuals differing

by race/ethnicity . . .—test users are responsible for providing evidence of comparability and for including cautionary statements whenever credible research or theory indicates that test scores may not have comparable meaning across these subgroups.

(p. 71)

Establishing fairness, such as comparability of the measure across time for relevant subgroups, requires additional considerations than those at a given time point as there are more "moving parts," including a shift in time and test content. The shift in time could produce shifts in test administration conditions and shifts within individual students in terms of not only their mastery of the construct, but also their individual characteristics or classifications (e.g., changes in gifted status, free-reduced-price lunch status, and maturity) that might not be a component of the intended construct but affect performance on the assessments. These shifts add complexity to evaluating fairness considerations as it may be difficult, for instance, to isolate any differences among subgroup cross-grade performance to psychometric inadequacies in the measure versus real differences in subgroup performance on the desired construct(s) across grade levels. Thus, generally, threats to validity with respect to scores measured at multiple time points are magnified relative to a single time point and additional fairness considerations can arise.

In this chapter, we highlight some key considerations when evaluating fairness related to measures comparing test scores across multiple grade levels for individual students from different subgroups and aggregated subgroup performance. We pose critical questions to guide this process and provide some examples for each measure of interest, but we do not purport to have all the answers. Rather, this chapter encourages further discussions and research to help establish clearer guidelines for testing programs to use and follow when collecting fairness evidence for their cross-grade comparison measures.

Key Definitions

Before positing fairness considerations, we define key terms or concepts integral to this chapter. First, "comparisons of test scores across grade levels" certainly corresponds to "student achievement growth" measures, but given that "growth" can take on various meanings depending on the context and purpose (Castellano & Ho, 2013a), we use the phrase "comparisons of test scores across grade levels" to clarify our use and employ a definition that applies to all the measures of interest.

Second, like Castellano and Ho (2013a), we define "model" loosely to refer not only to a statistical model but also to the entire "collection of definitions, calculations, or rules that summarizes student performance over two or more time points and supports interpretations about students, their classrooms, their educators, or their schools" (p. 16). We use "measure" to refer to the specific statistic used to describe student or subgroup cross-grade performance. For instance, the student-level measure in the gain score model is the gain or difference score, and an aggregated measure may be the average gain score.

Third, we focus on fairness issues related to the use of cross-grade comparison measures for comparisons of test scores of individual students or aggregated students over grade levels. We do not consider other uses for the cross-grade comparison measures, such as for evaluating educator effectiveness. See Haertel and Ho (this volume, Chapter 12) for a detailed discussion of fairness considerations when using student test scores to evaluate educator effectiveness. We highlight considerations for males and females in evaluating fairness for each of our cross-grade comparison measures. Gender subgroups have the advantage of large sample sizes for each subgroup, unlike for some special populations such as students with disabilities, making empirical analyses feasible without any needed considerations of small sample issues. However, our focus on gender subgroups does not mean that we are downplaying fairness considerations for other groups. Rather, we maintain that fairness should be evaluated for all groups in the target population for the tests of interest.

Fourth, we understand that various stakeholders and parties are involved in defining the purpose of comparisons of student scores across grade levels and in selecting the corresponding measure(s), as well as establishing any cut points or rules for interpreting the measure(s). Accordingly, we use the term "testing program," or simply "program," to encapsulate all entities involved in this process. These may include, for example, a state department of education, its constituents, such as principals, teachers, and parents, and its testing company vendor.

Considerations for All Measures of Interest

In this chapter, we consider three general approaches—using vertical scales (e.g., a gain score or trajectory model), conditional status or normative growth models (e.g., the Student Growth Percentile model), and comparing performance levels across grades (e.g., a value table model)—to compare test scores across multiple grade levels and time points, which differ by the type of test scores they use, the test scale assumptions they make, and the intended interpretations. Accordingly, we discuss particular considerations for each of these approaches one by one in subsequent subsections.

We first discuss some fairness considerations that pertain to all three approaches. Kolen (2006) asserts the quality of linking different assessments is affected by three key features of the test administrations: "test content," "conditions of measurement," and "examinee population." He indicates that these three key features work together to define the construct that is actually measured by the test, which we refer to as the "construct actually measured." The construct actually measured can be compared to the "desired construct" of the test developers, which Haertel and Ho (this volume, Chapter 12) refer to as the "developer construct." At a given point in time, test content, conditions of measurement, and examinee population together influence the construct actually measured. The construct actually measured by a particular grade-level, content area assessment can be compared for congruence with the developer construct for various examinee subgroups, and the degree of congruence can be considered in validating the assessment.

The three test administration features are also applicable in defining the "construct actually measured *over time*" versus the "desired construct *over time*" (or "desired cross-grade construct") and thus aid in evaluating the use of cross-grade comparison measures. In some cases, testing programs use grade-level assessments to measure cross-grade performance even if they did not explicitly develop the assessments so that they are aligned with the desired construct over time. In such instances, Haertel and Ho (this volume, Chapter 12) refer to the desired cross-grade construct as an "application construct" instead of a "developer construct" because the use of the test scores for cross-grade or "growth" comparisons is post hoc rather than incorporated into the development of the test by the test developers. They focus on the importance of validating any application constructs that may arise given post hoc uses of test scores.

Ideally, if programs are interested in making cross-grade comparisons, they would define their desired cross-grade construct a priori and develop the corresponding grade-level assessments in alignment with this construct. However, many possible scenarios may exist in which the development of the tests aligns in part, whole, or not at all with the desired cross-grade construct. For instance, programs may define a desired cross-grade construct in the early stages of test development, but then alignment to desired within-grade constructs may take priority, resulting in the tests only being partially developed to the desired cross-grade construct. In other cases, the desired cross-grade construct may never be explicitly defined even when test scores are used for making cross-grade comparisons and thus the program is trying to make inferences to a desired cross-grade construct that is only implicitly defined.

Throughout this chapter, we highlight the importance of anticipating cross-grade performance goals of test scores during the early stages of test development. In the remainder of this section, we discuss the three key test administration features that define the construct actually measured over time with the desired construct over time. We also provide an example that illustrates how considerations for fairness in measuring cross-grade performance can conflict with considerations for construct validity, and may result in programs having to weigh these competing priorities in test development or consider the use of a different set of tests for the purposes of assessing within-grade and cross-grade performance.

To aid in making fair cross-grade comparisons, some key *test content* considerations are:

(a) Over what content is cross-grade performance being defined?
(b) To what extent is the intended content across grades comparably assessed for all relevant subgroups?

The first critical question prompts testing programs to consider first what interpretations they want their cross-grade performance measure to afford. Clear definitions of the knowledge, skills, and abilities over which the program wants to be able to make statements of student change or progress—be it absolute or normative—pushes the discussion of cross-grade performance into the early stages of test development instead of choosing a measure post hoc to apply to tests that may or may not afford the desired interpretations. Such discussions can inform the selection of adjacent-grade common items if building a vertical scale and in defining performance level descriptors, which is particularly critical for comparison of performance level approaches. Clear definitions of the content over which the program is interested in making cross-grade performance inferences can also be important for conditional status models; that is, when the content is defined as following a developmental continuum, conditional status measures can afford student growth or progress inferences instead of only relative performance inferences.

This deliberate reflection over what content the program is interested in making cross-grade comparisons of student performance is also essential for being able to address the second question regarding the extent that the intended content across grades is comparably assessed for relevant subgroups. As with fairness content reviews for a given content area test, testing programs could conduct fairness reviews looking at content changes from one grade level to the next with a consideration of how such changes might differentially affect males and females (and other relevant subgroups) and if those changes align with the desired cross-grade construct.

For instance, suppose that in reviewing the content of eighth and ninth grade state mathematics tests, reviewers found that the ninth grade mathematics test emphasized applied word problems more than the eighth grade test, which may, for instance, involve inclusion of more constructed response items. The program may then observe in the data that females tend to perform better than males on the ninth grade test due to females generally having higher verbal ability. This change in mathematics content may align with the differences in desired within-grade constructs for grades 8 and 9.

However, this shift in content emphasis may result in fairness considerations when gauging cross-grade performance. In this scenario, the ninth grade assessment has two dimensions of content, albeit highly correlated, with one dimension reflecting high-verbal-demand mathematics content and the other low- to moderate-verbal-demand mathematics content. There is a gender difference on the first dimension but not the second. We are then comparing a single score that is a mixture of these two dimensions in ninth grade to a single score in eighth grade for each student that only reflects the low- to moderate-verbal-demand mathematics content. Thus, it might be argued that it is unfair to make this comparison across gender groups as by making the ninth grade test require higher verbal skills, the playing field is no longer level when comparing eighth grade to ninth grade scores for males and females. From a fairness perspective in making cross-grade performance inferences, using tests that only cover the intersection of material from the adjacent grades might be better substantiated, but from a (within-grade) construct validity perspective, a program would want to cover the content in the eighth grade and ninth grade tests fully as opposed to intentionally underrepresenting either content. In this scenario, we find that goals for construct representation and fairness in cross-grade comparisons might be in conflict.

This conflict arises in part because of a possible misalignment between the desired construct for each grade-level assessment and the desired cross-grade construct. Such a conflict might be addressed by developing separate assessments for the purpose of adequately covering each of these constructs. Alternatively, it suggests an empirical check for fairness in using cross-grade performance measures. If a program finds large differences in cross-grade performance between subgroups, such as males and females, it could re-estimate each subgroup's cross-grade performance using only the intersection of content across the grades of interest to determine if the difference is due to a difference in a rate of mastery of the intended content across grade levels or to differential performance on non-overlapping content. Consideration of the test content can potentially help explain observed differences between groups for any of the approaches of interest, but the implications may differ by approach. We thus return to this illustrative subgroup-by-content-interaction example in each of the subsequent sections.

Evaluating the extent to which content is assessed comparably across subgroups (question (b)) relates to how the assessed content for relevant subgroups is aligned to the desired cross-grade construct. To address this question fully, we need to consider all three test features—content, measurement conditions, and examinee population—which we do at the end of this section.

Another threat to accurate assessment across grades for relevant subgroups is shifts in the *conditions of measurement*. The following questions are thus useful to consider:

(a) Under what conditions should student test scores not be compared across time?
(b) To what extent do assignment rules and protocols for accommodations change across time, and do these changes affect score comparability in general or differentially by relevant subgroup?

Question (a) is a general question that should be one of the first questions posed to help guide inclusion and exclusion rules when estimating cross-grade comparison measures. With regard to question (b), consider, for instance, that the program changes the test timing accommodations assigned to students with attention deficit disorders from Time 1 to Time 2 so that the allotted extra time is more consistent with research on the amount of extra time such students need on a test. If a larger proportion of males in the student population are diagnosed with attention deficit disorders than the proportion of females, the change in testing conditions will have a higher relative impact on males than females.

Programs should evaluate how any changes in measurement conditions affect test scores and review the proportion of each relevant subgroup affected. Such evidence could be useful in explaining any differences found in subgroup performance. For instance, if the difference in the male and female mean gain scores (or Student Growth Percentiles for fourth grade mathematics given third grades scores) is consistent every year, but this difference changes substantially the year a change in time accommodations is implemented, then the accommodation change could be the reason for that performance change. Such a change is perhaps indicative of the program obtaining a more accurate assessment of the proficiency of students with attention deficit disorders, which affects the male mean more than the female mean.

If the program does observe a sudden change in the difference in average cross-grade performance measures, to investigate further, the program could look at the aggregated cross-grade comparison measure for male and female students who do not have attention deficit disorders and were not affected by the accommodation change. If those means are comparable, the accommodation change would explain the observed difference in male and female performance.

Just as defining the intended content and conditions of measurement over which a program wants to make cross-grade performance inferences is critical, so is defining the intended *examinee population*, making the following questions relevant:

(a) Who is the intended examinee population for the cross-grade comparisons?
(b) To what extent is the intended examinee population represented the same in the actual test taker sample in each grade? Does a particular subgroup's representation change over time?

Question (a) prompts the testing program to define clearly the intended population of students for whom they want to make cross-grade comparisons. Question (b) prompts an empirical analysis of the test taker sample to confirm whether the test takers represent the intended population and to take note of any demographic shifts in the test taker population over time that may then help in explaining any subgroup differences found on the cross-grade performance measure.

For instance, cross-grade comparison measures require at least two years of consecutive test score data, so differential missingness or longitudinal "matched" data rates can affect aggregate summaries of student cross-grade performance, as Lakin and Young (2013) discuss for English language learners. Here, suppose males have a lower match rate than females for data over Times 1 and 2, then when summarizing male and female cross-grade performance with the average gain score, Student Growth Percentile, or transition values, the male average may not adequately summarize the performance of males over time. This concern is particularly an issue if the students who are missing data at either

Time 1 or Time 2 are distinct from those students who do have complete data, which is generally the case. That is, migrant or economically disadvantaged students may be more likely to have missing data and tend to have lower achievement scores and different patterns (or trajectories) in change in performance over time than their affluent peers. Thus, it is important for programs to clearly define their intended population when making cross-grade comparisons and empirically verify the extent that the actual sample of students with available data matches this intended population. Any mismatch could help explain differences found in subgroup performance and should be documented.

Taken together, test content, conditions of measurement, and examinee population over multiple grades determine the construct that is actually measured versus the desired construct across those grade levels. To address the second test content question we posed regarding the extent the intended content *across grades* is comparably assessed for relevant subgroups, we recommend using targeted statistical analyses as is typically done for a given grade. We propose some possible methods that serve as starting points for establishing such procedures.

One such analysis involves comparing the factor structure across subgroups, such as males and females, over the current and prior grades of interest for the cohort of interest. More specifically, the program could compare the factor structures at Time 1, say for eighth grade, for males and females and then do the same at Time 2 for ninth grade. Subsequently, the program could compare changes across the genders in the factor structures from Time 1 to Time 2 and consider whether these changes are consistent with the desired cross-grade construct. See Liu and Dorans (this volume, Chapter 5) for further discussion of factor invariance studies.

A second method might be an application of DIF procedures to multiple grades. For instance, conduct DIF analyses by matching students on prior year scores and then investigating DIF for each individual item on the current year test across gender and other relevant subgroups. That is, compare the regressions for males and females of item scores from Time 2 on total score for Time 1. As with traditional DIF analyses, any flagged items need to be reviewed by content experts to determine whether the differences in regressions for males and females were due to differences in item functioning that was not expected given hypothesized differences for males and females in performance on the desired cross-grade construct. See Penfield (this volume, Chapter 4) for a more detailed consideration of DIF procedures.

Yet, a third procedure might involve investigating differential prediction, which Liu and Dorans (this volume, Chapter 5) discuss in detail. Such analyses involve determining the extent that regressions of current total scores on prior total scores are the same for males and females (as well as other relevant subgroups). Again, if any differential prediction is found, we would need judgmental follow-up analyses to determine why. Such determinations may be difficult to make, but we are arguing that careful deliberations that we are accustomed to making for a given grade-level test are exactly what are needed for evaluating fairness of cross-grade performance measures.

In the following sections, we consider three general cross-grade comparison approaches —using vertical scales, conditional status models, and comparing performance levels across grades—in more detail in their respective sections. We only briefly discuss comparing performance levels given this approach is not as widely used or considered for use as approaches that take advantage of vertical scales or model conditional status. We first describe each approach and then discuss additional fairness considerations in using the approach to describe cross-grade performance for relevant subgroups.

Vertical Scaling and Comparing Test Scores across Grade Levels

Vertical scaling (Kolen, 2006; Kolen & Brennan, 2014) involves placing scores on tests that are intended to assess a similar construct, but that differ in difficulty, on a common score scale. Vertical scaling has been used with elementary achievement test batteries such as the Iowa Tests of Basic Skills (ITBS) (Hoover, Dunbar, & Frisbie, 2003) and in state-based NCLB educational achievement batteries. More recently, the Partnership for Assessment of Readiness for College and Careers (2014) and Smarter Balanced Assessment Consortium (2014) assessment consortia are developing vertical scales for their assessments that are aligned to the Common Core State Standards (Council of Chief State School Officers & National Governors Association, 2014). Scores on vertically scaled tests typically are intended to be compared to one another. For example, consider a student who takes a vertically scaled test in a particular achievement area in grades 3 and 4. The difference between scores for this student in the two years is often interpreted as a measure of the amount the student has learned from third grade to fourth grade. The magnitude of this score change may also be compared with that of another student to compare the amount of learning from third grade to fourth grade for these two students.

The development of a vertical scale requires that: (a) tests at different grade levels are on a developmental continuum; and (b) data be collected that allow the placement of scores on tests that differ in difficulty on the same scale. We first review models for using vertical scales to compare test scores across grade levels. Subsequently, we pose critical questions and discuss pertinent evidence for addressing these questions when evaluating the fair use for relevant subgroups, such as males and females, of cross-grade comparison models that use vertical scales. Such discussion includes consideration of the development and properties of the vertical scale for the multiple grade-level tests of interest.

Models for Comparing Scores

The amount that an examinee's score changes from one year to the next provides a simple model for comparing scores across grade level. If one examinee's scores increase more than another examinee's scores, then the first examinee is said to have learned more during the year than the other examinee.

Scale anchoring studies (Kolen & Brennan, 2014) can also be conducted to augment a vertical scale by adding meaningful statements of what students know and are able to do across grades at various points along the score scale. Scale anchoring studies depend on subject matter experts developing descriptions, based on which items map to various points along the score scale representing performance at various grade levels. The use of a vertical scale with scale anchoring allows educators to develop descriptions of what a student knows and is able to do at Time 2 versus Time 1 when students take different grade level tests at each time point.

In addition to comparing scores at two points in time, student growth trajectories over multiple years can be fit when students have scores on the vertical scale over multiple years. Such trajectories can be fairly simple (e.g., the trajectory model) (Hoffer et al., 2011), or can be modeled with complex statistical models (e.g., growth curve models) (Rogosa, Brandt, & Zimowski, 1982; Singer & Willett, 2003). These models can be used for describing individual student trajectories as with growth curve models (e.g., shapes of curves, variation in initial status or rates of change, etc.) or in predicting future performance, as is typically done with the trajectory model to predict if students are on track to a target score (e.g., the "proficiency or college and career" readiness cut score in a future grade). Note that in the latter case, predicted scores result from extrapolating individual student trajectories to future time points, assuming, for instance, linear change, instead of with a prediction equation.

At the aggregate level, the average change in scores from one year to the next can be used as a description of the amount of change observed for the subgroup. Multilevel models can be used to examine growth trajectories for groups of students.

Considerations for Evaluating Fairness

The extent to which vertical scale approaches afford fair interpretations about the change in student performance over time for relevant subgroups depends on a number of factors related to the development of the test specifications, construction of the vertical scale, and technical properties of the resulting measure (e.g., precision of gain scores). However, to determine whether the vertical scale approach provides the same cross-grade performance interpretations for all relevant subgroups, a testing program must first answer the question: *What are the intended interpretations when using this approach?* This question may be more straightforward to address for vertical scale approaches than for the other two approaches considered in this chapter. Generally, when using a vertical scale to compare student performance over time, the goal is to measure how much students have learned from Time 1 to Time 2. For the vertical scale to support such interpretations, the test content across grades should represent a developmental continuum of the content area of interest, meaning that such a continuum must first be theorized and clearly defined (i.e., the desired cross-grade construct). Subsequent verifications involve a judgmental evaluation of the content specifications of the test within each grade, of how the content changes across grades, and how well the common items used to place scores on the scale represent the intended content changes across grades. Such evaluation requires the testing program to provide clear and complete information about the test content specifications both within and across grades.

Another fundamental assumption for a vertical scale to support cross-grade performance inferences is that the underlying vertical scale has equal interval scale properties. That is, a particular score difference from Time 1 to Time 2 indicates the same difference in achievement along the entire scale. For example, a gain of 10 points for a low scoring student is taken to indicate the same amount of increase in achievement as a score increase of 10 points for a high scoring student and likewise for a mid-scoring student. There is a thoughtful and ongoing debate in the field whether test scores can have this property (see, e.g., Ballou, 2009; Borsboom, 2005; Briggs, 2013; Domingue, 2014; Michell, 1997, 2008; Mislevy, 2006; Mosteller, 1958; Yen, 1986). But to use vertical scales to measure cross-grade performance, testing programs are tasked with substantiating this claim with supporting evidence.

Once the intended interpretation of using a vertical scale for measuring cross-grade performance is established, the key fairness question is then: *Are differences in scores appropriate for all relevant subgroups for describing cross-grade performance?* We first recall the gender by content interaction example about the shift in content from the eighth to ninth grade mathematics test to a greater emphasis on word problems that was presented in the introduction. If this shift in content is intended, then it should be reflected in the choice of adjacent grade common items or the content specifications of a scaling test, depending on which is used to create the vertical scale. We will focus on the selection of common items.

Consider the situation regarding eighth and ninth grade mathematics tests described in the first section of this chapter. Assume the following: (a) The program intends for the ninth grade mathematics test to have more applied word problems and, thus, to require a greater emphasis on reading than does the eighth grade test. (b) The common items that are used to assess change from eighth to ninth grade fully represent the content of the eighth and ninth grade tests. (c) Females have higher reading skills than males. In this case, a finding that females gained more than males from eighth to ninth grade on the vertical scale would be consistent with the shift in the intended content from grades 8 to 9.

On the other hand, if the common item set on the eighth and ninth grade tests contained only eighth grade items, due to fairness concerns that the ninth grade content will be too difficult for the eighth graders because they have not had yet an opportunity to learn the ninth grade content, then we might not observe a differential performance on common items by the ninth grade males and females. That is, the use of only eighth grade common items could potentially lead to different relative growth patterns for males and females on the grade-level assessments as compared to on the common items.

Even if the common items are a representative mix of eighth and ninth grade content, an observed higher mean gain for females could be misinterpreted as simply a higher gain in mathematics ability from eighth grade to ninth grade than for males if test users (e.g., school administrators, policymakers, etc.) are not aware of the shift in test content across these grade levels or how this shift differentially affects groups. Accordingly, fairness issues could potentially arise in interpretation even when the cross-grade performance measure accurately reflects true differences in changes in abilities over the tested content across time, which constitutes, in part, the construct actually measured as opposed to the desired construct. For fairness considerations in cross-grade inferences, programs may find that they are actually interested in the intersection of the content across grades instead of the union of the content. Accordingly, the desired cross-grade construct might be at odds with the desired within-grade constructs. Fairness and construct validity evidence for within-grade scores may be in conflict with fairness and construct validity evidence across grades. Ultimately, programs may decide they need two separate sets of tests to assess performance within and across grades adequately.

Another source of relevant evidence to determine whether gain scores are appropriate for all relevant subgroups is comparing effect sizes for subgroups across groups and time points. For instance, a program could compare the male/female effect size at Time 1 to that effect size at Time 2 on the administered tests to these gender effect sizes on the common items. This check assumes that the set of adjacent grade common items is the best representation of the program's definition of the construct over which they want to assess cross-grade performance and thus a mismatch between the comparability of the male/female effect size at Time 1 compared to Time 2 for the regular versus common items may indicate that one subgroup is being disadvantaged. This check could also be useful in determining if a content shift across time is the cause of a large difference between two subgroups' cross-grade performance by checking if effect sizes based on the entire tests versus those based on only the intersection of cross-grade content differ.

Another possible source of evidence is checking the population invariance of the vertical scaling. The vertical scaling could be conducted on different subgroups with the results compared to each other and to those from the combined population using population invariance procedures (Holland & Dorans, 2006). However, finding subgroup dependence in scaling is not necessarily evidence of unfairness against one of the groups. The program would have to investigate reasons for any differences and have established guidelines for determining the extent of differences with which they are comfortable proceeding forward.

Yet other empirical analyses include simple data/technical checks. For instance, measurement error affects the test scores at both time points, which results in gain scores also being contaminated with error. It may then be useful to compare the standard errors in the gain scores across groups to determine if students in particular groups have less precise estimates than others. Typically, students at the extremes have less precise scores for a given grade-level test, and this can be exacerbated when comparing across two tests (see Haertel, 2006, for a detailed discussion of the precision of gain scores). Thus, if one subgroup tends to have more low- or high-scoring students each year, their gain scores may be less precise than other groups. In addition, it is useful to examine floor and ceiling effects by subgroup as students at the floor may not have accurate scores, and students at the ceiling cannot exhibit growth.

The final analysis we will consider here is at the item level. As mentioned in the first section, testing programs may want to consider DIF procedures in which they condition on prior performance when evaluating differential performance on the current year's test items. With a vertical scale, another possibility may be comparing the performance of the subgroups on the common items over time. Programs can investigate the percentage of students within each subgroup who obtained each possible response pattern, such as those who improve. That is, students who generally respond incorrectly to the common items in the previous grade level assessment and then generally respond correctly in the current grade level assessment. Again, differences across groups may not be evidence of unfairness, but may provide reason to investigate further why such differences are occurring.

Conditional Status Models for Cross-Grade Performance Comparison

This section focuses on conditional status interpretations of cross-grade comparisons, which involve comparing current achievement status scores to expected achievement scores given, or conditional on, prior achievement and, potentially, other background variables (Castellano & Ho, 2013b, 2015). Conditional status is sometimes referred to as "normative" or norm-referenced growth or difference-from-expectation (Kolen, 2011). We first introduce conditional status models with a specific focus on the Student Growth Percentile model to ground discussions. We then provide considerations for fair cross-grade comparisons using this model for subgroups.

Conditional Status Models

Conditional status models typically use regression models to locate individuals' current status in empirically "comparable" reference groups conditional on their prior scores and/or other background variables. Conditional status models can accommodate as many prior years of scores as are available. In addition, these regression-based approaches do not require that the current score (the outcome) and the prior scores (the predictors) be on the same scale. That is, they do not require vertically scaled scores.

Some specific examples are the Student Growth Percentile Model (Betebenner, 2009), residual gain scores, projection models, and value-added models (VAMs). Residual gain scores that involve computing student residuals from the regression of Time 2 scores on Time 1 scores are not typically used by state testing programs, but see Castellano and Ho (2013a) for a discussion of this approach. Projection models involve applying a regression model estimated from an earlier cohort to *predict* scores in a future grade level given prior year scores for a focal cohort. In that case, the interest is not in describing cross-grade performance, but in predicting future performance so we do not discuss it in detail here but some of the same fairness considerations apply. McCaffrey, Lockwood, Koretz, Louis, and Hamilton (2004) provide an extensive review of value-added models in general, and Haertel and Ho (this volume, Chapter 12) discuss fairness considerations for the use of VAMs in particular. Given that inferences from VAMs tend to focus on teacher or leader effectiveness as opposed to comparing student achievement over grade levels (see, e.g., Briggs, 2011), we focus on the Student Growth Percentile model, and now provide further details about this approach.

The Student Growth Percentile Model allows for descriptions of current status through its Student Growth Percentile (SGP) measure and projections of future student status through its percentile growth trajectories and Adequate Growth Percentiles. In this chapter, we focus on the first of these two components of the model. SGPs are percentile ranks that describe the relative location of students' current status to the current scores of their academic peers, or students with same prior achievement history; that is, they just use prior scores as the conditioning variables. If a student's estimated SGP is 60, it is interpreted as: this student performed as well or better in the current year than 60% of his or her peers with the same prior observed scores.

As typically estimated operationally through the SGP package (Betebenner, Van Iwaarden, Domingue, & Shang, 2015) for R (R Core Team, 2015), SGPs use nonlinear parameterizations of the prior scores in quantile regressions (Betebenner, 2009), and thus do not require that the relationships between current and prior scores be linear unlike other conditional status approaches (e.g., residual gain scores and value-added models). Moreover, given the nonparametric nature of SGPs, they only require ordinal scores for each grade-level assessment (Briggs & Betebenner, 2009), whereas several linear-model-based conditional status approaches such as residual gain scores require interval-scaled scores.

To describe a higher-level unit, such as a subgroup, teacher, or school leader, programs aggregate the SGPs of students linked to the unit of interest using the median or mean. Betebenner (2008) recommended the use of the median due to the ordinal nature of percentile ranks, but Castellano and Ho (2015) demonstrate that the mean SGP has more desirable statistical properties than the median SGP. We use MGP to denote mean or median growth percentiles. Unlike value-added models, Betebenner (2008) characterizes MGPs as descriptive, rather than causal, statistics. However, in practice, with their use in teacher evaluation systems (e.g., Colorado Department of Eduction, 2013a; Georgia Department of Education, 2014), they are treated more like causal value-added effects, which necessitates stronger supportive empirical evidence. Given that the focus of this chapter is on comparing *student* scores over multiple grade levels, we focus on fairness considerations for the use of MGPs as a summary measure of student cross-grade performance rather than as a casual effect. However, see Diaz-Bilello and Briggs (2014), Walsh and Isenberg (2015), Wright (2010), Ehlert, Koedel, Parsons, and Podgursky (2012), Goldhaber, Walch, and Gabele (2014), and Guarino, Reckase, Stacy, and Wooldridge (2015) for guidelines or studies investigating SGPs and VAMs for this purpose.

Critical Questions for Evaluating Fairness

As in the second section, to evaluate whether a program's conditional status model results in fair cross-grade performance interpretations for all relevant subgroups, we first consider: *What are the intended interpretations when using this model?* Although conditional status models do not require vertically scaled scores, the interpretability of their conditional status inferences depends on the choice of conditioning variables. We could, for instance, estimate a student's SGP by estimating where a student's current observed mathematics score lies this year in the distribution of peers who have the same prior-year physical education score. However, such a conditional status measure would not likely yield meaningful information about the student's mathematics performance. To interpret SGPs as a *change* in performance across grades measure, the grade-level tests included in the SGP model (the predictors and the outcome) should align to a common construct. This admittedly extreme example highlights the utility in first defining the desired cross-grade construct over which the program intends to make conditional status inferences and using that in the construction of the tests and choice of conditioning variables.

Careful attention to the test content assessed by prior-year tests may also help explain differences found between relevant subgroups as well as in addressing the question: *Are SGPs appropriate for all relevant student groups in describing cross-grade performance?* To address this question, we first return to the gender-by-content-interaction example introduced in the first section. Under this example with the greater emphasis on problems that require higher verbal skills on the ninth grade mathematics test than the eighth grade mathematics test, we would expect to find that females, in general, have higher SGPs than males. In other words, a gender difference in mean SGPs could indicate a real difference in mastery over the tested content for males versus females, but interpretation of this difference is complicated by the content shift across grades.

As discussed in the previous sections, a question of fairness can still arise because the content shift means that the eighth grade performance does not level the playing field for the comparison of male and female performance and users may not be aware of this information. Thus, another way of looking at this fairness consideration is that there may be a misalignment between the user's assumptions about the conditioning and outcome variables and what they actually represent. In this case, users may assume that by conditioning on eighth grade scores, we have sufficiently accounted for prior mathematics ability, and any differences in ninth grade performance for males/females who have the same prior score are only due to differences in their increased mastery on the same developmental continuum of mathematics. However, in this example, the larger emphasis on word application problems on the ninth grade versus the eighth grade test is another factor that is affecting current ninth grade mathematics performance, and because the groups differ on this factor, we find differences in their SGPs. Thus, the desired cross-grade construct may actually be better represented by the intersection of eighth grade and ninth grade test content rather than their union, particularly for fairness considerations.

If a program decides, however, to use the tests and SGPs as is, test programs should include cautionary statements about this additional factor to assist users in correctly interpreting the gender MGP difference (as required by Fairness Standard 3.17). Such a statement could indicate that yes, females tended to outperform males of the same prior mathematics ability on the ninth grade mathematics test but that this is partly due to the shift in test content and differential performance by the subgroups on this shift.

A gender-by-content-interaction is only one example of an interaction that may affect current student performance differently by subgroup and result in a difference in SGPs, but that is not fully considered in the interpretation of the SGPs. That is, the MGPs may indicate real differences in relative student performance over time, but the key is understanding "relative to what" student performance is being compared, and depending on the extent of supporting interpretative materials, this may be easily misunderstood by or misrepresented to users and thus a question of fairness may still remain. For instance, there could be a shift in characteristics of the examinee population that disproportionately affects the relevant subgroups, such as males attending baccalaureate high schools at a greater proportion than females. In this example, users may falsely assume that, by conditioning on prior eighth grade score, they have a comparable sample of males and females, including that they had a similar education experience in the ninth grade. Under this assumption, users may interpret a higher male MGP as indicating that males generally improved more than similar achieving females without realizing that part of this improvement is due to differences in opportunities to learn and quality of instruction.

This discussion can be quite nuanced and challenging to investigate. We are arguing for not only empirical comparisons of relevant subgroup performance, but also consideration of *why* any differences are found and further checking if those differences represent a disconnect between desired constructs for each grade-level and cross grades or a misalignment with user assumptions of what the measure is conveying. Conditional status approaches can provide useful information, but the choice of conditioning variables and understanding of what is actually being controlled for by including those variables can be difficult.

One possible empirical check may be to estimate SGPs for a testing program separately by subgroup. This check is similar to the suggestion in the first section for fitting regressions of Time 2 on Time 1 scores separately by subgroup as a check of the extent to which the assessed content aligns with the developer cross-grade construct across subgroups. But here, instead of using linear regressions, we would use nonlinear, quantile regressions. A difference for males and females between their gender-specific SGPs and their combined-sample SGPs may indicate that some factor other than prior test score is affecting their current performance. Again, such evidence would not be conclusive of unfairness but an indicator that would require follow-up analysis, such as review of the content and the characteristics of the examinee population over time.

As discussed with gain scores in the second section, differential precision may also occur for SGPs. Measurement error in the prior and current year scores affects the accuracy of SGP estimates and can affect some subgroups more than others. McCaffrey, Castellano, and Lockwood (2015) investigate the effects of measurement error on the accuracy and precision of SGPs by comparing SGPs computed with observed scores (the "observed SGP") to those computed with true scores, or expected observed scores, (the "true SGP") under certain distributional assumptions. They show that the difference of the observed SGP minus the true SGP is positively correlated with prior true scores so that students with high prior true scores have overestimated SGPs on average, and vice versa for students with low prior true scores. Suppose, for instance, that males generally have higher true scores on the prior eighth grade mathematics test than females. Males will thus, on average, receive current ninth grade mathematics SGPs that are overestimates of their true SGPs, whereas females will receive SGPs that underestimate their true SGPs. Accordingly, we would find a difference in the mean SGP for males and females, but part of this difference would be due to measurement error in the test scores and not in real differences in relative cross-grade performance of males versus females. In practice, we may not observe large differences in prior mean scores of males and females, but we may see substantial differences in mean prior achievement for other relevant subgroups, such as White versus Black students or English learners versus non-English learners. In these cases, the correlation between the difference in observed and expected SGPs and true prior scores could result in larger differences in MGP for the relevant subgroups than if the test scores had no measurement error. In general, testing programs should consider differential accuracy and precision of the conditional status measure by each relevant subgroup to determine its appropriateness for each subgroup.

Some other empirical checks testing programs may consider when evaluating the fair use of SGPs include simple test score data checks and comparisons of results over time. These include investigating the extent floor and ceiling effects affect each subgroup of interest as the quantile curves may be poorly estimated at the extremes, resulting in imprecise SGP estimates. Plots can be useful diagnostic tools. For instance, the estimated quantile curves can be overlaid on the scatterplot of students' Time 2 on Time 1 scores with plotting symbols indicating subgroup membership (such as stars for males and circles for females) to visually check for issues with SGP estimation by subgroup.

In addition, subgroup SGP gaps can be monitored over time within and across cohorts to answer questions like: Is the difference in SGPs for sixth grade given prior scores by subgroup the same this year as it was last year? Is the subgroup difference in SGPs for the current sixth grade cohort similar to what it was last year when these students were in fifth grade? If students in one subgroup are continually earning lower SGPs than another subgroup over time, do we also see a continual decline in their status scores over time? With regard to this last question, if certain students (e.g., males) are continually performing worse than their peers with the same prior scores (i.e., low SGPs), we may expect to see a widening gap in their test scores each year against the other subgroup (e.g., females). If we do not, then this may be evidence that the SGPs are not appropriately measuring relative cross-grade performance for male students.

Another check may be a type of differential prediction analysis similar to those used in determining whether test scores for a particular grade-level assessment are comparable for relevant subgroups. For cross-grade performance, an analogous procedure may be evaluating how well student SGPs (instead of student current scores) predict some external criterion for each relevant subgroup to empirically investigate the fair and appropriate use of SGPs. It may be difficult though to choose an appropriate external criterion. If, for instance, we track students over time and then investigate how well their fifth grade SGPs predicted their ninth grade performance, we are only considering part of the picture. We may think that students who made significant progress relative to their peers from fourth to fifth grade (i.e., have high SGPs) will continue to make such progress and reach some target score in eighth grade (e.g., the proficiency cut score). However, we would also expect students who have a low fifth grade SGP but a very high fifth grade score to reach the target eighth grade score. Thus, it may be useful to compare subgroups' prediction of an external criterion separately for students with low and high current status scores.

Changes in Performance Levels across Grades

In this section, we briefly focus on cross-grade comparison measures that rely on vertically articulated performance (or achievement) levels (e.g., Basic, Proficient, and Advanced) over grades as opposed to vertically scaled scores as in the second section on vertical scaling. We first review the categorical model that involves changes in performance levels. Subsequently, we discuss pertinent evidence for evaluating the fair use of categorical models for relevant subgroups.

Categorical Models

The term categorical model is a general term for models that involve comparing performance levels across grades (Castellano & Ho, 2013a). Other terms include transition (matrix) models or value table models, which are often used interchangeably. These models generally involve comparing students' performance levels over two time points. They rely on programs defining performance-level descriptors of what students know and can do and setting cut scores on the grade-level test scales to distinguish among these levels through a standard setting process. They also involve making explicit the policy and program values on what changes or transitions are important given where students started by assigning point values to each transition (e.g., Delaware Department of Education [DE DOE], 2006). These point values are determined by an expert panel through a judgmental process similar to the standard setting for setting the cut scores for the performance levels.

The point values for the transitions in performance levels from Time 1 to Time 2 are typically represented in matrix form; hence, the names "value table model" and "transition matrix model." Figure 8.1 illustrates Delaware's value table that they used to meet NCLB accountability requirements (DE DOE, 2006). This table makes Delaware's values very clear; the magnitudes of the points indicate that they associate the greatest value with being at least Proficient (Level 3 or higher) with it receiving the greatest point value of 300, followed by movement toward proficiency, and a decrease in performance receiving no value. Note that the point values are not necessarily the same for the same performance level gain as the point values differ for the same gain of +1 performance level from Level 1A to Level 1B, Level 1B to Level 2A, and Level 2A to 2B: higher values are assigned to those transitions that bring the student closer to Level 3, the target proficiency level.

This choice of point values reflects Delaware's program values, but other point values could be possible to either reflect similar or different values. Iowa, for instance, considered students making positive performance level gains as "on-track," which essentially translates to assigning the same point value to all positive transitions (Hoffer et al., 2011). Both the Iowa and Delaware models were motivated by NCLB and thus valued moving students toward the proficiency level. Alternatively, a program could instead, for instance, value any positive movement, including that beyond the proficiency level.

Year 1 (Grade g – 1)	Year 2 (Grade g)						
	Below Proficiency				Proficiency	Above Proficiency	
	Level 1A	Level 1B	Level 2A	Level 2B	Level 3	Level 4	Level 5
Level 1A	0	150	225	250	300		
Level 1B	0	0	175	225	300		
Level 2A	0	0	0	200	300		
Level 2B	0	0	0	0	300		
Level 3 / Level 4 / Level 5	0	0	0	0	300		

Figure 8.1 Illustration of Delaware's Value Table

Considerations for Evaluating Fairness

To evaluate whether a program's categorical model results in fair cross-grade performance interpretations for all relevant subgroups, we first consider: *What are the intended
interpretations when using this model?* In one sense, categorical models are a chunkier
version of conditional status models (the third section) in that a student's current
status, performance level, is located and valued given or conditional on that student's
prior performance level. However, if the program's interest is in using categorical models
to interpret student movement toward the proficiency level as improvement or increased
mastery, as with the Delaware and Iowa examples, then the categorical models may
be more appropriately viewed as chunkier or coarser versions of the gain score model
(the second section). In this case, the performance level descriptors (PLDs) across the
grade levels of interest should be vertically articulated and aligned with increased mastery
over the desired cross-grade construct. And such processes should be carefully documented
and reported.

Specifically, when defining the PLDs and setting the corresponding cut scores for each
grade, a program needs to take into account the desired construct across grade levels
and not just within each grade level independently. For instance, programs may consider including teachers from adjacent grade levels on their standard setting panels, such
as including both third and fourth grade teachers on the third grade standard setting
panel. Moreover, it is useful to decide on the use of this cross-grade performance measure
during early stages of test development. In the Delaware example, the program valued
progress toward the proficiency standard so they decided to collapse all categories above
Proficient and subdivide lower performance levels (as shown in Figure 8.1) to be able
to make finer grain comparisons over time. In this case, the choice of cross-grade
comparison measure was not part of the test development process, prompting post hoc
changes to the performance levels and potentially undermining the deliberate standard
setting procedure that was originally used to establish the performance levels.

When using a categorical model, the key fairness question is: *Are the possible transitions
and assigned values appropriate for all relevant student groups in describing cross-grade
performance?* This question relates to understanding the practical consequences of
assigning students specific point values for each transition regardless of subgroup
membership.

When assigning the point values, programs need to consider their relevant subgroups
and whether some groups are more likely to transition between certain categories and
if specified point values allow for such groups to demonstrate improved cross-grade performance. Along the same lines, it may be useful for programs to compare the conditional
distributions by subgroup. For instance, using the Delaware example, the program could
compare the proportions of students within each Time 2 performance level who were
at Level 1A at Time 1 for males versus females and likewise for each of the other Time
1 levels. Differences in these distributions do not necessarily indicate unfairness; they
could reflect real differences in performance. However, any identified differences can
then be investigated, for example, by reviewing test content, the PLDs, and the alignment
of the content and PLDs with the desired cross-grade construct. Given the coarseness
of the performance levels and the different raw-to-scale-score conversions each year,
these distributions could be very sensitive to changes of one or two score points in the
cut scores or to slightly different raw-to-scale-score conversions each year. Test measurement error can also affect the accuracy of assigning students to each performance level
each year, making it important to have small conditional standard errors of measurement
for the cut scores of each grade-level assessment's performance levels. Taking all of these

factors together, it is useful to continually track each subgroup's conditional (Time 2 given Time 1) distributions and mean point values each year within and across cohorts to be able to detect any abnormal patterns.

We can also consider the gender by content interaction example for categorical models. If females outperform males on the ninth grade mathematics test with the greater emphasis on applied word problems, then we may expect females to make higher transitional gains in ninth grade than males who start at the same performance level in eighth grade. Thus, a review of the content can help explain differences by subgroups. But, more importantly, if the same tests are used for describing within-grade and cross grade achievement, this shift in emphasis in content should inform the definition of the PLDs and placement of the cut scores so that it is clear that a transition from Basic in eighth grade to, say, Proficient in ninth grade represents being able to solve numeric mathematics problems to being able to solve numeric and word mathematics problems. Alternatively, programs may find that focusing on only the intersection of content between grades allows for more interpretable and fair cross-grade performance measures, in which case they may need to narrow their focus to a subset of the tests' items that reflect common material and develop corresponding PLDs that reflect the cross-grade performance construct or develop separate tests altogether.

Other possible sources of evidence for determining the appropriateness of the assigned point values for all subgroups include longitudinal, qualitative data, such as principal, teacher, student, and/or parent surveys and interviews that ask these parties what resources were allocated to students making each transition. In addition, programs can collect observation data from school visits by internal or external evaluators on the allocation of resources or they can review documentation from the schools for how these entities use the information about student transitions to make instructional decisions, and if these decisions differ by subgroup.

Moreover, quantitative data on the percentage of students who reach the target achievement level by the target grade disaggregated by groups of students can provide further evidence that the measure operates the same for all relevant groups, such as males and females. Lakin and Young (2013) conducted such a study with a large California school district by English learner (EL) status. They found that the value table tended to have higher false negative rates for ELs, providing evidence that their value table model did not as effectively capture the change in student performance for ELs as accurately as it did for their English-proficient peers.

Using PLs to compare student performance across grades can facilitate interpretations of change in achievement as they are anchored to what students should know and can do in each grade, but it comes with many decisions, including two judgmental processes, setting cut scores and assigning point values, that should be fully substantiated.

Concluding Remarks

Fairness in comparisons of student test scores across grades is a validity issue, and as such requires the same rigorous substantiation and documentation of claims and evidence as for the test scores themselves. Just as there are often score differences in test scores by relevant subgroups, there are often differences in the cross-grade comparisons of test scores be it in their gain scores, value table points, SGPs, or other such measure. Due diligence is needed for investigating these differences and making informed decisions about whether they represent evidence of unfairness or not. Such efforts should be part of a larger validation effort, as Haertel and Ho (this volume, Chapter 12) discuss, to ensure that the cross-grade performance measures (i.e., derived scores) adequately assess the desired construct over time, which is sometimes more of an application construct than a developer construct given post hoc decisions to measure cross-grade performance rather than a priori planning and development of the tests themselves for this purpose. Establishing fairness and validity evidence for the use of test scores to assess achievement at a given point in time is not sufficient to establish such evidence for using scores from multiple time points to assess achievement over time. The reliance of these measures on longitudinal data also exacerbates many issues with evaluating fairness for status scores, including accounting for measurement error in multiple grade-level scores, higher missing data rates, and greater potential for errors in student records (e.g., issues with assignment of accommodations), as these now come into play over multiple time points.

These issues affect all cross-grade performance measures but may be realized and empirically checked in different ways. For instance, certain groups being more affected by floor or ceiling effects than others can result in less precise gain scores, issues with estimating their SGPs, and not being able to as accurately assign them to a performance level or demonstrate change in performance levels for these students. Moreover, we walked through a gender-by-content-interaction example in each approach's section, discussing how such an interaction may inform selection of common items for vertical scale approaches, the choice of conditioning variables for conditional status approaches, and definition of performance levels and their cut scores for the change in performance-level approaches.

In this chapter, we focused on evaluating fairness for using cross-grade performance measures for comparing performance across grades for relevant subgroups. However, testing programs may be interested in using these measures for school accountability or educator evaluations. These additional uses require additional substantiation and fairness considerations. References such as Hall (2014), Bell et al. (2012), Shepard (2012), and Jones, Buzick, and Turkan (2013) can help guide in collecting appropriate evidence as they provide frameworks that borrow from program evaluation and evidence-centered design frameworks to validate the use of educator effectiveness systems for educators that serve all student populations.

In choosing cross-grade comparison measures, programs are faced with challenges of balancing accuracy, transparency, interpretability, and other validity concerns, such as within-grade construct validity, that may be partially in conflict with fairness considerations for cross-grade inferences. The purpose of this chapter was not to burden test developers with another list of data checks, but to promote conscientious evaluation of fairness when using cross-grade performance measures so they provide the most useful information for students from all relevant subgroups and to satisfy the fairness standards (AERA et al., 2014). In places, we pose questions but do not provide all the answers, and in others, we make suggestions but understand that implementing them may bring up other practical considerations. This chapter thus encourages further discussions and research to help establish clearer guidelines for testing programs to use and follow when collecting fairness evidence for their cross-grade comparison measures.

Notes

1. The views expressed are those of the author and not necessarily those of the Educational Testing Service.
2. The views expressed are those of the author and not necessarily those of The University of Iowa.

References

American Educational Research Association (AERA), American Psychological Association (APA), & National Council on Measurement in Education (NCME). (2014). *Standards for educational and psychological testing.* Washington, DC: American Educational Research Association.

Ballou, D. (2009). Test scaling and value-added measurement. *Education Finance and Policy, 4*(4), 351–383.

Bell, C. A., Gitomer, D. H., McCaffrey, D., Hamre, B., Pianta, R., & Qi, Y. (2012). An argument approach to observation protocol validity. *Educational Assessment, 17,* 1–26.

Betebenner, D. W. (2008). *A primer on student growth percentiles.* Retrieved from www.doe. k12.ga.us

Betebenner, D. W. (2009). Norm- and criterion-referenced student growth. *Educational Measurement: Issues and Practice, 28*(4): 42–51.

Betebenner, D. W., Van Iwaarden, A., Domingue, B., & Shang, Y. (2015). *SGP: Student growth percentiles & percentile growth trajectories,* R package version 1.3-9.6

Borsboom, D. (2005). *Measuring the mind: Conceptual issues in contemporary psychometrics.* Cambridge: Cambridge University Press.

Briggs, D. C. (2011). *Making inferences about growth and value-added: Design issues for the PARCC consortium.* A White Paper Commissioned by the PARCC Large-Scale Assessment Consortium. Retrieved from www.parcconline.org/sites/parcc/files/BriggsPARCCGrowthFINAL022412. pdf

Briggs, D. C. (2013). Measuring growth with vertical scales. *Journal of Educational Measurement, 50,* 204–226.

Briggs, D., & Betebenner, D. W. (2009). *Is growth in student achievement scale dependent?* Paper presented at the annual meeting of the National Council for Measurement in Education, San Diego, CA. Retrieved from http://dirwww.colorado.edu/education/faculty/derekbriggs/Docs

Buzick, H. M. (2013). *PARCC accessibility and fairness technical memorandum.* Partnership for Assessment of Readiness for College and Careers. Retrieved from www.parcconline.org/sites/ parcc/files/AccessibilityandFairnessTechnicalMemo10-2-13.pdf

Buzick, H. M., & Laitusis, C. C. (2010). Using growth for accountability: Measurement challenges for students with disabilities and recommendations for research. *Educational Researcher, 39,* 537–544.

Castellano, K. E., & Ho, A. D. (2013a). *A practitioner's guide to growth models.* Washington, DC: Council of Chief State School Officers.

Castellano, K. E., & Ho, A. D. (2013b). Contrasting OLS and quantile regression approaches to student "growth" percentiles. *Journal of Educational and Behavioral Statistics, 38,* 190–215.

Castellano, K. E., & Ho, A. D. (2015). Practical differences among aggregate-level conditional status measures: From median student growth percentiles to value-added models. *Journal of Educational and Behavioral Statistics, 40,* 35–68.

Colorado Department of Education (CDE). (2013a). *Measures of student learning guidance for districts: Version 2.0.* Retrieved from www.cde.state.co.us/educatoreffectiveness/mslguidance forteachers

Colorado Department of Education (CDE). (2013b). *Colorado growth model: Brief report student growth percentiles and FRL status.* Retrieved from www.cde.state.co.us/accountability/colorado growthmodel

Council of Chief State School Officers & National Governors Association Center. (2014). *Common core state standards initiative.* Retrieved from www.corestandards.org

Delaware Department of Education (DE DOE). (2006). *Delaware's proposal for a growth model.* Retrieved from www.doe.k12.de.us/aab/accountability/accountability.shtml

Diaz-Bilello, E. K., & Briggs, D. C. (2014). *Using Student Growth Percentiles for educator evaluations at the teacher level: Key issues and technical considerations for school districts in Colorado.* Retrieved from www.cde.state.co.us/educatoreffectiveness/studentgrowthguide

Domingue, B. (2014). Evaluating the equal-interval hypothesis with test score scales. *Psychometrika*, *79*, 1–19.

Ehlert, M., Koedel, C., Parsons, E., & Podgursky, M. (2012). *Selecting growth measures for school and teacher evaluations*. Working Paper 80. National Center for Analysis of Longitudinal Data in Educational Research. Retrieved from http://eric.ed.gov/?id=ED535515

Georgia Department of Education. (2014). *Leader keys effectiveness system: Implementation handbook*. Retrieved from www.gadoe.org/School-Improvement/Teacher-and-Leader-Effectiveness/Pages/default.aspx

Goldhaber, D., Walch, J., & Gabele, B. (2014). Does the model matter? Exploring the relationship between different student achievement-based teacher assessments. *Statistics and Public Policy*, *1*, 28–39.

Guarino, C. M., Reckase, M. D., Stacy, B. W., & Wooldridge, J. M. (2015). A comparison of growth percentile and value-added models of teacher performance. *Statistics and Public Policy*, *2*(1), 66–76.

Hall, E. (2014). *The role of a theory of action for educator evaluation systems*. Paper presented at the National Conference on Student Assessment, New Orleans, LA.

Haertel, E. (2006). Reliability. In R. L. Brennan (Ed.), *Educational measurement* (4th ed., pp. 65–110). Westport, CT: American Council on Education/Praeger.

Hoffer, T. B., Hedberg, E. C., Brown, K. L., Halverson, M. L., Reid-Brossard, P., Ho, A. D., & Furgol, K. E. (2011). *Final report on the evaluation of the Growth Model Pilot Project*. Washington, DC: U.S. Department of Education.

Holland, P. W., & Dorans, N. J. (2006). Linking and equating. In R. L. Brennan (Ed.), *Educational measurement* (4th ed., pp. 187–220). Westport, CT: American Council on Education/Praeger.

Hoover, H. D., Dunbar, S. D., & Frisbie, D. A. (2003). *The Iowa tests: Guide to development and research*. Itasca, IL: Riverside.

Jones, N. D., Buzick, H. M., & Turkan, S. (2013). Including students with disabilities and English learners in measures of educator effectiveness. *Educational Researcher*, *42*, 234–241.

Kolen, M. J. (2006). Scaling and norming. In R. L. Brennan (Ed.), *Educational measurement* (4th ed., pp. 155–186). Westport, CT: American Council on Education/Praeger.

Kolen, M. J. (2011). *Issues associated with vertical scales for PARCC assessments*. Retrieved from www.parcconline.org/sites/parcc/files/PARCCVertScal289-12-201129.pdf

Kolen, M. J., & Brennan, R. L. (2014). *Test equating, scaling, and linking* (3rd ed.). New York: Springer.

Lakin, J. M., & Young, J. W. (2013). Evaluating growth for ELL students: Implications for accountability policies. *Educational Measurement: Issues and Practice*, *32*, 11–26.

McCaffrey, D. F., Lockwood, J. R., Koretz, D., Louis, T. A., & Hamilton, L. (2004). Models for value-added modeling of teacher effects. *Journal of Educational and Behavioral Statistics*, *29*, 67–101.

McCaffrey, D. F., Castellano, K. E., & Lockwood, J. R. (2015). The impact of measurement error on the accuracy of individual and aggregate-level SGPs. *Educational Measurement: Issues and Practice*, *34*(1), 15–21.

Michell, J. (1997). Quantitative science and the definition of measurement in psychology. *British Journal of Psychology*, *88*, 355–383.

Michell, J. (2008). Is psychometrics pathological science? *Measurement: Interdisciplinary Research and Perspective*, *6*(1), 7–24.

Mislevy, R. J. (2006). Cognitive psychology and educational assessment. In R. Brennan (Ed.) *Educational measurement* (4th ed., pp. 257–306). Westport, CT: American Council on Education/Praeger.

Mosteller, F. (1958). The mystery of the missing corpus. *Psychometrika*, *23*(4), 279–289.

Partnership for Assessment of Readiness for College and Careers (PARCC). (2014). *The PARCC assessment*. Retrieved from www.parcconline.org/parcc-assessment

R Core Team. (2015). *R: A language and environment for statistical computing* [computer software]. Vienna, Austria: R Foundation for Statistical Computing.

Rogosa, D., Brandt, D., & Zimowski, M. (1982). A growth curve approach to the measurement of change. *Psychological Bulletin, 92,* 726–748.

Shepard, L. (2012). *Evaluating the use of tests to measure teacher effectiveness: Validity as a theory-of-action framework.* Paper presented at the annual meeting of the National Council on Measurement in Education, Vancouver, British Columbia. Retrieved from www.cde.state.co.us/sites/default/files/NCME%202012%20Validity%20for%20Teacher%20Evaluation.pdf

Singer, J. D., & Willett, J. B. (2003). *Applied longitudinal data analysis: Modeling change and event occurrence.* New York: Oxford University Press.

Smarter Balanced Assessment Consortium (SBAC). (2014). *Smarter balanced assessments.* Retrieved from www.smarterbalanced.org/smarter-balanced-assessments

United States Department of Education (USDoE). (2009). *Race to the Top program: Executive summary.* Retrieved from www2.ed.gov/programs/racetothetop/executive-summary.pdf

United States Department of Education (USDoE). (2012). *ESEA flexibility.* Retrieved from www2.ed.gov/policy/elsec/guid/esea-flexibility/index.html

Walsh E., & Isenberg, E. (2015). How does a value-added model compare to the Colorado growth model? *Statistics and Public Policy, 2*(1), 53–65.

Wright, S. P. (2010). *An investigation of two nonparametric regression models for value-added assessment in education.* SAS White Paper. Retrieved from www.sas.com/whitepapers/indexAZ.html

Yen, W. M. (1986). The choice of scale for educational measurement: An IRT perspective. *Journal of Educational Measurement, 23*(4), 299–325.

9 Testing Individuals in Special Populations

Elizabeth A. Stone and Linda L. Cook[1]

Introduction

Test fairness has been a topic of central importance to test developers, test takers, and those who use test scores for many decades. The notion of what constitutes fair assessment has evolved over time and has psychometric, societal, and legal connotations. (See Phillips, this volume, Chapter 13, and Zwick & Dorans, this volume, Chapter 14, for a more extensive discussion of these factors.) In the most recent revision of the *Standards for Educational and Psychological Testing* (American Educational Research Association, American Psychological Association, & National Council on Measurement in Education, 2014), the connection between validity and fairness is emphasized in the text of Chapter 3, "Fairness in Testing." To quote the Standards, "Fairness is a fundamental validity issue and requires attention throughout all stages of test development and use" (p. 49). That is, unless one can be assured that an individual's test score is a bias-free measure of that individual's knowledge, skills, or abilities relevant to what is intended to be measured by the test, the resulting score will not be comparable with other resulting scores. Further, interpretation of the score for the original, intended use cannot be considered valid.

The fair and valid assessment of individuals in special populations can be challenging and requires creative approaches and careful planning to carry out adequately. Characteristics of individuals with disabilities or English learners (ELs), if not taken into consideration, could give rise to construct-irrelevant variance in test scores and thus disadvantage, or in some cases advantage, the individual test taker. Individuals with disabilities may have access limitations (difficulty accessing components of a test or testing process) that result from specific characteristics associated with their disability. Because of these limitations, assessment can be challenging for several reasons. For example, changes to testing conditions may help test takers to overcome barriers to demonstrating proficiency; however, some test changes may alter the construct being measured, leading to incomparable scores. By changes to testing conditions, we mean accommodations or modifications[2] and assistive technology. Similarly, individuals who are ELs face access limitations and may also use accommodations or modifications that could have an impact on the construct being assessed. In any discussion of the characteristics of individuals with disabilities and ELs, it is important to recognize that the two groups differ greatly from each other and also to recognize the heterogeneity within each of the two groups. Unfortunately, it is often the case that those interested in testing these two groups fail to take into account the differences between the needs of the two groups as well as the differences between the needs of the individuals that comprise the two groups. In particular, policymakers often fail to recognize the differences between these two groups and the heterogeneity within the groups and set policy that is less effective because it fails to take into account these differences.

Students with disabilities can have one or more of any number of disabilities such as medical, psychiatric, vision, hearing, physical, learning, and so forth. Each of these conditions may give rise to different barriers to fair assessment in a testing situation. As a further complication, a group of students may be classified, for example, as deaf; however, within this group, an individual's hearing may range from mildly hard of hearing to profoundly deaf. Students who are hard of hearing may be highly proficient in speaking, writing, and reading English, whereas a profoundly deaf individual may consider American Sign Language (ASL) to be their first language and may be less proficient in English than they are in ASL. These differences related to an individual's level of hearing will have a large influence on appropriate instruction, testing, and the type of accommodations or modifications that will be most useful.

Similarly, ELs are a very diverse group of individuals with different gifts, educational needs, cultural backgrounds, and levels of language proficiency. Some ELs come from homes where no English is spoken and some come from homes where only English is spoken; other students have been exposed to or use multiple languages. Some ELs live in communities that are strongly influenced by a single non-English-speaking culture where others live in communities where they are surrounded by non-EL families.

A challenging aspect of both instructing and testing ELs is that of understanding the implications of the lack of proficiency in English for both of these processes. According to the *Standards for Educational and Psychological Testing* (AERA et al., 2014):

> Individuals who differ culturally and linguistically from the majority of the test takers are at risk for inaccurate score interpretations because of multiple factors associated with the assumption that, absent language proficiency issues, these individuals have developmental trajectories comparable to those of individuals who have been raised in an environment mediated by a single language and culture.
>
> (p. 53)

In the United States, ELs are often treated as learners of English as a foreign language. The fact that developing a language and receiving formal instruction in a language are different processes, and the implications of this difference for instruction and testing, are rarely acknowledged.

In this chapter, we focus on ELs in the United States; however, many of the same fairness issues exist for linguistic minorities in other settings. The chapter begins by establishing an historical perspective on standardized testing and the education and testing of individuals with disabilities and individuals who are ELs. After establishing a perspective on fair assessment for these two groups, we provide a state-of-the-art summary of how to design and develop these assessments. This section of the chapter is followed by a discussion of administering tests and reporting scores to these individuals and other score users. The chapter concludes with a discussion of the importance of, and methods for, gathering evidence of the fairness and validity of assessments given to individuals from special populations.

Historical Perspective: Standardized Testing

Issues related to fairness in testing occur in a social context and often evolve or change over time. Ability and achievement tests, like those used in educational settings, are used for a number of purposes (e.g., to enhance learning and to support instruction). While they are typically intended to provide a measure of a specific ability or achievement, these tests are sometimes used as a factor in distributing resources such as admission to a college. Prior to the increased use of standardized assessments in the United States (before the early 1930s), most high-stakes decisions such as college admissions were made in the absence of objective measures and these decisions were often seen as both capricious and elitist (Conant, 1964). Standardized tests increasingly became viewed by stakeholders around the 1930s as a means of providing objective information that could be used as an aid in making fair decisions for a number of purposes.

As the use of standardized tests increased in areas such as employment, counseling, licensing, and education, and as test takers became increasingly diverse, educators as well as policymakers began questioning whether or not test results were fair and equitable for all subgroups of the test-taking population. Concern about the fairness of tests for subgroups in the United States initially focused on ethnic and racial groups but was later expanded to consider gender, and more recently has been expanded to include groups characterized by disabilities and diverse linguistic and cultural backgrounds.

Many of the initial concerns for fairness in education and testing in the United States found their roots in the Civil Rights movement of the 1960s. The 1960s were years in the United States that were marked with strife, including the Vietnam War and the assassination of national leaders such as John F. Kennedy, Martin Luther King Jr., and Robert F. Kennedy. During this period, education was at the forefront of most political agendas. The Civil Rights Act of 1964 (Pub. L. 88-352, 78 Stat. 241) outlawed discrimination based on race, color, religion, sex, or national origin. This Act was supplemented by Title IX of the Education Amendments Act of 1972 (Pub. L. 92-318, 86 Stat. 235), which prohibits sex discrimination in federally funded education programs and activities.

It was not until the mid-1970s that education of individuals with disabilities became more physically integrated with the mainstream classroom and more focused on the general classroom curriculum. The lives of children with disabilities were significantly changed by the passage of important legislation such as Section 504 of the Rehabilitation Act of 1973 (Pub. L. 93-112, Stat. 355), the Education of All Handicapped Children Act, passed in 1975 (Pub. L. 94-142), the passage of the Individuals with Disabilities Education Act in 1990 (IDEA: Pub. L. 1010476, 104 Stat. 1148), the reauthorization of this Act in 1997, and the passage of the No Child Left Behind Act in 2002 (NCLB: Pub. L. 107-110). This legislation attempted to assure that students with disabilities in the K-12 system receive appropriate accommodations during standardized testing (IDEA), and that all students between grades 3 and 12, regardless of disability or language proficiency, be tested to measure annual yearly progress (AYP) in the areas of reading and math (NCLB). It should be pointed out that even though the original NCLB accountability requirements have been modified somewhat, the requirement to include all students with disabilities and ELs in accountability testing with appropriate accommodations and to report their scores by subgroup to the public has remained unchanged.

Fairness and Testing Special Populations

The conceptualization of fairness as a fundamental validity issue has led testing professionals to emphasize that fairness to all individuals in the intended population of test takers, including individuals with disabilities and ELs, is an overriding foundational concern in the testing process. This perspective has led to the search for principles in the design, development, administration, and use of tests that minimize the possibility that test-taker characteristics (unrelated to the construct measured by the test) could give rise to construct-irrelevant variance in test scores and consequently interfere with the validity of test score interpretations. A common perspective among measurement practitioners is that a test that is fair measures the same construct(s) for all test takers and that scores from a fair test have the same meaning for all individuals in the intended population (Willingham & Cole, 1997). A frequently held belief is that a fair test does not advantage or disadvantage some individuals because of characteristics they may have that are irrelevant to the construct the test is intended to measure (AERA et al., 2014). Tests that reflect this perspective on fairness consider, to the degree possible, characteristics of all individuals in the intended test population throughout all stages of test development, administration, scoring, interpretation, and use so that barriers to fair assessment related to individual characteristics can be reduced. This conceptualization of the test design and test development process as considering the characteristics of all individuals in the intended test population is commonly referred to as Universal Design. (See Thurlow et al., 2009, for a discussion of the application of Universal Design to reading assessments for individuals with disabilities.)

A concept associated with fairness in testing that has become salient over the past few years is the concept of an accessible assessment (Thurlow et al., 2009). Accessibility is the idea that all individuals should have an opportunity to demonstrate their knowledge and skills on a construct of interest without having to overcome barriers that may arise in the testing situation. For example, if an individual who does not read English well is asked to take a mathematics test that is administered in English, he or she may perform poorly on the test because of insufficient English skills and not because of insufficient knowledge of mathematics. One way to increase the accessibility of the assessment and, consequently, to obtain a more valid measure of the mathematics construct (if the construct does not include a specific level of English language skill) might be to reduce the complexity of the language used on the mathematics test (Abedi, Hofstetter, & Lord, 2004).

A discussion of accessibility as it influences fairness titled "Fairness as Access to the Construct" has been added to the 2014 revision of the *Standards for Educational and Psychological Testing* (AERA et al., 2014). According to the Standards:

> Accessible testing situations are those that enable all test takers in the intended population, to the extent feasible, to show their status on the target construct(s) without being unduly advantaged or disadvantaged by individual characteristics (e.g., characteristics related to age, disability, race/ethnicity, gender or language) that are irrelevant to the construct(s) the test is intended to measure.
>
> (p. 52)

The notion that tests should be designed and developed with all intended members of the testing population in mind (including individuals with disabilities and ELs) is a very powerful one and requires, among other things, that careful thought be given to the construct(s) the test is intended to measure, as well as the format and administration of the test from the perspective of the intended test taker. For example, suppose a reading comprehension test is being designed, and it is decided that the construct of reading comprehension includes the skill of decoding printed words. If the intended population for the test includes individuals with visual impairments, they may need to use a screen reader in order to access the text of the reading passages. If the construct of reading comprehension has been defined as including decoding skills, the use of a screen reader will cause the construct to be underrepresented and invalidate the scores of individuals who use this accommodation. If the construct does not include decoding skills, the use of a screen reader will not necessarily lead to invalid inferences about the individual's reading comprehension test scores.

The importance of including both ELs and individuals with disabilities in all stages of test design and development cannot be overemphasized. For example, test developers have the responsibility of ensuring that these subgroups are included in field trials, focus groups, and cognitive interviews. Information that can be used to refine test questions, content, illustrations, and so forth should be collected early on in the test design and development process in order to promote fair testing for all individuals.

The next three sections of this chapter cover test design, development, and administration. Each section contains a discussion of how these processes influence the fairness of inferences made from test scores for individuals with disabilities and individuals who are ELs. The first topic that will be discussed is test design, particularly the use of Universal Design (UD) to increase the fairness and accessibility of an assessment.

Test Design and Fairness

As mentioned previously, tests that support fair and valid inferences about test scores are tests that minimize barriers to the construct(s) the test is measuring that are associated with test-taker characteristics that are not relevant to the construct. One way to consider the characteristics of all individuals in the intended test population in the design process is through the application of the principles of UD. UD is an approach to test design adapted from the field of architecture that has as a primary goal in the testing context: the provision of the most accessible assessments possible for all test takers in the intended test population.

UD strives to enhance the fairness of an assessment by designing the test in a way that minimizes, as much as possible, barriers for all test takers in the target population. Universally designed tests are designed with the characteristics of all members of the intended population in mind (e.g., age, gender, race, ethnic or language and cultural background, socioeconomic status, or disability).

The process of UD strives to minimize challenges to the accessibility of a test by taking into account test characteristics such as the choice of content, test tasks, response procedures, and test administration procedures that may impede access to the construct for certain test takers. The principles of UD would add changes to the testing process that would be useful for all students taking the test, including both ELs and individuals with disabilities. For example, a test can be made more accessible by providing user-selected font sizes in a technology-based test, by avoiding item contexts that would likely be unfamiliar to individuals because of their cultural background, by providing extended administration time when speed is not relevant to the construct being measured, or by minimizing the linguistic load of test items intended to measure constructs other than competencies in the language in which the test is administered (Thompson, Johnstone, & Thurlow, 2002).

It is important to note that the principles of UD and the resulting changes to a test or testing procedure are not made if these changes result in a test that is not reflective of the intended construct. In addition, as noted in the Standards (AERA et al., 2014), "Although the principles of Universal Design provide a useful guide for developing assessments that reduce construct irrelevant variance, researchers are still in the process of gathering empirical evidence to support some of these principles" (p. 58).

The principles of UD and the concept of developing items and tasks that are accessible to all members of the intended test population are very appropriate if the test developer anticipates that a test is going to be translated and adapted into several languages and used with groups of ELs who differ in language and cultural background from the majority of test takers. The principles of UD can be interpreted as suggesting minimizing access challenges for groups with different linguistic and cultural backgrounds by considering test characteristics such as content, format, test tasks, response procedures, and testing procedures that might present barriers to these groups at the design stage. Consequently, UD would require identifying the characteristics of the test takers in the different language and cultural groups and considering at the design stage of any assessment that will be translated and adapted into different languages how these characteristics will influence the interaction of test taker and test.

It is important to point out that the concepts of UD and accessibility go hand in hand. UD focuses on designing tests that maximize accessibility (i.e., minimize construct-irrelevant variance while avoiding construct underrepresentation) for all individuals in the intended population of test takers. The connection between accessibility, UD, and validity becomes clear if one thinks of these two concepts (accessibility and UD) as describing ways of reducing a fundamental threat to validity, construct-irrelevant variance. The reader is directed to Zieky (this volume, Chapter 2) for further discussion of fairness and test design. The next section of the chapter contains a discussion of the impact of the test development process on the fairness of the interpretations of test scores.

Test Development and Fairness

A significant threat to fair and valid interpretations of test scores for individuals with disabilities and ELs is the introduction, through the test development process, of test characteristics that may produce construct-irrelevant variance in test scores in a way that systematically lowers or raises scores for these test takers. These undesirable test characteristics may have a variety of causes such as inappropriate sampling of test content, inappropriate choice of task or item format, lack of clarity in test directions, or test questions or tasks with complexities that are unrelated to the construct being measured (Thurlow et al., 2009). In order to minimize the possibility that the test development process may introduce test characteristics that give rise to barriers for test takers in the intended test population, it is not enough simply to exercise care in the development of the items, tasks, and tests. The test developer also needs to try out the items and test and collect empirical information about their behavior when they are administered to subgroups of the population.

Test Content

Construct-irrelevant variance in test scores that may result in inferences that lack fairness and validity could be related to test content that differentially favors individuals from some subgroups over others. For example, a test that has been developed to measure critical reading should not include vocabulary that is associated with a particular occupation (e.g., technical terms that would require experience with or special training in the occupation), cultural background, socioeconomic status, ethnic group, or geographical location (unless this vocabulary can be justified as necessary to measure the intended construct). Failure to guard against this situation in the test development stage could lead to a confounding of the construct (the ability to read critically) with a test taker's prior knowledge and/or experience and is likely to advantage or disadvantage test takers from particular subgroups, such as individuals with disabilities or ELs who may not have the same background or experience as the majority of test takers.

Also, test content or situations that could be offensive or emotionally disturbing to some test takers should be avoided because they may affect a test taker's ability to engage with the test and to demonstrate his or her true level of skill or knowledge of the construct the test is measuring. An example of content that could be considered insensitive to test takers with visual impairments is the use of a poem such as "The Blind Men and the Elephant" by John Godfrey Saxe (see, e.g., Gardner, 1992, pp. 149–150), which describes the futile attempts of six blind men to identify an elephant based on separately feeling different parts of the elephant.

One way to guard against the inclusion of content in tests that may be unfair to some individuals with disabilities or ELs is to ask qualified persons to review the test content as well as the test tasks and test items. An effective practice for test developers is to employ independent panels of experts to review test and item content and format. These experts should be familiar with the characteristics of individuals with disabilities or ELs related to their linguistic or cultural background, disability, or other characteristics that may affect their performance on the test. The reviewers could look for content that may be inappropriate, confusing, or may function differently for these groups of examinees. The expert panel would be used to review test content for language, illustrations, graphics, examples, and other materials that might be more familiar to some groups of test takers than to other groups. The panel would also look for test material that might be interpreted differently by members of different subgroups or that might be offensive or emotionally disturbing to some test takers. (See Zieky, this volume, Chapter 2 or Thurlow et al., 2009, for an elaboration on the use of panels to promote fairness in the review process.)

The previous points about test content are particularly pertinent to the development of tests that may someday be translated or adapted for administration to groups of ELs with diverse linguistic or cultural backgrounds. If a test may someday be translated and adapted for administration in multiple languages, it is very important for the test developer to consider aspects of the group's culture or experience that might give rise to construct-irrelevant variance in the test scores if not addressed in the test development stage. For example, paying attention to the vocabulary used in a reading test that will be translated and adapted to ensure that this vocabulary will be accessible to different groups with different language and cultural backgrounds is an important consideration. (See ITC, 2010, and Sireci, Rios, & Powers, this volume, Chapter 10, for a more extensive discussion of test translation and adaptation.) In addition, consideration should be given to what might be emotionally disturbing or sensitive test material for the particular groups that are the target of the translation and adaptation, when deciding on the initial content of the test.

One accessibility approach that is used for tests with nonnative speakers of English is that of linguistic modification, in which the English language that is used is modified to be as simple as possible in structure, syntax, and vocabulary where there is no conflict with measurement of the construct. (See Abedi et al., 2004, for a discussion of the use of linguistic modification to improve accessibility of test items for ELs.)

Item and Task Format

The format of test items and the complexity of test tasks can also have an influence on the fairness and validity of inferences made from test scores. This may be particularly true for subgroups of the population such as test takers with disabilities and ELs. For example, a particular item type might require a level of fine motor coordination that not all examinees responding to the item possess. If this were the case, test takers who lack the level of fine-motor coordination required by the item would have a more difficult experience with the item than would other test takers. Or, an item intended to measure English language skills could be differentially difficult for ELs if it required the individual to read a train schedule. It could be that the EL is not as familiar with the format of train schedules as native speakers of English who have had experience with reading this type of schedule. Consequently, both of these items, if included in a test for these individuals, could give rise to construct-irrelevant variance in their test scores.

Test Directions

An important part of the test development process is the creation of directions for the test. A significant source of construct-irrelevant variance in test scores may be lack of clarity in test directions. It is important for both test directions and testing procedures to be simple, clear, and intuitive. Test directions and procedures need to be understandable regardless of a test taker's skills, abilities, knowledge, language proficiency, or experience; otherwise, areas of confusion are likely to become a barrier for some test takers and not for others, making the testing process unfairly difficult for some groups of test takers. This is a particular concern for individuals with disabilities or who are ELs who may, for various reasons, need to have the directions read aloud to them or presented to them in a modified form (for example, the use of American Sign Language to present test directions to test takers who are deaf or hard of hearing).

Item and Task Tryouts

An important component of the test development process is item and task tryouts. These tryouts should always be carried out using samples that include test takers with disabilities and ELs if they are members of the intended test-taking population. During the item and task tryout, the statistical properties of items and tasks can be evaluated before they are used to develop final versions of the test. Item and task statistics can be compared for different subgroups of the test population to examine how the properties of the items differ when the items are administered to the subgroups. For example, when sample sizes permit and there is a reliable and appropriate stratification variable available, differential item functioning analyses can be carried out to evaluate whether or not test items or tasks are performing similarly for all subgroups of the test population. When sample sizes for some subgroups are too small to support statistical analyses (which is often the case for groups with disabilities or ELs), qualitative procedures such as cognitive labs can be used to detect items or tasks that may lead to construct-irrelevant variance in the test scores for these test takers. We discuss these analyses and other methods of gathering fairness and validity evidence in the final section of the chapter.

If a test is being translated and adapted into several languages, it is important to carry out analyses of the items and tasks in order to demonstrate measurement equivalence for the different language and cultural groups that are the target of the translation and adaptation. (See Sireci, Rios, & Powers, this volume, Chapter 10, for an expanded discussion of test translation and adaptation.)

Test Tryouts

Statistical information such as test difficulty, reliability, and speededness that indicate how the items and tasks function as an intact test should be collected in field trials that include individuals with disabilities and ELs. There should be specific analyses carried out during these field trials that focus on whether there are aspects of the test design, item format, or test content that might give rise to barriers in the testing process that could lead to inferences from the test scores that lack validity or fairness for these test takers. When sample sizes are large enough, test properties such as reliability and speededness should be evaluated and compared for relevant subgroups. It is particularly important to include studies of fairness and validity for subgroups early on in the test development process.

It is also important to field trial test directions and test administration procedures, particularly procedures that might be used to administer any accommodations or modifications that are intended for use with the test. In addition, if a test has been adapted and translated into multiple languages, it is important to field trial the test directions and test administration procedures with language and cultural groups that make up the intended testing population. For further discussion of fairness and test development procedures, see Zieky (this volume, Chapter 2).

In the next section of this chapter, we focus on fairness for individuals with disabilities and ELs and the test administration process.

Test Administration and Fairness

Even if a test has been developed with fairness in mind, there are still challenges to fairness in terms of the accessibility of the test administration and score reporting. First, a test taker must be able to access the test registration materials and complete registration. Further, as stated in the *Standards for Educational and Psychological Testing* (AERA et al., 2014), fairness requires that all test takers have access to test preparation materials that are provided. For example, where possible, any materials should be available in Braille format for test takers who are blind, in large print for test takers who are visually impaired, and so forth. Individuals who are not native English speakers should have access to test preparation materials in their own languages, if possible. The accessibility of websites and other sources of test information is also important.

Nowhere else in the testing process is the conceptualization of fairness as comparable treatment of test takers more apparent than in the test administration process. There are many components of test administration (e.g., access to test content, test materials, and test sites) that can result in test takers being treated differently with a possibly negative impact on the validity and fairness of inferences made from their test scores. As just mentioned, reasonable access to the test administration site is an important aspect of fairness in testing. This implies, for example, that test sites that are inaccessible to test takers who require the use of a wheelchair be supplemented by alternate testing locations in a reasonably similar proximity. Some other components of the test administration process that have the potential to impact accessibility and, consequently, the fairness of inferences made from test scores are test security procedures, the use of technology to administer tests, testing conditions at test administration sites, and test accommodations and modifications. The goal of administering tests that are equally accessible and provide comparable measurement for all groups is important to strive for but may not always be achieved due to the numerous practical constraints and trade-offs that must occur.

The potential for each of the components of the test administration process to give rise to construct-irrelevant variance that systematically advantages or disadvantages some groups of test takers will be discussed next.

Test Security

Test security is one aspect of the test administration process that has important implications for the fair and valid interpretations of test scores. A test taker's score can only provide the basis for valid inferences about the test taker's knowledge, skills, and abilities if the score has been earned fairly (i.e., in the absence of cheating). Any form of cheating on a test such as copying, impersonation, and prior knowledge of the test content reduces the fairness and validity of the inferences made from the test scores. When tests are administered with accommodations and modifications, it is important to ensure that the same level of test security is enforced. However, test security concerns should not interfere with the appropriate administration of accommodations. Both forethought and a delicate balance are required to ensure that appropriate accommodations are administered without compromising any test materials. For example, test takers who need to take their tests in a separate setting from other test takers will require extra proctors so that they will be monitored just as carefully as the other test takers. These proctors, similarly, should have been carefully vetted and trained in the administration of accommodations. Additionally, care should be taken that materials that are provided beyond the typical test-taking materials (e.g., embossed Braille or other printed supports) are collected at the end of the testing session. A final area of test security that is on the rise for individuals who require accommodations and modifications is the challenge of how to individualize administration (e.g., through a bring-your-own-device approach) while ensuring that confidential test materials remain secure. (See Lazarus, Thurlow, Dominguez, Kincaid, and Edwards, 2014, for an examination of state policies regarding test security and the administration of accommodations, and the chapter by Wollack and Case, this volume, Chapter 3, for a comprehensive discussion of test security issues and fairness.)

Use of Technology to Administer Tests

Use of technology to administer tests raises particular concerns for the comparable treatment of test takers. If tests are administered using technology (e.g., computers), it is important that all test takers have access to the same or very similar equipment. Test results can be unfairly influenced if some computers are faster, newer, or have better screen resolution than others. In addition, it is important to ensure that all test takers are sufficiently familiar with the technology so that lack of familiarity with the computer used to deliver the test will not become a construct-irrelevant component in a test taker's score on the test. It should be noted that some disabilities may preclude the use of certain types of technology or that some ELs may not have the necessary experience with technology in order to be comfortable using the technology for testing. It is important to pay attention to the background and experience of the entire testing population when making decisions about appropriate technology to use for testing applications.

One issue for test takers with disabilities and ELs that computerized assessments are the ideal vehicle to address is that all tests are typically designed and developed with a target test-taking audience in mind. Individuals in special populations do not necessarily constitute the majority of this audience. Therefore, the test content, format, and difficulty level may not be well targeted for either test takers with disabilities or ELs. There are different ways to approach solving this problem. One way involves creating alternate assessments that are linked to grade-level standards but that hold students to different achievement standards. A different approach is to tailor test content based on test-taker proficiency. This is the goal behind computerized adaptive testing. This type of testing estimates test-taker proficiency after each item response and then targets the following item (in item-level) or set of items (in multi-stage) accordingly. The use of adaptive testing for individuals who may have divergent response profiles has been hypothesized as problematic (see, e.g., Stone & Davey, 2011); however, little empirical evidence currently exists to support or refute this idea.

Technology in the form of digital assessments provides additional options for fair testing for individuals in special populations, but also gives rise to additional challenges. Positive aspects include the ability to provide additional accommodations in a standardized way through the testing platform. In addition, accommodation usage can be tracked at the item level when the test is delivered electronically, which provides a mechanism for evaluating the ways that accommodations are actually used by test takers. Whether the possible benefits of technology are fully realized depends to a large extent on whether infrastructure can support the administration (e.g., available bandwidth). Administration of digital assessments requires some assumption that individuals are technologically literate enough that technical literacy will not result in an additional barrier to demonstrating proficiency. One way to consider this negative aspect as a positive is that it provides some exposure to technology, which individuals need in an increasingly technological world. A testing platform accessibility review may be performed to ensure that the accommodations presented are functioning appropriately and meet standards, and that test takers are able to navigate the system. (See Pommerich, this volume, Chapter 7, for a more extensive discussion of the fairness issues surrounding mode comparability and the research that has been done to examine these issues.)

Testing Conditions at Test Sites

Comparable treatment of test takers also requires that conditions at a test site should be reasonably comfortable (e.g., the furniture should be comfortable, the lighting adequate, the noise level low, and the temperature control adequate). Test takers have a right to expect that test administrators will be well qualified and trained and that they will administer the test and any required accommodations or modifications in a professional, sensitive and responsible manner. (See Wollack and Case, this volume, Chapter 3, for a more extensive discussion of testing conditions at test sites.)

Test Accommodations

As previously mentioned, providing fair or comparable treatment for some test takers may require a departure from standardized testing procedures; for example, the addition of test accommodations for individuals with disabilities is a common practice for most educational assessments. For some test takers with disabilities and ELs, comparable treatment at test administrations may require the provision of accommodations—changes in the test or testing procedures that are needed to overcome barriers in the test or testing process that may create construct-irrelevant variance in their test scores. An important component of a fair test administration for some individuals with disabilities or who are ELs is the use of test or testing accommodations.

The goal of test accommodations is to reduce construct-irrelevant variance in test scores and, thus, to enable test users to make comparable inferences about individuals based on their test scores. According to the *Standards for Educational and Psychological Testing* (AERA et al., 2014), this goal can be quite challenging. The Standards have the following to say about test accommodations:

> On the one hand, common, uniform procedures are a basic underpinning for score validity and comparability. On the other hand, accommodations by their very nature mean that something in the testing circumstance has been changed because adhering to the original standardized procedures would interfere with valid measurement of the intended construct(s) for some individuals.
>
> (p. 59)

The fairness of inferences made from scores obtained on accommodated tests rests on whether or not the scores measure the same construct(s) as the original test. However, the influence of accommodations on what is being measured is not always easily parsed. Consider the framework put forth by Dorans (2012). As an examinee, a test taker's true score on an item (the score we would expect from the test taker over many replications) is a function of the *construct of interest* and properties of the item. Dorans goes on to point out that the construct of interest can be replaced by the *attribute assessed*, which is a function of the construct of interest and specialized topic knowledge relevant to the item, pre-exposure to specific item material, and quality of test preparation relevant to the item. Similarly, we argue that without appropriate accommodations, the attribute assessed may be a function of some of the aspects listed by Dorans, as well as a function of the specific barrier created by the test taker's disability or other need. With appropriate accommodations, this additional influence is removed by providing access to the construct of interest. However, it should be noted that some test changes change the attribute assessed (which we refer to as the construct being measured) by acting on the construct of interest. As previously pointed out, these changes are called modifications. We discuss this distinction further with examples.

Accommodations sometimes encompass changes in the setting of the administration such as changes from a group administration to an individually administered test in order to avoid inappropriately administering the accommodation to or distracting other individuals (e.g., when a teacher must read the test aloud to a student). Accommodations can also include changes in the test presentation (e.g., administering a test in large print or Braille). Some accommodations include changes to scheduling (e.g., adding extra time to the administration of the test). Accommodations can also include changes to how an individual responds to a test item such as having a test taker circle answers directly in the test booklet rather than transfer to an answer sheet. Sometimes accommodations include adding individuals to the administration process such as a sign language interpreter or a scribe (Sireci, Scarpati, & Li, 2005).

For test takers who are ELs, accommodations may include those providing direct or indirect linguistic support. This taxonomy suggested by Rivera, Collum, Shafer Willner, and Sia (2006) distinguishes the type of accommodation based on whether it changes the text (direct) or the conditions (indirect). Which accommodation is most suitable for each test taker is strongly related to the individual test taker's background and characteristics.

In order to support fair and valid inferences from test scores, accommodations need to respond to an individual's needs (i.e., specific individual characteristics that may present barriers to testing such as low vision or a hearing disability). In addition, it is important that the accommodation removes the barrier from testing without changing the construct that is being tested or the meaning of the test scores. Accommodations should be administered in a standardized manner following well-developed procedures. In some cases, it may be necessary to train test administrators to administer accommodations. In all cases, what accommodations were used and how they were used should be documented. It is important, too, to consider whether the use of one accommodation necessitates additional test changes. This circumstance arises, for example, when test takers require parts of the test to be read aloud, need to use alternative formats such as large print, or need to make use of a bilingual dictionary or glossary. Similarly, when test material must be read aloud by a teacher or proctor, test takers may need to take the test in a separate room from the non-accommodated group in order to avoid the accommodation distracting other test takers and to avoid access to the accommodation for test takers who have not been approved to use it. In each of these cases, it may be necessary to provide extra time to complete the test, leading to a bundling of accommodations.

The term *accommodation* is often used as a catch-all to encompass the test changes previously mentioned. Some of these changes may change the construct being measured. For example, on a test designed to measure decoding of text, providing an accommodation that involves the test passages and questions being read aloud may prevent measurement of that construct. Another example is the allowance of a calculator for test takers with specific learning disabilities in mathematics on test items that measure ability to calculate as part of the construct. Test changes that change the construct measured by the test are typically referred to as modifications. Middleton and Dorans (2011) examined score equity in the presence of a modification (having a reading test read aloud) and quantified the effect on scores via correlations. For students who did not have a reading-based learning disability, the correlation between accommodated and non-accommodated scores was high (0.86–0.87 when corrected for attenuation). For students who did have a reading-based learning disability, the correlation between accommodated and non-accommodated scores was considerably lower (0.58–0.69 when corrected for attenuation). Middleton and Dorans argued that the lower correlations between tests under different accommodation conditions in the groups of students with reading-based learning disabilities indicated that the accommodation had a greater influence on the construct being measured than it did in the groups of students without learning disabilities. For English learners, modifications may include the use of glossaries that contain material related to the test content (e.g., for a science test). When modifications are used for a test, the resulting score is often not aggregated with the other scores from standard administrations from the test due to a lack of comparability. However, different states and testing agencies have different rules for what test changes are allowed on various tests and what, if any, consequences result with respect to the reporting of scores. The lack of consistency in state policies is based in part on how the construct under study is defined and can make it difficult to determine from state to state what constructs are being measured in the presence or absence of the specific test accommodations that are offered.

It is critical to ensure that tests given in different formats include the same information. For example, a review of the same test in standard paper format, large-print format, and Braille format found several differences, including different wording of directions given at the beginning of passages and the omission of some symbols and logos in the Braille form (Stone, 2007). An additional problem found in that review of test formats was that font sizes for footnotes to passages and items were not enlarged along with the rest of the text in the large-print form, and that line numbers for passages and poems in the Braille form were at times omitted or were located at a confusing distance from the body of the text. Finally, there were concerns raised about the representation of mathematical symbols in literary rather than Nemeth Braille code and whether particular Braille symbols would be familiar to target test takers. With regard to the latter issue, specifically, one symbol that is used to represent underlining or italics appeared in all items flagged as functioning differently for the Braille test takers when compared to students without disabilities taking the test under standard conditions. The test takers were fourth grade students, some of whom may not have been familiar with that symbol, and the students without disabilities performed differentially better on those items. These examples simply underscore the idea that fairness issues may arise in unexpected ways. An additional example includes scripting of mathematics test material for test takers who require the test to be read aloud, which must follow specific guidelines so that the way particular symbols or representations are read does not give away (cue) the correct answer. The potential for presenting an unfair advantage by cueing via altered intonation or pausing (e.g., lingering when reading the key, or correct option) is a concern in any human-read accommodation scenario. In this next section of the chapter, we discuss fairness for individuals with disabilities and ELs and score reporting.

Score Reporting

Two aspects of score reporting stand out as being important to evaluate for individuals from special populations. For individuals with disabilities, an historic concern has focused on whether flagging should occur. In other words, should scores from nonstandard test administrations be flagged so that those receiving and using the scores are aware of the different conditions under which the test was taken? The legal right for a testing company to flag scores obtained under an extended time accommodation has recently been struck down (see, e.g., Egelko, 2014). An argument that has been made against the practice of flagging is that test takers may not request needed accommodations if they know that their scores will be flagged because of it, because flagging essentially indicates to the score user that the test taker has a disability (see Sireci, 2005, and Phillips, this volume, Chapter 13, for a more extensive discussion of this issue).

Issues related to the use of scores are typically tied to validity; however, individual score interpretations are a matter of fairness. For English learners and other linguistic minorities, there is a legitimate concern that it is too easy to make assumptions about the role of English proficiency in demonstration of content proficiency (see, e.g., AERA et al., 2014, p. 53). For example, students who are educated in their native language, achieving subject matter proficiency, and are then tested in English will have different fairness issues to contend with than students who are educated in English, do not achieve English proficiency, and are then tested in English. The role of English proficiency in the first case may be entirely construct-irrelevant, depending on the subject matter being tested and the purpose of the test. However, limited English proficiency may have affected opportunity to learn as well as the material being tested, as well as reducing ability to demonstrate that knowledge, in the latter case. Therefore, the interpretations to be made from reported scores for ELs must be carefully considered. Further, it is important that score reports are available in a translated form, if feasible, so that parents and test takers who are not proficient in English are able to access the results.

Gathering Evidence of the Fairness and Validity of Assessments for Individuals with Disabilities and English Learners

A large portion of the evaluation of the fairness of a test administration takes place after the test has been administered and operational data have been collected. At this point, actual test-taker performance can be compared between groups to try to identify possible inequities that may not have been envisioned at earlier, pre-operational stages. While it would be impossible to evaluate performance for every possible subgroup, there are several common approaches to evaluating tests and test items for fairness issues that have been applied to individuals with disabilities and ELs. These approaches are applied to operational test data and to experimental data derived from carefully designed studies. It is important to note that there are challenges associated with using either type of data to obtain validity and fairness evidence for special populations who take tests under different testing conditions. Operational data may include individuals from the same disability or language category taking the test under various accommodations. However, it would not necessarily be appropriate to compare these groups to determine effects of the different accommodations because test takers were not assigned to those groups randomly. In other words, their assignment to use specific accommodations is based on their individual characteristics and IEPs. In order to isolate the effects of the accommodations from characteristics of test takers that might confound the inferences made from the study, experimental design can be used to assign testing conditions to randomly equivalent groups within disability or language category (see, e.g., Laitusis, 2010; Middleton & Dorans, 2011). This comes with a caveat, however—accommodations are frequently bundled in operational testing. For example, test takers who are linguistic minorities and have access to a glossary as an accommodation may require extended time as well to complete the test. Therefore, if it is to represent operational conditions, the experiment must be designed with this in mind, and all conditions must be accounted for in the design. Analysis methods for these data include differential item functioning (DIF), evaluation of item and test statistics for comparability between groups, evaluation of the appropriateness of the accommodation by testing the interaction hypothesis or differential boost hypothesis, and the investigation of test taker response processes through the use of cognitive labs. Finally, studies incorporating several of these methods can be summarized quantitatively using meta-analysis, capitalizing on the information in each study. It should be noted that while all of these procedures evaluate the effects of accommodations within groups, the appropriateness of accommodation assignments is very specific to each individual test taker.

Differential Item Functioning Analyses

Items that are problematic for a subgroup (e.g., test takers with a particular disability subtype or in a particular linguistic minority; test takers using accommodations) may be statistically flagged using DIF analysis (see Penfield, this volume, Chapter 4, for a thorough discussion of DIF). Should it be decided that DIF analyses will be carried out, there are aspects of these procedures that require specific consideration for test takers in special populations. We elaborate on several of the considerations for conducting DIF analyses presented by Penfield in the context of special populations.

Stratifying Variable

The stratifying variable used to match test takers based on their proficiency must be reliable, as noted by Penfield. The stratifying variable should also have the same factor structure (measurement invariance) for two groups that are compared, and it is useful to check that this is true prior to conducting DIF analyses. (See Liu & Dorans, this volume, Chapter 5, for a thorough explication of measurement invariance.) The test score as stratifying variable should also appropriately represent the test taker's proficiency, a more challenging claim to make when test takers in special populations are taking tests that result in scores that may be a less credible reflection of their ability than the scores of the group they are compared to. As we have discussed at length in this chapter, accommodations or other test changes may be necessary for eliminating barriers to a demonstration of proficiency for some groups of test takers. Therefore, the conditions under which the test was administered may determine whether or not the resulting score serves as a reasonable proxy of proficiency. This lends support for the use of accommodated test scores, where appropriate. However, when groups of test takers have taken a test under different conditions, it may not be appropriate to use DIF to compare their performance (Buzick & Stone, 2011). An additional possibility is the use of an external criterion for stratification in this case (see, e.g., Osterlind & Everson, 2009, for a discussion).

Sample Size

It should be noted that careful subgroup formation is important, especially in test-taking populations that are heterogeneous. While studies have, for example, grouped test takers as with or without disabilities, the membership of each subgroup is likely not described specifically enough to use as a basis for meaningful inferences. However, the more specific the group membership becomes, the smaller the resulting sample size. This can have a particularly strong impact when the subgroup of interest is a low-incidence disability subtype (e.g., visual impairments, experienced by only approximately 0.1% of the students in the United States from pre-K through twelfth grade). Further narrowing (e.g., to test takers who are blind using Braille on one particular test) may make DIF untenable because it would be impossible to obtain large enough samples to support the analyses.

Impact

Test takers in special populations may have observed proficiency distributions that are quite different than do test takers with which they are compared in the reference group. Thus, the need to evaluate and report on impact, or the difference in mean proficiency between groups, is even more important in this case. Further, it should be noted that having reduced overlap in the matching criterion distributions (e.g., different distributions over score points in the stratifying variable) will lead to even smaller sample sizes being used in the calculation of DIF statistics for some methods (e.g., Mantel-Haenszel), even if the mean proficiency scores are reasonably similar for the groups.

Interpreting the Cause of DIF

The cause of DIF for test takers in special populations may have more to do with access to the content, either physically or in terms of comprehension, than with potential bias in the item. Problematic aspects of an item may be difficult to identify, although it is often illuminating to listen to a test taker talk as they go through an item and try to solve it. This approach is part of the cognitive laboratory methodology, discussed subsequently. Either way, flagged items are typically removed from the scores of all test takers.

Comparison of Item and Test Statistics

The item-total, or point-biserial, correlation is a measure of the strength of the relationship between a given item score and the total test score. If an item is functioning appropriately and measures the construct of interest, we would expect that the tendency to answer that item correctly would be greater if the total test score were higher, and vice versa. At the test level, consistency of scores can be compared between groups by examining their reliability. Tests that are more reliable produce consistent scores across administrations and have relatively little random measurement error in the resulting scores. However, it should be noted that reliability and correlational analyses are sensitive to differences in group proficiency and should be evaluated with that caution in mind. The difficulty of the test overall provides a measure of fairness for test-taking subgroups. For example, a subgroup with scores hovering around chance level (e.g., 25 items correct on a 100-item test consisting of four-option multiple-choice items) is providing proficiency information about that subgroup of questionable value. While it is possible that the scores accurately reflect proficiency, it may alternatively be the case that either the subgroup has not mastered the test material or that the test takers are unable to access the test appropriately (and may need accommodations to help remove that obstacle). Thus, test difficulty (and, more specifically, item difficulty) that varies markedly by subgroup can be a red flag that there is construct-irrelevant variance contributing to the scores and that further investigation is warranted. Visual inspection via scatterplots also provides evidence of fairness across groups relative to item difficulty without the need for strong assumptions about consistency of overall test performance.

Predictive Validity

One measure of fairness for subgroups can be obtained by comparing consequential validity measures such as predictive validity for the groups. The underlying concept is that if a test is valid for two subgroups of the intended testing audience, the test scores that result should lead to the same consequences for the groups. One example is the evaluation of college admissions scores for test takers without disabilities versus test takers who are blind or visually impaired and require a Braille test form. If the test is fair for both groups, the regression of first-year grade point average (FYGPA) in college on admissions test score should be the same (lines having the same intercept and slope) for the two groups. Alternatively, using the common line derived from regressing FYGPA on admissions test score for all test takers (or the majority group) to predict FYGPA for subgroups should not result in significant residuals (or deviations) from the regression line. These analyses are important because if it is systematically the case that test takers achieving lower test scores on average still perform at a higher level in college, there may be fairness issues for that subgroup on the admissions test that will need to be investigated. The typically smaller sample sizes for groups of test takers with disabilities, in particular, may make very specific predictive validity analyses infeasible (e.g., those focusing on low incidence disability subtypes or low incidence accommodations) depending on the size and scope of the testing population; however, research to date has included test takers with learning disabilities taking the SAT with an extended-time accommodation (Cahalan, Mandinach, & Camara, 2002) and bilingual test takers taking the SAT (Pearson, 1993). In each case, the quality of predictions of first-year college grade point average using SAT score differed between the reference and focal groups.

Interaction Hypothesis/Differential Boost Paradigm

Evidence for or against the appropriateness of test accommodations can be obtained by comparing standardized mean scores for the group of individuals to whom the test accommodations are targeted (the studied group) and a group of individuals for whom the accommodation is assumed not to be appropriate (e.g., individuals without disabilities, or native English speakers). One major impetus for this approach is the concern that providing accommodations when they may not be needed by an individual could lead to artificial score inflation due to construct underrepresentation, whereas appropriate usage of accommodations reduces construct-irrelevant variance by removing the barriers that prevent test takers from demonstrating their proficiency. Therefore, it is of interest to determine whether the impact of the accommodation differs between the studied group (e.g., students with reading-based learning disabilities) and other groups for whom the accommodation is not hypothesized to be appropriate (e.g., students without disabilities). The two most common methods of evaluating appropriateness this way focus on obtaining evidence to support or refute one of two hypotheses: (1) the interaction hypothesis; and (2) the differential boost hypothesis. Each method involves determining whether there is an interaction between the effect of the accommodation and group identity. If there is a statistically significant interaction with a non-negligible effect size, it may be inferred that the strength of the relationship between the accommodation and changes in performance depends on the group. The magnitude of the effect size, which can be expressed in the test score metric, provides an indication of whether the difference between groups can be considered to be meaningful. In the presence of a significant interaction, therefore, it may be hypothesized that the accommodation is appropriate for the studied group if the score gain occurs for that group. In this case, the accommodation has a significantly greater effect for the group for whom it is hypothesized to be appropriate. The stronger of the two hypotheses requires that the studied group shows a significant boost from the accommodation (boost is measured as the accommodated minus the standard score) and the reference group shows no significant boost (*interaction hypothesis*) (see, e.g., Sireci et al., 2005). A weaker version allows both groups to have significant boosts but requires the boost for the studied group to be significantly greater than that for the reference group (*differential boost hypothesis*) (see, e.g., Cahalan-Laitusis, 2007; Fuchs & Fuchs, 1999). Note that if one of the groups under comparison has many test takers achieving very high scores, there may be a ceiling effect that prevents an accurate comparison of score gain between the groups. Laitusis (2010) reports that controlling for this by removing top performers did not lead to a change in the differential boost findings from that study. As was noted previously in the section on differential item functioning, it is critical to define the groups under comparison in a way that captures the differences of interest. For example, when comparing group performance with or without a read-aloud accommodation, the definition of the studied group should include a reading-based learning disability that includes a decoding deficit.

Cognitive Labs, Usability Studies, Surveys, and Focus Groups

Qualitative evidence of validity in the form of test-taker response processes can be obtained via interviews, surveys, focus groups, and cognitive laboratory techniques. These approaches may be useful for obtaining validity and fairness evidence when sample sizes are too small to allow for quantitative approaches; further, they are often only feasible if sample sizes are small enough because they are so time-intensive. While it is within the researcher's or practitioner's control to limit sample sizes to fit time constraints, the resulting information provided by the sample may not be generalizable if the study is not carefully designed and the sample and task content representative. The general cognitive lab methodology encompasses several specific methods, including think-aloud studies, cognitive interviews, and usability studies. These methods serve different roles in ascertaining whether a test is functioning fairly. Think-aloud studies use protocols in which test takers are encouraged to vocalize what they are thinking as they answer a test question. This provides information about their thought processes and evidence of whether the cognitive processes actually used are in line with those that should be enacted in order to obtain a valid measure of proficiency on the construct. For example, if a test taker is able to solve a problem by using some piece of knowledge or information irrelevant to the construct, there is evidence of construct-irrelevant variance present in the item, and the conclusions that can be drawn from a correct response are less obvious than if that were not the case. However, it can be difficult to explain one's thought process while that thinking is taking place. Therefore, cognitive interviews consisting of post hoc questions are often paired with the think-aloud protocol to allow test takers to reflect back and add to or clarify their thoughts on the test questions. Usability studies have a different focus. For those studies, with respect to special populations, we are usually interested in whether and how well individuals in the studied group are as able to navigate the test and its content. These studies can bring to light access issues that might not be obvious when just evaluating the test or platform design in the abstract. Surveys and focus groups can also be used to gather evidence of how test scores will be used, and consequently may be an important component of validity.

Meta-Analysis

One of the difficulties associated with analyzing experimental data for individuals with disabilities is the relatively small sample sizes that can typically be obtained by researchers. This leads to low power for the statistics that are used to detect differences. When we talk about statistical power, we mean the power of a statistical test to reject the null hypothesis. For example, if one were interested in comparing group means (e.g., of test scores for individuals with and without disabilities), one might choose to use a t-test. To determine the sample sizes required to result in power of 0.80 for this test, one could come up with an idea of what means and standard deviations are expected to be found based on previous analyses or theory and then calculate the required sample sizes to detect the resulting proposed difference. Unfortunately, there is a lot of interesting research on individuals with disabilities and ELs that was not designed with statistical power in mind; therefore, these studies suffer on their own from not being able to test what they are trying to test. Meta-analysis combines across studies to capitalize on information from each of them, weighting them (typically) by the sample sizes used, which is a proxy for the reliability of the information obtained. Average effect sizes can then be used to compare, for example, the effects of a particular accommodation in two different groups. As with investigations geared toward evaluating the interaction hypothesis or differential boost hypothesis, the magnitudes of the effect sizes can provide evidence to support or refute the appropriateness of the accommodation.

One of the main challenges with using meta-analysis to evaluate the appropriateness of accommodations is the question of whether or not to include non-peer-reviewed resources such as dissertations. These documents may include current and innovative research to answer these questions, particularly for research on accommodations that can differ significantly in implementation and can interact very differently with different test content; however, without the benefit of a peer-reviewed evaluation of the study design and methodology, any results may be questionable. An additional challenge specific to combining research studies focused on individuals in special populations using accommodations is that appropriate and effective analysis requires substantial information about the study design, instruments, and administration. For example, in an analysis of the read-aloud accommodation, it is important to know what parts of the test were read aloud, what specific constructs the test was designed to measure, how the read-aloud accommodation was administered, and details about test taker characteristics (e.g., specific disability subtype or language deficit), among other information. These particulars are often not included in published research to the extent desirable for categorizing and combining across studies.

Examples of meta-analysis studies evaluating accommodations (e.g., English dictionary or glossary, simplified English, bilingual dictionary or glossary, Spanish version, dual-language booklet, dual-language questions and read aloud in Spanish, and extra time) for test takers who are ELs include Francis, Rivera, Lesaux, Kieffer, and Rivera (2006), Kieffer, Lesaux, Rivera, and Francis (2009), and Pennock-Roman and Rivera (2011). Studies using meta-analysis methods to evaluate accommodations (e.g., extra time, read aloud) for test takers with disabilities include Gregg and Nelson (2012), Buzick and Stone (2014), and Li (2014). From each of these meta-analysis studies, a common theme arises about the importance of individual studies providing detailed information about test takers, tests, and accommodations for the purposes of drawing inferences about accommodation effects. Without this detailed information (e.g., about accommodation administration mode, specific disability subtype, linguistic background, details about test content as it might relate to accommodation effects), the challenges of drawing accurate inferences arise as in single studies and are compounded in a meta-analysis. One way that this deficient information affects the meta-analysis is in the unexplained variance due to these factors when they are not taken into account, weakening the statistical evidence.

Qualitative reviews of the accumulated literature on various accommodations for groups of test takers in special populations can provide very useful and effective tools for providing a comprehensive picture for informing implementation and policy. See Laitusis, Buzick, Stone, Hansen, and Hakkinen (2012), which provided critical analyses of studies focused on accommodations for students with disabilities for use in shaping accommodation policy. See also Abedi and Ewers (2013) for an evaluation of the validity and effectiveness of several EL accommodations with recommendations for usage and future research. However, while qualitative overviews do not directly make use of the data, meta-analysis (see, e.g., Hedges & Olkin, 1985) is able to do just that, making it a powerful tool for assessing fairness based on what is observed in practice.

Chapter Summary

We began this chapter by establishing an historical context for exploring fairness in testing individuals with disabilities and English learners. We noted that many individuals with disabilities have only recently, since the mid-1970s, been taught in classrooms in public schools along with students who do not have disabilities. We also noted the significant impact that the passage of NCLB legislation in 2002 has had on the inclusion of both individuals with disabilities and ELs in assessments used for public education accountability.

We discussed the concept of accessible assessments and how this concept plays an important role in the assessment of both individuals with disabilities and ELs. Accessibility is the idea that all individuals should have an opportunity to demonstrate their knowledge and skills on a construct of interest without having to overcome barriers that may arise in the testing situation. The importance of considering the characteristics of all test takers in the intended population, particularly individuals with disabilities and ELs, was emphasized.

We pointed out that one way to consider the characteristics of all individuals in the intended test population in the design process is through the application of the principles of Universal Design (UD). UD strives to enhance the fairness of an assessment by designing the test in a way that minimizes, as much as possible, barriers for all test takers in the target population.

We noted that the concepts of UD and accessibility go hand in hand. UD focuses on designing tests that maximize accessibility for as many individuals in the intended population of test takers as possible. We pointed out that the connection between accessibility, UD, and validity becomes clear if one thinks of these two concepts (accessibility and UD) as describing ways of reducing a fundamental threat to validity, construct-irrelevant variance.

We discussed developing fair and valid tests and emphasized that a significant threat to fair and valid interpretations of test scores for many individuals with disabilities and ELs is the introduction through the test development process, of test characteristics that may produce construct-irrelevant variance in test scores in a way that systematically lowers or raises scores for individuals with disabilities and/or ELs. We talked about factors that may precipitate construct-irrelevant variance in test scores such as inappropriate sampling of test content, inappropriate choice of task or item format, lack of clarity in test directions or test questions, or tasks with complexities that are unrelated to the construct being measured.

We emphasized that even if a test has been developed with fairness in mind, there are still challenges to fairness in terms of the accessibility of the test administration and score reporting. First, a test taker must be able to access the test registration materials and complete registration. Further, fairness requires that all test takers have access to test preparation materials that are provided. Reasonable access to the test administration site is an important aspect of fairness in testing. This implies, for example, that test sites that are inaccessible to test takers who require the use of a wheelchair be supplemented by alternate testing locations in a reasonably similar proximity.

We pointed out that providing fair or comparable treatment for some test takers may require a departure from standardized testing procedures; for example, the addition of test accommodations or modifications. For test takers with disabilities, comparable treatment at test administrations may require the provision of accommodations that are needed to overcome barriers in the test or testing process that may create construct-irrelevant variance in their test scores. An important component of a fair test administration for some individuals with disabilities or who are ELs is the use of test or testing accommodations or modifications.

We talked about score reporting for individuals with disabilities and ELs. We pointed out the importance of providing score reports in translated form so that test takers, their parents, or interested parties who are not proficient in English will be able to access the assessment results.

Finally, we discussed gathering evidence that inferences made from scores on assessments given to special populations are fair and valid. We talked about a variety of methods that can be used to demonstrate the equivalence of assessment results when the assessments are given to different subgroups of the testing population.

We are hopeful that this chapter illustrates both the extensive progress that has been made in providing fair and valid assessments to members of special populations over the past few years, but that it also highlights some of the work that remains to be done. Designing, developing, and validating assessments for special populations can be challenging and requires creative approaches and careful planning to carry out adequately. However, we believe it is the right of all members of the testing population to expect fair treatment throughout the entire testing process. To quote the *Standards for Educational and Psychological Testing* (AERA et al., 2014), "fairness is a fundamental issue for valid test score interpretation, and it should therefore be the goal for all testing applications. Fairness is the responsibility of all parties involved in test development, administration, and score interpretation" (p. 62).

Notes

1. The views expressed are those of the authors and not necessarily those of the Educational Testing Service.
2. In this chapter, we follow the definition of accommodations and modifications put forth in the 2014 edition of the *Standards for Educational and Psychological Testing* (AERA et al., 2014). Scores on tests taken with accommodations yield inferences that are comparable to inferences obtained from scores on the standard version. Scores on tests that are the result of modifications measure a different construct than that measured by the standard version of the test.

References

Abedi, J., & Ewers, N. (2013). *Accommodations for English language learners and students with disabilities: A research-based decision algorithm*. Olympia, WA: Office of the Superintendent of Public Instruction, Smarter Balanced Assessment Consortium.

Abedi, J., Hofstetter, C. H., & Lord, C. (2004). Assessment accommodations for English language learners: Implications for policy-based empirical research. *Review of Educational Research, 74*(1), 1–28.

American Educational Research Association, American Psychological Association, & National Council on Measurement in Education. (2014). *Standards for educational and psychological testing*. Washington, DC: American Educational Research Association.

Buzick, H., & Stone, E. (2011). *Recommendations for conducting differential item functioning (DIF) analyses for students with disabilities based on previous DIF studies* (ETS RR-11–34). Princeton, NJ: Educational Testing Service.

Buzick, H., & Stone, E. (2014). A meta-analysis of research on the read aloud accommodation. *Educational Measurement: Issues and Practice, 33*(3), 17–30.

Cahalan, C., Mandinach, E. B., & Camara, W. J. (2002). *Predictive validity of SAT(r) I: Reasoning Test for test-takers with learning disabilities and extended time accommodations* (ETS Research Report Series ETS RR-02-11). Princeton, NJ: Educational Testing Service.

Cahalan-Laitusis, C. (2007). Validity and accommodations: A variety of approaches to accessible assessments. In C. Cahalan-Laitusis & L. L. Cook (Eds.), *Large scale assessment and accommodations: What works* (pp. 71–83). Washington, DC: Council for Exceptional Children.

Conant, J. B. (1964). *Shaping educational policy*. New York: McGraw-Hill.

Dorans, N. J. (2012). The contestant perspective on taking tests: Emanations from the statue within. *Educational Measurement: Issues and Practice, 31*(4), 20–37.

Egelko, B. (2014). *Disabled law students settle suit over admissions tests*. Retrieved from www.sfgate.com/education/article/Disabled-law-students-settle-suit-over-admissions-5492705.php

Francis, D. J., Rivera, M., Lesaux, N., Kieffer, M., & Rivera, H. (2006). Research-based recommendations for the use of accommodations in large-scale assessments. *Practical Guidelines for the Education of English Language Learners. Book 3 of 3.* Houston, TX: Texas Institute for Measurement, Evaluation, and Statistics, University of Houston, Center on Instruction.

Fuchs, L. S., & Fuchs, D. (1999). Fair and unfair testing accommodations. *School Administrator, 56*(10), 24.

Gardner, M. (Ed.). (1992). *Best remembered poems*, Mineola, NY: Courier Dover Publications.

Gregg, N., & Nelson, J. M. (2012). Meta-analysis on the effectiveness of extra time as a test accommodation for transitioning adolescents with learning disabilities: More questions than answers. *Journal of Learning Disabilities, 45*(2), 128–138.

Hedges L. V., & Olkin, I. (1985). *Statistical methods for meta-analysis*. Orlando, FL: Academic Press.

International Test Commission (ITC) (2010). *ITC guidelines for translating and adapting tests*. Retrieved from www.intestcom.org/upload/sitefiles/40.pdf

Kieffer, M. J., Lesaux, N. K., Rivera, M., & Francis, D. J. (2009). Accommodations for English language learners taking large-scale assessments: A meta-analysis on effectiveness and validity. *Review of Educational Research, 79*(3), 1168–1201.

Laitusis, C. C. (2010). Examining the impact of audio presentation on tests of reading comprehension. *Applied Measurement in Education, 23*(2), 153–167.

Laitusis, C., Buzick, H., Stone, E., Hansen, E., & Hakkinen, M. (2012). *Literature review of testing accommodations and accessibility tools for students with disabilities*. Olympia, WA: Office of the Superintendent of Public Instruction, Smarter Balanced Assessment Consortium.

Lazarus, S. S., Thurlow, M. L., Dominguez, L. M., Kincaid, A., & Edwards, L. M. (2014). *Test security and students with disabilities: An analysis of states' 2013–14 test security policies* (Synthesis Report 95). Minneapolis, MN: University of Minnesota, National Center on Educational Outcomes.

Li, H. (2014). The effects of read-aloud accommodations for students with and without disabilities: A meta-analysis. *Educational Measurement: Issues and Practice, 33*(3), 3–16.

Middleton, K., & Dorans, N. J. (2011). *Assessing the falsifiability of extreme linkings* (ETS Research Report Series, Report No. RR-11-04). Princeton, NJ: Educational Testing Service.

Osterlind, S. J., & Everson, H. T. (2009). *Differential item functioning* (Vol. 7, No. 161). Thousand Oaks, CA: Sage.

Pearson, B. Z. (1993). Predictive validity of the Scholastic Aptitude Test (SAT) for Hispanic bilingual students. *Hispanic Journal of Behavioral Sciences, 15*(3), 342–356.

Pennock-Roman, M., & Rivera, C. (2011). Mean effects of test accommodations for ELLs and Non-ELLs: A meta-analysis of experimental studies. *Educational Measurement: Issues and Practice, 30*(3), 10–28.

Rivera, C., Collum, E., Shafer Willner, L., & Sia, J. K. (2006). An analysis of state assessment policies regarding the accommodation of English language learners. In C. Rivera and E. Collum (Eds.), *State assessment policy and practice for English language learners: A national perspective* (pp. 1–173). Mahwah, NJ: Lawrence Erlbaum Associates.

Sireci, S. G. (2005). Unlabeling the disabled: A perspective on flagging scores from accommodated test administrations. *Educational Researcher, 34*(1), 3–12.

Sireci, S. G., Scarpati, S., & Li, S. (2005). Test accommodations for students with disabilities: An analysis of the interaction hypothesis. *Review of Educational Research, 75*(4), 457–490.

Stone, E. (2007, October). *Investigation of some assessment issues for students who are blind or visually impaired*. Paper presented at the annual meeting of the Northeastern Educational Research Association, Rocky Hill, CT.

Stone, E., & Davey, T. (2011). Computer-adaptive testing for students with disabilities: A review of the literature. *ETS Research Report*, 11–32.

Thompson, S. J., Johnstone, C. J., & Thurlow, M. L. (2002). *Universal design applied to large scale assessments* (Synthesis Report 44). Minneapolis, MN: University of Minnesota, National Center on Educational Outcomes. Retrieved from http://education.umn.edu/NCEO/Online Pubs/Synthesis44.html

Thurlow, M., Laitusis, C. C., Dillon, D. R., Cook, L. L., Moen, R. E., Abedi, J., & O'Brien, D. G. (2009). *Accessibility principles for reading assessments*. Minneapolis, MN: National Accessible Reading Assessment Projects.

Willingham, W. W., & Cole, N. S. (Eds.) (1997). *Gender and fair assessment*. New York: Routledge.

10 Comparing Scores from Tests Administered in Different Languages

Stephen G. Sireci,[1] Joseph A. Rios,[2] and Sonya Powers[3]

Linking and Comparability Issues in Test Translation and Cross-Lingual Assessment

The world is rapidly becoming smaller, yet language still separates people more than any physical divide. For the measurement community, bridging the language divide is often attempted by translating, or more accurately *adapting*, assessments across languages. In fact, assessing individuals who communicate in different languages through the use of test translation appears to be one of the distinguishing features of assessment in the 21st century. Fifty years ago, translations of educational and psychological assessments were limited to a few cross-cultural researchers interested in studying the universality of psychological constructs. Today, international corporations assess the attitudes and skills of their global workforce using instruments translated into dozens of languages (Sireci, Yang, Harter, & Ehrlic, 2006), international comparisons of educational achievement are an annual occurrence, and licensure and certification practices often involve translating tests into several languages (Robin, Sireci, & Hambleton, 2003). Clearly, large-scale assessment activities have gone global, and test translation has made these activities possible.

Although test translation is becoming more popular, it is also controversial, especially when examinees who take different language versions of a test are compared to one another or when scores from such tests are aggregated for accountability purposes. In this chapter, we describe the issues involved in test translation and focus on the statistical, validity, and fairness issues associated with different language versions of educational tests. Our report begins with a discussion of why test translations are important for contemporary educational assessment programs and the degree to which test translations are being used. We then define the various terms associated with test translation, the different methods used for translating tests, and validity issues associated with interpreting and comparing scores from different language versions of a test. Next, we discuss issues and methods in linking score scales from different language versions of a test, and we provide recommendations for how to facilitate score comparability across multiple language versions of educational tests.

The Need for Test Translation

There are both practical and ethical reasons for the increased use of test translations. Practically, many organizations are international and need to compare the knowledge and skills of their employees, who function using many different languages. In addition, international comparisons of educational achievement, such as the Trends in International Mathematics and Science Study (TIMSS) (Mullis, Martin, & Foy, 2008), Program for International Student Assessment (PISA) (Organization for Economic Co-operation and Development, 2006), Progress in International Reading Literacy (PIRLS) (Baer, Baldi, Ayotte, Green, & McGrath, 2007), and the Program for the International Assessment of Adult Competencies (PIAC) (Statistics Canada & Organization for Economic Co-operation and Development, 2005) *must* use different language versions of their tests to accomplish their goals—to compare the educational achievement or literacy levels of students or adults across countries. The numbers of countries involved in these studies are staggering. In recent administrations, TIMSS involved 82 countries, and PISA, PIRLS, and PIAC involved 74, 60, and 50, respectively.

In the United States, translated and alternate-language forms of tests are used in many statewide educational assessment programs. In these states, assessing students in their native language is seen as the most valid way to measure their proficiency in subject areas that do not directly assess English proficiency (e.g., mathematics, science, etc.). For example, if students who are not fully proficient in English are given a math test in English, they may possess the math skills tested, but may not understand what is being asked or what they are required to do when responding to an item. In psychometric terms, English proficiency in this instance is a source of *construct-irrelevant variance*, since it is irrelevant to the construct measured by the test (math proficiency). Messick (1989) would describe English proficiency as a source of *construct-irrelevant difficulty* in this situation because the more English proficiency is needed to correctly answer the item, the more difficult the item will be for English learners.

The effect of language proficiency on test score interpretation has been acknowledged for some time (e.g., American Psychological Association, American Educational Research Association, & National Council on Measurement in Education, 1985). For example, the 1999 *Standards for Educational and Psychological Testing* repeated the following caution that originally appeared in the 1985 version:

> any test that employs language is, in part, a measure of [students'] language skills . . . This is of particular concern for test takers whose first language is not the language of the test . . . In such instances, test results may not reflect accurately the qualities and competencies intended to be measured.
>
> (AERA et al., 1999, p. 91)

Although this and similar cautions are found in the test validity literature (including the most recent version of the Standards, AERA et al., 2014), the issue is beyond a validity concern—it is an ethical concern. It is often inappropriate to test someone in a language in which they are not proficient enough to understand what they are being asked to do (Rodriguez, 1992).

Test translations are seen as one way to address this problem by removing the language barrier for examinees to access the assessment and demonstrate their true proficiencies. Testing students in a language in which they are not fully proficient will provide a misleading interpretation of their knowledge and skills, whenever something other than proficiency in the language tested is being measured. Thus, translating a test into a student's native language is seen as one way to promote fairness by allowing examinees to access and interact with the test in their native language, and hence providing more valid assessment (Pennock-Roman & Rivera, 2011).

Statewide Assessment Programs Using Native Language Assessment

In the United States, several states use translated or dual-language (defined later) versions of their state assessments to measure the proficiencies of students who are ELs. Others offer translation accommodations, such as reading the test material aloud in a student's native language. These alternate test forms are typically offered in math, science, or social studies, where measurement of English proficiency is *not* a purpose of the test. For example, Delaware administers Spanish versions of their math, science, and social studies tests, Massachusetts administers dual-language versions of math and science tests, and Michigan provides oral translations of their math, science, and social studies tests in Arabic and Spanish. Other states that offer alternate-language versions of their state assessments include Florida, New Mexico, Ohio, New York, and Utah. In many cases, the alternate-language versions are translations into Spanish, which represents the largest non-English language group in U.S. schools. Thirteen of the 50 states offer at least some form of native language translation in their statewide assessment system, with all 13 offering translated tests in Spanish. The most common subject areas translated are math and science, although some states also translate reading, writing, or social studies assessments. In addition to Spanish, other target languages include Chinese, Gujarati, Hmong, Korean, Portuguese, Russian, Somali, and Vietnamese. Many other states offer translation of the test directions. With respect to multistate K-12 testing consortia in the United States, the Smarter Balanced Assessment Consortium is translating their math assessments into Spanish, but the Partnership for Assessing Readiness for College and Careers is not planning on translating the assessments at the consortium level. Instead, they will leave that decision up to the individual states.

Cross-Lingual Assessment Definitions

There are several terms used in the cross-lingual assessment literature. Terms currently used to describe the process of adjusting test material for use in other languages include *translation, adaptation,* and the misnomer *transadaptation.* The term "translation" is typically used in its most general, everyday sense to describe the process of rendering words from one language into another. This term, however, may be viewed as implying a literal word-for-word substitution, which is not an accurate description of what happens when tests are adjusted for use across languages. For this reason, the term "adaptation" is preferable (Geisinger, 1994; Hambleton, 2005; Hambleton & de Jong, 2003), because in cross-lingual assessment, the intent is to retain the meaning of the test material, which often requires different words and phrases to be used to capture the essence of the test questions and related material.

The term "transadaptation" has also been used, and seems to be used to emphasize that the translation of test material is not a literal word-for-word translation. Bowles and Stansfield (2008) defined transadaptation as an emerging term used to describe "the standard direct translation of an assessment" (p. 17). In their view, transadaptation is a synonym for direct translation of test material that is thought to be straightforward from a content perspective.[4] In our view, transadaptation is an unnecessary term because it appears to have the same definition as adaptation, and the term adaptation is already codified in the International Test Commission's publications and other cross-lingual assessment literature.

Regardless of the vocabulary used to describe the process, the degree to which the translation or adaptation altered the original material needs to be ascertained, and accounted for in interpreting test results. In this paper, we use the term adaptation to refer to the process of translating test material from one language to another, with the goal of retaining the intent and meaning of the assessment material across languages.

Another term that appears in the test adaptation literature is a *dual-language* test or test booklet, which refers to a test administration booklet (or computerized presentation) in which two different language versions of each item are displayed together, typically side by side. Examples of dual-language test administrations have been used by the National Assessment of Educational Progress (Duncan et al., 2005) and in Massachusetts (Sireci & Khaliq, 2002), Ohio, and Oregon.

Two other terms that are common in the test adaptation literature are source language and target languages. Source language refers to the situation where a test has been developed in one language, and it represents the source from which the adaptation originates. The other languages into which the test is adapted represent the target languages. Other relevant terms refer to specific methods for adapting test material, which are described in subsequent sections.

Validity Issues and Guidelines for Cross-Lingual Assessment

The current version of the *Standards for Educational and Psychological Testing* (AERA et al., 2014) defines validity as "the degree to which evidence and theory support the interpretations of test scores for proposed uses of tests" (p. 11). This definition underscores the importance of understanding the intended purposes and uses of test scores because what needs to be validated is not the test itself, but the use of a test for a particular purpose.

The past three versions of the Standards have provided important guidance for promoting validity in the assessment of linguistic minorities and when testing across different languages. In addition, the most recent version (AERA et al., 2014) includes a chapter on "Fairness" that addresses important issues for cross-lingual assessment. Although the Standards acknowledge fairness can be defined in different ways, they state:

> this chapter interprets fairness as responsiveness to individual characteristics and testing contexts so that test scores will yield valid interpretations for intended uses ... A test that is fair within the meaning of the Standards reflects the same construct(s) for all test takers, and scores from it have the same meaning for all individuals in the intended population; a fair test does not advantage or disadvantage some individuals because of characteristics irrelevant to the intended construct.
>
> (p. 50)

An important fairness consideration in cross-lingual assessment is ensuring the construct measured is the same for all test takers. This importance is reflected in the Standards, which describe the evaluation of construct similarity as "especially important when the assessment crosses international borders and cultures" (p. 52).

Another way of saying that scores from a test "have the same meaning for all individuals" is to say scores from the same test are "comparable" across all examinees. In the "Fairness" chapter, the Standards describe "comparability of scores" as enabling "test users to make comparable inferences based on the scores for all test takers" (p. 59). Pommerich (this volume, Chapter 7) supported the definition of fairness in terms of comparability proposed by Willingham and Cole (1997) and Xi (2010), which states,

"Fairness is defined as comparable validity for individuals and groups at each assessment stage" (p. x).

When test scores are compared across examinees who take different language versions of a test, validity evidence will be needed to demonstrate that the scores from the different language versions of the test are comparable. The AERA et al. (2014) *Standards* specify five sources "that might be used in evaluating a proposed interpretation of test scores for a particular use" (p. 13). The sources are validity evidence based on: (a) test content; (b) response processes; (c) internal structure; (d) relations to other variables; and (e) consequences of testing. These sources of evidence can be used to evaluate the degree of score comparability across different language versions of an assessment (Sireci, Han, & Wells, 2008). If examinees' scores are only interpreted *within* each language group, then comparability across languages is not needed, and validity evidence would focus on demonstrating comparability of scores across subgroups within that single language of test administration. Thus, validity issues and validation responsibilities follow the intended purpose of the testing and how the test scores are used.

The AERA et al. (2014) *Standards* also speak directly to situations where tests are translated to facilitate testing in a student's native language or assessing across languages. They point out that translation itself cannot be considered to produce comparable scores:

> Simply translating a test from one language to another does not ensure that the translation produces a version of the test that is comparable in content and difficulty level to the original version of the test, or that the translated test produces scores that are equally reliable/precise and valid.
>
> (p. 60)

In such situations, the Standards require evidence that the scores on different language versions of a test are comparable.

This call for testing agencies to provide evidence of score comparability across different language versions of an assessment is also emphasized by another set of guidelines that are particularly relevant to test adaptations in cross-lingual assessment—the International Test Commission (ITC)'s *Guidelines for Translating and Adapting Educational and Psychological Tests*. The first version of these *Guidelines* was published in 1994 (Hambleton, 1994) and the most recent version was revised in 2010 (ITC, 2010; see also Hambleton, 2005). These *Guidelines* are organized into four categories: (a) context; (b) test development and adaptation; (c) administration; and (d) documentation/score interpretations. In each category, they provide valuable recommendations to facilitate valid score interpretations for adapted tests. For example, with respect to test development and adaptation, they provide recommendations regarding statistical analyses to facilitate equivalence across the different language versions of an assessment. The following four guidelines are particularly relevant in this regard:

> Test developers/publishers should ensure that the data collection design permits the use of appropriate statistical techniques to establish item equivalence between the different language versions of the test or instrument.
>
> Test developers/publishers should apply appropriate statistical techniques to (1) establish the equivalence of the different versions of the test or instrument, and (2) identify problematic components or aspects of the test or instrument which may be inadequate to one or more of the intended populations.

Test developers/publishers should provide information on the evaluation of validity in all target populations for whom the adapted versions are intended.

Test developers/publishers should provide statistical evidence of the equivalence of questions for all intended populations.

(ITC, 2010, pp. 2–3)

Clearly, these guidelines stress the importance of statistical evaluation of the quality of the adaptation and the degree to which such evaluations can inform test score interpretations and questions regarding validity. The *Guidelines* encourage test developers to use appropriate statistical techniques to evaluate item equivalence and to identify areas of a test that may be inadequate for one or more of the intended groups. More on potential statistical approaches for evaluating translated tests are described later.

Bias and Equivalence

Where score comparability across languages is needed, research should be conducted to evaluate potential biases that would invalidate cross-lingual comparisons. Van de Vijver and his colleagues stated that at least three types of bias could lead to a lack of comparability of test scores across languages: construct bias, method bias, and item bias (van de Vijver & Poortinga, 1997, 2005; van de Vijver & Tanzer, 1998). *Construct bias* refers to the situation where the construct measured, as operationally defined by the assessment, is nonexistent in one or more cultures or is significantly different across cultures. *Method bias* refers to a systematic source of construct-irrelevant variance that manifests at the test score level. Examples of method bias include improper test administration conditions, inappropriate or unfamiliar item formats, or improper test translations that make all test items easier or more difficult in one language, relative to the original language. *Item bias* refers to construct-irrelevant variance that affects performance at the item level.

When evaluating construct bias, there are three major levels of equivalence, which include configural, metric, and scalar equivalence. Configural (structural) equivalence assesses whether the same underlying latent variables are supported for all cultural or linguistic groups. Metric equivalence (invariance) is more restrictive in that it also requires that the measurement scales have the same units of measurement (i.e., an interval-level scale) (van de Vijver & Leung, 2011). From a confirmatory factor analytic framework, metric invariance requires that factor loadings are equal across groups. Lastly, scalar equivalence specifies that both configural and metric invariance are met, and the scale origin is equivalent across groups (Liu & Dorans, this volume, Chapter 5; van de Vijver & Leung, 2011).

If translated versions of tests achieve metric, but not scalar equivalence, the comparisons that can be made across groups are limited. Van de Vijver and Leung (2011) noted this situation would exist when a source of bias differentially shifts scores for different linguistic groups, but does not affect the relative scores of individuals *within* each group. In such a situation, one could say, for example, that women tend to have higher rank scores in math achievement than men across cultures (if within each culture women scored higher than men), but one could *not* say that women in language A score higher than women in language B. The reason for this indirect interpretation is that although the score intervals are equal across groups, the measurement units do not necessarily share the same origin of the scale.

Scalar equivalence subsumes both configural and metric equivalence, and adds the additional requirement that the scales of the latent construct possess the same origin.

In a factor analysis framework, this would require equal intercepts, which would signal the absence of differential item functioning, and would allow for direct comparisons of group means (Dimitrov, 2010). Most often, cross-cultural researchers are interested in obtaining this last form of equivalence as comparisons of group means are of upmost importance.

Equating, Linking, and Comparable Scores

The issues of structural, metric, and scalar equivalence found in the cross-cultural/cross-lingual assessment literature are subsets of the larger score comparability issues found in the more general area called "linking" or "equating" test scores. Equating refers to the practice of adjusting test scores across different forms of a test so that the scores from these different forms are placed on the same scale. Theoretically, if scores from different test forms are properly equated, there should be no difference in the expected scores for an examinee across the forms (Lord, 1980). In such cases, the scores can be considered "interchangeable" across test forms. In practice, however, it is difficult to achieve this ideal. With respect to equating tests translated across languages, such equivalence is elusive and so less strict forms of equating are typically sought (Sireci, 1997). These "weaker" forms of equating are typically described using different terminology such as score "linking."

There have been several classifications of methods for linking scores from different tests onto a common scale, or for making scores from different tests comparable in some other way. Classification systems have been proposed by Mislevy (1992), Linn (1993), Dorans (2004), and Kolen (2007), among others. Mislevy (1992) and Linn (1993) specified five levels of linking that differ according to the method and assumptions regarding similarity of the assessments to be linked. These levels range from equating, which has the most restrictive assumptions and the strongest degree of score comparability, to social moderation, which has the fewest assumptions and hence the weakest degree of score comparability. Dorans (2004) specified three types of linking—equating, concordance, and prediction.

Equating is the strongest type of linking in that when tests are equated, examinees would get essentially the same score on either test, within the expectations of measurement error, and the amount of measurement error would be roughly the same across tests. Equating requires that the same construct is measured and the different tests are developed from the same content specifications. Statistical methods for equating tests have strict data collection designs that require a common group of examinees, randomly equivalent groups, or common items.

Pommerich (this volume, Chapter 7) summarizes much of the literature regarding "weaker" forms of equating/linking and so we will not review it here. Instead, we borrow her distinction between "comparable scores" and "interchangeable scores." As she described, "comparable scores are not the same as interchangeable scores . . . Interchangeable scores are the ideal outcome of a linkage, while comparable scores imply a lower level of association" (p. 113). In describing "fairness" in testing with respect to score comparability, she reviewed the equating and comparability literature and came up with three aspects of equivalence to distinguish between interchangeable and comparable scores. As she describes, interchangeable scores imply three forms of equivalence: (a) distributional equivalence (identical score distributions); (b) construct equivalence (equivalence in the construct measured); and (c) predictive equivalence (equal prediction of external criteria). Comparable scores, on the other hand, imply only distributional equivalence. Although there is no universal acceptance of the different linking taxonomies or levels of score equivalence, Pommerich's framework is helpful for categorizing the cross-lingual assessment situation as clearly outside the realm of interchangeable scores.

Kolen (2007) discussed three features that affect the quality of the linking between scores on two different tests: (a) content similarity of the two tests; (b) administrative conditions under which the tests are given; and (c) characteristics of the populations to whom the tests are administered. This framework is helpful because it lists the three features on which the testing situation differs across languages in cross-lingual assessment (content, administration conditions, tested populations). Translated versions of tests typically involve the same construct and content specifications; however, the items cannot be considered "common" after they have been translated, and so the content cannot be considered equivalent. Similarly, language in which the test is administered is inconsistent across languages and so the administration conditions are also variable. Finally, the groups of examinees who take different language versions of an assessment cannot be considered randomly equivalent and so the last possibility for achieving interchangeable scores is removed. For these reasons, it is not possible to strictly equate translated tests and achieve interchangeable scores (Dorans & Middleton, 2012; Sireci, 1997, 2005). Instead, we need to be clear about the steps taken to approximate score comparability and put forth evidence to support the validity of any interpretations that are made within or across languages. In the next section, we review research and practice in cross-lingual assessment to illustrate methods that have been used to link scales across languages.

Review of Studies Linking Score Scales across Languages

Linking studies involve different data collection designs. One design is a common groups design where the same group of students takes the two test forms. Another design, the randomly equivalent groups design, randomly assigns test forms to groups. A third design uses a set of common items across forms to form a link. In some cases common-item linking is done using randomly equivalent groups; in other cases, non-equivalent groups are used. Complete descriptions of these designs can be found in Kolen and Brennan (2014).

All linking designs have important assumptions that must be satisfied, and in the case of test forms administered in the same language, satisfying the assumptions is typically feasible. For example, the randomly equivalent groups design assumes the average proficiencies of the groups taking each test form are equal up to sampling error. The single group design assumes there is no change in group proficiency between the first test administration and the second, and that there is no practice effect. These assumptions can often be tested, but in the case of test forms translated into different languages, satisfying the assumptions is more problematic.

For example, in the context of test translations, a common-person linking design requires a group of bilingual examinees. Assuming bilingual test takers are equally proficient in the construct measured in each language may not be defensible (Sireci, 2005). In addition, a randomly equivalent groups linking design is theoretically impossible, because examinees cannot be randomly assigned to a language version of the test, unless only bilingual examinees are used. Nevertheless, attempts have been made to link score scales across languages using monolingual groups of examinees.

Sireci (1997) claimed there are essentially three data collection designs for studies that attempt to link test scores across languages: (a) the separate monolingual groups design; (b) the matched monolingual group design; and (c) the bilingual group design. All designs have their limitations, some of which led Dorans and Middleton (2012) to refer to these attempts as "presumed linking" (p. 2) to emphasize the lack of tenability of their assumptions.

The separate monolingual groups design involves administering each language form of the test to the specific language group for which it was designed. The link is typically formed using a set of anchor items that are assumed to be invariant across languages. This assumption is typically justified via statistical analysis of differential item functioning (DIF) across languages. However, this justification is somewhat circular, because DIF analyses assume the variable on which examinees are matched is free of construct and method bias. Thus, this "justification" is more trust or hope than supporting evidence.

The matched monolingual groups design involves matching the examinees from the different groups on external criteria, rather than using a set of anchor items. The bilingual group design involves having a single group of examinees take both language versions of the test, or random assignment of one language to each bilingual examinee. In the next section, we describe these designs and some studies that have implemented them. Our description of these designs begins with the bilingual design.

Common Person (Bilingual) Designs

It is difficult to use a common person equating or linking design for translated versions of a test because typically only a small portion of the examinee population is bilingual. However, some researchers have used bilingual examinees to form a link across different language versions of a test (e.g., Boldt, 1969; Cascallar & Dorans, 2005; CTB/McGraw Hill, 1988; Ong & Sireci, 2008; Sireci & Berberoglu, 2000). There are essentially three variants of the bilingual design: (a) bilingual examinees take both language versions of a test (or of anchor items) in counterbalanced order; (b) two randomly equivalent groups of bilingual examinees each take one language version of the test; or (c) two randomly equivalent groups of bilingual test takers respond to a dual-language version of the test.

Ong and Sireci (2008) provided an example of a bilingual linking design. They analyzed data from Malay and English versions of a ninth grade math test. The students were thought to be fully bilingual because their math instruction was in English, but their native language was Malay. The exam was administered using dual-language test booklets, where the Malay version of the items appeared on one side of the test booklet and the English language versions appeared on the facing pages. English-only and Malay-only booklets were prepared, and the examinees took both language versions of the test in counterbalanced order. They first performed DIF analyses and found that 7 of the 40 items were flagged for DIF, with all having small effect sizes. Next, they performed linking using several methods including linear, equipercentile, and IRT, both with and without using the DIF items as part of the equating anchor. The equating resulted in a two-point adjustment across language versions of the test before the DIF items were removed, and a one-point difference if they were removed. Thus, they recommended screening items for DIF before conducting an equating.

Ong and Sireci (2008) also looked at differences in pass rates across the Malay and English versions. They found 81% passed the test regardless of language version, 3% passed only in English, and about 9% passed only in Malay, resulting in a decision consistency across languages of 0.89. When tests have achievement-level standards, decision consistency may be a helpful criterion for evaluating score comparability across bilingual test takers. The study results supported the policy of allowing students to take the test in the language they prefer (since some students would only pass the test in one of the languages) and illustrated the usefulness of bilingual examinees for evaluating score comparability or equating tests across languages.

Cascallar and Dorans (2005) also used bilingual students to evaluate different levels of score comparability across the Prueba de Aptitud Academica (PAA) and the Scholastic Aptitude Test (SAT). In addition to PAA and SAT scores, they also had English as a Second Language Achievement Test (ESLAT) scores for these bilingual students. They used equipercentile equating to establish concordance between the SAT and PAA, and multiple regression to predict math, verbal, and composite SAT scores. They found prediction preferable to equating, due in large part to the contribution of the ESLAT in the prediction, and they concluded that the PAA and ESLAT could be used to predict how well students in Puerto Rico might do in colleges in the United States.

Separate Monolingual Groups

Many studies have used separate groups of monolingual students to link test scores across languages, or to evaluate the comparability of different language versions of a test, typically using IRT (e.g., Angoff & Cook, 1988; Hulin, Drasgow, & Komocar, 1982; Hulin & Mayer, 1986; Woodcock & Muñoz-Sandoval, 1993). Although it is a popular procedure, a criticism of using IRT for cross-lingual linking purposes is that if the linguistic groups differ in ability, and the calibration procedure does not account for this difference, the parameters for the translated items will not be comparable to the source-language items (Sireci, 1997; see also Dorans & Middleton, 2012). Thus, these studies are not reviewed here. Instead, we focus on more recent work in college admissions testing in Israel.

Psychometric Entrance Test in Israel

One of the most interesting, high-stakes cross-lingual exams is the Psychometric Entrance Test (PET) used for college admissions in Israel. It is interesting because it is written in Hebrew and translated into five languages—Arabic, Russian, French, Spanish, and English. There are three tests in the battery: verbal reasoning, quantitative reasoning, and English. Verbal and quantitative reasoning are translated from Hebrew into the other languages. For the quantitative subtest, all items are translated, and DIF procedures are conducted for each language version using examinees who took the Hebrew version as the reference group. For the verbal subtest, only items in three content areas are translated (logic, reading comprehension, and sentence completion), while items measuring vocabulary and analogies are constructed uniquely in each language (Allalouf, Rapp, & Stoller, 2009). This combination of translation and independent item development is based on several research studies that illustrated vocabulary and analogy items are too different across languages to be translated.

DIF analyses are conducted across language versions of the PET to select items to be used to link the scales across languages. Items comprising these linking anchors must demonstrate a correlation of 0.80 or above with respect to their item difficulty parameters across languages. This criterion is less rigorous than the criteria typically used when evaluating anchor items in a usual equating study (e.g., Kolen & Brennan, 2014), which illustrates the lower level of linking that is being conducted. The linking anchor must also be at least 10 items in length. For the quantitative subtest, most of the items are used to create an anchor. For the verbal subtest, typically 25–65% of the items are used (Rapp & Allalouf, 2003).

Given the strong assumptions involved in the PET linking design ("extreme" assumptions as characterized by Dorans & Middleton, 2012), there have been several studies to evaluate and improve the process. Rapp and Allalouf (2003) proposed a unique method for evaluating the degree to which the linking process introduced equating error, relative to equating test forms in a common language. They used a "double linking plan" in which a test form is equated to two other forms. When a double-linking study is done in a single language, the typical course of action is to average the two separate equating results. Rapp and Allaouf used the design to compare equating PET Verbal test forms *within* each language to the cross-lingual equating (to the Hebrew form) described above. Their intent was to use the within-language equating to establish a baseline equating error and compare it to the equating error noted in the cross-lingual context.

The Rapp and Allalouf (2003) design capitalized on the fact that the PET verbal test contains a pair of parallel sections. These parallel sections could be equated within each non-Hebrew language (target language) using a common person design, and to the Hebrew versions (source language) using a set of linking items, as descried above. That is, each of the two sections within an exam was equated to each other (same language equating), but also equated to its Hebrew counterpart. Their study involved two non-Hebrew languages, one of which involved 12 separate test forms; the other involved nine separate test forms. They assumed the difference in equating results across the within-language and across-language equatings would reflect the instability associated with their operational practice of equating across languages.

Their results indicated that the average equating difference across test forms in the first target language was about 10 times what they observe for equating forms within a language (1–2 raw score points on average across the 12 forms in one of the language groups and about 0.6 points on average across the nine forms in the second language, compared to 0.1 to 0.2 points on a typical within-language equating). They concluded the within- and across-language double linking design was useful for evaluating cross-lingual linking stability. They also hypothesized six reasons for cross-lingual linking instability—translation differences for some items, cultural familiarity differences, item position effects, differences in anchor test lengths, differences in representativeness of anchor sets, and differences in the proficiency levels of examinees taking different language versions of the test.

The PET research illustrates how cross-lingual linking has been implemented and evaluated on a high-stakes test. Lower-stakes tests, such as TIMSS, PISA, and PIRLS, use a similar approach (i.e., translated items, DIF screening, and common-item linking). The approach is not perfect, as the viability of the linking anchor cannot be unequivocally established. The linking anchor may have items that differ across languages, but escape DIF detection, or it may underrepresent the construct the test is designed to measure (Sireci, 1997). As Allalouf et al. (2009) noted, "The issue at hand is whether it is better to have a superior, no-DIF link with an inferior representation of content or an inferior link (that includes some DIF items) with a superior representation of content" (p. 105). Several studies have illustrated the practice of cross-lingual linking (Allalouf et al., 2009; Allalouf, Hambleton, & Sireci, 1999; Beller, Gafni, & Hanani, 2005; Rapp & Allalouf,

2003), although all have raised caveats about achieving a relatively weaker form of linking than is desired. Nevertheless, it appears that in many situations the need to compare individuals who take the different language versions of an assessment outweighs concerns over strict score comparability, which remains an elusive goal.

Linking Cut-Scores via Statistical Moderation

Davis, Buckendahl, and Plake (2006) set pass/fail standards on English and French versions of high school reading and writing tests. To set the Standards, they convened separate panels of English and French reading and writing experts (teachers), but conducted the training simultaneously, using both an English-speaking and a bilingual (English-French) facilitator. The orientation and training was done first in English (with a French translation via headphones) and then in French (with an English translation via headphones).

Following the common orientation and training, the groups were split into language-specific panels, and the same process was used to derive passing scores on each language version of each test. The differences in the Standards set on each exam resulted in about 1–6% differences in the passing rate for each group of students, which was deemed acceptable by the authors, given that in Canada, English-speaking and French-speaking subgroups are often considered equivalent by the organizations who commission the tests (Wainer, 2011). The Davis et al. (2006) study illustrates that parallel standard setting processes could be used to set defensible standards on different language versions of an assessment. However, the utility of simultaneously setting the Standards deserves further study.

Evaluating Translated Assessments

In addition to *linking* assessments across languages, there has been a great deal of research in evaluating the *comparability* of tests that are adapted for use across languages. In this section, we describe some studies that have used these methods.

Statistical Methods for Evaluating Construct Bias

Statistical methods for evaluating construct bias can be classified as exploratory or confirmatory. Exploratory methods include exploratory factor analysis (EFA) and multidimensional scaling (MDS) (Fischer & Fontaine, 2011; Sireci, Patsula, & Hambleton, 2005). The most popular confirmatory procedure is multiple group confirmatory factor analysis (CFA). In this chapter, we focus on MDS and CFA because they allow for simultaneous evaluations of all language groups under consideration.

Multidimensional Scaling (MDS)

MDS is an exploratory method used frequently within cross-cultural research (Cleeland et al., 1996; Collazo, 2005; Robin et al., 2003; Wolff, Schneider-Rahm, & Forret, 2011). The objective of MDS is to provide a visual representation of the observed similarities among a set of objects (e.g., test items). A major advantage of MDS over EFA is that multiple group data can be analyzed simultaneously to determine the structural similarities across groups. This is accomplished by using an individual differences MDS analysis and evaluating the group weights to modify the common structure for each group

(Sireci et al., 2005; Sireci & Wells, 2010). An advantage of MDS relative to MGCFA is that because it is an exploratory procedure, there is no need to specify the dimensionality of the assessment a priori. This advantage is helpful when the dimensionality is either unknown, or the hypothesized dimensionality is not widely supported. The major disadvantage of MDS is that it is solely a descriptive technique. That is, it provides no statistical test to evaluate structural differences across groups (Fischer & Fontaine, 2011), requiring the researcher to rely primarily on visual interpretations and descriptive indices (e.g., patterns of group weights on dimensions).

Multiple Group Confirmatory Factor Analysis (MGCFA)

MGCFA is a theory-driven method used to evaluate formal hypotheses of parameter invariance across groups (Dimitrov, 2010). It is advantageous when evaluating construct comparability as it allows for: (a) simultaneous model fitting across multiple groups; (b) assessing various levels of measurement invariance; (c) disattenuation of the means and covariances of the latent constructs (controls for measurement error); and (d) direct statistical tests to evaluate group differences of the estimated parameters (Little & Slegers, 2005). MGCFA requires four hierarchical steps: (a) establishment of a baseline model across groups; (b) testing for configural invariance; (c) testing for metric invariance; and (d) testing for scalar invariance. This systematic process is known as *sequential constraint imposition*. In this process, one estimates a model with unconstrained parameters across groups. If adequate model fit is obtained, one constrains particular parameters (depending on the model) to be equal across groups and evaluates model fit. This process can theoretically continue until all parameters in the model are constrained equal across groups, providing that there is adequate model fit for less restrictive models. Comparison of hierarchically nested models can be conducted with two popular approaches: the likelihood ratio (x^2 difference) test, or the change in comparative fit index (CFI). The latter approach was developed as the traditional chi-square difference test has been suggested to be highly sensitive to sample size, while change in the CFI (ΔCFI) has been demonstrated in simulation studies to provide stable performance with various conditions, such as sample size, amount of invariance, number of factors, and number of items (Meade, Johnson, & Braddy, 2008). Based on simulation analyses, Cheung and Rensvold (2002) recommended that a ΔCFI $\leq$ .01 supports a hypothesis of invariance.

　　MGCFA has been widely used to evaluate construct bias in test adaptations (Davidov, 2011; Hattrup, Ghorpade, & Lackritz, 2007; Yen & Tu, 2011). Like MDS, it can handle a large number of groups in a single analysis. Ariely and Davidov (2011) used MGCFA to evaluate the factor structure of an attitudinal survey across 36 different countries, and Byrne and van de Vijver (2010) applied a two-stage technique across 27 countries (one stage involved eliminating some countries from the analysis).

Studies Evaluating Cross-Lingual Comparability

There is a large body of literature that focuses on evaluating the comparability of translated versions of tests across languages. These studies have evaluated comparability at both the item level (using DIF procedures) and at the test score level (using dimensionality assessment procedures). In this section, we review four of these studies: Allalouf et al. (1999), Gierl and Khaliq (2001), Ercikan and Koh (2005), and Oliveri, Olson, Ercikan, and Zumbo (2012).

Allalouf et al. (1999) summarized the results of studies conducted on the Hebrew and Russian versions of the verbal reasoning subtest of the PET. Previous research using MDS confirmed that the factor structures of the Hebrew and Russian versions of the exam were similar, but that analyses of DIF had found that several analogy and sentence completion items were not statistically equivalent across languages. Specifically, they found that the Russian versions of the analogy items flagged for DIF tended to be differentially easier in Russian, but that the sentence completion items flagged for DIF were inconsistent in the direction of DIF.

To better understand the potential causes of DIF, Allalouf et al. (1999) convened a group of eight Hebrew-Russian bilingual content specialists and translators to hypothesize and discuss reasons why the items flagged for DIF were inconsistent across languages. Four potential causes were identified: (a) differences in the familiarity of specific words across languages due to frequency of usage; (b) changes in the content of an item due to translation; (c) changes in the format or appearance of an item; and (d) differences in the cultural relevance of an item. This study illustrated how statistical analyses of DIF can be followed up by qualitative analyses to help interpret differences in test performance across examinees taking different language versions of a test, as well as the degree of comparability of the tests themselves.

Gierl and Khaliq (2001) also used focus groups to review DIF items to derive potential causes of DIF. Their study involved analysis of English and French versions of math and social tests administered in sixth and ninth grades in Canada. There were three stages to their study. The first stage involved using a simultaneous item bias procedure (SIBTEST) (Shealy & Stout, 1993) to flag items for DIF across the two languages. The second stage involved convening a group of eleven bilingual content specialists to review the English and French versions of the items flagged for DIF and come up with consensus opinions regarding the likely sources of the DIF. The third stage involved a subsequent team of two translators to use the sources of DIF identified by the content specialists to categorize items on a subsequent assessment that were flagged for DIF into one of the source categories put forward by the previous committee.

Their results illustrated how an iterative DIF screening process could be used to identify items that function differentially across languages and how the sources of DIF identified by bilingual content specialists could be used to explain subsequent items flagged for DIF. The sources of DIF identified by the content specialists were similar to those identified by the specialists in the Allalouf et al. (1999) study, even though the languages involved were very different. Furthermore, Gierl and Khaliq (2001) illustrated that sources of DIF could be used to evaluate the aggregate effect of translation and cultural relevance differences across items on students' test scores. They found the substantive interpretations of DIF to hold up over subsequent test forms and to affect score differences across the English and French versions of the assessments. They concluded, "The next step is to develop more refined and detailed [DIF] hypotheses where researchers identify content differences and predict group differences ... but also study the content-by-group interactions" (p. 183).

Ercikan and Koh (2005) evaluated the comparability of different language versions of TIMSS assessments. They looked at English and French math and science versions of 1995 TIMSS exams administered in Canada, England, France, and the United States. They evaluated both DIF and structural equivalence. DIF was evaluated by looking at the consistency of IRT parameters estimated separately for each language group and by using the Linn-Harnisch procedure. Structural equivalence was evaluated using MGCFA.

Their results indicated a lack of equivalence at both the structural and item levels. They found substantial levels of DIF in some comparisons (e.g., 59% of the math items were flagged for DIF across England and France, 79% of the science items were flagged for DIF across France and the United States). The global fit indices associated with the MGCFA illustrated relatively worse fit of the models to the data in those situations where the greatest amount of DIF was observed. They warned that when substantial amounts of DIF and inconsistencies in test structure are observed across translated assessments, comparisons of students who responded to different language versions of the items should not be made.

Oliveri et al. (2012) evaluated item- and test-level comparability of English and French versions of a test booklet from the 2003 PISA mathematics problem-solving subtest. Using three DIF detection methods, they found three of ten items functioned differentially across languages—two dichotomous items favored the French version, and one polytomous item favored the English version. However, when aggregating these results to evaluate differential test functioning (DTF), they found comparable test characteristic curves, suggesting comparability at the total test score level. They also found comparable factor structure using MGCFA. This study illustrates the importance of focusing on both the total test score and item levels, as DIF may cancel out at the total test score level, providing comparability of total scores even when item-level differences are present (Wainer, Sireci, & Thissen, 1991).

Caveats to These Studies

Although we note the comprehensive analyses that have been conducted to link or evaluate tests adapted for use across languages, the limitations and assumptions involved in these practices must be revisited. Dorans and Middleton (2012) criticized the lack of attention to the fact that cross-lingual assessment involves an inconsistency in measurement conditions across groups of examinees (i.e., different language versions), and like others (e.g., Sireci, 1997) noted it is not possible to fully evaluate the assumptions involved in the most common data collection setting—the monolingual groups design, which uses a "common" anchor of items after screening for DIF. They pointed out, "When comparisons are made between scores from two or more assessments that are built to different specifications and are administered to different populations under different conditions, the validity of the comparisons hinges on untestable assumptions" (p. 1). One way they proposed to evaluate the extreme assumptions is to test the invariance of the linking functions based on the separate groups and conditions.

Discussion and Recommendations

In this report, we described several issues related to cross-lingual assessment, including linking score scales across languages and evaluating the comparability of scores (and items) from different language assessments. We also described statistical methods that can be used to link assessments across languages or to evaluate the comparability of these assessments. Our review illustrates that statistical methods are available for evaluating comparability, but the results from studies that evaluated comparability vary widely across contexts. Thus, it is clear we cannot assume that tests translated from one language to another are equivalent with respect to psychometric properties, or that they produce scores that can be interpreted as if they are on the same scale. We can, however, conduct research to provide information regarding how similar translated versions of tests are with respect to item functioning, measurement precision, correlations with external criteria, and factor structure. The more similar the results are across languages, the more confidence we can have the scores are comparable. Thus, these analyses help us promote fairness in cross-lingual educational assessment.

Our review illustrates that much of the research conducted on translated tests has investigated validity evidence based on test content and internal structure (i.e., DIF and dimensionality). There have been some experimental studies using bilinguals, but these studies are rare, and we did not find any evaluating the consistency of relations between test scores and other variables across languages. Based on our review of the research and practices in this area, and of the professional guidelines, we offer a few recommendations for research and practice.

First, studies of DIF and structural equivalence may help shed light on items and tests that are (or are not) invariant across languages. Although such analyses involve assumptions that may be hard to justify, they have provided interpretable results that have helped improve translations. In addition, other analyses, such as evaluating the invariance of linking constants (Dorans & Middleton, 2012), can be used to provide other evidence of comparability (or lack thereof). Therefore, these statistical analyses should be conducted whenever appropriate sample sizes are available, and the results should be communicated to test developers to avoid future problems. Allalouf (2003), Allalouf et al. (1999), Elosua and López-Jaúregui (2007), and Ercikan et al. (2010) provide examples of how content experts can be used to explain the causes of DIF and inform item writers how to avoid future translation problems. Ercikan et al. (2010) and Benitez and Padilla (2012) also illustrate how think-aloud protocols or cognitive interviews can be used to understand the causes of cross-lingual DIF. In addition, Allalouf et al. (2009) illustrated how DIF analyses influenced the way in which the PET was linked across languages (e.g., exclude analogy items from the equating anchor).

It appears DIF screening of anchor items is a commonly accepted approach in cross-lingual linking. Although it is common, we suspect its popularity is borne out of necessity, given that it is technically impossible to link monolingual groups taking different language versions of an assessment (Dorans & Middleton, 2012; Sireci, 1997; Wainer, 2011). Thus, our second recommendation is to include other validity studies beyond DIF to evaluate the comparability of scores from tests linked across languages. Dorans and Middleton (2012) and Rapp and Allalouf (2003) illustrate innovative methods, but clearly more are needed. Although studies of DIF and construct equivalence are common, there are essentially no studies of the consistency of test-criterion relationships across languages (e.g., differential predictive validity) or more complex correlational studies.

We encourage more research to provide information regarding score comparability across languages in applied situations. The degree of evidence of comparability that should be required depends largely on how test scores are used. If scores are used to compare examinees across languages, a large body of evidence is needed to support those interpretations (Sireci et al., 2008). The *Standards for Educational and Psychological Testing* (AERA et al., 2014) specify five sources of validity evidence, but three of those sources—evidence based on response processes, relations with external variables, and testing consequences—have not been used to support the validity of cross-lingual assessments. Rios and Sireci (2014) found that most of the published literature on test translation ignores the ITC *Guidelines* and rarely reports even validity evidence based on internal structure.

When evaluating comparability after test forms have been administered, best practices in DIF and dimensionality detection suggest trying to account for large differences in group proficiency and sample sizes through matching strategies and drawing multiple random samples from the source language group (e.g., Sireci & Wells, 2010). Of course, statistical procedures require adequate sample sizes, which are not always available in cross-lingual assessment situations. Muniz, Hambleton, and Xing (2000) supported the use of sample sizes as low as 50 to identify items with large DIF in evaluating cross-lingual DIF. However, 200 examinees or more are probably required to identify DIF items of smaller magnitude.

We also recommend that, where possible, bilingual examinees be used to evaluate anchor items and other aspects of score comparability across languages. Although in many situations bilingual examinees may not represent the monolingual examinees for which the tests are designed, they can still be useful for evaluating the invariance of psychometric properties across different language versions of an assessment.

Current Limitations and Future Directions

As our review illustrated, the greatest limitation in cross-lingual assessment is the inability to link score scales across different language versions of a test without making strong assumptions. The assumptions that need to be made are probably too strong, in the sense that they cannot be unequivocally defended. When test items are translated across languages, they cannot be considered statistically equivalent, and thus cannot be used to link the score scales. Similarly, examinees who take different language versions of a test cannot be considered randomly equivalent; they are simply different populations. Thus, common-item and common-group equating designs are not directly applicable to the cross-lingual assessment situation. Given this situation, compromises must be made.

Fortunately, creative, approximate solutions to this problem have been researched. The most popular approach is to screen translated items for DIF to justify a set of linking items thought to be equivalent across languages. Another approach is to justify the comparability of assessments across language based on internal structure validity evidence (e.g., structural equivalence, invariance of linking functions). A third approach is to use bilingual examinees in common-group type linking studies. We believe these studies provide useful information. However, in the future, we would like to see all three types of studies integrated into a comprehensive test development and validation plan, rather than relying on single studies in isolation. In addition, we would like to see studies of test-criterion relationships across languages that involve both construct-relevant and construct-irrelevant criteria.

Finally, studies looking at the consistency of testing consequences across languages should be conducted. For example, if examinees who pass a test in one language show similar levels of success on the job or in college as examinees who pass a test in another language, we can have confidence the testing purpose is being similarly fulfilled across both language versions. If the consequence of offering a test in a second language is that more people from that language group attend college or enter a profession, that consequence provides important validity evidence.

One thing from our review is clear: cross-lingual assessment is a difficult endeavor that requires creativity at each stage of the process—in test development, in developing score scales, in setting standards, and in conducting validity studies. As the editor of this volume pointed out, "One way to do that is to approach the data from as many distinct perspectives as possible to see if the various linkages converge or diverge because the degree of agreement or disagreement should provide a sense of how much uncertainty has been reduced by examination of the data" (N. Dorans, personal communication, February 5, 2015). Creativity in conducting these studies will be needed more than ever, because assessing individuals who operate in different languages is in great demand—both nationally (due to increasing linguistic diversity within a nation) and internationally. Our review provided several examples of creative methods in test development, scaling, and validation. We hope future research and practice provides even better solutions to the difficult problems inherent in cross-lingual assessment.

Notes

1. The views expressed are those of the author and not necessarily those of the University of Massachusetts-Amherst.
2. The views expressed are those of the author and not necessarily those of the Educational Testing Service. Joseph A. Rios began this chapter while at the University of Massachusetts-Amherst.
3. The views expressed are those of the author and not necessarily those of Pearson.
4. Bowles and Stansfield claimed the term "adaptation" represents a substantial change to the test that involves the replacement of some items. However, this is not standard usage of the term. In its most common usage in the literature, adaptation refers to a flexible translation process that is not word for word, but rather one that sought to retain the overall meaning of the test material across languages. It does not necessarily signify a change in the construct measured.

References

Allalouf, A. (2003) Revising translated differential item functioning items as a tool for improving cross-lingual assessment. *Applied Measurement in Education, 16*(1), 55–73.

Allalouf, A., Hambleton, R. K., & Sireci, S. G. (1999). Identifying the sources of differential item functioning in translated verbal items. *Journal of Educational Measurement, 36*, 185–198.

Allalouf, A., Rapp, J., & Stoller, R. (2009). What item types are best suited to the linking of verbal adapted tests? *International Journal of Testing, 9*, 92–107.

American Educational Research Association, American Psychological Association, & National Council on Measurement in Education. (1999). *Standards for educational and psychological testing.* Washington, DC: American Educational Research Association.

American Educational Research Association, American Psychological Association, & National Council on Measurement in Education. (2014). *Standards for educational and psychological testing.* Washington, DC: American Educational Research Association.

American Psychological Association, American Educational Research Association, & National Council on Measurement in Education. (1985). *Standards for educational and psychological testing.* Washington, DC: American Psychological Association.

Angoff, W. H., & Cook, L. L. (1988). *Equating the scores of the Prueba de Aptitud Academica and the Scholastic Aptitude Test* (Report No. 88-2). New York: College Entrance Examination Board.

Ariely, G., & Davidov, E. (2011). Can we rate public support for democracy in a comparable way? Cross-national equivalence of democratic attitudes in the World Value Survey. *Social Indicators Research, 104*(2), 271–286.

Baer, J., Baldi, S., Ayotte, K., Green, P. J., & McGrath, D. (2007). *The reading literacy of U.S. fourth-grade students in an international context: Results from the 2001 and 2006 Progress in International Reading Literacy Study (PIRLS)* (NCES-2008-017). Washington, DC: U.S. Department of Education. Retrieved from http://nces.ed.gov/pubs2008/2008017.pdf

Beller, M., Gafni, N., & Hanani, P. (2005). Constructing, adapting, and validating admissions tests in multiple languages: The Israeli case. In R. K. Hambleton, P. F. Merenda, & C. D. Spielberger (Eds.), *Adapting psychological and educational tests for cross-cultural assessment* (pp. 297–320). Mahwah, NJ: Lawrence Erlbaum.

Benitez, I., & Padilla, J. L. (2012). *Bridging the gap between psychometrics and qualitative methods: A mixed-method approach to understand the lack of equivalence in cross-cultural testing.* 8th Mixed Methods International Conference. Leeds, UK.

Boldt, R. F. (1969). *Concurrent validity of the PAA and SAT for bilingual Dade School County high school volunteers* (College Entrance Examination Board Research and Development Report 68-69, No. 3). Princeton, NJ: Educational Testing Service.

Bowles, M., & Stansfield, C. W. (2008, January). *A practical guide to standards-based assessment in the native language.* Bethesda, MD: Second Language Testing.

Byrne, B. M., & van de Vijver, F. J. R. (2010). Testing for measurement and structural equivalence in large-scale cross-cultural studies: Addressing the issue of nonequivalence. *International Journal of Testing, 10*(2), 107–132.

Cascallar, A. S., & Dorans, N. J. (2005). Linking scores from tests of similar content given in different languages: An illustration of methodological artifacts. *International Journal of Testing, 5,* 337–356.

Cheung, G. W., & Rensvold, R. B. (2002). Evaluating goodness-of-fit indexes for testing measurement invariance. *Structural Equation Modeling, 9*(2), 233–255.

Cleeland, C. S., Nakamura, Y., Mendoza, T. R., Edwards, K. R., Douglas, J., & Serlin, R. C. (1996). Dimensions of the impact of cancer pain in a four country sample: New information from multidimensional scaling. *Pain, 67*(2–3), 267–273.

Collazo, A. A. (2005). Translation of the Marlowe-Crowne Social Desirability Scale into an equivalent Spanish version. *Educational and Psychological Measurement, 65*(5), 780–806.

CTB/McGraw Hill (1988). *Spanish assessment of basic education: Technical report.* Monterey, CA: McGraw Hill.

Davidov, E. (2011). Nationalism and constructive patriotism: A longitudinal test of comparability in 22 countries with the ISSP. *International Journal of Public Opinion Research, 23*(1), 88–103.

Davis, S. L., Buckendahl, C. W., & Plake, B. S. (2006, April). *When adaptation is not an option: An application of cross-lingual standard setting.* Paper presented at the 5th Conference of the International Test Commission, Brussels.

Dimitrov, D. M. (2010). Testing for factorial invariance in the context of construct validation. *Measurement and Evaluation in Counseling and Development, 43*(2), 121–149.

Dorans, N. J. (2004). Equating, concordance, and expectation. *Applied Psychological Measurement, 28,* 227–246.

Dorans, N. J., & Middleton, K. (2012). Addressing the presumed assumptions of extreme linking. *Journal of Educational Measurement, 49,* 1–18.

Duncan, G. D., del Rio Parant, L., Chen, W-H., Ferrara, S., Johnson, E., Oppler, S., & Shieh, Y-Y. (2005). Study of a dual-language test booklet in eighth-grade mathematics. *Applied Measurement in Education, 18,* 129–161.

Elosua, P., & López-Jaúregui, A. (2007). Potential sources of differential item functioning in the adaptation of tests. *International Journal of Testing, 7*(1), 39–52.

Ercikan, K., & Koh, K. (2005). Examining the construct comparability of the English and French versions of TIMSS. *International Journal of Testing, 5*(1), 23–35.

Ercikan, K., Arim, R., Law, D., Domene, J., Gagnon, F., & Lacroix, S. (2010). Application of think aloud protocols for examining and confirming sources of differential item functioning identified by expert reviews. *Educational Measurement: Issues and Practice, 29*(2), 24–35.

Fischer, R., & Fontaine, J. R. J. (2011). Methods for investigating structural equivalence. In D. Matsumoto and J. R. van de Vijver (Eds.), *Cross-cultural research methods in psychology* (pp. 179–215). New York: Cambridge University Press.

Gierl, M. J., & Khaliq, S. N. (2001). Identifying sources of differential item and bundle functioning on translated achievement tests: A confirmatory analysis. *Journal of Educational Measurement, 38,* 164–187.

Geisinger, K. F. (1994). Cross-cultural normative assessment: Translation and adaptation issues influencing the normative interpretation of assessment instruments. *Psychological Assessment, 6,* 304–312.

Hambleton, R. K. (1994). Guidelines for adapting educational and psychological tests: a progress report. *European Journal of Psychological Assessment, 10*, 229–244.

Hambleton, R. K. (2005). Issues, designs and technical guidelines for adapting tests into multiple languages and cultures. In R. K. Hambleton, P. F. Merenda, & C. D. Spielberger (Eds.), *Adapting psychological and educational tests for cross-cultural assessment* (pp. 3–38). Hillsdale, NJ: Lawrence Erlbaum.

Hambleton, R. K., & de Jong, J. H. A. L. (2003). Advances in translating and adapting educational and psychological tests (Editorial). *Language Testing, 20*, 127–134.

Hattrup, K., Ghorpade, J., & Lackritz, J. R. (2007). Work group collectivism and the centrality of work: A multinational investigation. *The Journal of Comparative Social Science, 41*(3), 236–260.

Hulin, C. L., Drasgow, F., & Komocar, J. (1982). Applications of item response theory to analysis of attitude scale translations. *Journal of Applied Psychology, 67*(6), 818–825.

Hulin, C. L., & Mayer, L. J. (1986). Psychometric equivalence of a translation of the Job Descriptive Index into Hebrew. *Journal of Applied Psychology, 71*(1), 83–94.

International Test Commission (2010). *Guidelines for translating and adapting tests*. Retrieved from www.intestcom.org

Kolen, M. J. (2007). Data collection designs and linking procedures. In N. J. Dorans, M. Pommerich, & P. W. Holland (Eds.), *Linking and aligning scores and scales* (pp. 31–55). New York: Springer.

Kolen, M., & Brennan, R. (2014). *Test equating, scaling, and linking: Methods and practices* (3rd ed.). New York: Springer-Verlag.

Linn, R. L. (1993). Linking results of distinct assessments. *Applied Measurement in Education, 6*, 83–102.

Little, T. D., & Slegers, D. W. (2005). Factor analysis: Multiple groups with means. In B. Everitt & D. Howell (Eds.) & D. Rindskopf (Section Ed.), *Encyclopedia of statistics in behavioral science* (pp. 617–623). Chichester: Wiley.

Lord. F. M. (1980). *Applications of item response theory to practical testing problems*. Hillsdale, NJ: Lawrence Erlbaum Associates.

Meade, A. W., Johnson, E. C., & Braddy, P. W. (2008). Power and sensitivity of alternative fit indices in tests of measurement invariance. *Journal of Applied Psychology, 93*(3), 568–592.

Messick, S. (1989). Validity. In R. Linn (Ed.), *Educational measurement* (3rd ed., pp. 13–100). Washington, DC: American Council on Education.

Mislevy, R. J. (1992, December). *Linking educational assessments: Concepts, issues, methods, and prospects*. Princeton, NJ: Educational Testing Service.

Mullis, I. V. S., Martin, M. O., & Foy, P. (2008). *TIMSS 2007 international mathematics report: Findings from IEA's trends in international mathematics and science study at the fourth and eighth grades*. Chestnut Hill, MA: TIMSS & PIRLS International Study Center, Boston College.

Muniz, J., Hambleton, R. K., & Xing, D. (2000). Small sample studies to detect flaws in test translation. *International Journal of Testing, 1*, 115–135.

Oliveri, M. E., Olson, B. F., Ercikan, K., & Zumbo, B. (2012). Methodologies for investigating item-level and test-level measurement equivalence in international large-scale assessments. *International Journal of Testing, 12*(3), 203–223.

Ong, S. L., & Sireci, S. G. (2008). Using bilingual students to link and evaluate different language versions of an exam. *US-China Education Review, 5*, 37–46.

Organisation for Economic Co-operation and Development (OECD). (2006). *Literacy skills for the world of tomorrow: Further results from PISA 2003*. Paris: OECD.

Pennock-Roman, M., & Rivera, C. (2011). Mean effects of test accommodations for ELLs and non-ELLs: A meta-analysis of experimental studies. *Educational Measurement: Issues and Practice, 30*(3), 10–28.

Rapp, J., & Allalouf, A. (2003). Evaluating cross-lingual equating. *International Journal of Testing, 3*, 101–117.

Rios, J. A., & Sireci, S. G. (2014). Guidelines versus practices in cross-lingual assessment: A disconcerting disconnect. *International Journal of Testing, 14*, 289–312.

Robin, F., Sireci, S. G., & Hambleton, R. K. (2003). Evaluating the equivalence of different language versions of a credentialing exam. *International Journal of Testing, 3*, 1–20.

Rodriguez, O. (1992). Introduction to technical and societal issues in the psychological testing of Hispanics. In K. F. Geisinger (Ed.), *Psychological testing of Hispanics* (pp. 1–15). Washington, DC: American Psychological Association.

Shealy, R., & Stout, W. (1993). A model-based standardization approach that separates true bias/DIF from group ability differences and detects test bias/DIF as well as item bias/DIF. *Psychometrika, 58*, 159–194.

Sireci, S. G. (1997). Problems and issues in linking tests across languages. *Educational Measurement: Issues and Practice, 16*(1), 12–19.

Sireci, S. G. (2005). Using bilinguals to evaluate the comparability of different language versions of a test. In R. K. Hambleton, P. Merenda, & C. Spielberger (Eds.), *Adapting educational and psychological tests for cross-cultural assessment* (pp. 117–138). Hillsdale, NJ: Lawrence Erlbaum.

Sireci, S. G., & Berberoglu, G. (2000). Using bilingual respondents to evaluate translated-adapted items. *Applied Measurement in Education, 35*(2), 229–259.

Sireci, S. G., & Khaliq, S. N. (2002, April). *An analysis of the psychometric properties of dual language test forms.* Paper presented at the annual meeting of the National Council on Measurement in Education, New Orleans, LA.

Sireci, S. G., & Wells. C. S. (2010). Evaluating the comparability of English and Spanish video accommodations for English language learners. In P. Winter (Ed.), *Evaluating the comparability of scores from achievement test variations* (pp. 33–68). Washington, DC: Council of Chief State School Officers.

Sireci, S. G., Patsula, L., & Hambleton, R. K. (2005). Statistical methods for identifying flawed items in the test adaptations process. In R. K. Hambleton, P. Merenda, & C. Spielberger (Eds.), *Adapting educational and psychological tests for cross-cultural assessment* (pp. 93–115). Hillsdale, NJ: Lawrence Erlbaum.

Sireci, S. G., Yang, Y., Harter, J., & Ehrlic, E. (2006). Evaluating guidelines for test adaptations: A methodological analysis of translation quality. *Journal of Cross-Cultural Psychology, 37*, 557–567.

Sireci, S. G., Han, K. T., & Wells, C. S. (2008). Methods for evaluating the validity of test scores for English language learners. *Educational Assessment, 13*, 108–131.

Statistics Canada & Organisation for Economic Co-operation and Development (OECD). (2005). *Learning a living: First results of the adult literacy and life skills survey.* Paris: Minister of Industry, Canada, and OECD. Retrieved from www.oecd.org/edu/highereducationandadultlearning/41529631.pdf

van de Vijver, F. J. R., & Leung, K. (2011). Equivalence and bias: A review of concepts, models, and data analytic procedures. In D. Matsumoto and J. R. van de Vijver (Eds.), *Cross-cultural research methods in psychology* (pp. 17–45). New York: Cambridge University Press.

van de Vijver, F. J. R., & Poortinga, Y. H. (1997). Towards an integrated analysis of bias in cross-cultural assessment. *European Journal of Psychological Assessment, 13*, 29–37.

van de Vijver, F. J. R., & Poortinga, Y. H. (2005). Conceptual and methodological issues in adapting tests. In R. K. Hambleton, P. Merenda, & C. Spielberger (Eds.), *Adapting educational and psychological tests for cross-cultural assessment* (pp. 39–63). Hillsdale, NJ: Lawrence Erlbaum.

van de Vijver, F., & Tanzer, N. K. (1998). Bias and equivalence in cross-cultural assessment. *European Review of Applied Psychology, 47*(4), 263–279.

Wainer, H. (2011). *Uneducated guesses: Using evidence to uncover misguided education policies.* Princeton, NJ: Princeton University Press.

Wainer, H., Sireci, S. G., & Thissen, D. (1991). Differential testlet functioning: Definitions and detection. *Journal of Educational Measurement, 28*, 197–219.

Willingham, W. W., & Cole, N. S. (1997). *Gender and fair assessment.* Mahwah, NJ: Lawrence Erlbaum.

Wolff, H. G., Schneider-Rahm, C. I., & Forret, M. L. (2011). Adaptation of a German multidimensional networking scale into English. *European Journal of Psychological Assessment, 27*(4), 244–250.

Woodcock, R. W., & Muñoz-Sandoval, A. F. (1993). An IRT approach to cross-language test equating and interpretation. *European Journal of Psychological Assessment, 9*(3), 233–241.

Xi, X. (2010). How do we go about investigating test fairness? *Language Testing, 27*(2), 147–170.

Yen, C. J., & Tu, C. H. (2011). Multiple-group confirmatory factor analysis of the scores for online social presence: Do they measure the same thing across cultural groups? *Journal of Educational Computing Research, 44*(2), 219–242.

11 Commentary on the Assessment of the Fairness of Comparisons under Divergent Measurement Conditions

David Thissen[1]

Apologia

At first glance, the topics of the four chapters in this section might appear almost unrelated; they have testing in common, but not much else. Computerizing paper-and-pencil tests, vertical scaling, test translation, and the development of accommodations and modifications for special populations are almost always distinct activities carried out by different groups of people. Each topic has its own experts, and its own areas of controversy.

However, under the umbrella of test *fairness*, all four topics are, in their own ways, examples of situations that require *linking disparate tests* to obtain scores that can be used interchangeably for some purpose. That may be a reason I was asked to write this commentary on a collection of chapters that are mostly on topics not central to my own research. I have previously been involved with projects or writing on the topic of linking disparate tests (Feuer, Holland, Green, Bertenthal, & Hemphill, 1999; Linn, McLaughlin, & Thissen, 2009; Thissen, 2007; Williams, Rosa, McLeod, Thissen, & Sanford, 1998). So linking will be the thread that stitches these four topics together in this commentary.

Disclaimer

In the interest of full disclosure, I should state that I have collaborated with two of the chapter authors (Sireci, Thissen, & Wainer, 1991; Thissen, Pommerich, Billeaud, & Williams, 1995; Wainer, Sireci, & Thissen, 1991; Williams, Pommerich, & Thissen, 1998), although not on the topics on which they have written for this volume. Given my history with those scholars and my respect for the intellectual stature of all of the chapter authors in this section, the reader should not expect this commentary to be *critical* in the sense of dictionary definition 2(a) "inclined to criticize severely and unfavorably"; instead, I hope to be critical in the sense of definition 2(c) "exercising or involving careful judgment or judicious evaluation" (*Merriam-Webster Dictionary*, n.d.).

A Little Background: Measurement, Contests, and Domain Score Estimates

A central idea in all four chapters in this section is the *construct* being measured by a test or assessment. Much of what Holland (2008) called the first three generations of test theory was concerned with the measurement of psychological constructs (Dorans, 2012). On the other hand, the idea of fairness is, on the surface, part of the more recent conception of the test as contest (Holland, 1994, 2008). Dorans (2011, p. 271) quotes Holland (1994) saying "tests are not just measuring instruments . . . that they are sometimes contests as well is the main reason that we care about fairness." So how does the idea of the construct being measured figure so heavily in these chapters on fairness? An answer lies in an integration of the ideas of the construct being measured by an assessment, and domain reference for its scores.

Bock, Thissen, and Zimowski (1997) set up the measurement of psychological constructs (or *traits*) and domain reference for scores in educational measurement as alternative conceptions, but it might be more useful to integrate the two ideas. We could say that the construct being measured by an educational achievement test is the proficiency needed to respond correctly to questions or to perform tasks that indicate mastery of the curricular content standards being assessed. In this conception, construct measurement and a contest based on domain-referenced scores are isomorphic. Dorans (2011, p. 271) offered a similar perspective when he wrote "The best way to resolve the contest/measurement conflict is . . . with better measurement. Better measurement should lead to fairer and more useful contests." Or, from the symmetrically opposite point of view, fairer tests (as contests) should lead to more valid tests (as measurement), because any lack of fairness is also a reflection of some source of extraneous, or construct-irrelevant, variance in the test scores.

What do these seemingly tangential remarks have to do with these chapters on fairness and computerization, vertical scaling, translation, and the provision of accommodations and modifications for special populations? It has to do with the relation of the construct being measured and the need for linking. If, in some imaginary world, there was only one test form that was the basis for either contest or measurement, in some senses questions of fairness, or indeed validity, would not arise: That single test would by (some) definition(s) be fair and valid in the sense that it would be an operational definition of the measurement, and it would be part of the rules of the contest. But these chapters are about situations in which there must be multiple different forms of assessment: different modes, or different languages, or different degrees of difficulty for higher or lower grades, or with and without accommodations or modifications. Scores on those different forms must be linked.

Castellano and Kolen (this volume, Chapter 8, p. 137) write that:

> Kolen (2006) asserts the quality of linking different assessments is affected by three key features of the test administrations: "test content," "conditions of measurement," and "examinee population." He indicates that these three key features work together to define the construct that is actually measured by the test, which we refer to as the "construct actually measured."

All of the chapters in this section are about changes to one or more of those three features of a test administration: mode and language, and some accommodations or modifications, change the conditions of measurement (Dorans & Middleton, 2012); language, difficulty shifts for vertical scaling, and accommodations/modifications are also for different examinee populations. Any of these changes may change content to some degree.

What, then, is the touchstone for *fairness*? Pommerich's chapter makes clear that there is no easy definition of fairness that will satisfy all, but in practice the working definition appears to make use of the integration, above, of construct measurement and domain-reference scores: The use of alternative test forms is considered *fair* if the same construct is measured on the same scale, so in the educational achievement setting, the score provides the same kind of estimate of domain mastery. Pommerich (this volume, Chapter 7) writes "Interchangeable scores as defined within an equating context (i.e., with regard to the equating requirements delineated by Dorans & Holland, 2000) appear to encompass the fairness properties of distributional equivalence, construct equivalence, and predictive equivalence." "Equivalence" is probably an unattainable standard for changes to assessments as substantial as computerization, development of more- and less-difficult forms for vertical scaling, translation, and the provision of accommodations and modifications for special populations. However, substantial lack of equivalence with respect to any of those features may lead to unfairness. So data analysis to avoid unfairness concentrates on the quality of the linking, by looking for evidence of any lack of distributional equivalence, construct equivalence, or predictive equivalence.

It Is All Linking

The production of scores that are interchangeable (for some purposes) is a goal in all four of the activities discussed in this section—computerization, vertical scaling, translation, and the provision of accommodations and modifications for special populations. However, entirely interchangeable scores, the products of *equating* between alternate forms, are *prima facie* not possible in any of those situations. It is widely agreed that equating between two tests requires that the tests be constructed with the same specifications and administered under the same conditions (Holland & Dorans, 2006; Kolen, 2007; Kolen and Brennan, 2014). All of the activities discussed in this section clearly change the test specifications. So consideration of the interchangeability of scores in those contexts falls in the more general category of test linking, which has only relatively recently been subject to taxonomy (Linn, 1993; Mislevy, 1992), and even more recently to evaluation (Dorans & Holland, 2000; Holland, 2005).

Dorans and Middleton (2012) summarize and extend work by Middleton and Dorans (2011) on ways to check, and potentially falsify, *presumed linkings* such as those that arise between translated tests or forms with accommodations. Expanding on methods used to evaluate actual linking, Dorans and Middleton recommend testing the invariance of the relationships among test forms that are administered under different measurement conditions, to (potentially) falsify a presumed linking: If alternate test forms do not have the same relative difficulty across languages, or across accommodations or modifications, that would be evidence that they do not measure the same construct, and that interchangeable use of their scores may be unfair.

The logic involved in testing the invariance of relationships among test forms can be applied to shorter and shorter tests, until one treats each item on a form as a one-item test. Then a second falsifiable assumption of linking is that the items within a test form have the same relative difficulty, or that they are in the same relative order with respect to other properties, such as discrimination, as well. This is essentially the null hypothesis tested by any number of methods of detecting differential item functioning (DIF) (Dorans & Holland, 1993; Thissen, Steinberg, & Wainer, 1993). Dorans and Middleton (2012) question the use of DIF analysis to examine presumed linkings on the grounds that one cannot always be assured that the so-called *matching variable* means the same thing in both groups (both languages, or populations tested with or without accommodations), but the question appears to be with the use of the term *DIF* rather than the functionality of the procedure. Indeed, Dorans and Middleton (2012) cite two studies, by Allalouf, Hambleton, and Sireci (1999) and Gierl, Rogers, and Klinger (1999), in which DIF analysis across translations suggested lack of invariance.

A third kind of evidence that has become prominent in the evaluation of the fairness of test linking in general is the caparison of group differences between the linked assessments. Dorans and Holland (2000) recommended this approach, and Dorans and Liu (2009) have described recent developments and summarized applications of this approach. Statistics such as RMSD and REMSD (Dorans & Holland, 2000) can be used to evaluate the extent to which two tests (translations or accommodated measures) order populations of examinees in the same way; if the two tests measure the same construct, then the relative positions of populations should be invariant, just as relative item difficulty or the relative difficulty of alternate forms should be invariant.

The bottom line is that, while we cannot be as assured of the quality of linking as we can be of the quality of equating between test forms constructed to the same specifications, we can check linking in ways that may show that the two tests measure different things, if they do.

One can conceive of the four topics covered by the chapters in this section on a branching continuum of linkings ranging from relatively straightforward to impossible to check empirically: The order would have changing mode of administration (in practice, computerizing paper-and-pencil tests) most straightforward to link and evaluate, followed by vertical scaling, which is also subject to empirical checks, but with more challenges. As previously mentioned, Dorans and Middleton use the term *presumed linkings* for linked scores when neither equivalent groups nor common anchor material are available, so linking is impossible. Linking accommodated or modified tests for special populations, and translations, fall in the category of presumed linking. Between those two topics, the continuum branches: The challenges involved in linking accommodated or modified tests for special populations to some parent assessment often involve small populations sizes as well as a lack of anchor material, while the translation problem may involve large populations and samples, but a complete lack of equivalent groups or anchor material.

Fairness across Modes of Administration

Pommerich (this volume, Chapter 7, p. 111) observes that while "fairness in testing has been addressed extensively in the measurement literature . . . the discussion typically focuses on a single test" and has not been extended to include tests administered in alternate modes, such as paper-and-pencil forms and computerized delivery. She further observes that mode comparability studies have tended to focus on overall comparisons of scores rather than issues of fairness, which would involve examination of subgroup performance. Thissen and Norton (2013) summarized an extensive review of the recent literature on mode effects and concluded similarly that the existing literature "is relatively silent on the question of whether gaps in scores among subpopulations may appear different, depending on whether computerized or paper and pencil tests are used."

Pommerich emphasizes the fact that examining fairness across modes of administration is formally the same as across linked tests, but then observes, "the fairness of comparing scores that have been linked across different tests has not been a focus of the linkage literature" either. She then describes ways to examine the fairness of score comparisons either across modes of administration or across linkages of disparate tests.

Pommerich provides an overview of the idea of fairness, noting that fairness is a property of test use, and is based on validity. Taking a comparable validity perspective on the idea of fairness, Pommerich notes that distributional equivalence of scores, construct equivalence, and predictive equivalence between modes of assessment are all needed for the interchangeable use of scores obtained with different modes of assessment to be truly fair. One could write exactly the same things about scores across grades (vertical scaling), or between languages, or between a standard assessment and versions administered with accommodations or modified; these ideas will recur.

In this commentary, we will follow Pommerich's use of words, in which *comparable* has a very limited meaning (distributional equivalence of scores) while *interchangeable* scores have distributional equivalence and also construct and predictive equivalence. We will, however, generally explicitly (or not) add the phrase "for some purpose" to the word *interchangeable*, because it is generally agreed that the only scores from different test forms that are interchangeable for any purpose arise from equating, and equating is off the table in this section.

As checks on the interchangeability of test scores between paper-and-pencil and computerized administrations, Pommerich suggests "evaluating the quality of a linkage, as recommended in Pommerich, Hanson, Harris, and Sconing (2004)." While that article is about SAT-ACT score concordance, it considers the relations among scores for subgroups, generalizability to other samples, and equity after cut scores are applied. All of those address questions one would want answered to have confidence in the comparison of scores obtained with such different conditions of administration.

Pommerich (this volume, Chapter 7, pp. 126–127) also notes:

> Population invariance of linking functions is another means by which to evaluate whether fairness is likely to be a concern for score linkages . . . Violations of population invariance are a threat to test fairness because examinees from different groups that have the same score on one test will have different linked scores on the corresponding test, resulting in potential disadvantages for some group members (Huggins & Penfield, 2012). Dorans (2004) recommended that score equity assessment be routinely addressed as a fairness consideration, along with differential item functioning and differential prediction.

There are aspects of the computerization of assessments that are unique. For example, Pommerich points out that "differential access to computers is a notable fairness concern associated with mode of administration, related to socioeconomic status." Commenting on an extensive review of recent studies of computerization, Thissen and Norton (2013, pp. 353–354) wrote that:

> Probably the most salient (unintended) individual differences variable that may be related to the results obtained with computerized assessments is computer familiarity, which is not a very well-defined term, but which includes skills with a keyboard and probably some other aspects of the idiom used in the computer interface. However, these effects have been rare historically, and can likely be eliminated with careful assessment design and thoughtful instructions and preparation.

In addition, many computerized tests also make use of internet delivery of items and collection of responses; Pommerich points to several recently well-publicized instances of failures of Internet test administration, which suggests that research and monitoring procedures are required to maintain confidence that Internet delivery of tests works as intended when used on a large scale.

Fairness across Grade Levels

In parallel with Pommerich's observation that issues of fairness have historically been addressed largely in the context of a single test, and not across modes of administration, Castellano and Kolen (this volume, Chapter 8, p. 135) open with similar acknowledgement that "at a single point in time, there are established procedures for investigating fairness considerations" but "no clear procedures have been established for investigating fairness considerations for measures comparing test scores across multiple time points." They observe that, if scores are to be compared across grades, evaluation of the quality of the scores should similarly be across grades. Like Pommerich, they consider the construct first, and write, "Ideally, if programs are interested in making cross-grade comparisons, they would define their desired cross-grade construct a priori and develop the corresponding grade-level assessments in alignment with this construct."

Castellano and Kolen then observe that "goals for construct representation and fairness in cross-grade comparisons might be in conflict." That is, indeed, a challenge. The classical solution is domain reference of the scores across grades, with the domain defined by curricular standards. Recently, Briggs and Peck (2015) suggested that learning progressions could provide a more rational basis for the description of the construct being measured by a vertical scale. It may be possible to integrate that with cross-grade domain reference, where the domain comprises a collection of learning progressions (Thissen, 2015).

Because the construction of vertical scales is widely considered to *be* a variety test linking, it is no surprise that Castellano and Kolen recommend the same kinds of data analysis to check vertical scales as are standards for linking: invariance of between-group differences in score distributions and DIF analysis, both within grades and across grades. They emphasize that "Fairness in comparisons of student test scores across grades is a validity issue, and as such requires the same rigorous substantiation and documentation of claims and evidence as for the test scores themselves." They also point out that "Establishing fairness and validity evidence for the use of test scores to assess achievement at a given point in time is not sufficient to establish such evidence for using scores from multiple time points to assess achievement over time." *Mutatis mutandis*, one could substitute "across modes of assessment" or "across languages" or "between administration with and without accommodations" for "across grades" or "over time" in those comments, and they would be equally true.

"And now for something completely different"
(Catchphrase from *Monty Python's Flying Circus*)

"The difficult we do immediately. The impossible takes a little longer." This motto, variously attributed to the U.S. Army Corps of Engineers (Bohle, 1967) or the U.S. Army Air Forces (*Newsweek*, 1943), could also be taken as the motto of psychometricians. For example, when I teach factor analysis, I begin with a description of the goal: to do regression analysis, with the response variable observed but the predictor variable unobserved. To be sure that is clear, I ask the students if they understand that to be impossible. When they agree that it is impossible, I say, "Alright, now we'll spend the rest of the class discussing how we do it."

Producing comparable scores for tests administered in different languages is similarly impossible, because there is no feasible data collection design to support linking. In general, two broad classes of data collection designs can be used to link tests (Holland & Dorans, 2006; Kolen, 2007; Kolen & Brennan, 2014): One makes use of a *common population* of examinees, and a sample taking both tests, or two random samples taking one test each. The other uses *common items* comprising an *anchor test* that is a linking subset of each of two tests administered to samples from distinct populations. Strictly speaking, neither possibility exists in any useful sense to link translations without making heroic assumptions. The only conceivable common population in which to link translations would be bilingual examinees; however, the entire point would be to draw inferences about the scores for monolingual examinees who are almost certainly different. So linking in the bilingual population cannot supply unambiguous evidence of score comparability for the intended (monolingual) populations. And there cannot be common items, because all items have to be in one language or the other. One can assume that some of the items are the same in translation, and use those as the common items, but again, the evidence so obtained cannot be unambiguous. So linking scores on tests administered in different languages is impossible; Sireci, Rios, and Powers (this volume, Chapter 10) provide a thorough summary of ways that it is done, and checks on validity and fairness.

Sireci, Rios, and Powers begin with the need for test translation, pointing out that international assessments (TIMSS, PISA, PIRLS, PIAC, and the like) are inconceivable without translation, and within countries many assessments (statewide tests in the United States, and other tests elsewhere) are administered in multiple languages to be fair in multilingual populations. While in everyday language we would use the word *translation* to refer to the process of rendering a test written in one language in another language, Sireci, Rios, and Powers (this volume, Chapter 9, p. 183) point out that:

> "translation" ... may be viewed as implying a literal word-for-word substitution, which is not an accurate description of what happens when tests are adjusted for use across languages ... the term "adaptation" is preferable ... because in cross-lingual assessment, the intent is to retain the meaning of the test material.

They emphasize that what one is trying to do in translation/adaptation is to measure the same construct in both (or all) languages, which is not the same in many cases as literal translation. In this regard, translation/adaptation is closer to accommodation or modification than to, say, a mode change.

Parallel with Pommerich's discussion of mode changes, Sireci, Rios, and Powers emphasize that the task of providing interchangeable scores (for some purpose) from translated/adapted assessments is one of test linkage, and they describe three data collection designs: "(a) the separate monolingual groups design; (b) the matched monolingual group design; and (c) the bilingual group design" and then remark that "All designs have their limitations" and elaborate on the limitations of each.

Interestingly enough, DIF analyses play perhaps the most prominent role among the four chapters in this section in the evaluation of cross-language linkages. That is surprising at first glance, because all DIF detection procedures require a *matching variable* (Dorans & Holland, 1993) or *anchor* (Thissen et al., 1993) set of items, and no items on any translated forms can be guaranteed to unambiguously serve that role. Nevertheless, DIF analysis can be informative: If standard DIF analyses show that a few items exhibit DIF between languages and most do not, then the few that show DIF might be repaired or set aside, and the agreement among those that do not show DIF is evidence that the items may be measuring the same construct in both languages. Sireci, Rios, and Powers also cite examples of translations in which many, even a majority of, the items exhibit DIF between languages; such findings were accompanied with a warning that "when substantial amounts of DIF and inconsistencies in test structure are observed across translated assessments, comparisons of students who responded to different language versions of the items should not be made."

DIF analysis can be used as part of the procedure to select common items for linkage across languages, in much the same way as it is often used to select linking items in vertical scaling. But Sireci, Rios, and Powers suggest that DIF analysis and linking are not sufficient to check the validity (and thereby fairness) of translation/adaptation, and recommend the use of "other validity studies beyond DIF to evaluate the comparability of scores from tests linked across languages." Sireci, Rios, and Powers describe uses of multiple group confirmatory factor analysis to examine the extent to which the structure of an assessment is the same across linguistic groups (and implementations). They cite suggestions by Dorans and Middleton (2012) and Rapp and Allalouf (2003) that are in agreement with procedures used in other contexts discussed in this section. But then they point out "there are essentially no studies of the consistency of test-criterion relationships across languages (e.g., differential predictive validity) or more complex correlational studies." To do those studies would buttress the validity of translation/adaptation, and serves as a connection between this topic and the computerization or vertical scales, for which Pommerich (this volume, Chapter 7) and Castellano and Kolen (this volume, Chapter 8) also indicate that predictive equivalence is evidence that two versions of a test measure the same construct.

Accommodations and Modifications and Fairness

Stone and Cook (this volume, Chapter 9) emphasize the relatively recently evolved notion that "tests should be designed and developed with all intended members of the testing population in mind" and in that process "careful thought be given to the construct(s) the test is intended to measure, as well as the format and administration of the test from the perspective of the intended test taker." The use of universal design (UD) principals in test design enhances fairness by minimizing the number of special populations that require any accommodations or modifications. Questions about the fairness of an assessment for members of special populations may still arise, but they can be investigated in the same way the general population assessment is checked for fairness for any subgroup.

Stone and Cook catalog a number of aspects of test design to consider, from the point of view of accessibility, including test content that may introduce construct-irrelevant variation in scores, item and task format that may be more familiar or easier for some populations than others, and instructions that may be more clear for some groups than others. They emphasize the usefulness of item and test tryouts to acquire statistical evidence that the items, and assembled test forms, measure the construct as intended. They also explain ways in which conditions of administration may enhance or reduce fairness. They point out that the goal of test accommodations, where they remain required after the test is constructed following the principles of UD, is "to reduce construct-irrelevant variance in test scores and, thus, to enable test users to make comparable inferences about individuals based on their test scores."

Stone and Cook observe that the same kinds of statistical evidence discussed in other chapters in this section can, in principle, be applied to the investigation of the fairness of tests for special populations that require accommodation. They specifically mention DIF analysis and predictive validity, as well as the "interaction hypothesis/differential boost paradigm." The latter forms of analysis are unique to accommodation:

> Evidence for or against the appropriateness of test accommodations can be obtained by comparing standardized mean scores for the group of individuals to whom the test accommodations are targeted (the studied group) and a group of individuals for whom the accommodation is assumed not to be appropriate (e.g., individuals without disabilities, or native English speakers).
>
> (Stone and Cook, this volume, Chapter 9, p. 174)

This kind of evidence may be expensive to obtain, because it involves data collection beyond standard test administration, but it clarifies the effects of accommodations. Stone and Cook also point out the usefulness of cognitive labs, usability studies, surveys, and focus groups to provide qualitative evidence of validity when sample sizes are too small to permit quantitative approaches.

As an illustration of challenging conditions that can render the very idea of statistical evidence of score interchangeability unthinkable, consider accommodations for special populations required of the assessment being developed by the ELPA21 (English Language Proficiency Assessment for the 21st Century) consortium (www.elpa21.org). That consortium of 10 states supports the development of an assessment system for English learners (ELs), measuring proficiency in four language domains: reading, writing, listening, and speaking. Scores on the assessment are to be used as part of the decision-making process for entry to, and exit from, EL programs. Stone and Cook discuss the EL population as a special population with respect to the reference general population, but the target population for the ELPA21 assessment is the EL population, so it is already relatively small and diverse.

Within that population, there are special populations of students with specific needs for accommodations, even after a test development process that follows Stone and Cook's suggestion that the assessment be designed with accessibility in mind. For example, students who are blind or have low vision require an assessment that uses alternative methods of item presentation, such as text-to-speech, realia, and read-aloud items (ELPA21 Administration, Accommodations and Accessibility, & Item Acquisition and Development Task Management Teams, 2015). Further, there are several item types on the ELPA21 assessment that make use of visual displays to reduce the dependence of the writing and speaking scores on listening or reading skills; those items must be completely replaced with alternatives for students who are blind or have low vision, if domain coverage is to be kept close to that of the test for the general EL population. In the end, an assessment that has been changed in many ways for students who are blind or have low vision is required to produce scores that are interchangeable, at least for the purpose of qualifying students for entry to or exit from EL programs. Because the prospective population size is so small, statistical evidence of score comparability in this context is unthinkable. In its place, the plan is to "produce scores for these students that are comparable in terms of the constructs assessed and proficiency level domain scores to those based on the general test" (ELPA21 Administration et al., 2015). The idea is to assure that the items on the form for students who are blind or have low vision stand in the same relation to the domain of standards as the items on the general test. It is possible that score comparability will be achieved with the use of parallel standard setting for the general test and the modified assessment.

This takes us back to the beginning of this commentary: The construct being measured is the proficiency needed to respond correctly to questions or to perform tasks that indicate mastery; an assessment that is *fair* measures that same construct for all students. In the case of accommodations or modifications with extremely low volume, the only evidence of comparability may be judgment about the similarity of domain coverage, and social moderation of qualifying scores. If the special populations making use of accommodations or modifications are sufficiently large, the statistical techniques discussed earlier, in the context of mode effects, vertical scaling, and translation may be used to investigate the possibility of a lack of comparability.

Conclusion

All four chapters in this section emphasize that fairness involves measuring the same construct on the same scale in all modes in which the test is used and for all subpopulations. While there is no statistic with a range of values indicating that "these two tests measures the same construct," there can be statistical evidence that a test, or some items on a test, do *not* measure the same construct. These kinds of statistical evidence can be used to falsify the "same construct" hypothesis, and thereby cast doubt on fairness. So all four chapters suggest the use of those kinds of statistical analysis where practical.

Prototypical among statistical approaches to check the hypothesis that a test measures the same construct across groups has been DIF analysis, since its inception in the 1970s (Angoff & Ford, 1973; Lord, 1977). DIF analysis works backward from the idea that, if a set of items measure the same construct for two (or more) groups, then the items should be in the same relative order of difficulty, and/or discrimination, for those groups. That forms a null hypothesis that can be tested statistically. DIF analysis can be used between groups tested under different administrative conditions, like computerized or paper-and-pencil, or between grades on a vertical scale, or between linguistic groups, or between the general population and groups with special needs, if sample size permits.

The idea that item statistics within groups should be in the same order across groups for a test that measures the same construct within each group can be generalized above the item level, to suggest that the distributions of scores on alternate test forms should be in the same order across groups. More creatively, this can also be generalized to say that group differences in scores should be the same across tests that are to be linked (Dorans & Holland, 2000), which has come to be a fundamental statistical test for the viability of linking. Because all of the topics in this section come down to linking, this idea is applicable to all.

Non-statistical evidence that two tests measure the same construct is also essential. In this section, "two tests" may be what appears to be the same test administered under different conditions (modes of assessment), or in different grades (vertical scaling), or in different languages, or with accommodations or modifications. In the context of educational achievement testing, the construct is the proficiency needed to respond correctly to questions or to perform tasks that indicate mastery of the curricular content standards being assessed. So evidence that the items span the domain, and are free of construct-irrelevant sources of variation in the test scores, is also crucial support for the idea that the "two tests" measure the same construct, and therefore that comparisons between scores are fair.

Continued vigilance is required. There is no way to guarantee that a use of a test is fair. All that can be done is to catalog carefully the ways in which comparisons could be unfair, and then check, with either statistics or reasoned judgment, whether unfairness exists. The chapters in this section do that cataloging task well, and should provide the standards of vigilance for some time to come.

Note

1. The views expressed are those of the author and not necessarily those of the University of North Carolina, Chapel Hill.

References

Allalouf, A., Hambleton, R. K., & Sireci, S. G. (1999). Identifying the causes of DIF in translated verbal items. *Journal of Educational Measurement, 36*, 185–198.

Angoff, W. H., & Ford, S. F. (1973). Item-race interaction on a test of scholastic aptitude. *Journal of Educational Measurement, 10*, 95–106.

Bock, R. D., Thissen, D., & Zimowski, M. F. (1997). IRT estimation of domain scores. *Journal of Educational Measurement, 34*, 197–211.

Bohle, B. (1967). *The home book of American quotations*. New York: Dodd, Mead.

Briggs, D. C., & Peck, F. A. (2015). Using learning progressions to design vertical scales that support coherent inferences about student growth. *Measurement, 13*, 75–99.

Dorans, N. J. (2004). Using population invariance to assess test score equity. *Journal of Educational Measurement, 41*, 43–68.

Dorans, N. J. (2011). Holland's advice for the fourth generation of test theory: Blood tests can be contests. In N. J. Dorans & S. Sinharay (Eds.), *Looking back: Proceedings of a conference in honor of Paul W. Holland* (pp. 259–272). New York: Springer.

Dorans, N. J. (2012). The contestant perspective on taking tests: Emanations from the statue within. *Educational Measurement: Issues and Practice, 31*, 20–37.

Dorans, N. J., & Holland, P. W. (1993) DIF detection and description: Mantel-Haenszel and standardization. In P. W. Holland & H. Wainer (Eds.), *Differential item functioning* (pp. 35–66). Hillsdale, NJ: Lawrence Erlbaum Associates.

Dorans, N. J., & Holland, P. W. (2000). Population invariance and the equitability of tests: Basic theory and the linear case. *Journal of Educational Measurement, 37*, 281–306.

Dorans, N. J., & Liu, J. (2009). *Score equity assessment: Development of a prototype analysis using SAT mathematics test data across several administrations* (ETS Research Report No. RR-09-08). Princeton, NJ: Educational Testing Service.

Dorans, N. J., & Middleton, K. (2012). Addressing the extreme assumptions of presumed linkings. *Journal of Educational Measurement, 49*, 1–18.

ELPA21 Administration, Accommodations and Accessibility, & Item Acquisition and Development Task Management Teams. (2015, April). *Issue Brief: ELPA21 accessibility for students who are blind or have low vision*. Washington, DC: Council of Chief State School Officers.

Feuer, M. J., Holland, P. W., Green, B. F., Bertenthal, M. W., & Hemphill, F. C. (1999). *Uncommon measures: Equivalence and linkage among educational tests*. Washington, DC: National Academy Press.

Gierl, M., Rogers, W. T., & Klinger, D. (1999). Using statistical and judgmental reviews to identify and interpret translation differential item functioning. *Alberta Journal of Educational Research, 45*, 353–376.

Holland, P. W. (1994). Measurements or contests? Comments on Zwick, Bond and Allen/Donoghue. In *Proceedings of the Social Statistics Section of the American Statistical Association* (pp. 27–29). Alexandria, VA: American Statistical Association.

Holland, P. W. (2005). Assessing the validity of test linking. In C. A. Dwyer (Ed.), *Measurement and research in the accountability era* (pp. 185–195). Mahwah, NJ: Lawrence Erlbaum.

Holland, P. W. (2008, March). *The first four generations of test theory*. Paper presented at the Association of Test Publishers on Innovations in Testing, Dallas, TX.

Holland, P. W., & Dorans, N. J. (2006). Linking and equating. In R. L. Brennan (Ed.), *Educational measurement* (4th ed., pp. 187–220). Westport, CT: American Council on Education/Praeger.

Huggins, A. C., & Penfield, R. D. (2012). An NCME instructional module on population invariance in linking and equating. *Educational Measurement: Issues and Practice, 31*(1), 27–40.

Kolen, M. J. (2006). Scaling and norming. In R. L. Brennan (Ed.), *Educational measurement* (4th ed., pp. 155–186). Westport, CT: American Council on Education/Praeger.

Kolen, M. J. (2007). Data collection designs and linking procedures. In N. J. Dorans, M. Pommerich, & P. W. Holland (Eds.), *Linking and aligning scores and scales* (pp. 31–55). New York: Springer.

Kolen, M. J., & Brennan, R. L. (2014). *Test equating, scaling, and linking: Methods and practice* (3rd ed.). New York: Springer.

Linn, R. L. (1993). Linking results of distinct assessments. *Applied Measurement in Education, 6,* 83–102.

Linn, R. L., McLaughlin, D., & Thissen, D. (2009). *Utility and validity of NAEP linking efforts.* Washington, DC: American Institutes for Research, NAEP Validity Studies Panel.

Lord, F. M. (1977). A study of item bias, using item characteristic curve theory. In Y. H. Poortinga (Ed.), *Basic problems in cross-cultural psychology* (pp. 19–29). Amsterdam: Swets & Zeitlinger.

Merriam-Webster Dictionary (n.d.) *Critical.* Retrieved from www.merriam-webster.com/dictionary/critical

Middleton, K., & Dorans, N. J. (2011). *Assessing the falsifiability of extreme linkings* (ETS Research Report Series, Report No. RR-11-04). Princeton, NJ: Educational Testing Service.

Mislevy, R. J. (1992). *Linking educational assessments: Concepts, issues, and prospects.* Princeton, NJ: Educational Testing Service.

Newsweek (1943, March 8). Impossible is possible. *Newsweek, 21*(10), 34–35.

Pommerich, M., Hanson, B. A., Harris, D. J., & Sconing, J. A. (2004). Issues in conducting linkages between distinct tests. *Applied Psychological Measurement, 28,* 247–273.

Rapp, J., & Allalouf, A. (2003). Evaluating cross-lingual equating. *International Journal of Testing, 3,* 101–117.

Sireci, S. G., Thissen, D., & Wainer, H. (1991). On the reliability of testlet-based tests. *Journal of Educational Measurement, 28,* 237–247.

Thissen, D. (2007). Linking assessments based on aggregate reporting: Background and issues. In N. J. Dorans, M. Pommerich, & P. W. Holland (Eds.), *Linking and aligning scores and scales* (pp. 287–312). New York: Springer.

Thissen, D. (2015). Growth through levels. *Measurement, 13,* 128–131.

Thissen, D., & Norton, S. (2013). What might changes in psychometric approaches to statewide testing mean for NAEP? In F. B. Stancavage & G. W. Bohrnstedt (Eds.), *Examining the content and context of the Common Core State Standards: A first look at implications for the National Assessment of Educational Progress.* San Mateo, CA: American Institutes for Research, NAEP Validity Studies Panel.

Thissen, D., Pommerich, M., Billeaud, K., & Williams, V. S. L. (1995). Item response theory for scores on tests including polytomous items with ordered responses. *Applied Psychological Measurement, 19,* 39–49.

Thissen, D., Steinberg, L., & Wainer, H. (1993) Detection of differential item functioning using the parameters of item response models. In P. W. Holland & H. Wainer (Eds.), *Differential item functioning* (pp. 67–113). Hillsdale, NJ: Lawrence Erlbaum Associates.

Wainer, H., Sireci, S. G., & Thissen, D. (1991). Differential testlet functioning: Definitions and detection. *Journal of Educational Measurement, 28,* 197–219.

Williams, V. S. L., Pommerich, M., & Thissen, D. (1998). A comparison of developmental scales based on Thurstone methods and item response theory. *Journal of Educational Measurement, 35,* 93–107.

Williams, V. S. L., Rosa, K. R., McLeod, L. D., Thissen, D., & Sanford, E. (1998). Projecting to the NAEP scale: Results from the North Carolina End-of-Grade testing program. *Journal of Educational Measurement, 35,* 277–296.

Part III

Perspectives on Fair Assessment

The third part of the volume contains three chapters that are devoted to various perspectives on fair assessment, including a chapter on score use that examines the implications of using test scores that were designed for one purpose (assessing the educational achievement of individual test takers) for a variety of other purposes, including evaluating teachers or classifying schools according to their success in meeting accountability goals; a chapter that considers fairness from a legal perspective; and a chapter that considers diverse philosophical perspectives on how fair assessment contributes to a just society.

In the chapter titled "Fairness Using Derived Scores," Haertel and Ho consider potential threats to fairness that arise when tests are used to measure *different constructs* from those for which they were originally designed. In particular, the authors examine fairness issues associated with increasingly prevalent uses of educational achievement test scores for such purposes as judging college and career readiness, measuring growth over time, or aggregated to the level of teachers or schools, evaluating teachers or classifying schools according to their success in meeting accountability goals. Any use of test scores to measure a different construct than that originally intended may give rise to different sources of construct underrepresentation and construct-irrelevant variance, which in turn may be associated with new sources of unfairness. These issues are developed and illustrated for several prominent score uses.

The next chapter by Phillips, "Legal Aspects of Test Fairness," discusses how legal issues influence the fairness of educational tests. It begins with a review of federal laws that are most often cited in legal cases challenging educational tests. Subsequent sections discuss specific legal issues and court cases related to the fairness of tests in different educational contexts, including high-stakes decisions regarding students and educators, test construction practices, and test administration procedures. The chapter concludes with a discussion of legal challenges related to the fairness of educational tests that may be likely to occur in the future.

In "Philosophical Perspectives on Fairness in Educational Assessment," Zwick and Dorans introduce different definitions of fairness as forms of the just distribution of opportunity and goods. Different forms of distributive justice are considered, including an equality of outcome, equality of opportunity, meritocracy, reward for effort, justice based on a social contract such as the original position of John Rawls, and a free-market libertarian perspective. Examples in an educational setting where these contrasting perspectives may play out are admissions to college, accountability, international assessments, and end-of-year examinations. The authors describe the educational examples, introduce the fairness perspectives, and then examine the examples from these contrasting perspectives.

Worrell closes out the third part of this book with a commentary that critiques and synthesizes these three chapters on various perspectives on test fairness.

12 Fairness Using Derived Scores

Edward Haertel[1] and Andrew Ho[2]

In testing, performances are elicited under standardized conditions, and one or more scores are then derived from those performances. Different scores often correspond to distinct constructs. One familiar case is the use of two or more scoring rubrics to evaluate several dimensions of the same performance, as when an essay is scored both for content and for grammatical usage. Another example is the reporting of both subtest and total scores, where the total score references a broader construct encompassing the more specific constructs referenced by the subtests. Sometimes, new scores may be created to measure constructs quite different from those envisioned when a test was first designed. In one early example, Jackson and Messick (1961) constructed new scales for the Minnesota Multiphasic Personality Inventory (MMPI) to measure response acquiescence and social desirability. They did so in part to study these new constructs directly, but also to investigate the validity of the MMPI by quantifying and investigating potential sources of what Messick (1989, p. 34) would later term "construct-irrelevant variance," that is, "excess reliable variance that is irrelevant to the interpreted construct."

Various types of scores have been created to support different interpretations using educational achievement test data. These interpretations may be supported by additional sources of evidence, but they may also introduce additional sources of construct-irrelevant variance and threaten the validity and fairness of score use. In this chapter, we address the logic of validation for uses and interpretations of such derived scores. As a framing example, we first discuss "Adequate Yearly Progress" (AYP), which is the annual determination under the No Child Left Behind Act (NCLB) of whether each public school in the United States is "In Need of Improvement" versus making "Satisfactory Progress." This example shows how complex derived scores are built up layer by layer from simpler scores, and how these layers can be unpacked to frame interpretation and use arguments (IUAs) for validity.

Following this overview example, we proceed with five examples of more circumscribed derived score uses, offering more detailed consideration of specific operations (judgmental standard setting, score aggregation, score adjustment, score linking) used in creating derived scores intended to measure distinct constructs. For each example, we describe how issues of fairness in test use might arise in connection with construct under-representation or construct-irrelevant variance. These potential threats to validity in turn suggest additional studies or kinds of evidence that can support validation of uses and interpretations based on these derived scores.

Defining Constructs

The *Standards for Educational and Psychological Testing* (American Educational Research Association, American Psychological Association, & National Council on Measurement in Education, 2014, p. 11) define the term *construct* as follows:

> Validation logically begins with an explicit statement of the proposed interpretation of test scores . . . [which] includes specifying the construct the test is intended to measure. The term construct is used . . . to refer to the concept or characteristic that a test is designed to measure. Rarely, if ever, is there a single possible meaning that can be attached to a test score or a pattern of test responses. Thus, it is always incumbent on test developers and users to specify the construct interpretation that will be made on the basis of the score or response pattern.

We would argue that in this single paragraph, the Standards have conflated two quite distinct definitions of *construct*: the construct that a test is *designed* to measure and the construct that it is *intended* (or *used*) to measure in a given measurement application. In this chapter, we examine situations in which a test designed to measure one construct is used in some testing application to measure a different construct. We will refer to the construct the test is designed to measure as the *developer construct*, and the construct it is used to measure as the *application construct*.

Developer construct definitions pertain to the test scores and score uses originally created and validated by the test developer. These may include uses and interpretations based on raw scores, scale scores, and often, one or more additional derived scores (e.g., percentile ranks or grade equivalents). It is certainly possible for users to attach extended interpretations (implicitly, new construct definitions) to these original scores, just as it is possible for a patient to use a drug for an off-label use. In this chapter, however, we are primarily concerned with cases where new derived scores are created, whose uses extend beyond those envisioned or validated by the test developer, with the intent of measuring different constructs.

We use the term *derived score* broadly, including classifications, such as "proficient," "English Learner," or "In Need of Improvement," as well as scores derived from multiple observations or incorporating non-test data, such as gain scores, teacher effectiveness estimates from value-added models (VAMs), or score scales from one test that are used to support interpretations of performances on different tests. An application construct is defined, implicitly or explicitly, by actual uses and interpretations made of derived test scores, reaching beyond those warranted by developers' efforts in test design and validation. When a use or interpretation extends beyond those that developers validate, and particularly when a secondary user derives a score to facilitate this use, we will refer to the difference between the developer construct and the application construct as a *construct shift*.[3] A central observation of our chapter is that construct shifts are increasingly common and predictable, raising systematic threats to the fair use of derived scores.

Our examples in this chapter illustrate several common operations used to generate such derived scores. One operation is *judgmental standard setting*, creating discrete score scales with levels such as "Below Basic," "Basic," "Proficient," and "Advanced." A second is *score adjustment*, as when end-of-course scores are adjusted for pretest performance to measure growth. A third is *score aggregation*, changing the object of measurement from individual students to schools, for example. Score adjustment and aggregation are sometimes combined, as in VAMs intended to measure teacher effectiveness. A fourth operation, *score linking*, creates a projection from one test score scale to another, often in cases where the test score scales were created for different purposes. This list is not exhaustive. Under NCLB, in addition to judgmental standard setting and score aggregation, the operations required to determine AYP status also include aggregation across tests used at different grade levels and across the content areas of reading and mathematics, as well as decision rules for indices that incorporate patterns of subgroup performance, test participation rates, and other considerations.

When tests are scored in new ways to support new interpretations and uses, implicitly or explicitly invoking new application constructs, these new constructs require validation, including the consideration of fairness for particular groups. Jackson and Messick (1961) could not infer the validity of their new MMPI scores from research on established MMPI scales. Whenever a new kind of score is derived from test data, its intended interpretation and use, and the application construct that it implies, should be made explicit, and interpretation/use arguments (IUAs) (see Kane, 2013) should be reframed accordingly. We extend Kane's IUA framework to derived scores and then apply it in the examples that follow.

Interpretation/Use Arguments (IUAs) for Application Constructs

Kane (2006, 2013) proposed the *interpretation/use argument* (IUA) as an approach to validating test score interpretations and uses. The IUA sets forth the chain of reasoning from eliciting or observing examinee performances through the creation of scores and onto the descriptions or decisions those scores inform. Once the IUA is formulated, test validation proceeds by assembling and integrating evidence for and against the propositions in that chain of reasoning.

Kane (2006) organizes the IUA into four broad stages, namely scoring, generalization, extrapolation, and, finally, use or interpretation. At the risk of oversimplification, we sketch an interpretation of these four stages as follows:

- *Scoring* is the link from a particular examinee performance to the resulting test score. At the scoring stage, a validator asks whether the test score is an accurate and undistorted reflection of the relevant qualities evidenced by that particular test performance. It is here that construct-irrelevant variance might first be considered.
- *Generalization* is the link from the test score to a hypothetical universe of possible replications of the observation (e.g., on different occasions or with alternate test forms) and of the scoring process (e.g., with different raters). It is here that score reliability is considered.
- *Extrapolation* moves beyond this hypothetical universe of possible test scores out to the broader domain of performances or situations where the target construct should matter. It is here, primarily, that construct underrepresentation might come into play. For achievement tests, this would include the fidelity of test content to the intended construct.
- *Use or interpretation* takes up the relevance of the score for a particular interpretation and the utility and appropriateness of proposed decisions or other actions based on that score.

For most developer constructs, the four stages of scoring, generalization, extrapolation, and use or interpretation require investigations that are well established and fairly common in practice. As an example, consider a multiple-choice reading comprehension test. Scoring might address clarity of items and test instructions, accuracy of the scoring key, and considerations such as test speededness. Generalization would address score reliability, perhaps including the stability of scores across repeated test administrations or across alternate forms intended to be parallel. Extrapolation might take up the limitations of the multiple-choice format and the relation between reading performance as elicited by the test versus reading called for in real-world settings. Interpretation or use would address the suitability of whatever decisions or interpretations were based on the scores, perhaps the assignment of students to different reading groups within their classrooms. At this fourth stage, one might ask whether score-based decisions were in fact better than decisions that would have been reached otherwise.

For application constructs based on derived scores, however, IUAs can become more complex and multilayered. We show that derived scores generally require an IUA that builds on the IUA for the developer construct. This extended IUA can begin by addressing the validity of original score uses in the context of the developer construct (most often related to individual examinees), looping through scoring, generalization, extrapolation, and use. Much of this evidence is likely to have been gathered by the developer for the originally intended use. The derived score, which can be seen as an extension of the original score that measures an application construct, should require a second round of validation, looping through scoring, generalization, extrapolation, and use a second time. This investigation should have the same rigor as the validation of any other score use, in the context of test score construction, reliability, relevance, benefits, and costs. Thus, the construction and use of most derived scores motivate a revisitation of each of the four IUA stages. Such extensions of the original IUA to address uses and interpretations of derived scores are rare, consistent with an unexamined assumption that IUAs for uses of original scores extend automatically to IUAs for uses of derived scores.

An IUA for AYP Status under NCLB

Consider the construction of the binary school-level "AYP status" score, representing "Satisfactory Progress" versus "In Need of Improvement" under NCLB. The IUA for use or interpretation of such a complex score might be organized in various ways. Kane (2006, pp. 53–54) used this accountability classification as an illustrative example and presented one such IUA. In his discussion, he treated the scoring and generalization stages of the IUA as a repetition of the considerations for individual student scores. In contrast, we prefer to describe AYP status as a derived score itself, because it is used and interpreted as a meaningful and consequential indicator. We also highlight two additional kinds of derived scores that are created, used, and interpreted en route from the original student achievement test scores to the final, binary school-level AYP status determination. The first of these is a student achievement level designation (e.g., "Basic" or "Proficient") and the second is a "percentage proficient" score for schools or demographic subgroups within schools. Thus, our proposed IUA for AYP status actually calls for four loops through scoring, generalization, extrapolation, and use. The first loop, which we do not discuss further, addresses the original developer construct; the second attends to valid interpretation of student achievement levels; the third takes up aggregate "percentage proficient" scores; and the final loop examines the binary, school-level "Satisfactory Progress"/"In Need of Improvement" AYP determination. The structure of our IUA is illustrated in Figure 12.1.

Validation would begin with the test developer's investigation of achievement tests used to measure reading and mathematics achievement on continuous scales. Then, a second looping through Kane's four stages would address the derived scores created when scale scores are mapped into "Below Basic," "Basic," "Proficient," and "Advanced" according to cut scores defined by a judgmental standard setting process. The second-round scoring stage might investigate the judgmental standard setting process itself and also whether by and large, test performances classified as "proficient," for example, matched the textual definition of the "proficient" level. Generalization and extrapolation might then be engaged a second time, examining achievement level classification consistency across repeated measurements (generalization) and the accuracy of inferences concerning the proficiency of "proficient" examinees in nontest settings (extrapolation). Use and interpretation might take up the manner in which the meaning of these achievement level designations is communicated and interpreted to parents (per NCLB requirements) or other audiences, including efforts to convey their degree of precision and the actions, if any, that a school or district might recommend parents take on the basis of this information.

Under NCLB, achievement level scores are next further collapsed to proficient-or-above versus not proficient-or-above. These binary scores for students at different grade levels, based on different tests, are then pooled together and aggregated to obtain school-level reading and mathematics "percentage proficient" scores for all students at tested

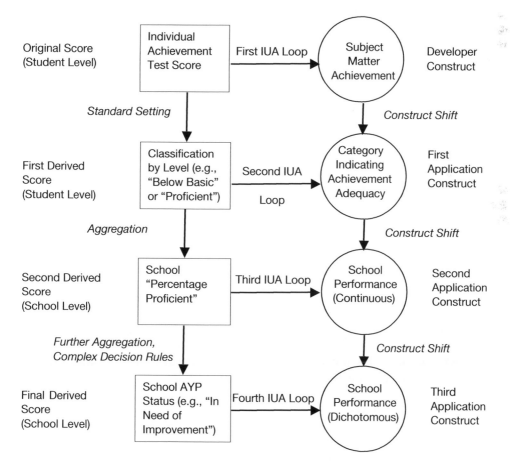

Figure 12.1 Relations among Developer Constructs, Application Constructs, Original Scores, and Derived Scores

grade levels and also for various subgroups within a school. Because these group-level "percentage proficient" statistics are reported and interpreted, we treat them as another kind of derived score, triggering a third loop through the IUA. Regarding scoring, the averaging of students' (binary) "proficient-or-above" scores across grade levels would seem to call for some thought as to the meaning of that average—the implications of "proficient" for a third grader versus an eighth grader might differ. Setting that aside, however, simple aggregation from the student level to the school level might not in itself raise scoring concerns. Generalization would need to be re-examined, however, because precision of the aggregated score would reflect sampling error (regarding the tested students as representative of some larger potential student population) in addition to measurement error. If the school percentage of proficient students is regarded as measuring some school-level attribute, then extrapolation considerations arise when one asks what qualities of the school, beyond student test performance itself, that school-level "percentage proficient" measure is intended to represent and whether such intended inferences are warranted. Common but problematic uses and interpretations of these school-level "percentage proficient" scores include reporting of score gaps between demographic groups, tracking of trends over time, and tracking of trends in gaps over time (Ho, 2008).

Judgmental standard setting then comes into play again as school-level "percentage proficient" scores are compared to year-specific thresholds called "Annual Measureable Objectives" (AMOs) to judge whether school performance is satisfactory. Actual decision rules are still more complex, also factoring in test participation rates, safe-harbor provisions (which are based on year-to-year changes in percentages of proficient students), margin-of-error adjustments (not envisioned in the original legislation), and other significant details. The final result is a binary determination as to whether each school is "In Need of Improvement" or not. Extending the IUA through a fourth round to examine these final school-level scores, one might first consider the logic of the scoring rules in the light of this binary application construct. Generalization would address decision consistency, perhaps best investigated using bootstrap or other resampling procedures. Extrapolation might revisit the same questions as for the school "percentage proficient" scores, again asking what school qualities the "In Need of Improvement" label is intended to signify and whether such intended inferences are warranted. Use or interpretation would take up the manner in which mandated annual reports to parents convey the meaning of schools' AYP status, as well as the effectiveness of the remedies prescribed for schools in need of improvement. As Kane (2006) observes:

> The arguments for [current accountability] testing programs tend to claim that the program will lead to improvements in school effectiveness and student achievement . . . [yet] the validity arguments developed to support these ambitious claims typically attend only to the descriptive part of the interpretive argument (and often to only a part of that). The validity evidence that is provided tends to focus on scoring and generalization to the content domain for the test. The claim that the imposition of the accountability requirements will improve the overall performance of schools and students is taken for granted.
>
> (p. 57)

Fairness becomes a concern in the interpretation and use of these binary school scores because student background characteristics outside the school's control give rise to construct-irrelevant variance, making it far more difficult for some schools than others to meet AMO performance expectations. Construct underrepresentation becomes a concern to the extent that the "In Need of Improvement" label takes on surplus meaning as a more general description of the school, incorporating attributes beyond those captured by student test scores. Fairness concerns also arise at the level of individual students and groups of students. Kane (2006, p. 53) notes that "test-based accountability programs have a range of potential benefits and costs . . . [and their] positive and negative consequences are likely to have different impacts on different groups and in different schools."

In considering our examples for this chapter, we concluded that IUAs for application constructs are often vague and ill-specified, but we found it a valuable exercise to try to clarify them. Issues of fairness arise when the performance of an identifiable subgroup is differentially affected by some construct-irrelevant influence on test scores, or occasionally when some subgroup is advantaged or disadvantaged due to construct underrepresentation (when a test measures only a portion of the construct the score is intended to represent).[4] Consideration of IUAs for derived scores measuring new application constructs may highlight new sources of construct-irrelevant variance and construct underrepresentation, pointing to matters of unfairness or other deficiencies that could otherwise go unnoticed.

Examples

Our first example is that of an English language proficiency test used (typically in conjunction with other measures) to determine students' English learner (EL) status. This example illustrates how judgmental standard setting can produce a construct shift, giving rise to new sources of construct-irrelevant variance with implications for fairness in test use. Our second example is the use of achievement tests in mathematics and English language arts to measure "college and career readiness" (CCR). In contrast to the EL classification example, the use of scores to measure CCR implies a larger shift from the developer construct measured by the achievement tests to the CCR application construct, raising issues of construct underrepresentation. Our third example is the use of trajectories of student-level achievement test scores to describe student growth over time. Here, multiple scores are combined to create a new derived score intended to measure an application construct involving a rate of academic progress or a status beyond expectations given past scores. Our fourth example, VAMs measuring teacher effectiveness, illustrates aggregation as well as score adjustment, as the measurement target shifts from students to their teachers. Finally, we turn to fairness considerations that may arise when linkages are constructed across different tests that may be or seem similar in name or in purpose. Our third and fifth examples are relatively brief, as we defer to other chapters in this volume that cover these topics in greater depth (Castellano & Kolen, this volume, Chapter 8; Pommerich, this volume, Chapter 7).

In our concluding section, we argue for greater attention to application constructs measured by new kinds of derived scores, and to the IUAs supporting them. Such scores are often created and used with little or no involvement on the part of the original test developers, which muddies the question of responsibility for validation. Conscientious test developers may collect evidence supporting their test's appropriateness to measuring the developer construct, but they cannot be expected to attend to all potential application construct definitions entailed by new uses, nor to accompanying fairness issues. Nonetheless, through these illustrations, we demonstrate that these kinds of test uses are not only increasingly common in modern educational research, policy, and practice, but also increasingly predictable. Our hope is that these examples ultimately encourage a more proactive and preemptive accumulation of evidence to ensure that such uses are fair.

EL Classification Example

Suppose that a test of English language proficiency is used to determine which students should be classified as "English learners" (ELs). This EL designation in turn has a range of consequences, such as a requirement that students be provided with 30 minutes daily of "English Language Development" (ELD) instruction. We might describe and begin to justify this test use by saying: (1) the developer construct[5] is English language proficiency; (2) for ease and efficiency in allocating funds and meeting diverse students' needs, the students are classified into those who are versus those who are not ELs, based on English language proficiency; such that (3) based on theory and empirical research, we expect ELs to need (or to benefit from) daily ELD instruction, "sheltered" academic subject matter lessons in English,[6] or other targeted interventions. This description suggests that the original test score and the EL classification based on that score refer to the same construct. On closer examination, however, it might be argued instead that a distinct application construct is created in this process.[7] A first construct shift occurs when proficiency levels are established via judgmental standard setting for a test designed to measure language proficiency. A second construct shift occurs when these proficiency levels then contribute to the measurement of a binary attribute of examinees intended to distinguish those who are best served by EL instructional services versus those best served by the instructional program designed for native speakers. These construct shifts raise the possibility of new sources of construct-irrelevant variance, with attendant implications for fairness.

Construct Shift Due to Judgmental Standard Setting

For purposes of EL and RFEP (Reclassified Fully English Proficient) designations, language proficiency test scores are interpreted relative to cut scores defining levels such as "Beginning," "Early Intermediate," "Intermediate," "Early Advanced," and "Advanced." These categories are created by a judgmental standard-setting process, which relies upon, or in some cases modifies or generates, text describing the meaning of each level. The standard-setting process establishes cut scores on a specific test form that serve to define the levels operationally. Once cut scores are established, they may then be re-expressed as scale scores so that their meaning may be preserved via equating across current and future alternate forms of the same test.

Clearly, standard setting per se—the attaching of labels to score bands—does not change what the test actually measures.[8] Nonetheless, judgmental standard setting both encourages and is motivated by a construct shift, creating a distinct application construct with the potential for new sources of construct underrepresentation and construct-irrelevant variance. This construct shift occurs because the text describing proficiency levels provides new interpretations, potentially adding new meaning to the score scale.[9] A sampling of such level descriptions for several states' proficiency tests is provided in Appendix A of a report by the National Research Council (2011, pp. 181–207). A few phrases from these descriptions will serve to illustrate how they lend additional meaning to test scores. At the lowest level on one test, students "speak in English and understand spoken English that is below grade level and require continuous support." Students at or above specified levels on one or another test may be expected to "process, understand, produce, or use specific and some technical language of the content areas," "begin to combine the elements of the English language in complex, cognitively demanding situations," "communicate effectively with various audiences on a wide range of familiar and new topics to meet social and learning demands," or "write at grade level in a manner similar to non-English language learners."

An IUA for judgmental standard setting was briefly described in the discussion of AYP status. As in that case, the IUA for English language proficiency levels might begin with scoring, generalization, extrapolation and use or interpretation for the continuous scale score (the developer construct). Extending the developer construct IUA to address the use and interpretation of proficiency levels might include an evaluation of the judgmental standard setting process itself (scoring) and decision consistency based on alternate test forms (generalization).

At the extrapolation stage, substantive claims about the meanings of different language proficiency levels might raise two related questions (cf. Haertel & Lorié, 2004). First, one might ask whether there exists *any* score on a given test for which the proficiency level description is warranted. Claims about effective communication "with various audiences on a wide range of . . . topics" or language use in "complex, cognitively demanding situations," for example, or even about "specific and some technical language of the content areas," might reach beyond the range of performances either sampled by the test or shown empirically to be predicted by test scores. Second, assuming the test does in fact measure or predict the capabilities referred to in the proficiency level descriptions, one might then ask whether the cut scores are set at appropriate levels. It is in principle an empirical question whether the cut score results in an optimum ratio of false positive errors (where examinees who in fact do not meet the standard nonetheless score above the cut) to false negative errors (where examinees who in fact do meet the standard nonetheless score below the cut).[10] Of course, one could also ask about the accuracy of the examinee classifications yielded by the test and cut score. We would hope not only for an optimum ratio of false positive to false negative errors, but also for as few classification errors as possible, in either direction.

As with achievement levels, the use and interpretation stage of the IUA for language proficiency levels might attend to communication to various audiences concerning the meaning of these designations, their accuracy, and any recommendations for action.

Construct Shift Due to English Learner Determination

The previous discussion addressed one construct shift, due to judgmental standard setting. We now turn to a second construct shift, from English language proficiency levels to EL status determinations.

The English proficiency tests and the procedures used to determine EL status vary from state to state, but typically, initial EL classification is based on test scores in conjunction with a home language survey (HLS) (National Research Council, 2011, pp. 80–82). The HLS triggers English language proficiency testing for students with a first language other than English, and low test scores then trigger the EL designation. EL status is intended to be transitional. EL students are provided with instructional supports designed to help them develop sufficient English proficiency that those supports are no longer necessary. At that point, students may move from EL to RFEP status. Whereas entry into the EL category is typically based solely on home language background and English proficiency test scores, there are usually additional criteria that must be satisfied to exit the EL category. In addition to language proficiency test scores, decision rules for reclassification may involve academic achievement test scores, teacher recommendations, parent or guardian input, and other criteria. As a consequence, many students remain classified as EL even though they would not be so designated solely on the basis of their language proficiency test scores (National Research Council, 2011).

As described by Robinson (2011), the EL classification is associated with a distinct bundle of educational services and instructional conditions. Teachers of EL students may be required to hold some special certification, and instructional programs for EL versus non-EL students are likely to differ, featuring ELD instruction, "sheltered" instruction in academic content, and so forth. In describing EL status as a distinct application construct, we are suggesting that the practical use of the EL designation in schools and districts is consistent with a model under which, for each student, at a given point in time, there is a true, unobservable EL/non-EL status, which is measured imperfectly by established classification and reclassification procedures. A student's standing with respect to this application construct indicates which of the two available bundles of educational services and instructional conditions, the EL bundle or the non-EL bundle, is more suitable for that student. Note further that the description of a student as EL versus non-EL has important consequences over and above the language proficiency test score on which it is (partially) based. EL status may impinge on students' personal identities. In addition, the number of EL students in a school or district influences educational funding. In summary, EL status functions as a significant attribute of the examinee, over and above English language proficiency.

The tests and procedures used to operationalize EL status, including but not limited to the prior procedure of mapping scores into categories defined by cut points, may result in a correct classification (i.e., one that matches a student's true status) or otherwise. Faulty classifications may arise not only due to random error, but also due to faulty standard setting. If reclassification criteria are too lenient, a disproportionate number of students with inadequate language skills may be placed in regular classrooms, whereas too stringent criteria may subject disproportionate numbers of students with adequate English fluency to unnecessary ELD instruction and other language supports (Robinson, 2011). Any such systematic misclassifications represent a source of unfairness in test use, affecting primarily those students in the ranges of the English language proficiency distribution where misclassifications and consequent inappropriate educational placements are most likely to occur.

The IUA for this second application construct might build upon the IUA for the language proficiency level designations. Scoring might examine EL entry and exit criteria to assure that to the extent possible, decision rules were based on the relevant attributes of examinees and not on extraneous factors. Generalization might address the accuracy of EL determinations. Extrapolation and use/interpretation would address the question of whether students designated as EL were, in fact, best served by the EL bundle of educational services and instructional conditions, and conversely. Robinson (2011) illustrates the use of a regression discontinuity design to investigate this question, arguing that if EL exit criteria are appropriate, then for students right at the boundary between these two categories, it should be a matter of indifference which bundle of services they receive.

College and Career Readiness (CCR) Example

Recent state and federal education policies have used the concept of "college and career readiness" (CCR) to motivate K-12 educational reform, framing CCR as a purpose of a K-12 education to which standards and assessments should be aligned. The summary document for the Obama administration's 2010 blueprint for reform was titled *College-*

and Career-Ready Standards and Assessments (U.S. Department of Education, 2010). Similarly, the documentation for the Common Core State Standards Initiative (n.d.) describes the Standards as "a clear set of shared goals and expectations for the knowledge and skills students need in English language arts and mathematics at each grade level so they can be prepared to succeed in college, career, and life" (p. 2).

Following this reasoning, we consider the developer construct for these assessments to be the knowledge, skills, and abilities at each grade level that are directly or, via a progression across grades, ultimately relevant for college and careers. The IUAs for the developer construct concern interpretations and uses of proficiency estimates related to relevant knowledge, skills, and abilities such as those articulated by the Common Core State Standards. Uses of these scores can include targeting feedback, guiding instruction, and focusing teacher and student attention on standards. In practice, part of the validation of these IUAs has rested on alignment of tests to these standards, either by developing tests aligned to these standards, such as those by the assessment consortia (Partnership for Assessment of Readiness for College and Careers, 2013; Smarter Balanced Assessment Consortium, 2013), or by evaluating and augmenting alignment of existing tests.

We contrast this developer construct (student proficiency with CCR-relevant skills) with an application construct: student readiness for college and careers. As in the previous section, we focus on threats to fairness that arise not from the use of individual student scale scores, but from the use of derived scores following a judgmental standard setting procedure: dichotomous student readiness/non-readiness or probabilities of readiness. Although we recognize that the application construct may not be readiness but binary proficiency/non-proficiency with CCR-relevant skills—a weaker claim representing a smaller shift—we argue that the policy rhetoric around "college-ready standards" is strong enough to shift the interpretation to a judgment about readiness or at least whether a student is "on track" (U.S. Department of Education, 2010). Here, we describe the stages of the extended IUA necessitated by this construct shift, from a developer construct of continuous student proficiency with CCR-relevant skills to an application construct of binary student college/career readiness itself.

The scoring stage concerns the scoring rule, its application, and any bias imparted. At this stage, potential bias can emerge due to the predictive basis of the standard setting. The judgmental standard setting procedure for CCR standards is often informed by empirical relationships between tests and future outcomes—for example, college grades. Examples from college admissions testing include ACT "benchmarks" where students "have approximately a 50% chance of earning a B or better and approximately a 75% chance or better of earning a C or better in the corresponding college course or courses" (ACT, 2014, p. 24). The College Board defines its SAT benchmarks as "the SAT score associated with a 65% probability of earning a first-year GPA of 2.67 (B–) or higher" (Wyatt, Kobrin, Camara, & Proestler, 2011, p. 5). Similar methods are used by state departments of education as part of a process known as evidence-based standard setting (McClarty, Way, Porter, Beimers, & Miles, 2013), where convergent evidence from multiple sources of data defines neighborhoods within which experts then exercise judgment.

The predictive nature of this standard setting procedure is a scoring challenge that can represent a serious threat to fairness. Students with different individual-level and school-level demographic characteristics can be shown empirically to have different predicted college grades. A central tenet of the Standards movement and NCLB has been that proficiency standards cannot differ by students based upon student or school background characteristics (No Child Left Behind, 2002). Hess and Petrilli (2004) describe this as a "no excuses" mantra representing a bipartisan consensus in Washington, a political and ultimately, it was hoped, pedagogical signal to students that everyone can achieve proficiency. However, in the case of CCR standard setting, the interpretation of the derived score may be more plainly predictive. Even if the generating statement is probabilistic (e.g., a 65% chance), the dichotomous score suggests that a student is on track to college or career readiness, or not. To the extent that two students with the same scores come from families or schools with different college- or career-relevant resources, there will be systematic bias in the predictive inferences supported by dichotomous CCR scores.

At the generalization stage, there are questions about the replicability of judgmental standard setting processes in general, as well as the replicability of predictive links that may inform panel judgments. When predictive links are generated from convenience samples of students for whom test scores and college grades are available, questions of both bias and replicability across samples arise. Additionally, as in the previous section, consistency of student-level classifications is addressed in the generalization stage. Even if the judgmental cut score were perfectly replicable and unbiased, misclassification probabilities could be sizable, particularly for students close to the cut score.

At the extrapolation stage, many concerns that may be more muted for continuous CCR scores can become more salient for dichotomous scores that support "on track" inferences. Consistent in the use of CCR terminology in policy documents is a lack of clarity about whether the knowledge, skills, and abilities articulated by CCR standards are necessary or sufficient for CCR. Recent conceptions of CCR present the construct as multifaceted. Conley and McGaughy (2012) note that career readiness and college readiness share common elements but are not the same construct. Fields (2014) summarized results from more than 30 studies that investigated whether twelfth grade results from the National Assessment of Educational Progress (NAEP) could be interpreted in terms of CCR. He concluded that the research supported inferences about academic preparedness for college but not for job training. Even setting aside career readiness, for college readiness alone, Conley (2007) describes many facets that are rarely the target of measurement for educational tests, including contextual skills and awareness, academic behaviors, and key cognitive strategies. Citing Conley, Fields (2014) emphasized a distinction between academic preparedness for college, on the one hand, and college readiness, on the other, stating that "readiness is broadly understood to include both academic preparedness and other characteristics needed for success in postsecondary education" (p. 2).

In contrast, CCR and, more frequently, college readiness are treated as singular constructs in both political rhetoric (U.S. Department of Education, 2010) and score reporting. Both ACT and the College Board occasionally conflate "college and career readiness standards" and "college readiness standards" (ACT, n.d.; College Board, 2011), and they report results in achievement bands or metrics labeled with "college readiness." The two general assessment consortia supporting the Common Core State Standards Initiative differ in their use of the term, with one describing proficiency as a "college- and career-ready determination" (Partnership for Assessment of Readiness for College and Careers, 2013) and the other narrowing the description of achievement levels to concern "college content-readiness" (Smarter Balanced Assessment Consortium, 2013). Although all of these organizations offer distinctions between career readiness and college readiness, and between college readiness and college academic preparedness, in their associated documentation, we argue that the reification of CCR or college readiness in common usage and as a reporting scale nonetheless represents a naming fallacy, where the application construct (CCR, college readiness) is underrepresented by the developer construct that the instrument measures (student proficiency with CCR-relevant skills, often referred to as college academic preparedness).

The IUA builds to interpretation and use, where the consequences of this construct underrepresentation for fairness becomes salient. As before, consider two students who have the same ninth grade test scores but are enrolled in schools with different resources. Considering only these test scores, the students may both exhibit the same evidence of academic preparedness for college, but to the extent that the schools or the students have different resources available to support non-academic factors of college readiness, one student would not meet more holistic criteria for college readiness due to insufficient non-academic support, and the other would. Roderick, Coca, and Nagaoka (2011) provide empirical evidence for precisely this phenomenon.

We can extend this example to two school-level populations of students with equal test scores but different non-academic resources for students. Even if both school populations appeared equally ready on the basis of their test scores, the low-resource school population would be, empirically and on average, less likely to be on track than their high-resource counterparts. If an intended use of the scores is to assign additional support to students or schools that are not "college ready," the high-resource school and its students would receive an inappropriately high share of this support. And, if an intended use of the scores is to sanction students or schools that do not have "college ready" students, the high-resource school and its students would receive an inappropriately high share of these sanctions.

When we interpret achievement test scores for different audiences, we tend to emphasize those test score determinants over which each intended audience might exercise some control. Thus, for students, we emphasize the importance of individual initiative; for teacher evaluation, we emphasize the role of individual teachers; for school accountability, we emphasize the importance of school policies and practices. We often derive and describe scores differently to impart these different emphases. It seems unhelpful, indeed unwise, in interpreting scores for individual students, to draw undue attention to factors beyond their own control, nor would we want to absolve schools of all responsibility for achievement gaps simply because out-of-school differences contribute substantially to those gaps. But in the case of a school's responsibility to assure CCR for all of its students, it would seem best to provide the fullest and most accurate possible interpretation of score meanings. A test score above some CCR threshold is not an end in itself. If test scores are interpreted in context, using multiple sources of available information and tailoring instructional interventions accordingly, fairness is better served. As with validation exercises broadly, attention to differences between developer constructs and application constructs facilitates improved contextualization and appropriate use.

Student Growth Trajectories

In the previous two examples, judgmental standard setting generated derived scores whose application constructs risked construct-irrelevant variance and construct under-representation. We have shown how IUAs can be extended in these situations to raise new issues and motivate the collection of additional evidence. In this example, we briefly discuss another common operation generating derived scores: summarization of longitudinal trajectories to support interpretations about the growth, progress, or conditional status of individual students.

This section is brief, and we do not demonstrate full IUAs, deferring instead to the chapter in this volume about growth (Castellano & Kolen, this volume, Chapter 8). However, we believe that our perspectives cast that chapter in a complementary light in at least three ways. First, by distinguishing between developer and application constructs, we place greater emphasis on the likelihood that longitudinal analyses are not anticipated in the assessment design process. It is quite common for assessments that may not have been designed with the goal of supporting growth interpretations to nonetheless come to be used to support them, usually after approval by a state or local educational agency (e.g., Reform Support Network, 2014).

Second, our perspective is that these derived scores and construct shifts are often common enough to be predictable, and this is certainly true in the case of growth measurement. The predictability of growth uses warrants acknowledgment by developers, particularly when growth is not a developer construct, and preemptive cautions against growth uses may be warranted when they are clearly unsupported by the extant evidentiary base.

Third, we locate growth measures in a larger framework of derived scores. We describe growth as an "adjustment" operation, where the adjustment is by one or more prior scores and perhaps other covariates. Castellano and Kolen (this volume, Chapter 8) delve into the vast variation among possible growth adjustments and demonstrate how each raises different risks to fairness. We show similar variation in the particularities of other derived scores and emphasize, similarly, that the details of score derivations matter.

Teacher Value Added

In VAMs used to estimate teacher effectiveness, tests originally designed to measure individual students' academic achievement at one point in time are used instead to measure teachers' influence on multiple students' academic progress over the course of a school year. Both the object of measurement (teachers rather than students) and the application construct (instructional effectiveness rather than academic achievement) depart from those envisioned in the original test design.

There are several distinct types of value-added models (McCaffrey, Lockwood, Koretz, Louis, & Hamilton, 2004). In broad outline, they share the same logic as aggregated versions of the conditional status models reviewed by Castellano and Kolen (this volume, Chapter 8). Prior test scores are used to predict students' end-of-current-year scores, and these predicted scores are subtracted from students' actual scores to obtain "residuals." If the observed score exceeds the predicted score (a positive residual), this provides evidence that the teacher's effectiveness was above average for that student, and conversely. These (positive or negative) residuals, averaged across each teacher's students, serve as the basis for teacher VAM scores. Value-added models may incorporate additional predictors, including student demographic variables and sometimes adjustments for overall average achievement of schools or districts. Teachers' estimates may be averaged across years or subject areas. Bayesian methods may be used to shrink teacher VAM estimates toward the overall mean, with the degree of shrinkage depending on the precision of each teacher's estimate. Estimates may be rescaled or otherwise transformed for ease of interpretation.

These statistical adjustments, largely based on prior-year test scores, are intended to account for the facts that students are assorted into schools and also into classrooms (and thereby assigned to teachers) according to mechanisms that are nonrandom and imperfectly known, and that teachers are likewise assigned to schools by such mechanisms.

As with our earlier examples, an IUA for teacher VAM scores might be built by extending the IUA for the original developer construct. If student achievement tests are poorly constructed, unreliable, or poorly aligned with the prescribed curriculum, the validity of teacher VAM estimates based on those tests will suffer. Failings of individual student achievement test scores even for their original purposes may take on new significance when they serve as the basis for teacher effectiveness estimates. The use of achievement tests that address only a subset of intended learning outcomes (construct underrepresentation) may be tolerable for some test uses, but may create incentives to distort curriculum and instruction if the tests are used for high-stakes purposes (Koretz, 2008). As another example, when tests are used to quantify student achievement at one point in time, alignment and scaling across achievement test forms at successive grade levels may not matter, but value-added models make stronger assumptions about the interval properties of test score scales, and some models also impose assumptions about the scaling of test scores across years (Ballou, 2009).

IUA for Construct Shift to VAM Estimates

In deriving teacher VAM estimates, intermediate results (e.g., individual students' adjusted gain scores) are not reported or interpreted. Thus, in extending the IUA for the developer construct, the entire series of operations linking individual student scores to teacher VAM estimates may be organized as a single added round of scoring, generalization, extrapolation, and use or interpretation.

The scoring stage might consider whether value-added estimates for various groups of teachers are affected systematically by practices in the assignment of students to teachers that are not fully accounted for in the model. Consider, for example, teachers regarded by their principals as especially effective in working with English learners, who are therefore assigned a disproportionate number of such students. Because these students face the dual task of improving their English proficiency at the same time as they learn academic content, and because a portion of their school day is devoted to ELD, their test scores may increase more slowly than those of native speakers. Conversely, if these students' prior-year test scores were depressed due to limited English proficiency and improvements in language skills enabled them to better demonstrate their knowledge when tested at the end of the current school year, then their test score improvements might be exaggerated. More generally, consider teachers who for whatever reason are working predominantly with students significantly above or below grade level. If (as is the case under NCLB) achievement tests at each grade level are limited to content specified for that grade alone, then these tests may be insensitive to the academic progress of students in the tails of the achievement distribution, and their teachers may be penalized if consequences are attached to their VAM scores.

Teachers working in schools or districts with less adequate resources may be penalized by VAMs that fail to fully account for such resource differences (including average teaching experience of that teacher's peers and class size as well as material resources). Additional factors that are outside the teacher's control, which may vary systematically with student demographics, and which may influence VAM scores, include student peer culture and peer interaction effects. If students' initial achievement levels influence instructional pacing, for example, then teachers of low-performing students may be penalized simply because they cannot cover as much content.

The generalization stage of the IUA would examine VAM reliability. There is ample evidence that VAM estimates are much less reliable than are tests typically used for consequential decisions about individuals (Chetty, Friedman, & Rockoff, 2011; McCaffrey, Sass, Lockwood, & Mihaly, 2009; MET Project, 2010), constraining the appropriate use of teacher VAM estimates for consequential descriptions or decisions.

The extrapolation stage of the IUA would examine the extension from VAM scores to notions of teacher effectiveness more broadly conceived. If the student achievement tests underlying VAM estimates fail to represent the full range of learning outcomes teachers are expected to foster, then that construct underrepresentation in the student achievement tests leads directly to construct underrepresentation in teacher VAM estimates. VAM estimates show limited generalizability to other tests in the same subject area (Lockwood et al., 2007; Papay, 2011).

Finally, the IUA stage addressing score uses and interpretations might consider unintended consequences that might reasonably be anticipated from typical teacher VAM score applications. Numerous discussions of appropriate and inappropriate uses of VAM estimates have appeared elsewhere, including discussions of unintended consequences (e.g., Baker et al., 2010; Braun, 2005; Darling-Hammond, Amrein-Beardsley, Haertel, & Rothstein, 2012; Goldhaber & Hansen, 2010; Hill, Kapitula, & Umland, 2010; Rubin, Stuart, & Zanutto, 2004). As indicated, VAM estimates of teacher effectiveness may be unfair to teachers working with more challenging student populations, those teaching students with unusual characteristics (e.g., English learners, students with disabilities, gifted and talented students), or those working in schools with limited resources, although the thoughtful inclusion of appropriate covariates in value-added models can help to redress bias related to student demographics.

In summary, teacher effectiveness estimates from value-added models may be regarded as derived scores created by a complex measurement procedure to measure an application construct far removed from individual student scores obtained at a single point in time. As with other kinds of scores, their uses and interpretations may be examined using established psychometric frameworks. There is little argument that VAM estimates are generally superior to unadjusted means of students' end-of-year test scores for use as outcome variables in research on teacher effectiveness. Nonetheless, an IUA for high-stakes uses of VAM estimates as significant factors in the evaluation of individual teachers highlights serious problems of low reliability, bias, fairness, and plausible unintended negative consequences. Obviously, if teacher evaluations employ VAM scores in combination with other kinds of information (e.g., student surveys or classroom observations), the validity of these other sources of information should also be scrutinized.

Linking Different Tests

Test linking and equating are among the most common behind-the-scenes procedures undertaken by testing experts. Equating is generally an effort to use a single test score scale for different test forms over time. With increasing frequency, however, secondary analysts and practitioners are estimating links between different test score scales and modes of administration and using them to support a broader range of uses and interpretations. Pommerich (this volume, Chapter 7) reviews fairness issues that arise in these contexts, including a review of linkages between ACT and SAT score scales in college admissions. We defer to her chapter for an in-depth discussion. As with our growth example, we consider our perspective as complementary. We emphasize the frequency and predictability with which linkages across different tests occur and the fairness concerns that can arise as a result. Consistent with previous examples, we argue that the application construct is shifted from the developer construct implicitly or explicitly in accordance with the use of derived scores, raising concerns about fairness.

Other recent examples reviewing fairness in linking are policy-oriented and focused not on students but aggregates. Thissen (2007) provides numerous examples of aggregate-level test linking efforts that were recent at the time, and those efforts have proliferated since. The mapping of state standards to the NAEP scale (Bandeira de Mello, 2011) involves an implicit link across all state tests and NAEP. The link between NAEP and the Trends in International Mathematics and Science Study (TIMSS) (National Center for Education Statistics, 2013) represents a more explicit link between two tests in an effort to compare particular U.S. states to different countries, and vice versa. These link-ages have long been anticipated with serious cautions raised about appropriateness of resulting inferences (Feuer, Holland, Green, Bertenthal, & Hemphill, 1999). Nonetheless, researchers, too, are active in linking different tests to common scales—for example, across NAEP, TIMSS, and the Programme for International Student Assessment (PISA) (e.g., Hanushek & Woessmann, 2011) or across different subjects, grades, and time points in efforts to estimate and compare value-added scores, as reviewed in the previous section.

When the targets of inference are not students directly, but aggregates of students in structures such as schools and states, the fairness implications of poor and drifting linkages between tests are not as well reviewed. In the case of the NAEP-state standard mapping (Bandeira de Mello, 2011), there is an implicit construct shift from state achievement tests to the knowledge, skills, and abilities measured by NAEP. When the linkage fails, whether due to differing constructs, populations tested, or administration protocols, standard mappings will appear to drift over time, even when cut scores themselves have not actually changed.

Haertel and Ho (2007) anticipated that a state's standard mapping will shift over time in the direction and to the degree that its NAEP trend exceeds its state test score trend, and this has indeed manifested in the mappings over time. On the one hand, this may seem unfair to those state policymakers whose standards appear to fall, given the importance of high standards in the rhetoric of educational policy, and the fact that the cut scores may not have actually changed. On the other hand, because falling standards are a manifestation of state test score gains that outpace NAEP gains, these linkages set up an indirect incentive for state policymakers to ensure that gains in student achievement generalize across both state tests and NAEP. This can benefit states that have designed their state test to be similar to NAEP. In these intricate ways, secondary linkages like the NAEP-state standard mapping raise fairness considerations far downstream from those that are evaluated under standard test design protocols.

Discussion/Conclusion

In the simplest case, individuals' test scores obtained on a single occasion are used to quantify some attribute of those individuals. This simple case covers a great range of testing applications, and it is clear from other chapters in this volume, especially the chapters by Penfield ("Fairness in Test Scoring") and Liu and Dorans ("Fairness in Score Interpretation"), that significant fairness concerns can arise even when original scores are used to measure developer constructs. In this chapter, we have illustrated how individuals' test scores also enter into increasingly complex calculations to create scores of different kinds. Continuous scores may be used to classify students into elaborately described categories with complex meanings and implications. Scores obtained at multiple points in time may be combined to measure some construct of "growth" or to determine which students are "on track" to reach "college or careers." Individual students' scores may be aggregated to construct measurements of teachers or schools. Linkages may be constructed so that scores on one test may be used as if they were scores on some other test.

These new kinds of scores are sometimes created or sanctioned by measurement specialists and sometimes not. Often, they are not regarded as derived scores, leading to a blind spot in test score validation. Even though their uses and interpretations often have significant consequences, they may not be subjected to the kinds of scrutiny called for in the measurement field's professional standards (AERA et al., 2014). It bears repeating that the examples given here are merely illustrative. However, we also argue that they are representative of increasingly common practices that follow familiar, even predictable, patterns of inference and use. Any quantitative indicator similarly derived in whole or in part from one or more test scores should be subjected to an examination of fairness considerations, as we have outlined here.

Our focus within this brief chapter has been on sources of construct-irrelevant variance and construct underrepresentation in derived scores used to measure shifted constructs, giving rise to predictable biases for identifiable subgroups of students, teachers, or schools. A fuller consideration of these new kinds of scores and their uses might address the context of their use in a more systematic fashion, including the theories of action whereby scores were intended to accomplish various policy goals, the interests in each case of different stakeholder groups, the costs and benefits of policy alternatives, and plausible unintended consequences.

Notes

1. The views expressed are those of the author and not necessarily those of Stanford University.
2. The views expressed are those of the author and not necessarily those of Harvard University.
3. The term *construct shift* has been used differently in other contexts. For example, Martineau (2006) and Li and Lissitz (2012), in the context of vertical scaling, use construct shift to refer to changes in the meaning of constructs at successive grade levels.
4. The *Standards for Educational and Psychological Testing* (AERA et al., 2014) frame fairness issues primarily as absence of test bias, but also in terms of accessibility and universal design. Test bias may occur when identifiable subgroups differ with respect to their distributions of some source of construct-irrelevant variance.
5. It is widely recognized that multiple constructs are entailed in language proficiency, including at a minimum reading, writing, speaking, and listening, which for some measurement purposes could be further subdivided. The simple reference here to a single construct is for ease of exposition. The logic of the argument would be unchanged if multiple constructs were recognized.
6. Goldenberg (2008, p. 22) defines sheltered instruction as an instructional model "in which English-only teaching and texts are modified to make them more comprehensible as [ELs] learn academic English and content."
7. For consistency, we refer to this new, binary examinee attribute as the application construct, even though it may in fact have been anticipated when the test was designed, and even though the test developer may have been involved in the judgmental standard setting whereby it was specified.
8. However, it is possible that proficiency levels and the consequences associated with them would influence students' motivation or teachers' choices of instructional activities (e.g., test preparation) and their allocation of instructional time and resources, thereby influencing students' performance, especially for English learners undergoing mandated annual retesting.
9. Paradoxically, at the same time as this additional meaning is introduced, the actual information available from the scores is reduced. When scale scores are mapped into broader proficiency categories, distinctions among scale scores within the same category are lost.
10. The optimum ratio of these two kinds of misclassifications might depend on their relative costs, provided these costs can be defined.

References

ACT (2014). *Technical manual: The ACT.* Iowa City, IA: ACT. Retrived from www.act.org/aap/pdf/ACT_Technical_Manual.pdf

ACT (n.d.). *What college and career readiness scores mean.* Retrieved from www.act.org/standard

American Educational Research Association, American Psychological Association, & National Council on Measurement in Education (AERA, APA, & NCME). (2014). *Standards for educational and psychological testing.* Washington, DC: American Psychological Association.

Baker, E. L., Barton, P. E., Darling-Hammond, L., Haertel, E., Ladd, H. F., Linn, R. L., Ravitch, D., Rothstein, R., Shavelson, R. J., & Shepard, L. A. (2010, August 29). *Problems with the use of student test scores to evaluate teachers* (Economic Policy Institute Briefing Paper #278). Retrieved from www.epi.org/publications/entry/bp278

Ballou, D. (2009). Test scaling and value-added measurement. *Education Finance and Policy*, 4(4), 351–383.

Bandeira de Mello, V. (2011). *Mapping state proficiency standards onto the NAEP scales: Variation and change in state standards for Reading and Mathematics, 2005–2009* (NCES 2011-458). Washington, DC: National Center for Education Statistics, Institute of Education Sciences, U.S. Department of Education.

Braun, H. (2005). *Using student progress to evaluate teachers: A primer on value-added models.* Princeton, NJ: Educational Testing Service. Retrieved from www.ets.org/Media/Research/pdf/PICVAM.pdf

Chetty, R., Friedman, J. N., & Rockoff, J. E. (2011). *The long-term impacts of teachers: Teacher value-added and student outcomes in adulthood* (NBER Working Paper 17699). Retrieved from www.nber.org/papers/w17699

College Board. (2011). *The SAT college and career readiness benchmark.* Retrieved from http://media.collegeboard.com/digitalServices/pdf/sat/12b_6661_SAT_Benchmarks_PR_120914.pdf

Common Core State Standards Initiative. (n.d.). *Frequently asked questions.* Retrieved from www.corestandards.org/wp-content/uploads/FAQs.pdf

Conley, D. T. (2007). *Redefining college readiness.* Eugene, OR: Educational Policy Improvement Center.

Conley, D. T., & McGaughy, C. D. (2012). College and career readiness: Same or different? *Educational Leadership*, 69(7), 28–34.

Darling-Hammond, L., Amrein-Beardsley, A., Haertel, E., & Rothstein, J. (2012). Evaluating teacher evaluation. *Phi Delta Kappan*, 93(6), 8–15.

Feuer, M. J., Holland, P. W., Green, B. F., Bertenthal, M. W., & Hemphill, F. C. (1999). *Uncommon measures: Equivalence and linkage among educational tests.* Washington, DC: National Academy Press.

Fields, R. (2014). *Towards the National Assessment of Educational Progress (NAEP) as an indicator of academic preparedness for college and job training.* Washington, DC: National Assessment Governing Board. Retrieved from www.nagb.org/content/nagb/assets/documents/what-we-do/preparedness-research/NAGB-indicator-of-preparedness-report.pdf

Goldenberg, C. (2008). Teaching English language learners: What the research does—and does not—say. *American Educator*, 32(2), 8–23, 42–44.

Goldhaber, D., & Hansen, M. (2010). *Assessing the potential of using value-added estimates of teacher job performance for making tenure decisions* (National Center for Analysis of Longitudinal Data in Education Research [CALDER] Working Paper 31). Washington, DC: The Urban Institute. Retrieved from www.urban.org/publications/1001369.html

Haertel, E. H., & Lorié, W. A. (2004). Validating standards-based test score interpretations. *Measurement: Interdisciplinary Research and Perspectives*, 2(2), 61–103.

Hanushek, E. A., & Woessmann, L. (2011). How much do educational outcomes matter in OECD countries? *Economic Policy*, 26, 427–491.

Hess, F., & Petrilli, M. (2004). The politics of No Child Left Behind: Will the coalition hold? *Boston University Journal of Education, 185*(3), 13–25.

Hill, H. C., Kapitula, L., & Umland, K. (2010). A validity argument approach to evaluating teacher value-added scores. *American Educational Research Journal, 48*(3), 794–831.

Ho, A. D. (2008). The problem with "proficiency": Limitations of statistics and policy under No Child Left Behind. *Educational Researcher, 37*(6), 351–360.

Ho, A. D., & Haertel, E. H. (2007). *(Over)-interpreting mappings of state performance standards onto the NAEP scale.* Paper commissioned by the Council of Chief State School Officers.

Jackson, D. N., & Messick, S. (1961). Acquiescence and desirability as response determinants on the MMPI. *Educational and Psychological Measurement, 21*(4), 771–790.

Kane, M. (2006). Validation. In R. L. Brennan (Ed.), *Educational measurement* (4th ed., pp. 17–64). Westport, CT: American Council on Education/Praeger.

Kane, M. (2013). Validating the interpretations and uses of test scores. *Journal of Educational Measurement, 50*(1), 1–73.

Koretz, D. (2008). *Measuring up: What educational testing really tells us.* Cambridge, MA: Harvard University Press.

Li, Y., & Lissitz, R. W. (2012). Exploring the full-information bifactor model in vertical scaling with construct shift. *Applied Psychological Measurement, 36*(1), 3–20.

Lockwood, J. R., McCaffrey, D. F., Hamilton, L. S., Stecher, B., Le, V., & Martinez, J. F. (2007). The sensitivity of value-added teacher effect estimates to different mathematics achievement measures. *Journal of Educational Measurement, 44*(1), 47–67.

McCaffrey, D., Lockwood, J., Koretz, D., Louis, T., & Hamilton, L. (2004). Models for value-added modeling of teacher effects. *Journal of Educational and Behavioral Statistics, 29*, 67–101.

McCaffrey, D. F., Sass, T. R., Lockwood, J. R., & Mihaly, K. (2009). The intertemporal variability of teacher effect estimates. *Education Finance and Policy, 4*(4), 572–606.

McClarty, K. L., Way, W. D., Porter, A. C., Beimers, J. N., & Miles, J. A. (2013), Evidence-based standard setting: Establishing a validity framework for cut scores. *Educational Researcher, 42*, 78–88.

Martineau, J. A. (2006). Distorting value added: The use of longitudinal, vertically scaled student achievement data for growth-based, value-added accountability. *Journal of Educational and Behavioral Statistics, 31*(1), 35–62.

Messick, S. (1989). Validity. In R. L. Linn (Ed.), *Educational measurement* (3rd ed., pp. 13–103). New York: American Council on Education/Macmillan.

MET Project. (2010). *Learning about teaching: Initial findings from the Measures of Effective Teaching Project* (MET Project Research Paper). Seattle, WA: Bill & Melinda Gates Foundation. Retrieved from www.metproject.org/downloads/Preliminary_Findings-Research_Paper.pdf

National Center for Education Statistics (2013). *U.S. states in a global context: Results from the 2011 NAEP-TIMSS linking study* (NCES 2013-460). Washington, DC: Institute of Education Sciences, U.S. Department of Education.

National Research Council. (2011). *Allocating federal funds for state programs for English language learners.* Panel to Review Alternative Data Sources for the Limited-English Proficiency Allocation Formula under Title III, Part A, Elementary and Secondary Education Act. Committee on National Statistics and Board on Testing and Assessment. Division of Behavioral and Social Sciences and Education. Washington, DC: The National Academies Press.

No Child Left Behind (NCLB) Act of 2001, Pub. L. No. 107–110, § 115, Stat. 1425 (2002).

Papay, J. P. (2011). Different tests, different answers: The stability of teacher value-added estimates across outcome measures. *American Educational Research Journal, 48*(1), 163–193.

Partnership for Assessment of Readiness for College and Careers. (2013). *PARCC grade- and subject-specific performance level descriptors (PLDs) frequently asked questions.* Retrieved from www.parcconline.org/sites/parcc/files/PARCCPLDFAQsJuly2013.pdf

Reform Support Network. (2014). *A toolkit for implementing high-quality student learning objectives 2.0.* Retrieved from www2.ed.gov/about/inits/ed/implementation-support-unit/tech-assist/toolkit-implementing-learning-objectives-2-0.pdf

Robinson, J. P. (2011). Evaluating criteria for English learner reclassification: a causal-effects approach using a binding-score regression discontinuity design with instrumental variables. *Educational Evaluation and Policy Analysis, 33*(3), 267–292.

Roderick, M., Coca, V., & Nagaoka, J. (2011). Potholes on the road to college: High school effects in shaping urban students' participation in college application, four-year college enrollment, and college match. *Sociology of Education, 84*(3), 178–211.

Rubin, D. B., Stuart, E. A., & Zanutto, E. L. (2004). A potential outcomes view of value-added assessment in education. *Journal of Educational and Behavioral Statistics, 29*(1), 103–116.

Smarter Balanced Assessment Consortium. (2013). *Initial achievement level descriptors and college content-readiness policy.* Retrieved from www.smarterbalanced.org/wordpress/wp-content/uploads/2012/11/Smarter-Balanced-ELA-Literacy-ALDs.pdf

Thissen, D. (2007). Linking assessments based on aggregate reporting: Background and issues. In N. J. Dorans, M. Pommerich, & P. W. Holland (Eds.), *Linking and aligning scores and scales* (pp. 287–312). New York: Springer-Verlag.

U.S. Department of Education. (2010). *College- and career-ready standards and assessments.* Retrieved from www2.ed.gov/policy/elsec/leg/blueprint/faq/college-career.pdf

Wyatt, J., Kobrin, J., Wiley, A., Camara, W. J., & Proestler, N. (2011). *SAT benchmarks: Development of a college readiness benchmark and its relationship to secondary and postsecondary school performance* (College Board Research Report #2011-5). Retrieved from http://research.college board.org/sites/default/files/publications/2012/7/researchreport-2011–5-sat-college-readiness-benchmark-secondary-performance.pdf

13 Legal Aspects of Test Fairness

S. E. Phillips

Background[1]

The primary impetus for legal challenges to testing programs is unresolved allegations of unfairness. Unfairness is often alleged when groups or individuals are differentially denied something of value or subjected to an undesirable outcome as a result of their test scores. Federal laws as interpreted by court decisions and applied to testing programs confer rights and impose responsibilities that must be satisfied by both testing entities and test takers for test use to be judged fair.[2] Judicial decisions based on professional standards have generally required equal opportunity and equal access but not equal outcomes because group differences, although worthy of further investigation, are not per se indicators of a biased or unfair testing program (2014 *Test Standards*, p. 54).[3]

Federal laws addressing aspects of fair treatment in educational testing include the due process and equal protection clauses of the fourteenth amendment to the U.S. Constitution, Title VI of the Civil Rights Act (1964), the Americans with Disabilities Act (ADA, 1990), Section 504 of the Rehabilitation Act (1973), the Individuals with Disabilities Education Act (IDEA, 1991), the No Child Left Behind Act (NCLB, 2000), and the Equal Educational Opportunity Act (EEOA, 1974).[4] The sheer number of legal cases in which courts have addressed allegations of unfairness for groups and individuals affected by testing programs precludes a comprehensive review here. Instead, the focus of the chapter is on the following three broad fairness questions addressed by precedential testing litigation:

1. *Graduation testing*: When is it fair to require minority, special education, and ELL students with differential success rates and educational experiences to pass a graduation test to earn a high school diploma?
2. *Testing accommodations*: What are fair policies for providing testing accommodations to test takers with disabilities that concurrently achieve the goals of access, full representation of the intended construct, and comparable scores for all test takers?
3. *Test security*: When is it fair for a testing program to keep test items secure, to withhold/cancel test scores, or to discipline educators for test security violations?

Courts have generally answered these testing fairness questions by limiting the conditions under which the challenged action may be upheld or by accepting settlement agreements drafted by the parties. A court decision applies prospectively only to situations that are factually similar to the case from which it originated, so it is important to review the factual basis of judicial decisions when evaluating their applicability in new contexts. The remainder of this chapter does so for key testing cases that have addressed each of these fairness questions.

Legal Considerations Related to the Fairness of Graduation Tests

In answering the question of what process is due students subject to a graduation test, the landmark *Debra P. v. Turlington* (1984) case established two new legal requirements: (1) testing what has been taught in the schools (curricular validity, also known as opportunity to learn); and (2) adequate notice of the testing requirement. *Debra P.* was a Florida class action lawsuit brought by African-American students who failed a graduation test of applied basic mathematics and communication skills instituted with about 1½ years notice. On the first administration of the graduation test, 78% of the African-American students failed one or more sections while only 25% of the majority group students did so.

The trial court held the graduation test to be valid and reliable but the notice period insufficient and the test in violation of equal protection due to the perpetuation of the effects of the state's past intentional discrimination via statutorily segregated schools. The court enjoined the use of the graduation test until 1983 and, on appeal, the case was remanded back to the trial court to determine the test's curricular validity. For the second trial, the state offered curricular validity evidence from a study conducted by a private educational consulting firm that analyzed four types of data: (1) teacher surveys of instruction on tested skills; (2) district surveys of grade-level curricula; (3) site visits; and (4) student surveys. The results of the study indicated that each student received instruction on the tested skills an average of 2.7 times, which the study's author opined exceeded the single instructional exposure required for an instructionally valid and fair test (*Debra P.*, 1983, pp. 180–181).

The challengers disputed the study results, claiming that the state was required to demonstrate that every teacher taught the tested knowledge and skills to every student. The trial court declined to adopt this impossible state burden, defining an appropriate standard for curricular validity as "the skills [are] included in the official curriculum and ... the majority of the teachers recognize them as being something they should teach" (*Debra P.*, 1983, p. 186). The trial court held that Florida had produced sufficient evidence to support the curricular validity of the test and its use as a necessary remedy for any vestiges of past discrimination. The injunction was lifted and affirmed on appeal, allowing Florida to award high school diplomas based on the test results. The *Test Standards* subsequently adopted curricular validity standards in the 1985 (Standard 8.7), 1999 (Standard 13.5), and 2014 (Standards 3.19, 12.8) editions.

GI Forum v. Texas Education Agency (2000)

A decade and a half later, the *GI Forum* case reaffirmed the *Debra P.* notice and curricular validity requirements while reiterating states' rights to mandate graduation tests despite differential performance by minority groups. Nonetheless, the *GI Forum* case was factually distinguishable from the *Debra P.* case in several respects. Texas had a state-mandated curriculum; Florida did not. African-American and Hispanic minority students subject to the graduation test requirement in Texas had not been required by statute to attend segregated schools like the Florida students in the *Debra P.* case. Moreover, graduation testing was not a new concept in Texas as it had been in Florida. At the time, the *GI Forum* case was filed in 1997, high school graduation tests had been in existence nationwide for nearly two decades and in Texas for a decade, beginning with the challenged test's predecessor implemented in 1985. Consistent with the ruling in the *Debra P.* case, the state asserted that even if there had been prior discriminatory conduct by some educators in Texas, the graduation test would help to remedy any potential vestiges of past discrimination.

Disparate Impact[5]

The challengers in the *GI Forum* case alleged the graduation test, an academic skills test of reading, mathematics and writing skills, discriminated against African-American and Hispanic students in violation of Title VI Regulations (1999)[6] and constitutional due process. They asked the court to issue an injunction prohibiting the state from using the graduation test to award diplomas and requiring the school districts of the named challengers to issue their diplomas. For 1998 first-time test takers in tenth grade, initial passing rates were 85%, 55%, and 59%, respectively for Caucasian, African-American and Hispanic students. Corresponding cumulative pass rates for seniors in the Class of 1998 were 94%, 82%, and 83%, respectively (Phillips, 2000). Based on the 80% rule (*EEOC Uniform Guidelines*, 1978), values of 68% and 75% for the initial and cumulative passing rates, respectively, the presumption of disparate impact for racial minorities was supported by the initial passing rate differences but not the cumulative values.

The court concluded that cumulative statistics were more appropriate than initial passing rates for evaluating relative subgroup performance and applied the 80% rule to assess the significance of the observed disparate impact. However, the court also credited inappropriate statistical tests applied to subpopulation differences that identified majority/minority group passing percentage differences of less than 1% as significant due to the large numbers of students tested in each subpopulation. A test of practical significance using a more stringent judgmental criterion (e.g., a 90% rule or a fixed difference of 10 percentage points) would have provided a more technically sound basis for a finding of disparate impact.

Nonetheless, after finding disparate impact, the court held that the state had met its burden of demonstrating an educational necessity for the test in establishing minimum academic standards for all students and identifying inequalities in minority student achievement and remediating them. The court further determined that the challengers had not met their burden of identifying a valid and effective alternative to the graduation test. In doing so, the court rejected the challengers' arguments for combining test scores with teacher grades (a different standard) or substituting a compensatory total passing score (high test scores in one subject offsetting low scores in another) in place of the existing conjunctive passing scores.

Due Process

The factual issue in dispute under the challengers' due process claim was whether the implementation and use of the graduation test was a substantial departure from accepted professional standards. In finding the Texas graduation test constitutional under the due process clause, the court made extensive findings of fact related to test construction and adherence to professional standards, holding that the test met applicable legal standards for notice and curricular validity and satisfied relevant professional standards for content validity, reliability, and standard setting for the intended uses and interpretations of the test scores.[7]

The challengers argued that Texas should have collected exactly the same curricular validity evidence as Florida presented to the court in the *Debra P.* case. However, the

GI Forum court found that: (1) the widely disseminated, state-mandated curriculum; (2) surveys of teachers and curricular materials for the prior graduation test based on the same curriculum; (3) adequacy of preparation reviews by Texas educator committees and bias review panels; (4) eight testing opportunities with mandated remediation; (5) distribution of study guides; and (6) availability of released tests provided sufficient evidence to satisfy the curricular validity requirement. The court also held that three years' notice prior to initial administration in 10th grade and five years' notice prior to graduation satisfied due process notice requirements.

Item Selection Criteria

The *GI Forum* challengers also argued that the state should have considered a *Golden-Rule*-type procedure for selecting test items.[8] The court disagreed, rejecting testimony by the challengers' expert that attempted to demonstrate test bias using correlations between item majority/minority p-value differences and item point-biserials. The court expressed concern for the extent of differential performance in the test data, but held that the graduation test was constructed according to professional standards and the state was not required to choose test items that minimized disparate impact for particular minority groups.

Precedents

One important lesson learned from the *GI Forum* lawsuit was that state testing programs must not only follow legal and professional standards, but they must also produce detailed documentation of those efforts and be prepared to explain and defend all the psychometric properties of the test in court. The challengers elected not to appeal, perhaps because there was a substantial likelihood the court's decision would have been affirmed.

Graduation Testing of Students with Disabilities

The fairness of applying graduation testing requirements to students with disabilities has been challenged in several states. Although state court cases have limited applicability, they may be cited and applied by analogy in other jurisdictions. Key decisions from the 1980s to the 2000s follow.

Brookhart v. Ill. State Bd. of Educ. (1983)

The *Brookhart* case addressed the due process requirements for graduation tests applied to students with disabilities. This case involved a minimum-competency test of reading, language arts, and mathematics mandated by a local school district. Students who scored 70% correct or better on all three subtests were awarded diplomas while those who did not pass received certificates of completion. The testing requirement was imposed in the spring of 1978 and became effective for the spring of 1980 graduating class. Students had five opportunities to pass the test prior to their scheduled graduation and could retest until they passed or reached age 21.

   Several students with disabilities who had successfully completed their individualized educational programs (IEPs) but who had failed the graduation test and been denied diplomas filed a lawsuit to challenge the testing requirement. They alleged that their due process rights had been violated by insufficient advance notice and lack of instruction on the tested skills. The court held that students with disabilities may be subject to a graduation test requirement if parents and educators have made an informed decision regarding whether the test objectives should be included in a special education student's IEP. But the court also ruled that 1½ years is not sufficient notice for a special education student to prepare for a graduation test.

Because many of the challengers had been out of school for several years, the court determined that it would be unreasonable to expect them to return to school for further remediation and instead ordered their districts to award them diplomas as a remedy for the due process notice violation. In addition, the court distinguished between factors that prevented students with disabilities from demonstrating the degree of their learning and altering the tested content because they were unable to learn it. Thus, the court interpreted the *reasonable accommodations* requirement of Section 504 to include Braille or wheelchair access but not *substantial modifications* such as changing the test questions.

Rene v. Reid (2001)

The *Rene* case was a graduation test class action lawsuit filed by a group of students with disabilities from the class of 2000 who had previously been exempted from standardized tests, had not been taught the tested content, and/or had been denied certain testing modifications listed in their IEPs. They alleged violations of their due process rights and IDEA requirements. The Indiana graduation test covered English language arts (ELA) and mathematics, and the class of 2000 was the first to be subject to the testing requirement.

The court held that three to five years' notice provided adequate preparation time and that the remediation opportunities provided to students with disabilities were an adequate remedy for any prior failure of the schools to teach them the tested skills. The court also held that the IDEA did not require Indiana to honor all modifications in students' IEPs for the graduation test if the state had determined they would fundamentally alter the tested skills and produce non-comparable scores (e.g., a reader for the reading test) (see Samuels, 2014b).

Chapman v. Cal. Dept. of Educ. (2002)

The *Chapman* case was a challenge to the applicability of a California graduation test requirement to students with disabilities. The challengers complained that some special education students were unable to access the graduation test because they needed an alternate assessment. At that time, NCLB and IDEA required alternate assessments for school accountability tests but not specifically for graduation tests. For some of the student challengers, it appeared that inability to access the graduation test meant that their IEP teams had judged the tested high-school-level content instructionally inappropriate for them and had substituted elementary level IEP objectives.[9]

The court ordered that students with disabilities be permitted to take the graduation test with any accommodations or modifications provided in the students' IEPs for any standardized or classroom tests without having to reconvene an IEP team meeting. California was also ordered to develop an alternate assessment for the graduation test as soon as practicable. But the court reserved for future consideration the issue of whether test scores obtained with unapproved modifications or on alternate assessments would count as satisfying the graduation testing requirement. Prior to trial in the *Chapman* case, the legislature intervened and by law provided that special education students who met certain procedural requirements and all other graduation requirements, were entitled to a high school diploma after three unsuccessful attempts to pass the graduation test (Senate Bill 517, 2006). On May 30, 2008, the court approved a final settlement of the case releasing all claims from the classes of 2001–2011 and requiring the state to contract for an independent study to inform recommendations to the legislature regarding graduation testing of students with disabilities.

Graduation Testing of English Language Learners (ELLs)

ELLs are a growing segment of the school population and represent over 100 languages in some states. States differ in their approaches to educating and testing ELLs. For example, Texas provides bilingual instruction and testing in Spanish in the elementary grades while California favors English immersion unless parents opt out. ELLs challenged both states' graduation tests administered in English and both tests were upheld.

Valenzuela v. O'Connell (2006)

The challengers in the California *Valenzuela* case unsuccessfully argued that ELLs should be awarded high school diplomas without passing the graduation test due to inequities in educational opportunities and failure of the state to provide native language testing or certain ELL modifications. Similar to the *disparate impact* claims of minority groups, the challengers cited differences in passing rates between ELL and non-ELL students as evidence that the graduation test was unfair. This analogy was inappropriate because *disparate impact* was intended to describe test score differences between sub-groups whose members are identified by characteristics judged construct irrelevant to the tested academic skills while ELLs are members of that subgroup precisely because they have academic skill deficits in English that may be judged construct-relevant to the tested skills.

The state argued that awarding unearned diplomas to ELLs who had not passed the graduation test devalued the diplomas of the substantial number of ELLs who had passed it and that the appropriate remedy for some ELLs' lack of proficiency on the tested skills was additional remedial education. The court agreed, holding that the potential injury to the ELL challengers was the loss of educational opportunity to learn the tested skills, not the denial of the diploma, and the appropriate remedy for that injury was provision of the missed instruction, not removal of the test requirement or the award of diplomas by court order.

ELL "Accommodations"

The use of the term "accommodations" to describe testing alterations for ELLs is technically inappropriate because classification as an ELL has not been legally recognized as a disability covered by Section 504 or the ADA. ELLs are not disabled because they can become proficient in English through instruction.

However, during the period in which ELLs are acquiring English language proficiency and states are required to include them in accountability testing (NCLB, 2000), a partial measure of the intended construct may be obtained by providing linguistic supports such as language simplification, dual language dictionaries, translation glossaries, or translated/adapted tests. When such testing modifications that change the tested construct are provided, the 2014 *Test Standards* view the resulting tests as new tests for which the user is responsible for demonstrating adherence to relevant psychometric standards in areas such as validity, reliability, standard setting, equating, etc. (Standards 3.9, 3.11, 3.12, p. 61).

In addition, testing programs that develop translated/adapted tests in one or more native languages may be confronted with an equal protection challenge from test takers for whom a native language test is not available. These ELLs could argue that the state has effectively created similarly situated majority and minority ELL groups that are not yet English language proficient but are treated differently when tested. Majority group ELLs are instructed and tested in their native language but minority group ELLs are not, often because the state has insufficient resources to do so. Using numerical dominance to justify providing the benefit of native language testing for some ELL test takers but not others may be unfair to the ELLs who do not receive the benefit and may constitute an equal protection violation.[10]

Legal Considerations Related to the Fairness of Testing Accommodations Policies

When an individual with a disability is unable to access a tested construct due to construct-irrelevant factors, to be fair and to support the validity of the intended inferences from the resulting test scores, ADA Regulations (1991) and the 2014 *Test Standards* require accommodations to be provided (§36.309; Standard 9.14). Judicial decisions use the term *reasonable accommodations* to describe testing alterations that afford test takers access without compromising the validity of the intended test score interpretations (Phillips, 2011) and the 2014 *Test Standards* distinguish between *accommodations* that preserve the measurement of the intended construct and the comparability of test scores and *modifications* that alter the tested construct and result in scores that are not comparable to scores obtained from standard administrations of the original test (pp. 59–61; Standard 3.9).

When measuring the achievement of content knowledge and skills, eliminating construct-irrelevant factors without creating construct underrepresentation or compromising score comparability may be more challenging when testing alterations relate to cognitive disabilities rather than to physical disabilities because cognitive disabilities often are directly relevant to the focal construct of the test. For example, the physical skill of sight is construct relevant for a bus driver but not essential for an attorney, so a Braille version of a written test is appropriate for a bar examination but not for a commercial driver's license. Alternatively, it is more difficult to evaluate whether the cognitive skills of decoding or computation are construct-relevant for a reading or a mathematics test. When the purpose of the test is to measure a test taker's relative standing on a construct or attainment of specified proficiencies, testing modifications prevent test takers from fully accessing the construct and create scores with construct underrepresentation that invalidates the intended normative (e.g., percentile ranks) or criterion-referenced (e.g., pass/fail) score interpretations (2014 *Test Standards*, p. 61; Standard 9.9):

Test Score Annotations

One of the most contentious accommodations issues has been the use of score annotations (also referred to as "score flags") to identify reported test scores as having been obtained from nonstandard test administrations. Test score annotations are controversial because (1) there are differences of opinion about whether specific testing condition alterations are construct-relevant and affect score comparability, and (2) the inclusion of score annotations on test reports may violate test takers' privacy rights by revealing the existence of a disability to third parties.

(2014 *Test Standards*, pp. 61–62; Standard 9.19)

Common testing alterations for some physical disabilities, such as Braille versions, are known to require more testing time. However, for many physical disabilities that cause fatigue, decreased manual dexterity, or frequent needs for restroom breaks, it is difficult to quantify the exact amount of extra time required to alleviate manifestations of the disability without providing an unfair advantage relative to test takers tested under standard time limits.

Two legal challenges to test score annotations for extended time, *Doe v. National Board of Medical Examiners* (NBME, 2006; medical licensure) and *Breimhorst v. Educational Testing Service* (ETS, 2000; professional admissions affecting college admissions) are instructive. At the time these cases were litigated, neither the ADA nor its guidelines specifically addressed test score annotation and the 1999 *Test Standards* recommended that when evidence of score comparability was lacking, annotations should identify the altered testing conditions to facilitate appropriate score interpretations by test users (Standards 10.11 and 10.4).[11]

Annotations for Extended Time for Physical Disabilities: The Doe Case

John Doe had multiple sclerosis, which caused problems with muscle spasticity, fine motor coordination, and bathroom urgency, that required extra testing time. The NBME annotated Doe's medical licensure test scores, indicating that they had been obtained under nonstandard conditions.[12] Doe argued that he had been injured because the test score annotations invaded his privacy and, against his will, identified him as disabled to residency programs selecting candidates for interviews. At the time, nearly half of the nonstandard administrations provided on the medical licensure tests were for extra time and approximately two-thirds of the test takers with disabilities who were granted extra time had learning disabilities (Phillips, 2010). Upon inquiry by a state or residency program administrator, the NBME policy was to identify the nonstandard condition (e.g., extra time) but not the disability (e.g., multiple sclerosis).

NBME staff stated a belief that Doe received a performance benefit from the extra time when compared to test takers tested under standard time limits. While Doe conceded that it was theoretically possible for him to continue thinking about the test questions during his mini-breaks, he also stated he was unable to read text or mark answers during that time, suggesting that the amount of time he was actually able to work on the test and alleviate his discomfort simultaneously was negligible. In addition, if Doe had used the extra time to work on the test questions, one would have expected him to consistently use more time on all test sections of comparable content and difficulty but the evidence was to the contrary.[13]

Legal Standard for Score Annotation

The trial court granted Doe's motion for a preliminary injunction requiring the NBME to report his medical licensure scores to residency programs without annotations. This decision was reversed on appeal because the court held Doe had not provided sufficient evidence that his scores with extra time were comparable to scores from standard time administrations. In response to the absence of an explicit prohibition on annotating in the ADA and its Regulations, the appeals court crafted its own legal standard for determining when a test score should not be annotated, stating:

> If Doe were to establish either that his scores are psychometrically comparable to the scores of candidates who take the test under standard time conditions, or that his scores will be ignored by the programs to which they are reported, he might [prevail on his ADA claim].

(2000, pp. 156–157)

Doe's expert argued that the appeals court standard only required Doe to demonstrate that his scores, not those for a group of test takers with similar disabilities, were comparable and that the credible evidence required by the 1999 *Test Standards* (Standard 10.11) to avoid annotation could be either empirical evidence or professional judgment. The 1999 *Test Standards* did not specifically address whether or how individualized determinations of score comparability could be formulated but did state that it should be construed consistent with applicable law (pp. 4, 101–102). Based on these interpretations and the totality of available information, including extensive data for Doe, his expert concluded that his scores were essentially comparable to those from standard administrations (Phillips, 2010). Doe's expert was convinced that but for the interference of his physical disability, Doe would have had no difficulty completing the tests within standard time limits, that Doe's test scores did not overestimate his true knowledge and skills, and that it was unfair to penalize Doe with annotated scores simply because he was unable to determine in advance and with precision how much extra time he would need and when he would need it. In addition, Doe's expert argued that annotation would have been unnecessary if the NBME had been willing to provide a computerized version of the test that permitted pausing between items.

Without expressing any opinion regarding the comparability of Doe's scores, the NBME's expert argued that under the 1999 *Test Standards*, credible empirical evidence of score comparability was lacking and the score annotations should be retained (Brennan, 2008). He argued that it was the "accommodation" that was annotated, not the disability or the test taker. The NBME's expert was also not convinced that lack of speededness of the test for Doe, even if true, would indicate psychometric comparability. He observed that the extra time was in part a buffer for Doe's anxiety about taking the test under standard conditions and speculated that if non-disabled test takers were also given extra time, the resulting decrease in anxiety for some might have a positive effect on their test scores.[14]

Feasibility of Case-by-Case Annotation Decisions

Admittedly, individual inquiries are time-consuming and potentially costly for testing organizations with large test taker populations. However, legal and psychometric standards require testing entities to evaluate and respond individually to all requests by test takers for testing accommodations. Since only a small fraction of test takers with disabilities are physically impaired, it may not be too great a burden for testing entities to also consider score comparability and the appropriateness of annotation when evaluating the requests for testing alterations from test takers with physical disabilities.

To address the issue of the feasibility of a testing organization making individualized determinations of score comparability, Doe's expert used the results from the individualized inquiry concerning the comparability of Doe's scores to develop a set of criteria that a testing entity administering high-stakes, cognitive achievement tests, such as the NBME, could use to determine when there is a substantial likelihood that scores obtained with extra time are essentially comparable to scores from standard test administrations and should not be annotated (Phillips, 2010). The NBME's expert in the *Doe* case was skeptical about the feasibility of case-by-case annotation decisions and distinguished the responsibilities of test developers and test users, arguing that it is the responsibility of the test user (e.g., the residency program), not the test developer (e.g., the NBME), to consider multiple sources of collateral information such as academic record when making decisions about a test taker (Brennan, 2008).

Case Resolution

Following the completion of discovery and submission of the expert reports, both parties filed motions for summary judgment. Doe argued that there were no disputed facts and that its expert had more than satisfied, by a preponderance of the evidence, the "comparability" requirement articulated by the appeals court in order to establish an ADA violation (Brief of Appellant John Doe, 2006). The NBME, on the other hand, argued that Doe failed to demonstrate an injury caused by the NBME's actions, that if Doe were injured by being identified as disabled it was due to the actions of third parties (e.g., residency programs), not the NBME, and that the requested relief of removing the annotation would not redress the alleged injury because his disability had already been disclosed in other ways (e.g., Doe's gait when walking, Doe's references).

The trial court ruled that the potential future harm to Doe was too speculative to justify ordering the NBME to remove the annotations. In the interim while the case was pending, Doe had been accepted to the residency program of his choice and been licensed in multiple states using the annotated score reports. The trial court held that Doe's possible move to California and application for licensure or a fellowship program were not sufficient to confer standing to pursue his ADA claim. The appeals court affirmed this decision. Because neither the trial court nor the appeals court decided the issue of comparability, it is still an open question what the legal requirements are for demonstrating score comparability sufficient to sustain an ADA challenge for removal of a score annotation.

Annotations for Extended Time for Cognitive Disabilities: Effects of the Breimhorst Case

In 2000, the then-current ETS policy of annotating test scores obtained with extra time on its admissions and licensure tests was challenged in a federal court in California. The test taker with a disability had taken the Graduate Management Admissions Test (GMAT) on a computer with a track ball (replacing the mouse) and 25% extra time to compensate for the physical disability of having no hands. His scores were annotated with the notation "Scores obtained under special conditions." ETS denied his request to remove the annotation and he (and two advocacy groups) filed suit.

The challengers argued that the ETS annotation policy violated the rights of test takers with disabilities under Sections 309 and 503(b) of the ADA and Section 504 because ETS had no evidence scores obtained with extra time were not comparable to scores from standard administrations. ETS argued that when scores were obtained under nonstandard conditions, accurate reporting of that information to test users was consistent with the 1999 *Test Standards*, caused no injury, and violated no applicable laws.

ADA Examination Section

Under § 309 of the ADA specific to examinations, the *Doe* court held that annotating test scores was not prohibited, stating that although this section required testing entities to provide accommodations to test takers with disabilities, it did not require "that the resulting scores be declared psychometrically comparable to the scores of [test takers] who take the test under standard conditions" (2000, p. 156).[15]

The *Breimhorst* court, however, held that the ADA did not focus narrowly on accessibility of the test to persons with disabilities, but had a broader goal of equal opportunity that required the test itself to provide results that reflected the true abilities of persons with disabilities regardless of the burden to the testing entity. If testing entities met this burden, the court said, there would be no need to annotate scores. Nonetheless, the *Breimhorst* court ruled that whether an accommodated test administration might differ significantly enough to warrant annotation despite the testing entity's best efforts was a factual matter to be decided at trial.

Section 504

Section 504 Regulations stated that colleges may only inquire about a disability confidentially post-admission to identify needed accommodations (34 C.F.R. § 104.42(b)(4)). Office for Civil Rights (OCR) interpretations added that colleges could use test scores from nonstandard administrations if they were not devalued and were not the sole criterion for admission (*Duke University*, 1993; *SUNY*, 1993). However, stating that the Section 504 Regulations and OCR interpretations did not address the issue of whether a testing entity could be liable for discrimination for supplying the annotated test scores, the *Breimhorst* court held that the challengers had stated a viable claim challenging the underlying assumption of differential interpretation of annotated scores.

Settlement

ETS settled the *Breimhorst* case in 2001 by agreeing to discontinue annotating scores obtained with extra time on the GMAT, GRE, TOEFL, and Praxis tests beginning in the fall of 2001 and the College Board agreed to convene an expert panel to study doing the same for the Scholastic Assessment Test (SAT).[16] By agreement of the parties, the expert panel consisted of three college professors specializing in disability research, two psychometricians, one college administrator, and a nonvoting chair. Each party provided the expert panel with a written report and an oral presentation. In a 4–2 decision, the panel recommended that the College Board stop annotating SAT scores obtained with extra time (Gregg, Mather, Shaywitz, & Sireci, 2002).

Expert Panel Opinions

The expert panel issued multiple opinions.[17] The majority opinion appeared to view equal access in terms of the benefit of access to college and future careers available to test takers with high test scores.[18] The focus of the minority opinion was on the validity and accuracy of the test score interpretations (Brennan & Saleh, 2002). This distinction between access to the test itself and access to the benefits of performing well on the test appeared to be the crux of the disagreement between the majority and minority opinions.

The majority opinion did not provide evidence that test takers with learning disabilities would be unable to access the test without the extra time—only that their scores would be higher with extra time due to removal of the effects of their lack of reading fluency. This view seemed to treat reading fluency as construct-irrelevant variance for persons with identified learning disabilities but as construct-relevant variance for non-disabled test takers who were slow readers for unknown reasons. This inconsistency in construct relevance depending on disability status is contrary to professional standards that define construct relevance as a test-centered, not a group-centered, characteristic (1999 *Test Standards*, Standard 1.2; 2014 *Test Standards*, Standard 1.1, p. 62).

In addition, the majority may have misunderstood the intent of a primarily power test. The fact that most test takers are able to finish the test in the allotted time does not necessarily mean that speed of work is unimportant or irrelevant. It may mean the test is intended to be non-speeded for test takers with a reasonable level of facility with the tested knowledge and skills, but not for slow readers, poor analyzers, or those with marginal skill acquisition who are unable to apply their skills efficiently. In this view, the construct is a unified measure of skill acquisition that brings together a constellation of skills to produce a desired performance within reasonable time limits.

Fragmented and Shifting Constructs

Alternatively, if the focal construct is fragmented into smaller pieces of skills, for which groups of test takers demonstrate different combinations of pieces, the construct shifts from group to group depending on the portions removed and is no longer a unified measure of the intended skill for all test takers. The 2014 *Test Standards* impose a duty on testing programs that do so to provide evidence of the comparability of the resulting test scores (Standards 3.11, 5.17, 9.9). In addition, a fragmented construct that shifts depending on different judgments of construct relevance for different test taker groups is contrary to the ADA and Section 504 cases stating that testing programs are not required to lower standards or fundamentally alter the constructs the test measures.

Psychometric Opinions

The two psychometricians split their votes and issued separate opinions (Brennan, 2002; Sireci, 2001). They agreed that the existing ETS policy for annotating test scores obtained with extra time was in conformity with the 1999 *Test Standards*, that the reliability and factor structures of standard and extra time versions of the SAT were similar, and that scores from standard administrations demonstrated higher predictive validity, but they disagreed on the issue of comparability. One psychometrician said the scores were *not comparable* and the other was *not sure* (Psychometric Committee, 2001).[19]

Final Decisions

Subsequently, the College Board and ETS announced that SAT scores obtained under nonstandard conditions would no longer be annotated and the American College Testing (ACT) Program followed suit for extended time administrations of the ACT Assessment (ACT, 2002; College Board, 2002). Although the original *Breimhorst* challenger had a physical disability, these decisions to discontinue annotating scores obtained with extra time also applied to test takers with cognitive disabilities.

Alternatives

ETS and the College Board were not bound to accept the expert panel recommendation. In addition to offering a standard administration with more generous time limits or nonstandard administrations with annotated scores to any test taker, they could have defended their score annotation policy. The lack of credible evidence of score comparability and the existence of credible evidence of non-comparability might have convinced the court. But doing so would not have resolved the troubling question of whether to continue to annotate the scores of the small number of test takers with physical disabilities given the extra time necessary to deal with the non-cognitive, physical manifestations of their disabilities.

Responsibility for Proving Comparability

When addressing the legality of test score annotations, the *Doe* and *Breimhorst* courts split on the issue of what evidence is required and which party is responsible for producing it. In the *Doe* case, a federal appeals court placed the burden on the test taker with a disability for demonstrating his scores were comparable. But in the *Breimhorst* case, a federal trial court placed the burden on the testing entity to produce evidence that the scores of the test taker with a disability were not comparable.[20] This makes a difference both legally and practically. The party assigned the burden of evidence production will have the greater expense of information collection and analysis and will lose the case if unable to produce sufficient evidence. The 2014 *Test Standards* appears to have resolved this issue by placing an affirmative responsibility on test developers and/or users to document empirical or judgmental evidence of score comparability (Standards 3.11, 9.9; pp. 60, 62).

Legal Considerations Related to the Fairness of Test Security Policies

Fair enforcement of reasonable test security policies is an essential requirement for ensuring the validity and integrity of the intended test score interpretations for all test takers (2014 *Test Standards*, Standard 6.6). Test security and release, aspects of due process fairness, implicate a combination of rights and responsibilities for both test takers and test administrators. Test takers have the right to a fair test and fair treatment, but they also have a responsibility to be prepared, follow instructions, protect the security of test materials, and refrain from dishonest conduct that produces scores that misrepresent their actual levels of achievement (2014 *Test Standards*, p. 132). Test administrators have a responsibility to act in good faith, strictly adhere to standardized administration procedures, and to proactively seek out and investigate evidence of misconduct to ensure that no test taker obtains an unfair advantage. These shared rights and responsibilities have created tensions between test administrators and test takers, educators, parents, and the media over the reasonableness of test security policies (Phillips, 2012).

Test-Taker Misconduct

Most cases of test-taker misconduct investigated by testing entities involve threatened score invalidation and are settled without going to court. When test-taker misconduct cases are settled judicially, courts generally have upheld the right of testing entities to cancel scores for which the validity of the score interpretations is questionable provided they have fairly considered all available evidence, including that supplied by the test taker whose scores have been questioned, and have followed the written procedures accepted by the test taker during the registration process.

One of the methods used by testing entities to identify potential cases of misconduct when retest score gains are large is similarity analysis, a statistical procedure designed to compare the answers of the suspect test taker to those of test takers seated nearby to evaluate the probability that copying occurred. While such analyses do not prove beyond a reasonable doubt that misconduct occurred, they provide an important piece of circumstantial evidence. Such evidence is probative when combined with other consistent evidence of misconduct and subject to doubt in the face of additional conflicting evidence (*Langston v. ACT*, 1989). Illustrative cases decided for and against the test taker follow.

Misconduct in College Admissions Testing

In the early days of college admissions testing, there were few cases, and the courts generally upheld the test publisher's right to offer retests, cancel scores, and notify score recipients when they had reason to believe misconduct had occurred. A short paragraph in the registration bulletin was sufficient to notify prospective test takers of the policy. For example, in *DePina v. ETS* (1969), ETS requested that the test taker retest to confirm his scores after comparing his answer sheet with another test taker and concluding that he had cheated. DePina refused to retest and filed suit to prevent ETS from canceling his scores and notifying recipient colleges. The court sided with ETS.

The results in more recent misconduct cases involving college admissions tests have been mixed, with less deference given to the test publisher, greater benefit of the doubt accorded the test taker, more convincing evidence required for canceling scores, and more detailed advance notification of test security policies expected. Lists of regulations included in the registration bulletin have been lengthened, and the options available to test takers accused of misconduct have been expanded.

SAT Examples: The Dalton and Murray Cases

The *Dalton v. ETS* (1995) and *Murray v. ETS* (1999) cases are examples of test takers challenging ETS decisions to cancel scores based on large retest score gains. In both cases, the court was asked to decide whether ETS had acted in good faith in its investigation of questionable scores and its decision not to report those scores to the test takers' designated colleges. At that time, when the scores of retesters increased significantly, ETS investigated the handwriting on the answer sheets and registration materials and conducted a similarity analysis.

Dalton's 410-point score increase triggered such an ETS investigation. Believing that an imposter had taken the second test, ETS refused to release the scores. Dalton filed suit and the court held that ETS had not conducted a bona fide investigation because it had arbitrarily relied solely on handwriting evidence to the exclusion of alternative explanations and evidence. As a result, the court concluded that Dalton was entitled to the benefit of his contract and ordered ETS to release Dalton's retest scores "without comment or qualification." On appeal, the court agreed that ETS had breached its contract with Dalton but held that release of his scores was not the proper remedy. Instead, the court ordered ETS to conduct a good-faith reconsideration of the exculpatory material submitted by Dalton.

In the *Murray* case, the retest score gain was 600 points. ETS conducted a similarity analysis and found an unusual correspondence between Murray's answers and those of another test taker seated diagonally in front of him. Statistically, the number of Murray's incorrect answers that matched those of the other test taker had a probability of 1 in 3.3 million of occurring by chance when pairs of answer sheets were compared. ETS also conducted an erasure analysis revealing that a substantial number of items with erasures had apparently been changed to answers matching those of the other test taker. Similar to the *Dalton* case, the *Murray* court did not determine whether the test taker had cheated, but only ruled on the contract issue of whether ETS had acted in good faith. But unlike *Dalton*, the *Murray* case was decided in federal rather than state court and reached an opposite result. The *Murray* court found that the facts were undisputed and held that ETS had a right and duty to report only valid scores to institutions, to protect its own reputation, and to assure all test takers that no other test taker had received an unfair advantage.

Cheating Conspiracies

In addition to dealing with low-tech cheating behavior by test preparation companies and individual test takers, ETS has also uncovered high-tech cheating schemes implemented by groups of test takers. For example, in 2002, ETS temporarily suspended computer administration of the GRE in China, South Korea, and Taiwan, and switched to paper-and-pencil administrations (Wheeler, 2002). This action was taken in response to a cheating scheme involving websites where test takers posted questions they had memorized. An ETS investigation had revealed that toward the end of the cycle in which a pool of questions had been used, national average scores on the verbal section of the test had increased by 100 points in China, 50 points in South Korea, and 50 points in Taiwan.

Criminal Prosecution

The usual consequence of test taker misconduct is cancellation of scores. However, on occasion, cheating allegations result in criminal prosecution. For example, in 1992, ETS investigated a tip that a Maryland high school student had cheated on the SAT (Associated Press, 1992). Although ranking in the bottom quarter of his class, the student's combined SAT score was 1,410 (out of a possible 1,600). A handwriting discrepancy was discovered, and the student filed suit to prevent ETS from notifying score recipients that the validity of the score interpretations was questionable. At trial, the student testified that he had taken the SAT but later admitted that he had paid $200 to a friend to take the test for him (Associated Press, 1992). The judge sentenced him to six months in jail for perjury.

Procedural Irregularities

A test score can also be challenged by test administrators or test takers when standardized test administration protocols have been violated. For example, the court upheld the test publisher's cancellation of scores when proctors reported a test taker's repeated refusal to stop working when the testing time expired (*ETS v. Hildebrant,* 2007). Conversely, in *Mindel v. ETS* (1990), the test taker alleged that multiple administration irregularities, including the borrowing of her test booklet by a proctor to resolve an inquiry from another test taker, adversely affected her test performance. She filed suit to compel ETS to schedule a special compensatory test administration so she could obtain retest scores in time to meet college early application deadlines. The court held that the proctor's taking of Mindel's test booklet created a sufficient irregularity to mandate an unscheduled makeup test.

Educator Malfeasance

In the past, many states and school districts have chosen to assume their educators are honest and ethical and that serious test security violations only occur in other jurisdictions. Recent high-profile cases in multiple cities and states have proved them wrong (Perry, Vogell, Judd, & Pell, 2012). No longer can states avoid the reality that the high-stakes use of test scores for accountability has created a climate in which some educators have felt justified in engaging in prohibited and unethical behaviors that undermine the validity of student test score interpretations. In a few notable cases, the adult offenders avoided detection for several years.

Answer Sheet Tampering

In an early case in an affluent Connecticut school district, officials became suspicious of an elementary school with extremely high Iowa Tests of Basic Skills (ITBS) achievement test composite scores (none below the 98th percentile rank) when they discovered an abnormally high number of erasures on student answer sheets (Lindsay, 1996). A high percentage of the erasures were from wrong answers to right answers and in a few cases from the right answer to the same wrong answer.

In an unannounced retest in the target school and two control schools, proctored by District personnel, erasures and student scores declined at the target school to levels similar to the demographically comparable control schools. In addition, analyses of state test results by a different test publisher for the same elementary schools demonstrated the same pattern of substantially greater numbers of erasures and suspicious answer changes in the target school. There was an outcry of protest from parents when these results became public because students in the target school had consistently outscored those in the district's other eight elementary schools over the previous five years and educators in the target school had won several prestigious awards for educational excellence.

Parents and educators at the target school were particularly upset and denied that any misconduct had occurred. They insisted that their students had been taught a special test-taking strategy that caused the excessive erasures and common responses. An extensive follow-up investigation was supervised by a retired judge and involved inquiries by the state crime laboratory and law enforcement professionals, as well as additional statistical analyses. Based on all the facts and circumstances, the District concluded that the school principal had tampered with the answer sheets, and his employment was terminated.

Recent Epidemic

Several states and school districts have recently faced public embarrassment and loss of credibility in their testing programs due to well-organized schemes by adult educators to artificially inflate test scores over extended periods of time. For example, in March

2013, 35 Atlanta educators were indicted for altering student answer sheets after an extensive investigation triggered by excessive erasures and phenomenal test score improvements over 10 years (Wilson, Bowers, & Hyde, 2011). The investigation implicated a total of 178 educators, 82 of whom confessed. Nearly all resigned, were fired, or lost their teaching licenses at administrative hearings. Other schemes to falsify test scores have also been exposed in New York City, Washington, DC, Houston, Los Angeles, and Philadelphia school districts (Mezzacappa, 2014; Strauss, 2013).

Test Security Lapses

Sometimes inappropriate access to test materials occurs without any intentional dishonesty but because enforcement of test security procedures has been lax. Test security can be compromised especially quickly when secure information is posted on the Internet. For example, in 2003, Georgia was forced to cancel census testing in some grades and subjects because 270 live test items had been posted to an Internet practice item bank available to teachers, parents, and students (Olson, 2003).

In another case in Michigan, a public school allowed a reporter from a local newspaper to observe in a classroom (Bunkley, 2007). In the ensuing article about the state tests, the newspaper revealed two of the writing essay topics. Because many districts had not yet administered the writing test and anyone could have read the article online, the state determined that fairness for all schools and students had been compromised and elected to retest all 260,000 fifth and sixth grade students in the state with a new writing test. Although the District apologized for violating test security procedures, the state announced that penalties against the District were also being considered.

Whistleblower Case

Educators who report inappropriate test preparation activities may become a target for retaliation. For example, an assistant principal who refused to implement a scheme to provide teachers with copies of test items for review prior to test administration and reported it to state officials was demoted and transferred to another school (*Canary v. Osborn*, 2000). Canary sued the school board. The board claimed legislative immunity but the court held that the board's actions were personnel decisions subject to challenge. The parties apparently settled the case nonjudicially.

Test Preparation Courses

Preparing students for undergraduate and graduate college admissions tests is a thriving business. Over the years, there have been organized attempts by some test preparation course sponsors to surreptitiously acquire current secure items to provide an advantage to their course clients and increase future business. The test publisher of the SAT and GRE tests fought back with federal copyright infringement suits and won injunctions halting the infringement and ordering the offenders to return copies of pirated items (*ETS v. Kaplan*, 1997; *ETS v. Katzman*, 1986).

Maintaining the Security of Test Items

There are three main reasons why a high-stakes testing program may need to maintain the security of its test items: reuse of items, maintaining equivalent passing scores, and item field testing. But convincing test takers, parents, educators, taxpayers, and the media that tests are fair is challenging when test items remain confidential. After protracted litigation and negotiation in many states, partial item release on a periodic basis has become the norm in large volume testing programs and occasional limited release is common in small volume testing programs.

NY "Truth in Testing" Law

The New York Standardized Testing Act (STA, 1980) was enacted to remove the secrecy surrounding standardized testing by subjecting test questions, data, and technical information to public scrutiny. The STA was designed primarily to regulate admissions testing in the state by requiring test publishers to file certain documents with the state that then became subject to disclosure under a freedom of information request. In addition, certain information, including scored test items and answers, had to be provided to test takers with their score reports.

Several test publishers engaged in protracted litigation and negotiation with the state over the number of test forms required to be released. The state argued that the required disclosures under the statute fell within the *fair use* exception of the Copyright Act while the test publishers insisted that test takers in New York were disadvantaged by the law because fewer testing dates were offered there to limit the number of test forms required to be released.

The test publishers entered into an agreement with the state temporarily allowing fewer test forms to be disclosed. The AAMC agreed to disclose one MCAT form every four years, GMAC agreed to disclose all of their tests, GRE agreed to 60%, the College Board agreed to 80% for the SATs, and ETS agreed to 42% for TOEFL. Additional negotiations with the state extended the reduced disclosure agreements for additional years and the court ultimately ratified a modified version of its court order enforcing the current agreement between the parties requiring some but not all administered forms to be disclosed (*College Bd. v. Pataki*, 1995).

Parental Rights and Privacy Concerns

Test security measures that maintain the confidentiality of test items may be in conflict with legitimate concerns of parents about exposure of their children to content inconsistent with their values and interference with their right to review instructional materials provided to their children. Courts and legislatures have responded by mandating annual release of test items in some states, creating financial, technical, and resource challenges for the state testing program (*Maxwell v. Pasadena Ind. Sch. Dist.*, 1994; *State ex. rel. Rea v. Ohio Dep't of Educ.*, 1998). While the disclosure legislation in Texas and Ohio defused claims of inappropriate item content, it also substantially increased testing costs due to the need to field test a much larger number of items each year. In addition, the increased complexity of equating designs necessary to ensure a comparable standard across administrations increased the cost of test development and analysis. After several years of annual disclosure, the Texas legislature sought to decrease costs by modifying the law to reduce the frequency of disclosure to every other year and then later reduced it again to every third year (Phillips, 2010). However, unlike Texas and Ohio, a Florida appeals court held that its graduation test was not a public record subject to release at the request of a parent (*Fla. Dep't of Educ. v. Cooper*, 2003).

Media Access

Citing the public's right to know, media outlets have sought access to secure test items from high-stakes educational tests under state freedom of information laws. For example, high failure rates on an Arizona graduation test led to a request from a major state newspaper to inspect and copy the test (*Phoenix Newspapers Inc. v. Keegan*, 2001). The state responded that it would provide a limited viewing period on two conditions: that notes and copying were not allowed, and that the newspaper sign a nondisclosure agreement. The newspaper refused and filed suit to compel the disclosure. The trial court ordered release of all items except the anchor items owned by a test publisher. The state subsequently settled the case by agreeing to establish a timetable for releasing test forms except for a small number of items reserved for reuse.

NY Browniegate

Most court cases involving test security have dealt with misconduct or the refusal of a test developer to release test items post-administration. But choosing to release test items voluntarily can also generate controversy, particularly in the "court of public opinion." In particular, the Internet's accessibility to a large audience at minimal cost can be an equally, if not more, effective tool than a newspaper article in stirring controversy about a test. It can also provide an effective forum for a minority viewpoint that otherwise might be ignored. The New York *Browniegate* incident is one such example (Herszenhorn, 2006).

Brownie was a cow portrayed in a children's fable used for a New York state NCLB fourth grade listening comprehension test. The story described how Brownie the cow had initially been nice to an arrogant rooster but eventually tricked him into getting up early each morning to crow. The story was read aloud to students twice while they listened and took notes. They were then asked to write a short essay explaining how the behavior of Brownie the cow had changed during the story. This essay was worth 1.8 points out of a test total of 43 points.

The parents of some tested students wanted the question invalidated because they believed it inappropriately required students to psychoanalyze a cow and they created a website to publicize their concerns. The state responded that the challenged question had been field-tested and that most fourth graders answered it correctly. The dispute was picked up by the *New York Times* and other national media outlets. The website became a forum for some disgruntled parents of high-performing students and continued to criticize the state test.

Future Directions for Legal Challenges Related to the Fairness of Educational Tests

This section provides a brief glimpse into evolving fairness issues that may become the focus of future testing litigation.

Graduation Testing

In 2013, 24 states had graduation tests, many of which were end-of-course (EOC) tests (Diplomas Count, 2013). For example, in 2007–2009, the Texas legislature passed an ambitious reform package requiring high school graduates to pass three EOCs each in ELA, mathematics, science, and social studies (Texas Education Agency, 2012).

Performance standards in each subject area required minimum scores on each EOC test and a minimum compensatory total score for the subject area. ELA III and Algebra II tests were also required to have college readiness standards based on external empirical evidence, and EOC tests for earlier courses in the sequence had proficiency scores linked to predicted success in the next level course. One of the issues raised by critics was whether it was fair to require all students to demonstrate EOC proficiency in Algebra II (Robelen, 2013). After several years of planning and implementation, the program was scaled back by the legislature in favor of a more flexible set of graduation alternatives that value both vocational training and college readiness. States requiring high school graduates to achieve college and career readiness standards on consortia- or state-developed tests could face similar challenges.

Substantive Due Process: Mode Effects

When a testing program administers tests in both paper-and-pencil and computer formats, the 2014 *Test Standards* recommends investigation of differential performance due to the test administration format, also known as *mode effects* (Standard 5.17). When the items administered in different formats are based on the same test blueprint and mode effects are statistically and practically significant, it is advisable to adjust the results of the two administrations to a common scale via an appropriately designed linking process. This ensures that students tested via computer are not advantaged or disadvantaged relative to those who tested with paper-and-pencil forms. Computer adaptive tests also pose challenges for establishing the comparability of student scores from different numbers and sets of items and the fairness of pattern scoring when three parameter logistic models are utilized.

As more state tests transition to a computer-administered format, many are seeking to decrease the length of the testing window and reduce testing costs by administering tests on a variety of computer platforms, including laptops and tablets. Because the interfaces are different on each of these devices, different computer skills are needed to navigate a test successfully. For example, tablets use touchscreen technology, where the width of the answer choice or hot spot for an item needs to be larger than required for a pointing device such as a mouse (Strain-Seymour, Craft, Davis, & Elbom, 2013). Tablets also use touchscreen keyboards where touch typing is ineffective because fingers cannot rest on the keyboard without triggering an input and there may be a lack of auditory and sensory feedback to indicate when an input has been triggered. These differences in computer platform characteristics may raise equity and fairness issues because the testing experience may be more challenging on some devices than others, and experience with the device may be critical to accurate responses and test-taker engagement. Comparability studies similar to those for evaluating paper-and-pencil and computer-administered tests will be important to determine if scoring adjustments are needed. Support may also be needed to assist districts in selecting and configuring appropriate testing technology to deliver tests that provide all students with an equal opportunity to demonstrate their focal construct knowledge and skills.

Disparate Impact

Research indicates that the achievement gap between majority and minority students in public schools is increasing the fastest among the highest-achieving students (Viadero, 2008). These findings suggest the possibility that if disparate impact statistics were calculated separately for majority and minority students scoring in the highest performance category on a state accountability test, they might fall short of the 80% criterion, despite that criterion having been satisfied at the proficient level. The question for the court, then, would be whether disparate impact for an identifiable subset of high-achieving minority students is sufficient to trigger further test scrutiny.

Parental Objections to Testing

The distinction between actions that constitute unconstitutional establishment of religion and actions that unconstitutionally interfere with an individual's free exercise of religion can be challenging for public agencies and school districts and has been the subject of extensive federal litigation (see, e.g., *Bd. of Educ. of Kiryas Joel Village Sch. Dist. v. Grumet,* 1994; *Sch. Dist. of Grand Rapids v. Ball,* 1985). For computer-administered tests, this issue may surface when parents hold religious beliefs requiring avoidance of the use of technology, raising the question of whether schools can require computerized test administrations for students whose parents object or whether the school must accommodate the religious objection by providing an alternative testing method such as paper-and-pencil. In *Stark v. Ind. Sch. Dist. No. 640* (1997), the court upheld a Minnesota district's opening of a new school with technology-free curricula requested by a religious group whose children were the only students enrolled. Taxpayers had challenged this arrangement as an impermissible establishment of religion but the court held that the district's actions did not violate the first amendment because non-affiliated children had not been excluded and curricular exemptions were available to all parents in the district regardless of religious affiliation or the reason for the request.

A substantial number of parents have also chosen to opt their children out of state testing in Chicago and New York for a variety of reasons, including objections to the amount of testing and to the Common Core Standards (Associated Press, 2014; Reid, 2014). If many parents in a district or state do so, there may be adverse consequences for school accountability measures, teacher evaluations, item field testing, and individual student graduation decisions.

Cash Incentives

In some cases, efforts to raise students' test scores have not produced the desired gains so some districts have experimented with monetary rewards for students who achieve specific levels of performance on state tests. For example, in 67 high schools in seven states, the ExxonMobil, Gates, and Dell foundations funded rewards of $100 to $200 for advanced placement test scores that earned college credit in the 2008–2009 school year (Jones, 2008). Such incentive programs may be challenged if data indicate differential receipt of rewards for disadvantaged groups. There may also be privacy concerns if students receiving rewards are recognized publicly. Challenges related to eligibility rules, fairness when only limited grades/schools can participate in consecutive years, transfer students lacking prior year data for calculating gains, or other special circumstances are also possible.

Testing Accommodations

Testing accommodations policies continue to be an area of contention and litigation as testing programs wrestle with defining constructs clearly and identifying convincing evidence of score comparability. As many states are preparing to administer new Common Core aligned tests developed by the two federally funded consortia, some are facing testing accommodations policies that differ from those previously implemented (Heitin, 2014; NCEO, 2013). For example, Oregon and Connecticut previously prohibited read-aloud for their ELA tests, arguing that read-aloud changes the construct of the demonstrated skill from text comprehension to listening comprehension and could assist low-achieving students who may not be eligible for this testing adaptation (Phillips, 2011; Samuels, 2014b). However, they have adopted the Smarter Balanced Assessment Consortium (SBAC) tests that permit read-aloud in grades 6 and above. The SBAC policy is based on a determination by its content experts that decoding and reading fluency are construct relevant in grades 3 through 5 but the reading skill intended to be measured by the ELA tests in the upper grades is comprehension.

Conversely, Massachusetts and Tennessee previously allowed read-aloud for their ELA tests for students with disabilities but have adopted the Partnership for Assessment of Readiness for College and Careers (PARCC) tests that annotate scores when that testing adaptation is provided. PARCC explained that the intent of its tests is to measure independent reading and comprehension of texts at all grade levels. PARCC settled a lawsuit filed by the National Federation of the Blind challenging the lack of Braille access on 2014 field tests by agreeing to provide field tests compatible with accessibility devices or electronic files from which hardcopy Braille forms and tactile graphics could be produced locally (Samuels, 2014a).

PARCC and SBAC also differ on their policies for translating tests into languages other than English with SBAC providing Spanish translations for its mathematics tests and PARCC doing so only if a state orders and pays extra for it (Heitin, 2014). This means that students with disabilities and ELLs residing in different states will likely continue to be tested under different conditions as they were previously but with more adaptations available for all students through computer delivery platforms. ELLs with native languages other than Spanish may also be tested differently, creating a potential equal protection issue.

Test Security

External Intervention

In some of the instances of educator malfeasance discussed earlier in relationship to test security, the incentive to investigate and take action was provided by an outside source, such as the governor's office or the media, rather than internally by testing program administrators (e.g., Atlanta) (see Wilson et al., 2011). Such incidents have served as a wake-up call to states and school districts to be more proactive in their test security policies, particularly as they transition from paper-and-pencil to Web-based computer administrations of the new Common Core aligned assessments under development by the Consortia and other vendors. Although digital cheating may be harder on computer-administered tests with adaptive features, secure browsers and plagiarism-detecting software, states with such tests have faced many technical problems that have threatened the validity of some students' test scores (Davis, 2013, 2014). In addition, a recent report by the USDE Inspector General found lax test security policies in five states and recommended that the USDE review test security in future NCLB peer reviews of state accountability testing programs (McNeil, 2014b).

Increased Pressures for Educator Malfeasance

States awarded federal Race to the Top Grants and NCLB waivers are required to focus on measuring student growth, closing achievement gaps and implementing more rigorous teacher evaluation procedures that include measures of improvement in student achievement (Klein, 2014; McNeil, 2014a). These additional high-stakes uses of student achievement data may increase the pressure on educators to improve test scores by appropriate and inappropriate activities. And as states transition to new Common Core or alternative post-secondary readiness standards and assessments in ELA and mathematics, pressure on educators will further increase as they are expected to teach more rigorous and demanding content to students who had not previously been expected to master such material. Under such pressures, educators who seek monetary rewards, who believe their jobs are at risk if test scores remain low, or who believe that their primary responsibility is student success may be even more tempted than in the past to engage in behaviors that threaten the integrity and validity of state test results.

A 2006 Josephson Institute poll of 36,000 students reported that 60% admitted cheating on a test during the previous year (Gewertz, 2007). Some researchers who were interviewed excused the behavior as survival tactics while others faulted adults for not punishing unethical behavior more consistently and seriously. Similar to the challenges facing antivirus software providers, it remains to be seen whether test security efforts can keep pace with and foil the efforts of academically dishonest test takers. In addition to secure test administration procedures and data forensics, testing programs must also be vigilant now for copyrighted test items posted on the Internet, sharing of secure test content on social media sites, and malware designed to interfere with fair test administration, scoring, data reporting, and other testing functions on computers and/or the Internet.

College Admissions State Census Testing

A University of Chicago research team found that extensive practice with ACT test questions in area high schools in 2005 was ineffective (Samuels, 2008). The research team estimated that teachers of high school juniors in core courses were spending as much as one month of instructional time on practice ACT questions but their students achieved lower scores on the ACT college admissions test than students of teachers who spent less than 20% of their class time on test preparation practice. Nonetheless, 83% of high school juniors surveyed indicated a belief that test-taking skills are the primary determinant of high ACT scores. Illinois is one of several states that require all juniors to take the ACT exam. When states implement census testing of high school juniors with a college admissions test and use it for school accountability and as part of teacher evaluations, there may be increased pressure for educators to engage in inappropriate testing practices and/or cheating. Educators may also contest any associated sanctions for such activities.

Conclusion

The brief overview above of potential future testing litigation around fairness issues suggests that many policy issues are still in dispute and the associated rhetoric remains robust. Testing programs have learned much from prior litigation and many have improved their legal defensibility substantially over the years. As attorneys learn more about testing and psychometricians increase their knowledge of legal requirements, legal adversaries may be able to engage in more constructive substantive negotiations about testing fairness issues that may in turn facilitate resolution of their differences more often outside the courtroom.

Notes

1. Portions of this chapter have been adapted from Phillips (2010) and Phillips and Camara (2006). This chapter is not intended to provide specific legal advice; the views expressed are those of the author. Its purpose is to provide a broad outline of the legal, psychometric, and policy issues involved in the topics discussed. In applying these principles, testing entities are advised to seek individual legal counsel.
2. Also, according to professional standards for educational testing, testing entities and test takers share the responsibility for ensuring fairness (2014 *Test Standards*, pp. 131–132; Standards 3.0, 8.0, 9.0). The most appropriate edition of the *Test Standards* for evaluating the fairness of a specific testing application is the edition in effect at the time the test was developed and administered (1985 or 1999 for most cases included here). The 2014 edition applies to tests revised or developed post-release and is referenced here where relevant to specific topics. Because multiple standards documents devised by different organizations may be relevant to judging the fairness of a test (see Phillips & Camara, 2006), the author has chosen to refer to the AERA/APA/NCME *Standards for Educational and Psychological Measurement* in shortened form as the *Test Standards* preceded by the year of publication of the referenced edition.
3. Professional standards assume a central role in testing litigation. Courts have routinely recognized the 1985 and 1999 *Test Standards* as an appropriate source of authority for expert opinions in testing cases. When evaluating the credibility of expert opinions, judges typically consider the expert's qualifications, demeanor on the witness stand, quality and quantity of supporting evidence, and ability to withstand cross-examination. Expert witnesses, who are qualified by training and experience to offer opinions, are distinguishable from fact witnesses such as test directors and school superintendents, who are qualified by job description to testify about factual matters related to testing in their districts.
4. See Phillips (2000, 2010, 2011, 2012) and Phillips and Camara (2006) for descriptions of the requirements for legal cases broadly classified as disparate impact, due process, disability rights, or school accountability challenges under these federal laws and their corresponding regulations.
5. Disparate treatment involves overt discrimination, whereas disparate impact does not require evidence of subjective discriminatory intent. The Civil Rights Act of 1991 allocated shifting burdens of proof to plaintiffs and defendants consistent with *Griggs v. Duke Power Co.* (1971). Plaintiffs start by producing statistical evidence of disparate impact on a protected minority group. Then the defendant must show educational necessity by citing an important educational objective. To prevail, the plaintiff must then identify an equally effective but less discriminatory alternative.
6. Note that in 1999, when the *GI Forum* case was litigated, challenges based on Title VI Regulations required proof of disparate impact but not intent to discriminate. Subsequently, the U.S. Supreme Court held that, consistent with its earlier holdings with respect to the Title VI statute, Title VI Regulations also require proof of intent to discriminate (*Alexander v. Sandoval*, 2001).
7. See Phillips (2012) for more information about legal issues related to setting performance standards.
8. The original *Golden Rule* procedure was part of an out-of-court settlement of a challenge to an insurance licensure test that required items with majority/minority p-value differences of less than 15% to be preferred (*Golden Rule Life Ins. Co. v. Washburn*, 1984). No adjustments were made to compare groups of equal ability and the procedure was later discredited by psychometricians and renounced by the testing entity that had agreed to it. For more information on the *Golden Rule* case, see Phillips (2010).
9. Note, however, that some other states do award high school diplomas to special education students who have completed IEPs prescribing content and skills below a high school level.

10. The 2014 *Test Standards* supports testing students in the language in which they receive instruction (Standard 3.13), but in many states resource limitations may preclude offering bilingual instruction in more than one language. ELLs for whom instruction in English is the only option might question whether they are being treated fairly relative to ELLs who also have the option of bilingual instruction.

11. The 2014 edition notes a lack of agreement on appropriate action when credible evidence is lacking (pp. 61–62).

12. The pseudonym John Doe was used in the litigation to keep Doe's identity confidential. The score report contained the notation *Testing Accommodations* and a comment explaining that a review and approval process was followed in granting the test taker's request.

13. For example, on one section, Doe used three minutes less than the standard testing time, but on another he used all of the extra testing time. The average difficulty of the two sections was 0.79 and 0.82 and Doe's scores for these sections were 22 and 20, respectively (Phillips, 2010).

14. Note that one could distinguish between anxiety due to ordinary nervousness about one's ability to efficiently engage in the tested cognitive skills and anxiety due to unpredictable interruptions from physical symptoms outside the test taker's control. While the former type of anxiety is directly related to the test taker's test-taking skills and facility with the tested content and is arguably part of the tested construct, the latter anxiety stems from an extraneous interference arguably unrelated to the tested construct.

15. The cited case was the first appeals court decision in the Doe case in which the court held that identification of a person as disabled against his will during the application process constituted a cognizable injury that satisfied the standing requirement. Ironically, the court later changed its mind once Doe had been accepted to and completed a residency program. The court then ruled that Doe no longer had a sufficient injury to provide standing to challenge the annotation of his test scores. Apparently, because he was accepted despite the annotated scores that identified him as disabled against his will, and because the problem would not recur in the future, the court no longer viewed that disclosure as an injury.

16. The ETS decision to discontinue annotating scores obtained with extra time to settle the *Breimhorst* case was reminiscent of the ETS settlement in the *Golden Rule* case. In both cases, the social policy goal of increasing the success rate for a particular group of test takers was achieved by potentially compromising the validity of the test score interpretations. Alternatively, these social policy goals could probably have been achieved more directly by transparent affirmative action policies enacted following open discussion and debate.

17. A Boston, Massachusetts, attorney specializing in education law observed that "[from the start, the makeup of the seven-person panel . . . should have sent a warning signal to anyone who is concerned about valid testing standards . . . The panel was tilted toward those with a special commitment to students with disabilities . . . The differences between the two sides were so great that the minority wrote the scholarly equivalent of a judicial dissent" (Freedman, 2003).

18. The majority opinion did not directly address the score comparability issue. Rather, they seemed to believe that extra time was a reasonable accommodation because test takers with disabilities benefitted from it more than non-disabled test takers. The psychometrician who joined the majority opinion suggested that the College Board consider equating extra time administrations to standard administrations under the analogy that extra time resulted in an easier test (Sireci, 2001). Aside from the technical problems of implementing such a solution, this recommendation was probably not included in the main report because such equating would have eliminated most of the score increases needed to achieve the majority's goal of qualifying more students with disabilities for college admission.

19. In Standard 10.11, the 1999 *Test Standards* states that test scores obtained under nonstandard conditions should be annotated when there is evidence that they are not comparable *or when evidence of comparability is lacking*. Having reached similar conclusions that evidence of comparability was lacking and that there was some credible evidence of non-comparability, and if they had strictly followed Standard 10.11, one would have expected the two psychometricians to have agreed that scores obtained with extra time should be annotated. Instead, apparently giving differential weight to the lack of comparability evidence and other non-psychometric factors, they split their votes, one voting in favor of retaining the score annotations and the other voting for removal.

20. A related federal case in Oregon also considered the comparability of nonstandard administrations for graduation and other statewide tests (*Advocates for Special Kids v. Oregon Dep't of Educ.*, 2001). The case involved a ban on the use of computer spellcheck on the tenth grade writing test for which 40% of the score was based on spelling, grammar, and punctuation. The challengers claimed the ban discriminated against students with learning disabilities. In a settlement agreement based on the recommendations of an expert panel, the state agreed to permit all requested nonstandard administrations on its tests unless it had research proving that a specific nonstandard administration produced non-comparable scores. Because definitive empirical research evidence may be unobtainable due to small sample sizes or prohibitively expensive, this decision rule permitted the use of virtually any feasible testing alteration, irrespective of its logical relationship to the tested construct. Advocates also used it to pressure other states.

References

Advocates for Special Kids v. Oregon Dep't of Educ., No. CV99-263 KI (Feb. 1, 2001).

American Educational Research Association, American Psychological Association, & National Council on Measurement in Education. (2014, 1999, 1985). *Standards for educational and psychological testing.* Washington, DC: AERA [*Test Standards*].

Americans with Disabilities Act [ADA], 42 U.S.C. § 12101 *et seq.* (1990).

Americans with Disabilities Act [ADA] Regulations, 28 C.F.R. § 36.101 *et seq.* (1991).

Alexander v. Sandoval, 532 U.S. 275 (2001).

American College Testing Program [ACT] Press Release. (2002, July 26). *ACT will end practice of annotating test scores under extended time.* Iowa City, IA: ACT.

Associated Press. (1992, October 24). Student given jail for lie on paying friend to take test. *NY Times*, B6.

Associated Press. (2014, April 16). Parents pull thousands from New York tests. *Education Week*, 4.

Bd. of Educ. of Kiryas Joel Village Sch. Dist. v. Grumet, 512 U.S. 687 (1994).

Breimhorst v. Educational Testing Service [ETS], No. C-99-3387 WHO (N.D. Cal. 2000).

Brennan, R. L. (2002). *On the comparability of extended-time vs. standard-time scores for College Board standardized tests: Psychometric report submitted to the blue ribbon panel on flagging.* New York: College Board.

Brennan, R. L. (2008, August 30). Personal communication based on Doe v. NBME expert witness report, *Doe v. NBME*, No. 99-4532 (E.D. Pa. Jan. 24, 2004).

Brennan, R. L., & Saleh, D. A. (2002). *Flagging scores for extended time on College Board standardized tests: A minority report.* New York: College Board.

Brief of Appellant John Doe, *Doe v. NBME*, No. 05-2254 (3rd Cir. 2006) (redacted public version).

Brookhart v. Illinois State Bd. of Educ., 534 F. Supp. 725 (C.D. Ill. 1982); *rev'd*, 697 F.2d 179 (7th Cir. 1983).

Bunkley, N. (2007, October 13). After news article on test, Michigan orders retesting, *NY Times*, A12.

Canary v. Osborne, 211 F.3d 324 (6th Cir. 2000).

Chapman v. Cal. Dep't of Educ., 229 F. Supp.2d 981 (N.D. Cal. 2002).

College Board Press Release (2002, July 17). *The College Board and Disabilities Rights Advocates announce agreement to drop annotating from standardized tests.* New York: College Board.

College Bd. v. Pataki, 893 F. Supp. 152 (N.D. N.Y. 1995).

Dalton v. ETS, 155 Misc.2d 214 (N.Y. Sup. 1992); *aff'd as mod.*, 87 N.Y.2d 384 (N.Y. 1995).

Davis, M. R. (2013, May 8). Online testing suffers setbacks in multiple states. *Education Week*, 1.

Davis, M. R. (2014, March 13). Preventing digital cheating. *Education Week*, 34.

Debra P. v. Turlington, 474 F. Supp. 244 (M.D. Fla. 1979); *aff'd, in part, rev'd, in part*, 644 F.2d 397 (5th Cir. 1981); *on remand*, 564 F. Supp. 177 (M.D. Fla. 1983); *aff'd*, 730 F.2d 1405 (11th Cir. 1984).

DePina v. ETS, 31 A.D.2d 744 (N.Y. A.D. 1969).

Diplomas Count. (2013, June 6). Graduation policies for the class of 2013. *Education Week*, 27.

Doe v. Nat'l Bd. of Med. Examiners (NBME), No. 99-4532 (E.D. Pa. 1999); *rev'd*, 199 F.3d 146 (3rd Cir. 2000); *on rem.*, No. 99-4532 (E.D. Pa. 2005); *aff'd*, 210 Fed. Appx. 157 (3rd Cir. 2006).

Duke University, 4 Nat. Disability Law Rep. ¶ 87, Compl. No. 04-91-2124 (OCR Apr. 2, 1993).

Educational Testing Service [ETS] v. Kaplan, 965 F. Supp. 731 (D. Md. 1997).

ETS v. Katzman, 793 F.2d 533 (3rd Cir. 1986).

ETS v. Hildebrant, 923 A.2d 34 (Md. 2007).

Equal Educational Opportunity Act [EEOA], 42 U.S.C. § 1703 (f) (1974).

Equal Educational Opportunity Commission [EEOC]. (1978). *Uniform guidelines on employee selection procedures* (Title VII Regulations), 29 C.F.R. § 1607.2B (1978) [*Uniform Guidelines*].

Fla. Dep't of Educ. v. Cooper, 858 So.2d 394 (2003).

Freedman, M. K. (2003, Fall). Disabling the SAT. *Education Next, 3*(4), 36–43.

Gewertz, C. (2007, December 19). Poll raises questions about extent of teen cheating. *Education Week*, 8.

GI Forum v. Texas Education Agency, 87 F. Supp.2d 667 (W. D. Tex. 2000).

Golden Rule Life Ins. Co. v. Washburn, No. 419–76 (Ill. Cir. Ct. Nov. 20, 1984).

Gregg, N., Mather, N., Shaywitz, S., & Sireci, S. (2002). *The annotating test scores of individuals with disabilities who are granted the accommodation of extended time: A report of the majority opinion of the blue ribbon panel on annotating.* New York: College Board.

Griggs v. Duke Power Co., 401 U.S. 424 (1971).

Heitin, L. (2014, April 23). Testing plans differ on accommodations. *Education Week*, S30, S6.

Herszenhorn, D. M. (2006, October 18). Brownie the cow has some parents alleging an unfair test. *NY Times*, B3.

Individuals with Disabilities Education Act [IDEA], 20 U.S.C. § 1400 *et seq.* (1991).

Jones, D. (2008, September 11). CEOs split on paying for good grades. *USA Today*, 1B.

Klein, A. (2014, April 16). Race to the top: A roadmap. *Education Week*, 20.

Langston v. ACT, 890 F.2d 380 (11th Cir. 1989).

Lindsay, D. (1996, October 2). Whodunit? Someone cheated on standardized tests at a Connecticut school. *Education Week*, 25.

McNeil, M. (2014a, January 15). Some waiver states struggle in key areas, ed. dept. says. *Education Week*, 15.

McNeil, M. (2014b, April 2). Auditors fault education department, states for test-security problems. *Education Week*, Politics K-12 blog.

Maxwell v. Pasadena Ind. Sch. Dist., No. 92–017184 (Tex. Dist. Ct., Dec. 29, 1994).

Mezzacappa, D. (2014, January 29). Cheating case implicates Philadelphia educators. *Education Week*, 1.

Mindel v. ETS, 559 N.Y.S.2d 95 (N.Y. Sup. Ct. 1990).

Murray v. ETS, 170 F.3d 514 (5th Cir. 1999).

National Center for Educational Outcomes [NCEO]. (2013, October 30). Patchwork of policies. *Education Week*, S21.

No Child Left Behind Act [NCLB], 20 U.S.C. §§ 6301 *et seq.* (2000).

Olson, L. (2003, April 16). Ga. suspends testing plans in key grades. *Education Week*, 1.

Perry, J., Vogell, H., Judd, A., & Pell, M. B. (2012, March 25). Cheating our children: Suspicious school test scores across the nation. *The Atlanta Journal-Constitution*, A1.

Phillips, S. E. (2000). *GI Forum v. TEA*: Psychometric evidence. *Applied Measurement in Education, 13*, 343–385.

Phillips, S. E. (2010). *Assessment law in education*. Phoenix, AZ: Prisma Graphic. Retrieved from www.sephillips.dokshop.com

Phillips, S. E. (2011). U.S. legal issues in educational testing of special populations. In S. N. Elliott et al. (Eds.), *Handbook of accessible achievement tests for all students* (pp. 33–68). New York: Springer.

Phillips, S. E. (2012). Legal issues for standard setting in K-12 educational contexts. In G. J. Cizek (Ed.), *Setting performance standards: Foundations, methods, and innovations* (2nd ed., pp. 535–569). New York: Routledge.

Phillips, S. E., & Camara, W. J. (2006). Legal and ethical issues. In R. L. Brennan (Ed.), *Educational measurement* (4th ed., pp. 733–755). Westport, CT: American Council on Education/Praeger.

Phoenix Newspapers Inc. v. Keegan, 35 P.3d 105 (Ariz. App. 2001).

Psychometric Committee. (2001). *Blue ribbon panel on flagging: Report of the psychometric committee.* New York: College Board.

Reid, K. S. (2014, March 12). Testing skeptics' advice: Just say "no." *Education Week*, 1.

Rene v. Reed, 751 N.E.2d 736 (Ind. App. 2001).

Robelen, E. W. (2013, June 12). Questions arise about algebra 2 for all students. *Education Week*, 1.

Samuels, C. A. (2008, June 4). ACT test-prep backfiring in Chicago, study warns. *Education Week*, 6.

Samuels, C. A. (2014a, March 15). National Federation of Blind settles suit against PARCC. *Education Week*, 4.

Samuels, C. A. (2014b, March 26). Read-aloud option boosts NAEP achievement, study finds: Testing supports are subject of debate. *Education Week*, 15.

Sch. Dist. of Grand Rapids v. Ball, 473 U.S. 373 (1985).

Section 504 of the Rehabilitation Act [Section 504], 29 U.S.C. § 701 *et seq.* (1973).

Section 504 Regulations, 45 C.F.R. § 84 (1990).

Senate Bill 517 (January 30, 2006) (amending CEC § 60851 and adding CEC § 60852.3).

Sireci, S. G. (2001). *Equating non-standard and standard SAT test administrations: Opinion paper submitted to the Blue Ribbon Panel on flagging.* New York: College Board.

Standardized Testing Act [STA], N.Y. [Truth in Testing] Educ. Law, §§ 340–348 (McKinney Supp. 1980).

Stark v. Ind. Sch. Dist. No. 640, 123 F.3d 1068 (8th Cir. 1997).

State ex. rel. Rea v. Ohio Dep't of Educ., 692 N.E.2d 596 (Ohio 1998).

Strain-Seymour, E., Craft, J., Davis, L., & Elbom, J. (2013, July). *Testing on tablets: Part I of a series of usability studies on the use of tablets for K-12 assessment programs.* Austin, TX: Pearson White Paper.

Strauss, V. (2013, April 1). Atlanta test cheating: Tip of the iceberg. *The Washington Post*, Answer Sheet blog.

SUNY Health Science Ctr. at Brooklyn, 5 Nat. Disability Law Rep. ¶ 77, Compl. No. 02-92-2004 (OCR Aug. 18, 1993).

Texas Education Agency (TEA). (2012, August 17). STAAR EOC assessments: Standard setting technical report. Austin, TX.

Title VI and Title VII of the Civil Rights Act, 42 U.S.C. §§ 2000d, 2000e *et seq.* (1964).

Title VI Regulations, 34 C.F.R. § 100.3 (1999).

Valenzuela v. O'Connell, No. JCCP 004468 (Cal. Sup. Ct., May 12, 2006); *rev'd, O'Connell v. Superior Court*, 47 Cal.Rptr.3d 147 (Cal. App. 2006).

Viadero, D. (2008, April 16). Black-White gap widens faster for high achievers. *Education Week*, 1.

Wheeler, D. L. (2002, August 16). Testing service says GRE scores from China, South Korea, and Taiwan are suspect. *Chronicle of Higher Education*, A41.

Wilson, R. E., Bowers, M. J., & Hyde, R. L. (2011, June 30). *Investigative report of test tampering in the Atlanta public schools.* Atlanta, GA: Governor's Office.

14 Philosophical Perspectives on Fairness in Educational Assessment

Rebecca Zwick[1] *and Neil J. Dorans*[2]

Philosophical Perspectives on Assessment Fairness

In Michael Young's dystopian satire, *The Rise of the Meritocracy*, purportedly written in 2034, admission to schools, selection and promotion in the workplace and the military, and access to government subsidies are all dependent on intelligence test scores, which are stored in a national registry. From the point of view of the elite (the high scorers), the system is a marvel, eliminating all manner of difficult decisions. The approach is even considered progressive, since it is in opposition to the rule of the aristocracy. ("Nobody should be born with a silver spoon in his mouth, or if he is, it should choke him" [Young, 1994, pp. xii–xiii].) All appears to go smoothly until the inevitable revolution, in which the alleged author of the manuscript is himself killed.

In real life, test scores and other assessments of individuals do have a substantial impact on the allocation of important societal goods, though fortunately not to the nightmarish extent envisioned by Young in 1958, when his book was first published. Access to schools, special educational programs, scholarships, jobs, and promotions often depend, at least in part, on tests. According to the 2014 *Standards for Educational and Psychological Testing*:

> [t]he central idea of fairness in testing is to identify and remove construct-irrelevant barriers to maximal performance for any examinee. Removing these barriers allows for the comparable and valid interpretation of test scores for all examinees. Fairness is thus central to the validity and comparability of the interpretation of test scores for intended uses.
>
> (American Educational Research Association, American
> Psychological Association, & National Council on
> Measurement in Education, 2014, p. 63)

But how do these technical principles mesh with more general philosophies of fairness and justice? In this chapter, we consider three real-world fairness cases in light of principles of *distributive justice*, which provide guidance for the allocation of benefits and burdens in society. Philosophers in this field seek to establish what kinds of distribution frameworks are morally preferable (Lamont & Favor, 2014).

As our illustrative examples, we have selected scenarios from college admissions, graduation testing, and scholarship competitions. In the first section of the paper, we describe these scenarios and enumerate some of the questions they raise. In the next section, we outline some principles of distributive justice that could be used to address these questions. In the final section, we revisit the three scenarios from the perspective of these principles.

Assessment Fairness Scenarios

Castaneda v. The Regents of the University of California: University Admission Criteria[3]

In 1999, a suit was filed in Federal District Court by five civil rights organizations on behalf of more than 750 African-American, Latino, and Filipino-American applicants to the University of California, Berkeley. The plaintiffs charged that the university did not take into account the full range of indicators of merit and therefore denied admission to people of color with strong academic records (American Civil Liberties Union of Northern California, 2003; Nieves, 1999). In particular, the complaint alleged that Berkeley gave undue weight to admissions test scores and unfairly favored those who had taken Advanced Placement (AP) courses. These courses were assigned bonus points in the computation of applicants' high school grade point averages. Lawyers for the case argued that Black, Latino, and Filipino-American high school students were less likely than other students to have access to test preparation courses and AP classes. The suit came in the wake of Proposition 209, an amendment to California's constitution that banned affirmative action in public education, employment, and contracting and led to steep decreases in the numbers of Black and Latino students at Berkeley.

The case was settled (on behalf of the specific plaintiffs only, not on behalf of a class of applicants) through a consent decree (*Castaneda v. The Regents of the University of California*, 2003) in which UC Berkeley made a commitment to provide certain information to the plaintiffs' counsel for five years, including current admissions policies and procedures and admissions statistics by ethnic group, and to use "comprehensive review" for every applicant. In Berkeley's comprehensive review procedure, all student records are judged in terms of 14 criteria, which consist of 10 academic factors and four "supplemental" factors. The comprehensive review policy includes the requirement that academic accomplishments be evaluated "in light of an applicant's experiences and circumstances," which include "low family income, first generation to attend college, need to work, disadvantaged social or educational environment, [and] difficult personal and family situations" (University of California, 2001, p. 2).

The *Castaneda* case raises a number of questions: Does unequal access to test preparation courses make it unfair to use standardized test scores as admissions criteria? Should applicants get more credit for taking AP courses than for other courses, despite the uneven availability of these courses? Without affirmative action, how should universities take into account the lesser educational opportunities of students of color?

Debra P. v. Turlington: Opportunity to Learn High School Material

In 1976, the State of Florida put in place a high school graduation test called the State Student Assessment Test, Part II (SSAT-II). The test was a "multiple-choice assessment of basic communication and math skills applied to real life situations" (Phillips, 1993, p. 10; see also Phillips, this volume, Chapter 13). Students were allowed to take the test more than once. Those who did not pass, but met other graduation requirements, received a completion certificate instead of a diploma. After three administrations, the failure rate was 2% for White students and 20% for Black students. Because the test was considered a "functional literacy examination" (indeed, this was originally the name of the test), those who failed were sometimes referred to as "functionally illiterate" (Phillips, 1993, p. 29).

A lawsuit was filed in 1978 on behalf of "present and future twelfth grade students who had failed or would fail the test" (*Debra P. v. Turlington*, 1984), charging that the SSAT-II was racially biased, that it was administered without sufficient notice, and that its use was designed to resegregate schools by placing Black students in remedial classes. The suit claimed that the use of the test to withhold diplomas violated Title VI of the Civil Rights Act of 1964, the due process and equal protection clauses of the Fourteenth Amendment to the Constitution, and the Equal Educational Opportunity Act (EEOA).

The case consisted of five proceedings that took place in federal district and appeals courts between 1979 and 1984. According to the initial ruling, the use of the test to deny diplomas did in fact perpetuate past discrimination and was in violation of the Civil Rights Act, the Fourteenth Amendment, and the EEOA. Although the test's content was ruled valid, the state was enjoined from using it to award diplomas until 1983, as detailed below.

A subsequent appeal led to a re-examination of the fairness and validity of the test and an investigation of the students' opportunity to learn the material, as well as further consideration of the role of past racial discrimination. The opportunity to learn issue had two dimensions: First, how did the state's history of discrimination and school segregation affect Black students' opportunities to learn? More generally, could it be demonstrated that Florida schools were actually teaching the material included on the test?

Florida maintained a dual public education system, with entirely separate school systems for Black and White students, through 1967. In some counties, segregation continued unabated through at least 1971. The facilities, curricula, and textbooks for the Black schools were "obviously inferior," as noted in a court transcript (*Debra P. v. Turlington*, 1979). Almost all the Black *Debra P.* plaintiffs had attended these inferior schools, and the initial court ruling held that this "past purposeful discrimination" was perpetuated by the use of the SSAT II to withhold diplomas. The initial *Debra P.* court enjoined the state of Florida from using the test to deny diplomas until 1983 for two reasons: to allow adequate notice to test takers, and to ensure that they would have had the opportunity to complete 12 years of schooling in integrated schools.

The state of Florida took a number of steps in response to the lawsuit. To address the more general question of whether Florida students were being taught the material on the test, the Florida Department of Education commissioned a study that consisted of a teacher survey, a district-level survey, a series of site visits, and a student survey. In a subsequent court proceeding, the state also provided evidence of the remedial support available to those who initially failed the SSAT II, as well as data on the pass rates for the class of 1983. For Black students, the pass rate (after multiple administrations) was 99.5% on the communications portion and 91% on the math portion. Two district court hearings that included presentation of this material were decided in favor of the state of Florida. Ultimately, a federal appeals court confirmed in 1984 that the test could be used to award diplomas.

Debra P. raised a number of interesting and important issues. Here, we focus on opportunity to learn, which proved to be central to the case (*Debra P. v. Turlington*, 1984). According to the 2014 *Standards for Educational and Psychological Testing*:

In settings where the same authority is responsible for both provision of curriculum and high-stakes decisions based on testing of examinees' curriculum mastery, examinees should not suffer permanent negative consequences if evidence indicates that they have not had the opportunity to learn the test content.

(American Educational Research Association et al.,
2014, p. 72)

So must graduation tests be restricted to material that is specifically taught, or can they include information that high school graduates "should know?" And is it fair to impose uniform high school graduation requirements if educational opportunities vary substantially across student groups?

The PSAT/NMSQT: Test Content and Scholarship Eligibility Scores

The Preliminary SAT/National Merit Scholarship Qualifying Test (PSAT/NMSQT) is a program cosponsored by the College Board and the National Merit Scholarship Corporation (NMSC). The test is intended to measure skills in reading, math problem-solving, and writing. The PSAT/NMSQT serves as a practice SAT and is used in identifying approximately 16,000 semifinalists for the National Merit Scholarships. The student guide (National Merit Scholarship Corporation, 2013) describes the process that begins with 1,500,000 test takers and ends with about 9,000 scholarship recipients.

Here, we focus on the issue of whether the test content or the semifinalist qualifying scores should be modified so as to achieve equal outcomes for various demographic groups. This issue has arisen in two contexts. The fact that boys, on average, scored higher than girls became the subject of a gender bias complaint filed in the 1990s. More recently, the fact that the qualifying scores for National Merit Scholarships vary by state has garnered some unfavorable publicity for the program.

In 1994, the American Civil Liberties Union and the National Center for Fair and Open Testing—the watchdog organization widely known as FairTest—filed a complaint with the U.S. Department of Education against the College Board and Educational Testing Service,[4] charging that the PSAT/NMSQT, which then consisted only of math and verbal sections, was biased against girls and should not be used as a criterion for identifying National Merit semifinalists. The Selection Index, which ranged from 60 to 240, was simply the sum of the PSAT/NMSQT math score and twice the PSAT/NMSQT verbal score. These Selection Index scores were used for selecting semifinalists, who were then required to submit additional materials to compete for the scholarship awards and to take the SAT for score verification. Fewer girls than boys became semifinalists, primarily because of differences in performance on the math portion of the examination, even though girls outnumbered boys among test takers and earned higher grades in both high school and college.

To settle the complaint, a multiple-choice writing skills test was added to the PSAT/NMSQT in 1996. The Selection Index was redefined as the sum of the PSAT/NMSQT math, verbal, and writing scores. Because secondary school girls typically outperform boys on writing tasks, this change was expected to improve girls' combined test scores. But although girls' combined PSAT/NMSQT scores did increase, girls continued to win fewer National Merit Scholarships than boys, leading test critics to complain that the test was still biased against females.[5] "This was a Band-Aid for a fundamental problem, and one that would not close the wound," a FairTest representative said in 1998. "Girls are still cheated of their fair share of National Merit Scholarships" (Reisberg, 1998). What *is* girls' fair share of these scholarships? Should it be 50%? Should it be equal to the proportion of girls taking the test? Or should it be larger because of girls' higher grades in high school? Should the content of tests be adjusted in order to obtain a particular pattern of results? If so, should tests be modified to obtain equivalent results across racial or ethnic groups?

A related question has arisen regarding the Selection Index qualifying scores for each state. In 2013, as it has in the past, FairTest posted on its website a listing of the qualifying scores for each state.[6] The qualifying scores listed by FairTest range from 203 to 224. Moving from Virginia (222) to West Virginia (203), it turns out, could substantially increase a student's chances of qualifying. FairTest referred to these cutoffs as "previously secret," and indeed, the *Chronicle of Higher Education* reported in 2010 that the NMSC "used legal pressure to stop an independent college counselor from publishing the state-by-state cutoff scores" (Hoover, 2010). According to the *Chronicle*, the NMSC did not want the cutoffs "out there for public consumption" because this kind of public airing would lead to "confusion and invalid conclusions."

Just how are these state qualifying scores determined? The 2013 PSAT/NMSQT *Guide* notes that:

> an allocation of Semifinalists is determined for each state, based on the state's percentage of the national total of high school graduating seniors. For example, the number of Semifinalists in a state that enrolls approximately two percent of the nation's graduating seniors would be about 320 (2 percent of the 16,000 Semifinalists). NMSC then arranges the Selection Index scores of all National Merit Program participants within a state in descending order. The score at which a state's allocation is most closely filled becomes the Semifinalist qualifying score. Entrants with a Selection Index at or above the qualifying score are named Semifinalists. As a result of this process, Semifinalist qualifying scores vary from state to state and from year to year.
>
> (National Merit Scholarship Corporation, 2013, p. 6)

The qualifying score for each state, then, is set in such a way as to select a predetermined number of students that is based on the number of graduating seniors in the state. States in which it is more difficult to obtain the desired number of semifinalists have less stringent qualifying scores. Again, this raises the question of whether test use should be adjusted so as to obtain a particular desired outcome. Is it better to have a national qualifying score and let the chips fall where they may, or to make an adjustment so that the number of semifinalists in a state is related to the number of graduating seniors? If state-by-state adjustments are legitimate, should similar adjustments be made to allocate scholarships more equitably across racial, ethnic, and gender groups?

Philosophical Perspectives

In this section, we describe three philosophical perspectives on distributive justice and their implications for fair assessment. The first is a perspective that traces its lineage to the Aristotelian concept of virtue described in his *Politics*, which dates to the 4th century BC. We then discuss a free-market libertarian perspective articulated by Robert Nozick (1974) and a conception of justice as fairness based on John Rawls's (1999) *A Theory of Justice*.[7]

We consider these particular approaches because they represent distinct perspectives on fairness. Aristotle's approach aligns the just distribution of goods with the worthiness of the individual, which may be based on his natural talents or potential for accomplishment, the fruits of his labor, or the importance of his contribution to social goals. The libertarian approach emphasizes the right of individuals to maximize their gains and seeks to limit the role of society to activities that protect individual liberty. The approach put forth by Rawls also places an emphasis on the rights of individuals but permits inequalities in the distribution of goods to occur provided that these inequalities grant the greatest benefit to the least advantaged. Our goal in this section is to describe these three perspectives and provide an idea of how they might be applied in the context of educational assessment. In the next section, we examine the three assessment scenarios from these three viewpoints.

Aristotelian Perspective

The Aristotelian perspective holds that individuals (which in our case consist of college applicants, high school students, and scholarship candidates) should be honored and rewarded for their virtues and accomplishments, rather than receiving goods solely because of their ancestry.[8] As noted by Michael Sandel (2009), Aristotle perceived justice as being determined by the *telos*—the purpose or nature—of the activity in question. In *Politics*, Aristotle said:

> When a number of flute players are equal in their art, there is no reason why those of them who are better born should have better flutes given to them; for they will not play any better on the flute, and the superior instrument should be reserved for him who is the superior artist. If what I am saying is still obscure, it will be made clearer as we proceed. For if there were a superior flute-player who was far inferior in birth and beauty, although either of these may be a greater good than the art of flute-playing, and may excel flute-playing in a greater ratio than he excels the others in his art, still he ought to have the best flutes given to him, unless the advantages of wealth and birth contribute to excellence in flute-playing, which they do not.
> (Aristotle, 2005, p. 47)

In the world of assessment, certain tests are intended to serve the purpose (*telos*) of determining whether an individual deserves an honor, such as a scholarship or award. For example, many educators would consider a well-constructed math test to be an appropriate merit-based tool for identifying the recipients of a math award. Giving people what they deserve on the basis of their talents and accomplishments is the gist of Aristotelian justice.

Nozick's Libertarian Perspective

The libertarian approach espoused by Nozick (1974) focuses on protecting the freedom of the individual to engage in just acquisitions and transfers of goods. The principle of justice in acquisition is rooted in the idea of self-ownership promoted by John Locke in his *Second Treatise of Civil Government*, which was published in 1690. Locke, one of the first philosophers to promulgate the concepts of liberty and limited government, argued that we own ourselves and hence we own whatever is produced by the fruits of our labor.

According to Nozick, the activities of a state should be restricted to "the protection of the rights of life, liberty, property, and contract" (Mack, 2014). Nozick advocated a three-part entitlement theory:

1. A person who acquires a holding in accordance with the principle of justice in acquisition is entitled to that holding.
2. A person who acquires a holding in accordance with the principle of justice in transfer, from someone else entitled to the holding, is entitled to the holding.
3. No one is entitled to a holding except by (repeated) applications of 1 and 2.

(1974, p. 151)

What do justice in acquisition and justice in transfer mean? As Nozick states:

[s]ome people steal from others, or defraud them, or enslave them, seizing their product and preventing them from living as they choose, or forcibly exclude others from competing in exchanges. None of these are permissible modes of transition from one situation to another

(1974, p. 152)

Nozick requires that each step in an acquisition or transfer start from a prior state in which all previous acquisitions and transfers were just (part 3 of the entitlement theory). For example, suppose a somewhat dim applicant to an elite college is admitted only because of a large donation from his mother, who acquired it through her illicit entanglement with a Wall Street inside trader. From this libertarian perspective, the source of the donation renders the candidate's admission illegitimate.

A libertarian perspective on testing would hold that test takers should take advantage of any legitimate opportunities afforded to them by life. If their wealth, or that of their relatives, allows them access to the best high schools, the most effective test coaching courses, and unlimited opportunities to take the test, they are at liberty to use these advantages to improve their test performance. The opportunity to exploit one's legitimately acquired assets is a right available to all. Attempts to equalize capital assets (or to impose any particular distribution of assets) violate a person's right to justly acquire goods—in this case, educational opportunities.

It is also possible to consider a libertarian perspective on testing from the vantage point of the agency that uses test scores. Any attempt to restrict how an agency uses a test score might be viewed as a violation of its basic right to conduct its business as it sees fit.

We now turn to a very different perspective on justice, that of John Rawls.

Rawls's Justice as Fairness Perspective

A widely debated philosophy of distributive justice was proposed by John Rawls in *A Theory of Justice* (1999), originally published in 1971, and revised in *Political Liberalism* (1993). Central to Rawls's (1999) philosophy is a thought experiment he called the *original position*. The original position is a hypothetical scenario in which a group of people who represent different aspects of society are brought together to identify the roles and rules that will define that society. Each representative stakeholder is to deliberate from behind a "veil of ignorance."

According to philosopher Catherine Audard (2007), the stakeholders behind the veil of ignorance of Rawls's original position would have access to general information about society but not particulars that pertain to them. Those behind this thick veil of ignorance would not know their specific place in society or their social class. They would not know their share of natural talents and abilities, their race, ethnic group, or gender. They would also be ignorant of their personal vision of the good life and their religious, moral, or philosophical perspective. They are ignorant of the particular political and economic circumstances of their society and its degree of civilization. Although they do not know where they fit in as individuals, they do, under the terms of this thought experiment, have access to all relevant general facts about human society, including the bodies of knowledge that have emerged from the physical and social sciences. They have no knowledge of what rights and liberties are protected in successful societies, but they know they have to develop rules fit for a democratic regime, and they use reason to do so. The society they create will be subject to the principles of justice agreed upon from behind the veil of ignorance. Rawls argued that, from this original position of equality, these hypothetical citizens, who don't know where they will end up in the system, are unlikely to design a structure that is unfair to individuals on the basis of factors like race, gender, and wealth.

Rawls (1999) claimed that two principles of justice would emerge from the original position:

(1) Each person is to have an equal right to the most extensive scheme of equal basic liberties compatible with a similar scheme of liberties for others.
(2) Social and economic inequalities are to be arranged so that they are both
   (a) to the greatest benefit of the least advantaged members of society, consistent with the just savings principle, and
   (b) attached to offices and positions open to all under conditions of fair equality of opportunity.

(p. 266)

The just savings principle in 2a refers to intergenerational justice, the requirement that the current generation leave enough material resources to the next generation to allow just institutions to be preserved over generations.

According to Audard (2007), the basic liberties noted by Rawls include:

(1) Freedom of thought and liberty of conscience
(2) The political liberties and freedom of association and the freedoms specified by the liberty and integrity of the person
(3) The rights and liberties covered by rule of law.

(p. 95)

At first glance, the emphasis on basic liberties may resemble that of the libertarian perspective. Unlike Nozick (1974), however, Rawls (1999) did not view all liberties as basic. "[L]iberties not on the list, for example the right to own certain kinds of property (e.g., means of production) and freedom of contract as understood by the doctrine of laissez-faire are not basic; and so are not protected by the priority of the first principle" (Rawls, 1999, p. 54).

Rawls's *difference principle* has been debated extensively for more than four decades. It allows inequalities to occur if they benefit the least advantaged members of society.

Rawls's concern focused on the *absolute* position of the least advantaged members rather than their *relative* position. If inequalities in society serve to raise the absolute position of the least advantaged, then the difference principle permits increasing inequality up to that point where the absolute position of the least advantaged can no longer be raised. In the educational realm, we might say that increasing the rewards for effective teachers makes sense if the effect of their teaching is to raise the educational level of the least advantaged.

Ordered from most important to least important, Rawls's justice as fairness can be expressed as the principle of the greatest liberty, the principle of (fair) equal opportunity, and the difference principle, with each principle subordinate to the preceding one. Consequently, basic rights and liberties cannot be sacrificed to foster equality of opportunity or a greater quantity of goods, even if this aids the least advantaged.[9]

Revisiting the Assessment Fairness Scenarios

In this section, we return to the three cases described at the beginning of this chapter and examine them from each of our philosophical perspectives.

Castaneda v. The Regents of the University of California

How might the *Castaneda* case be viewed from our three philosophical perspectives?[10] To what degree should grades, test scores, ethnic and socioeconomic background, and access to educational opportunities, such as Advanced Placement courses, be considered in admissions decisions?

According to an Aristotelian approach, just distribution depends on the purpose of the good that is being distributed. Thus, those who can best fulfill the purpose of the university should be admitted to it.[11] If the university's purpose is simply to nourish scholarly excellence, it can be argued that academic admissions criteria, such as grades, test scores, and the rigor of the students' high school classes, should be the primary, or perhaps the sole, criteria. If these measures provide a valid representation of the intellectual worth of the candidate, the admissions process would be fair from the Aristotelian perspective.

But in the eyes of many, a university's role encompasses the promotion of certain societal goals, such as fostering diversity. From this point of view, a society in which people of all races, cultural groups, and socioeconomic classes occupy key roles in the community contributes to the common good. In that case, race, ethnicity, and social class should be considered in admissions decisions, with an eye to increasing the diversity of the college-educated population. Given the large inequities in the American educational system and the associated achievement gaps, an effort to increase diversity might well involve de-emphasis of traditional admissions criteria, such as test scores and high school grade point averages (e.g., see Sackett, 2005). Factors other than a test taker's academic skills would need to be taken into account.

According to the libertarian perspective espoused by Nozick, inequality is not in itself unjust, provided that it did not result from improper acquisitions or transfers of property. Therefore, the fact that some applicants have had greater access to educational opportunities than the Castaneda plaintiffs is not of any particular importance. If an applicant can legitimately buy admission to a top-notch high school, enroll in the best SAT prep courses, and engage the services of a high-priced private college admissions coach, the libertarian sees no objection. These are free exchanges of goods that should not be regulated. Likewise, a university policy that gives admissions preferences to those who have benefitted from the greatest opportunities is not problematic from the libertarian perspective. Universities should be able to determine their own admission policies, unfettered by government rules. In fact, there should be no objection to auctioning college admission to the highest bidder, a possibility facetiously suggested both by Sandel (2009) and Klitgaard (1985).

John Rawls took the position that we don't deserve to be rewarded for our natural talents because we can't take credit for nature's endowments. More controversially, he also believed that we don't deserve to be rewarded for effort or hard work either. He argued that the ability to put forth effort was itself a function of luck and opportunity. Those individuals born into families that emphasized hard work and grit received social advantages that were not available to those who were born into homes haunted by defeatism. Neither a perfect GPA, nor an Olympic medal, nor a year volunteering in an inner-city soup kitchen would automatically "merit" admission to UC Berkeley, from a Rawlsian perspective. Most of today's admissions practices, then, would seem discordant with Rawls's beliefs since they involve—at least in part—a determination of which applicants' talents and efforts most deserve to be rewarded. This approach would be considered unacceptable unless it could be shown to help raise the level of the least advantaged members of society. For example, admissions preferences and perquisites could be awarded to applicants who wished to study medicine if an increase in the number, quality, or diversity of doctors would benefit the least advantaged.

Rawls's original position also needs to be considered in determining what he might regard as fair in an admissions setting. How would higher education be allocated by a group of people who were unaware of what their own status as college candidates would be—if indeed they were to become candidates at all? These decision-makers would not know if they were to emerge from affluent families or impoverished ones, and they would not know what their accomplishments, talents, and limitations would be. It seems that the type of admissions policy that would result from this debate would be a flexible one that allowed candidates multiple ways of demonstrating their eligibility and improved the outcomes for the least advantaged in society. In the *Castaneda* case, Rawls might well have supported the plaintiffs' argument that an admissions process that rewards applicants who have taken AP courses does not provide equality of opportunity. AP courses are not available to all candidates, and this lack of availability is clearly not to the benefit of the least advantaged.

In summary, the three fairness perspectives provide different lenses through which to view the Castaneda case. In the Aristotelian approach, valid measures of academic preparedness would likely be viewed as being essential to the admissions process, assuming it had been established that the primary mission of the university was to encourage intellectual growth. Factors unrelated to academic skills would be regarded as irrelevant. To the extent that admissions test scores and AP course taking are related to academic preparedness, they should be considered. The libertarian would dismiss the argument offered by Castaneda et al., provided that those who gained admission in preference to the plaintiffs had not benefited from advantages acquired through illegitimate transactions. The Rawlsian perspective would likely support Castaneda and her co-defendants because the opportunity to take advantage of premier test preparation and AP courses is not distributed equally and these inequities would likely translate into more significant disparities in subsequent quality of life. Rawls (2007, p. 215) puts it simply: "Injustice . . . is simply inequalities that are not to the benefit of all."

Debra P. v. Turlington

The *Debra P.* case raises key issues about the opportunity to learn. Must graduation tests be restricted to material that is specifically taught? Is it fair to impose uniform high school graduation requirements if educational opportunities differ substantially across racial groups?

Aristotle held the view that honors and rewards should be based on achievements. If the graduation test itself is fair (suggesting that the racial gap in scores is due to unequal educational opportunity, rather than a flaw in the test), then there is no obstacle to using it to determine who will receive a diploma.

As noted earlier, unequal opportunities and unequal outcomes are not, in and of themselves, troubling to the libertarian. If White students performed better than Black students on the high school graduation test due to greater educational opportunities, that would not necessarily be an injustice. However, the question of just acquisition could arise in this case. In Florida, the opportunities of Black children were obviously restricted because they had no choice but to attend segregated and inferior schools. Would Nozick regard the White students' acquisition of a superior education as an ill-gotten gain? Perhaps. Nozick acknowledges that in some cases, past injustices provide legitimate grounds for remediation (Sandel, 2009, p. 63).

Rawls would likely consider this case to have much in common with *Castaneda*. The policy for awarding diplomas was not developed through a deliberative process and the inequalities of educational opportunity that were demonstrated were obviously not to the benefit of the least advantaged. In short, the process of granting diplomas, the school's instructional practices, or both, would be viewed as unjust and would need to be changed.

The PSAT/NMSQT

The PSAT/NMSQT case raises a question of whether test content or test use should be adjusted so as to obtain a particular desired outcome. Should the number of semifinalists in a state be adjusted relative to the number of graduating seniors? Should results be adjusted to achieve gender equity? If these adjustments are legitimate, should similar adjustments be made to allocate scholarships more equitably across racial and ethnic groups?

In the Aristotelian view, honors and rewards are tied to accomplishments. If everyone has an opportunity to take the test, the test scores are accurate reflections of the attributes the test purports to measure, and the measured characteristics are the ones that are important for academic success in college, then the test is an appropriate way of identifying those who are worthy of an award. The PSAT/NMSQT is widely available and its scores are reliable measures of skills (reading, writing, and math) that are deemed important for academic success. Hence, its use for rewarding students is aligned with the Aristotelian perspective. Using state of residence or gender as factors in the selection of semifinalists runs counter to Aristotelian logic.

From the perspective of a libertarian test taker, state-by-state quotas, racial quotas, or gender quotas would be viewed as roadblocks having nothing to do with scholastic proficiency. Viewing the issue from the scholarship agencies' perspective, however, a libertarian might regard the state-by-state qualifying scores, the requirement that semifinalists take the SAT for score verification, and the submission of supporting material as falling within the purview of the scholarship grantors. The National Merit Scholarship

Corporation and the corporations and colleges who sponsor scholarships should have the freedom to set their own rules and run the competition as they see fit. For a libertarian, whether non-academic factors may be used depends on whether the issue is viewed from the eyes of the test taker or the eyes of the scholarship agencies.

From behind the veil of ignorance provided by Rawls's original position, the wide availability of the PSAT/NMSQT would be viewed as a plus. It is unlikely that the emergent Rawlsian perspective would favor using test scores as the sole basis of selection of semifinalists because of the inequalities associated with opportunity to prepare for the test. The final rules would probably contain more than test scores and state of residence. Gender, race, and parental income or other proxies for disadvantage might be part of the process for identifying semifinalists.

Conclusions

We have considered three practical situations where test scores have been used to make decisions about admissions, graduation, and scholarship eligibility. We have introduced and applied three philosophical perspectives to these situations: Aristotelian, libertarian, and Rawlsian. One philosophical approach that we elected not to consider in detail is utilitarianism. The utilitarian doctrine, which has its roots in the work of Jeremy Bentham and John Stuart Mill, focuses on what is good for society overall, ignoring potentially negative consequences that may exist for individuals. Bentham (1789) focused on the maximization of pleasure over pain and believed that the utility of all actions could be placed on a single pleasure-pain scale. John Stuart Mill (1863) shifted the focus from pleasure to happiness or fulfillment. In all varieties of utilitarianism, the process of maximizing utility is amenable to mathematical formulation. It requires assigning values (which may be positive or negative) and importance weights to various outcomes and then calculating the weighted sum of these values over all individuals. We excluded this perspective because it does not spell out what is to be maximized and thus does not provide any specific guidelines on fairness. The utilitarian approach, however, can be useful as a tool for analyzing the three philosophical perspectives we do consider. In particular, what utilities are maximized in the application of the Aristotelian, Nozickian, and Rawlsian perspectives? We consider this question in revisiting the three perspectives.

The Aristotelian fairness perspective assigns awards and honors on the basis of moral character and intrinsic talents. Hence, those who deserve to be admitted to college, graduate from high school, or receive a scholarship on the basis of their virtues and aptitudes should be awarded these honors. Other factors should not come into play. Thus the Aristotelian philosophy could be said to maximize the alignment of reward with merit (at least for those qualified to be citizens; see note 6). However, a narrow focus on individual merit undercuts an institution's ability to further particular societal goals. Aristotelian distributive justice principles do not take into account the varying opportunities available to the possible recipients of societal goods. Therefore, for those who believe it is important to consider inequalities of opportunity in distributing educational benefits—and we count ourselves among them—the Aristotelian view must be viewed as incomplete. If an Aristotelian approach to just distribution were adopted as the sole basis for making all decisions pertaining to selection, placement, and promotion, we might end up in a world dangerously like the stratified society described by Michael Young.

Nozick's libertarian perspective is concerned with maximizing the degree to which individuals are free to pursue their goals in life. Test takers should be at liberty to pursue graduation from high school, attend their college of choice, and compete for scholarships by every means possible, provided the means were not obtained illegally. This libertarian viewpoint does not target any particular distribution of goods; as long as each acquisition or exchange is "just," all is well. Enforced reallocations of goods or opportunities—such as affirmative action programs—are regarded as infringements on personal freedom. Individuals may exploit any advantages that exist because of inequalities in opportunity, provided their actions do not interfere with the liberties of others. Again, if inequality of opportunity is a concern, this perspective cannot be considered acceptable.

Rawls differs sharply from Aristotle and Nozick in his concern for equality of opportunity. According to Rawls, our gender, race, and talents are all determined by a "natural lottery" and the degree to which our family and community are able to nurture us and support the development of our abilities is determined by a "social lottery." To the extent that our accomplishments and talents are influenced by these natural and social lotteries, opportunities to achieve are unequal. Therefore, students' aptitudes, efforts, and attainments are not in themselves deserving of reward, in Rawls's view. The ultimate goal of educational policies should be to improve the welfare of all, including the least advantaged. Rawls's focus on the importance of opportunity and the remediation of disadvantage seems consonant with the needs and realities of American society today.

Unlike the Aristotelian and libertarian perspectives, which can be cast as straightforward maximization problems, Rawlsian philosophy involves a so-called maximin principle that involves the comparison of several possible scenarios: A person behind the veil of ignorance would, as a rational being, choose the social system in which the worst outcome—the circumstances of the least well off—was better than the worst outcome of all other feasible systems (Freeman, 2014). She would not choose a utilitarian system because it would allow her own well-being to be sacrificed to maximize the overall well-being of the society. Under the Rawlsian principles of justice, the comfort and security of the least advantaged members of society would be maximized relative to the situations they would encounter under competing social systems, provided that basic liberties have been respected and equal fair opportunity has been afforded to all.

Can our three, or any, philosophical perspectives provide conclusive answers to our fairness dilemmas? We don't think they can. Reading Aristotle will not tell us what attributes are most important for college students, nor will libertarian doctrine tell us what acquisitions are just or how to compensate for those that aren't. Rawls cannot tell us what inequalities will ultimately better the situation of the least advantaged in society. However, these philosophical perspectives can provide us with alternate lenses through which to view assessment fairness issues and can at least encourage us to ask the right questions.

Notes

1. The views expressed are those of the authors and not necessarily those of the Educational Testing Service or the University of California, Berkeley.
2. The views expressed are those of the author and not necessarily those of Educational Testing Service.
3. Initially, the case was named *Rios v. The Regents of the University of California*. Rios subsequently dropped out as a plaintiff.
4. Even though the National Merit Scholarship Corporation (NMSC) administers the scholarship programs, it was not included as a defendant in this case because it does not receive federal funds. It is important to note that the case was brought against the use of the PSAT/NMSQT to select semifinalists, and not the process used to allocate scholarships per se.

5. Many press accounts appear to confuse the process for selecting semifinalists on the basis of the PSAT/NMSQT with the final scholarship selection process used by the NMSC, in which the PSAT/NMSQT does not play a role. While the NMSC does publish the overall number of awards by state, we are not aware of any breakdown by gender.

6. These qualifying scores apply to the high school class of 2014: Note that the PSAT/NMSQT score scale changed in 2015.

7. In the field of philosophy, these three perspectives are considered "ideal theories" in that they each describe a vision for a perfectly just society. Even though they express unrealistic goals, these philosophical perspectives provide us with alternate lenses through which to view fairness issues in assessment and frameworks from which to ask questions about fairness in nonideal settings.

8. Our account of Aristotle's philosophy would be incomplete without reference to his defense of slavery and his views on women's role. It was his contention that some men were well suited to serve as slaves and that for them, slavery is "both beneficial and just" (Sandel, 2009, p. 202). The resulting hierarchy, in which some men were masters and others slaves, was not only acceptable, but natural, in Aristotle's eyes. Like slaves, women were ineligible for citizenship in Aristotle's view (Sandel, 2009, p. 200). According to Aristotle, "the relation of male to female is one of superior to inferior, and ruler to ruled" (see Stauffer, 2008, p. 935). Women's role was to liberate men from concern with everyday household matters, allowing the men to pursue the important issues of the community (Stauffer, 2008, p. 939). We have elected not to discuss these positions about who was eligible for citizenship in order to focus on Aristotle's definition of fair treatment—his perspective on aligning reward with virtue, accomplishment, or value to society.

9. Rawls's approach is complex, and this ordering helps resolve conflicts that can occur between the desiderata of protecting basic liberties, providing equal opportunity, and maintaining concern for the least advantaged. Consider the following simplistic illustration. Assume that society recognizes that a college education tends to improve quality of life. Rawls probably would oppose the practice of legacy preferences because it violated his equal opportunity principle. Assume society seeks to provide all families with the opportunity to send at least one child to college. Rawls probably would argue against a policy that stated that students with siblings who had attended college should have their right to attend college restricted to ensure that all families could send at least one child to college. Although this restriction would enhance opportunities for the least advantaged families, it would do so at the expense of other individuals' liberty to attend college.

10. See Meyer (2013) for another discussion of philosophical perspectives on fairness in university admission. Further discussion of fairness in college admission can be found in Zwick (to appear).

11. See Sandel (2009, pp. 190–191) for a related discussion.

References

American Civil Liberties Union of Northern California. (2003, June 18). *Castaneda v. The Regents of the University of California.* Retrieved from www.aclunc.org/our-work/legal-docket/castaneda-v-regents-university-california

American Educational Research Association, American Psychological Association, & National Council on Measurement in Education (2014). *Standards for educational and psychological testing.* Washington, DC: AERA.

Aristotle. (2005). *Politics* (trans. B. Jowett). Stilwell, KS: Digireads.

Audard, C. (2007). *John Rawls (Philosophy Now Book 10).* Montreal: McGill-Queen's University Press.

Bentham, J. (1789). *An introduction to the principles of morals and legislation.* Oxford: Clarendon Press. Retrieved from www.econlib.org/library/Bentham/bnthPML.html

Castaneda v. The Regents of the University of California, 3:99-cv-00525-SI (2003). Proposed consent decree. Retrieved from www.aclunc.org/sites/default/files/asset_upload_file854_3466.pdf

Debra P. v. Turlington, 474 F. Supp. 244 (M.D. Fla 1979). Retrieved from www.courtlistener.com/flmd/b52Q/debra-p-v-turlington

Debra P. v. Turlington, 730 F.2d 1405 (1984). Retrieved from http://law.justia.com/cases/federal/appellate-courts/F2/730/1405/345196

Freeman, S. (2014). Original position. In E. N. Zalta (Ed.), *The Stanford encyclopedia of philosophy* (Fall 2014 Edition). Retrieved from http://plato.stanford.edu/archives/fall2014/entries/original-position

Hoover, E. (2010, February 19). How the National Merit Scholarship Corporation tried to muzzle a blogger. *Chronicle of Higher Education, 56*(23), A24–A25.

Klitgaard, R. E. (1985). *Choosing elites.* New York: Basic Books.

Lamont, J., & Favor, C. (2014). Distributive justice. In E. N. Zalta (Ed.), *The Stanford encyclopedia of philosophy* (Fall 2014 Edition). Retrieved from http://plato.stanford.edu/archives/fall2014/entries/justice-distributive

Locke, J. (1690). *Second treatise of government.* Retrieved from https://archive.org/details/osthistory-second_treatise_of_government

Mack, E. (2014). Robert Nozick's political philosophy. In E. N. Zalta (Ed.), *The Stanford encyclopedia of philosophy* (Fall 2014 Edition). Retrieved from http://plato.stanford.edu/archives/fall2014/entries/nozick-political

Meyer, H-D. (2013). Reasoning about fairness in access to higher education: Common sense, normative, and institutional perspectives. In H-D. Meyer, E. P. St. John, M. Chankseliani, & L. Uribe (Eds.), *Fairness in access to a higher education in a global perspective* (pp. 15–40). Rotterdam: Sense Publishers.

Mill, J. S. (1863). *Utilitarianism.* London: Parker, Son, & Bourn. Retrieved from https://archive.org/details/a592840000milluoft

National Merit Scholarship Corporation. (2013). *Official student guide to the 2013 Preliminary SAT/National Merit Scholarship Qualifying Test.* Retrieved from www.nationalmerit.org/student_guide.pdf

Nieves, E. (1999, February 3). Civil rights groups suing Berkeley over admissions policy. *New York Times,* A11

Nozick, R. (1974). *Anarchy, state and utopia.* New York: Basic Books.

Phillips, S. E. (1993). *Legal implications of high-stakes assessment: What states should know.* (North Central Regional Educational Laboratory Rept. No. RPIC-HS-93). Retrieved from http://eric.ed.gov/?id=ED370985

Rawls, J. (1993). *Political liberalism (The John Dewey Essays in Philosophy, Book 4).* New York: Columbia University Press.

Rawls, J. (1999). *A theory of justice (revised edition).* Cambridge, MA: Harvard University Press.

Rawls, J. (2007). Justice as fairness [excerpt]. In M. J. Sandel (Ed.), *Justice: A reader* (pp. 203–221). New York: Oxford University Press.

Reisberg, L. (1998, January 23). Girls' scores on PSAT rise slightly, but critics aren't appeased. *Chronicle of Higher Education,* A42.

Sackett, P. R. (2005). The performance-diversity tradeoff in admission testing. In W. J. Camara & E. W. Kimmel (Eds.), *Choosing students: Higher education admissions tools for the 21st century* (pp. 109–125). Mahwah, NJ: Erlbaum.

Sandel, M. J. (2009). *Justice: What's the right thing to do?* New York: Farrar, Straus, & Giroux.

Stauffer, D. J. (2008). Aristotle's account of the subjection of women. *The Journal of Politics, 70*(4), 929–941.

University of California (2001). *Comprehensive review.* Retrieved from www.ucop.edu/news/factsheets/2001/comprev.pdf

Young, M. (1994). *The rise of the meritocracy.* New Brunswick, NJ: Transaction.

Zwick, R. (to appear). *Who gets in? Strategies for fair and effective college admissions.* Cambridge, MA: Harvard University Press.

15 Commentary on Perspectives on Fair Assessment

Frank C. Worrell[1]

The three previous chapters in this section introduce us to several perspectives on fairness in the assessment arena. Haertel and Ho (this volume, Chapter 12) highlight the importance of fairness in the context of using derived scores, Phillips (this volume, Chapter 13) presents the legal aspects of test fairness, and Zwick and Dorans (this volume, Chapter 14) discuss philosophical perspectives on assessment. In my opinion, these chapters and, indeed, this volume, signal a heightened attention in society and the educational arena in particular to fairness in assessments, driven in large part by ongoing concerns about the seemingly intractable achievement gap (American Psychological Association, 2012; Aud, Fox, & KewalRamani, 2010; Aud et al., 2013; Plucker, Burroughs, & Song, 2010; Plucker, Hardesty, & Burroughs, 2013). Concerns about the achievement gap have resulted in the increased use of tests and assessments to measure both student progress (Barton, 1999; Weingarten, 2011) and teacher effectiveness (Baker et al., 2010; Worrell et al., 2014). These concerns have also resulted in the development of more rigorous standards for K-12 education. These newly adopted standards—known as the Common Core Standards (2014)—have been adopted by over 40 states, and there is hope that these Standards will help to eliminate the achievement gap (Powers, 2014), provided they are implemented successfully and survive the political challenges they face.

In this chapter, I begin with a brief overview of the concept of fairness in the most recent edition of the *Standards for Educational and Psychological Testing* (referred to as the Standards henceforth) (American Educational Research Association, American Psychological Association, & National Council on Measurement in Education [AERA, APA, & NCME], 2014), as well as previous editions of the Standards. Next, I discuss the perspectives on fairness raised in the three chapters and comment on how these perspectives relate to discussions of fairness with regard to the achievement gap. I conclude with comments on the multiple perspectives on fairness put forward in the previous chapters in this section and what these perspectives contribute to ongoing debates on fairness.

Fairness in the *Standards for Educational and Psychological Testing*

In the testing and assessment arena, validity and reliability have always been preeminent constructs—the *Big Two*, one might say—and developers of assessment instruments used in practice or research are expected to provide reliability and validity evidence supporting the use of the instrument's scores. To date, there have been several versions of technical recommendations or standards related to educational and psychological testing. The first two of these were published separately for psychology (APA, AERA, & National Council on Measurements Used in Education [NCMUE], 1954) and education (AERA & NCMUE, 1955) in the mid-1950s, with joint editions coming out in each decade through the end of the 20th century (AERA, APA, & NCME, 1985, 1999; APA, AERA, & NCME, 1966, 1974). All of the editions of the Standards have included chapters on validity and reliability. In the 1974 edition, they were placed in a section by themselves, and in all subsequent editions, validity and reliability have been covered in the first and second chapters, respectively, signaling their importance.

The concept of fairness was mentioned for the first time in the 1974 edition: "Some unfairness may be built into a test, for example, requiring an inordinately high level of verbal ability to comprehend the instructions for a nonverbal test" (APA et al., 1974, p. 2). As with the 2014 edition, the 1974 edition of the Standards acknowledged that (a) there were different definitions of fairness; (b) evidence in support of fairness should be provided for subgroups; (c) mean differences in subgroup means were not necessarily evidence of unfairness, but should trigger additional scrutiny; and (d) test users should actively work "to minimize unfairness in test use" (APA et al., 1974, p. 12). Although fairness was not mentioned explicitly before 1974, issues related to fairness (e.g., bias, adequate sampling of population, adequate coverage of items, use of independent samples for cross-validation) were mentioned in previous editions of the Standards (Worrell & Roberson, 2016).

Since its introduction in 1974, the concept of fairness has continued to gain prominence. The 1985 *Standards* included an Applications section with chapters on testing linguistic minorities and individuals with handicaps, and the 1999 *Standards* named the section with those chapters "Fairness in Testing," and the section began with an opening chapter entitled "Fairness in Testing and Test Use." In 2014, the Standards went even further by moving the Fairness chapter to the opening section, Foundations, and expanding the Big Two to the *Big Three*—validity, reliability, *and fairness*. As the Standards note, "Fairness is a fundamental validity issue and requires attention throughout all stages of test development and use" (AERA et al., 2014, p. 49). Issues of fairness were also incorporated into all of the chapters in the 2014 edition. Camara and Lane (2006) pointed out that there were no standards on fairness in the 1985 *Standards* and 12 in the 1999 *Standards*. Chapter 3, "Fairness in Testing," of the 2014 *Standards* contains 20 standards, and the number of standards on fairness is even greater when one considers standards related to fairness in other chapters of the 2014 edition. It is not a coincidence, I think, that the concept of fairness has increased in importance over the past 60 years, given the increased attention to the issue of fairness in society and the increasing number of legal rulings related to the issue of fairness in assessments in education, credentialing, and the workplace.

The 2014 *Standards* highlight four views of fairness. The first of these is fair treatment during testing. From this viewpoint, fairness is intended to ensure that all examinees get to demonstrate what they know on a test, and this view of fairness is typically associated with standardization of test administration and scoring. The second viewpoint of fairness involves lack of measurement bias in scores (e.g., Warne, Yoon, & Price, 2014), typically demonstrated by examining scores for differential item and test functioning, differential prediction (e.g., looking at slope and intercept differences by subgroup), different estimates of precision, different factor structures, or differences in the meaning of the construct. Fairness in accessing the construct is the third viewpoint: the issue here is does each examinee have the opportunity to show their *true* standing on the construct (i.e., minimizing construct-irrelevant variance)? The fourth view of fairness "concerns the validity of individual score interpretations for intended uses" (AERA et al., 2014, p. 49).

For example, are these scores appropriate to use in classifying Person A as gifted and Person B as learning disabled? Finally, the 2014 *Standards* acknowledge test content, context, and response, as well as opportunity to learn, as potential sources of construct-irrelevant variance. I now turn to the chapters in this section.

Fairness Using Derived Scores

Haertel and Ho (this volume, Chapter 12) dive into the fairness issues with derived scores, or scores that differ from the scores that the test developer intended when creating the test. These authors distinguish developer constructs ("the constructs that the test is designed to measure") from application constructs ("the constructs that the test is used to measure") (p. 218), a situation that they argue is becoming increasingly common. Some of the more controversial uses of derived scores in education at the moment involve using scores from tests of student achievement to make decisions about teachers and schools. For example, value-added measures combine student achievement scores over individuals and years to make inferences about teacher effectiveness, with implications for merit and even termination decisions. Another example involves using student achievement scores to classify schools as effective and ineffective, with consequences ranging from dismissing principals and teachers to closing and reconstituting schools.

A less visible but increasingly common example of derived scores being used in education stems from the increasing popularity of cross-battery assessment in psycho-educational evaluations of students (e.g., Flanagan, 2000). Cross-battery assessment involves combining scores from different tests to more accurately reflect the Cattell-Horn-Carroll (CHC) theory of cognitive abilities (McGrew, Flanagan, Keith, & Vanderwood, 1997). Importantly, the cross-battery assessment approach combines scores from subtests drawn from different validated instruments (e.g., the Wechsler scales and the Stanford-Binet) and bases inferences about performance and need for special education services using the *derived* combined scores. Proponents of this approach contend that this approach is "a more valid and defensible way of deriving meaning from test scores" since the approach is theory-driven (Flanagan, 2000, p. 295). Moreover, Flanagan, Ortiz, and Alfonso (2007) put forward the Culture-Language Interpretive Matrices (C-LIMs) as a cross-battery approach for assessing children from diverse cultural and linguistic backgrounds; these authors suggested that even non-verbal tests are culturally loaded and argued that C-LIMS is a less-biased—in essence, *fairer*—alternative. However, other researchers have questioned the utility of cross-battery assessment (Parkin & Beaujean, 2012) as well as the validity and fairness of C-LIMs (e.g., Kranzler, Flores, & Coady, 2010). Importantly, Kranzler et al., in keeping with Haertel and Ho (this volume, Chapter 12), argued that more research needs to be conducted before drawing inferences from these derived scores. Pommerich (this volume, Chapter 7) addresses the technical issues associated with comparing scores obtained from different instruments that purport to measure the same construct.

The fundamental issue articulated by Haertel and Ho (this volume, Chapter 12) is the validity of the inferences derived on the basis of derived scores, and whether these decisions can be fair. For example, although value-added measures are under tremendous scrutiny and these scores have been criticized with regard to reliability and validity (Baker et al., 2010), much of the concern seems to center on evaluating teachers, with the concerns about validity, reliability, and fairness being used to say that teachers should not be evaluated. However, as Worrell et al. (2014) pointed out, teachers are being evaluated by a variety of methods, so the concerns should be with using the best available methods—that is, the ones that allow for the best inferences about teacher effectiveness. In other words, as Haertel and Ho ask, does the use of these derived scores introduce construct-irrelevant variance such that the scores are not fair and appropriate for interpretation and use for decisions about teachers, students, and schools?

The solution to this problem is evidence in support of the interpretation and use of these derived scores for the decisions that they are being used to make. Another example of the use of derived scores provided by Haertel and Ho (this volume, Chapter 12) is the use of English Language proficiency scores to decide which English language learners are proficient and which are not, with implications for placement into different programs in school. A third example that these authors provide is the use of achievement test scores to classify students as *college and career ready*. Importantly, Haertel and Ho are not suggesting that derived scores not be used. Rather, they are saying (a) that evidence should be provided in support of derived scores, and not just those being used to evaluate teachers and schools; and (b) that tests users need to recognize when they have moved from the developer construct to an application construct using derived scores, so that we avoid "a blind spot in test score validation" (p. 234).

Legal Views of Fairness

Phillips (this volume, Chapter 13) discusses the legal aspects of fairness. In addition to using a high school graduation test like Zwick and Dorans (this volume, Chapter 14), Phillips also reports on cases related to testing accommodations and test security. The perspective here is legal and determined by the rulings made in courts, although rulings by different courts are not always congruent. Phillips points out that courts have generally rejected the notion of equal outcomes as the appropriate standard for fairness, giving due deference to the Standards and the expert opinions that it reflects. Instead, the concern of courts has typically been about equal opportunity and access, which is also in keeping with expert opinion. I now turn to how these fairness concerns play out in legal proceedings.

Graduation Tests

According to Phillips (this volume, Chapter 13, p. 240), the two primary legal considerations with regard to fairness are "adequate notice of the testing environment" and opportunity to learn, or "curricular validity." With regard to opportunity to learn, the court and professionals engaged in testing and assessment are in strong agreement. Adequate notice of the testing environment is an interesting requirement, which seems to be more legal than technical: Do students know that they are going to be tested so that they can prepare adequately? It is also important to know that, in general, the courts (a) recognize the importance of having minimum education standards; (b) recognize that well-constructed tests are one way to assess student competence, including the competence of students with disabilities and English language learners; and (c) defer to the Standards with regard to construct validity in the broadest sense. In other words, test users, including school districts, that follow the Standards and provide adequate notice and opportunity to learn are considered to be fair in their practice.

Testing Accommodations

As Phillips (this volume, Chapter 13) points out, although the legal system recognizes the distinction between accommodations (i.e., alterations to a test that increase access to the construct without changing the construct) and modifications (i.e., alterations to a test that *change* the construct), the major issue that courts have addressed around this issue has to do with whether scores from tests given with accommodations should be annotated or flagged, so that individuals receiving the test scores are aware that the testing conditions were altered in some way. The concern here, of course, is adverse impact.

From the perspective of fairness, a central issue is, are the test scores given under accommodated conditions *truly* comparable to scores given under the standard conditions used for norming? If one answers "yes" to this question, then flagging is unfair and should not be used. In most cases, however, there is little evidence of comparability, as the studies have not been done. As Phillips (this volume, Chapter 13) notes, courts have split on whether scores should be flagged or not, with one court suggesting that the test taker should provide evidence of comparability and another court placing the burden on the test user to show that the scores are not comparable. As the 2014 *Standards* take the latter position, placing the onus on test developers and test users, these groups will have to conduct considerably more research on this topic.

However, the Standards also highlight the principle of universal design in the Fairness chapter, "an approach to test design that seeks to maximize accessibility for all intended examinees" (AERA et al., 2014, p. 50). Although it may not be possible to make tests accessible to absolutely everyone, designing tests so that they are accessible to individuals with the most commonly occurring disabilities that require accommodations (e.g., learning disabilities, visual impairments) will go a long way to ensuring fairness by removing the need for accommodations, and may even result in less litigation around this issue.

Test Security

The issue of test security is the last one raised by Phillips (this volume, Chapter 13). To the extent that a test is supposed to assess a person's standing on the construct, release of test items that are still in use is a major fairness issue, creating multiple adverse impacts. In addition to disadvantaging individuals who do not have access to the inappropriately released items, there are also negative consequences for test developers, schools, employers, and, ultimately, clients of individuals whose performance on the tests that led to their selection is due to knowledge of the items rather than their actual standing on the construct. For example, there have been instances of previous and current editions of IQ tests available for sale on eBay, and I remember a situation where a child who was being assessed for possible "gifted" classification at a clinic that I worked at saying, "Oh, the blocks, again. I like these." Given the negative consequences of test security failures, the Standards place responsibility for test security on all individuals who have access to the test, including test takers.

The need for test security and intellectual property rights of test developers have come into conflict with the right to information on the part of parents and the media, and different court cases have resulted in selective release of items under certain conditions (e.g., after a certain amount of time). An important fairness question that has not been addressed is this: Are there finite or infinite numbers of new items in a domain? To the extent that the number is finite, periodic releases of items may eventually result in a situation where it is not possible to assess anyone's standing on a particular construct, as most of the test items are in the public domain. Although this scenario may seem far-fetched, in this brave new world of the Internet, this scenario is quite possible, and could be very costly in real dollars to test developers and test users.

Philosophical Views of Fairness

Zwick and Dorans (this volume, Chapter 14) presented three scenarios—use of tests for awarding high school diplomas, making college admissions decisions, and awarding of National Merit Scholarships—that are representative of a wide range of important decisions in society based on testing. Zwick and Dorans interpreted these scenarios from three different philosophical perspectives on fairness: Aristotelian (accomplishments *and not status* should determine rewards), libertarian (individuals should have maximum freedom within legal boundaries to pursue rewards), and Rawlsian (inequality in rewards is permissible, if these inequalities ultimately result in greater benefits to the least advantaged members of society). Let's play out the three perspectives of fairness in the context of the scenarios presented.

Using Tests in the Awarding of High School Diplomas

Zwick and Dorans (this volume, Chapter 14) focus on the question of opportunity to learn in the *Debra P.* case. When there was differential opportunity to learn, the court ruled in favor of the plaintiff, and it seems as if both Aristotelian and Rawlsian perspectives on fairness are violated. Zwick and Dorans indicate that the libertarian position is not necessarily clear here, turning on the question of if the "superior education is an ill-gotten gain" (p. 277). To the extent that the families who are benefitting are not the ones who set up the unequal system—a tenuous assumption, I admit—libertarians would see the graduation tests as fair.

However, assuming the legal criteria of opportunity to learn and notice of the testing environment have been met, from an Aristolelian perspective, the use of these tests are fair, in that an individual's score on the test—that is, his or her accomplishment—determines the awarding of a high school diploma. A libertarian analysis would also see this use of tests as fair. From the libertarian perspective, the fact that parents with greater financial resources are able to pay for test preparation classes outside of school is irrelevant. For example, consider the substantial increase in charter schools over the past two decades (National Alliance for Public Charter Schools, 2015). Many charter schools, which are public schools, have been opened specifically to serve low-income students of color (Fleischman & Heppen, 2009; Wohlstetter, Smith, & Farrell, 2013), and some of these schools have had tremendous success in increasing the graduation rates of low-income minority students (Center for Research on Education Outcomes, 2009; KIPP, n.d.; RTI International, n.d.). A low-income family's decision to enroll their son in a high-performing charter school rather than the regular public school is akin to the high-income family's decision to pay for a test preparation course, with the goal of both options being higher scores on the high school graduation test. This analysis is in keeping with the court's decision to allow the test to be used for awarding of diplomas after 1984. In this latter scenario, however, given the absence of information on the societal beneficiaries of a high school diploma, the Rawlsian perspective is unclear.

Using Tests for College Admission Decisions

The college scenario (Zwick & Dorans, this volume, Chapter 14) was based on a lawsuit filed against the University of California, Berkeley, in 1999 subsequent to the 1996 state proposition banning the use of race/ethnicity by public institutions, including college admissions decisions. The lawsuit contended that the campus gave undue weight to admissions test scores including results from the Advanced Placement examinations because not all schools offer AP courses in all AP areas. The idea of undue weight being given to test scores has also been raised in the context of classifying students as gifted and talented (Erwin & Worrell, 2012; Ford, 2008; Worrell, 2003, 2013).

UC Berkeley now uses a holistic review process—excluding race, ethnicity, gender, and religion—with the goal of identifying students "who are most likely to contribute to Berkeley's intellectual and cultural community and, ultimately, to the State of California, the nation, and the world" (University of California, Berkeley, Office of Undergraduate Admissions, n.d.). Holistic review focuses on academic achievement in high school, personal qualities (e.g., leadership, character, motivation), contributions to intellectual and cultural vitality, standardized test scores, and academic achievement outside of high school, all "considered in the context of the opportunities an applicant has had" (University of California, Berkeley, Office of Undergraduate Admissions, n.d.). On the basis of the new admission policy, 17% of UC Berkeley undergraduates are first-generation college students and more than 60% qualify for some financial aid.

How do the three perspectives on fairness apply to the *Castaneda* case and to the holistic review policies that UC Berkeley uses? Both the Aristotelian and libertarian perspectives would dismiss the Castaneda complaint about fairness, as rigorous coursework in high school is associated with college success. These positions would suggest that the university has the right to choose individuals who meet the academic criteria that predict success in college. This position would also apply to the holistic review process from the libertarian perspective—related to the university's right to choose criteria, provided they were being applied to all applicants, who were free to use the means at their disposal to meet the criteria. However, Aristotelians would need to be shown data indicating that holistic review was as predictive of college success as academic indicators for them to deem that process fair. Although the use of merit-based criteria might appear to be in conflict with the Rawlsian position, I contend that the holistic review used by UC Berkeley would come the closest to passing the Rawlsian test. As Zwick and Dorans (this volume, Chapter 12, p. 276) indicate, acceptable criteria from a Rawlsian perspective would have "to help raise the level of the least advantaged members of society" and a decision on criteria made using Rawlsian principles would be a flexible one that allowed candidates multiple ways of demonstrating their eligibility.

It can be argued that UC Berkeley's holistic review, with its inclusion of individual opportunities in context, is based on a Rawlsian interpretation of fairness, because the holistic review process at UC Berkeley and five other UC campuses has resulted in them being the leading colleges serving low-income students (Leonhardt, 2015), assuming all of the social and socioeconomic benefits that accrue on the basis of a college degree. Leonhardt's conclusion is based on the College Access Index, which assesses the economic diversity of the top universities in the United States. As noted in the 2015 figures, six of the top seven on that index are UC campuses. Thus, although the *Castaneda* case suggested a lack of fairness on the basis of ethnicity, the College Access Index suggests fairness on the basis of income, which may be as close to a Rawlsian perspective as we can get in the current age.

Gender Differences in National Merit Scholarships

In the third scenario, Zwick and Dorans (this volume, Chapter 14) turn their attention from race/ethnicity to gender. The central question here is this: Is using PSAT scores to assign the National Merit Scholarship semi-finalists fair? This question was raised in the

290 Frank C. Worrell

context of two concerns. The first is purported outcome bias as males were receiving more scholarships than females due to superior male performance on the mathematics portion of the test. It is worth noting that the total score that was used consisted of the math score plus twice the verbal score. Moreover, the remedy that was applied—that is, adding a writing component—so that the total scores consisted of math plus verbal plus writing did not eliminate the outcome bias favoring males. The second concern is that individual states used different cut scores, so that students in less competitive states receive scholarships with scores lower than students in more competitive states.

Aristotelians and libertarians would argue that the use of the tests to award scholarships is fair for different reasons. The former would condemn the use of different cut scores by state, and would suggest that scholarships be awarded purely on merit, even if that resulted in some states getting many scholarships and some getting none. Libertarians, to the extent that they apply the same notion of freedom to companies as they do to individuals, would not have a problem with the different cut scores by state. As Zwick and Dorans note, Rawlsians would want additional factors to be considered beyond the scores on a test. These could include scholarship recipients being required to provide service to impoverished communities upon completion of their degrees, or awarding more scholarships to states with the most disadvantaged populations. However, a Rawlsian perspective would find any system based purely on test scores unfair if the decisions did not ultimately result in greater benefits to the least advantaged individuals and, possibly, states.

Conclusion

The three chapters in this section provide an important overview of the fairness issues from a variety of perspectives—measurement-oriented, legal, and philosophical—and highlight the fact that fairness involves a broad set of concerns that are likely to be around for many years to come. I invoked the achievement gap at the beginning of this piece, and suggested that society's growing concern with fairness may be tied to this issue, as the achievement gap has much broader societal implications (e.g., socioeconomic and health disparities). America is often described as a meritocracy, the Aristotelian ideal, although individuals who are concerned about the lack of equity and social justice are more likely to see it as a libertarian zone and distinctly non-Rawlsian (Education Trust, 2014; Rogers, Terriquez, Valladares, & Oakes, 2006).

With regard to legal issues, the courts recognize the importance of professional standards in testing and assessment. However, as the Standards now put the onus on test developers and test users to show comparability of scores, unless testing programs respond affirmatively to this call using robust empirical evidence or universal design principles in developing tests, there will be increasing court challenges based on issues such as annotating scores, especially given the increase in the numbers of individuals who are getting diagnoses leading to accommodations such as extra time in testing situations. It is also probable that there will be a growing set of legal challenges to the use of derived scores as well, as their use becomes more prevalent.

Well-constructed tests are important and vital tools in helping professionals make decisions in a variety of spheres: high school graduation, awarding of scholarships, college admissions, teacher and school effectiveness, hiring and credentialing, and the list goes on. However, testing is misunderstood by the general public, the utility of test scores is undervalued, and tests are frequently maligned and blamed for doing what they were designed to do, that is, providing a fair and accurate assessment of an individual's standing on the construct of interest. Philosophical, legal, and measurement-based concerns about fairness all contribute to the mistrust of test scores by the public. Many individuals *believe* that unequal outcomes are an indicator of unfair tests, a position that continues to be put forward by some "experts" (e.g., Ford & Helms, 2012), and mistrust is only heightened when different courts consider similar cases and come to different decisions, in large part because judges are not experts in testing. Moreover, the range of philosophical perspectives in society on test fairness exceeds the range of perspectives raised by Zwick and Dorans (this volume, Chapter 14). Finally, the 24-hour access to data and opinions via the web and news channels provide numerous examples of disparities in test results by cultural groups (American Psychological Association, 2012; Erwin & Worrell, 2012). Thus, concerns about fairness in testing will not go away go away in the foreseeable future.

In conclusion, I would argue that the most important concerns that these chapters raise are related to communications and public relations issues. The Fairness chapter of the Standards suggests that

> As research on contextual factors (e.g., stereotype threat) is ongoing, test developers and test users should pay attention to the emerging empirical literature on these topics so that they can use this information if and when the preponderance of evidence dictates that it is appropriate to do so.
>
> (AERA et al., 2014, p. 55)

It is incumbent upon test developers, test users, and measurement professionals to not only design tests that yield reliable and fair scores from which valid inferences can be generated, but also to proactively communicate with and educate the public and policymakers about testing, test construction, test utility, and test *fairness*. Failing to meet the communication and public relations challenges that unequal outcomes inevitably raise may result in tremendous damage to the testing industry even if society gets to a time and place when all the tests are fair.

Note

1. The views expressed are those of the author and not necessarily those of the University of California, Berkeley.

References

American Educational Research Association, American Psychological Association, & National Council on Measurement in Education. (1985). *Standards for educational and psychological testing*. Washington, DC: American Psychological Association.

American Educational Research Association, American Psychological Association, & National Council on Measurement in Education. (1999). *Standards for educational and psychological testing*. Washington, DC: American Educational Research Association.

American Educational Research Association, American Psychological Association, & National Council on Measurement in Education. (2014). *Standards for educational and psychological testing*. Washington, DC: American Educational Research Association.

American Educational Research Association, & National Council on Measurements Used in Education. (1955). *Technical recommendations for achievement tests*. Washington, DC: National Education Association.

American Psychological Association, American Educational Research Association, & National Council on Measurements Used in Education. (1954). *Technical recommendations for psychological tests and diagnostic techniques.* Washington, DC: American Psychological Association.

American Psychological Association, American Educational Research Association, & National Council on Measurement in Education. (1966). *Standards for educational and psychological tests and manuals.* Washington, DC: American Psychological Association.

American Psychological Association, American Educational Research Association, & National Council on Measurement in Education. (1974). *Standards for educational and psychological tests.* Washington, DC: American Psychological Association.

American Psychological Association, Presidential Task Force on Education Disparities. (2012). *Ethnic and racial disparities in education: Psychology's contributions to understanding and reducing disparities.* Retrieved from www.apa.org/ed/resources/racial-disparities.aspx

Aud, S., Fox, M., & KewalRamani, A. (2010). *Status and trends in the education of racial and ethnic groups* (NCES 2010-015). Washington, DC: U.S. Department of Education, National Center for Education Statistics. Retrieved from http://nces.ed.gov/pubs2010/2010015.pdf

Aud, S., Wilkinson-Flicker, S., Kristapovich, P., Rathbun, A., Wang, X., & Zhang, J. (2013). *The condition of education 2013* (NCES 2013-037). Washington, DC: U.S. Department of Education, National Center for Education Statistics. Retrieved from http://nces.ed.gov/pubs2013/2013 037.pdf

Baker, E. L., Barton, P. E., Darling-Hammond, L., Haertel, E., Ladd, H. F., Linn, R. L., & Shepard, L. A. (2010). *Problems with the use of student test scores to evaluate teachers.* Washington, DC: Economic Policy Institute. Retrieved from www.epi.org/page/-/pdf/bp278.pdf

Barton, P. E. (1999). *Too much testing of the wrong kind; too little of the right kind in K-12 education.* Princeton, NJ: Educational Testing Service. Retrieved from www.ets.org/Media/Research/pdf/PICTOOMUCH.pdf

Camara, W. J., & Lane, S. (2006). A historical perspective and current views on the standards for educational and psychological testing. *Educational Measurement: Issues and Practice, 25*(3), 35–41.

Center for Research on Education Outcomes. (2009). *Multiple choice: Charter school performance in 16 states.* Stanford, CA: Center for Research on Education Outcomes. Retrieved from http://credo.stanford.edu/reports/MULTIPLE_CHOICE_CREDO.pdf

Common Core Standards. (2014). *Common core state standards initiative: Preparing America's students for college & career.* Retrieved from www.corestandards.org

Education Trust. (2014). *Access and success in higher education: Can we do more?* Paper presented at the annual conference of the Northeast Association for Institutional Research, Philadelphia, PA.

Erwin, J. O., & Worrell, F. C. (2012). Assessment practices and the underrepresentation of minority students in gifted and talented education. *Journal of Psychoeducational Assessment, 30*, 74–87.

Flanagan, D. P. (2000). Wechsler-based CHC cross-battery assessment and reading achievement: Strengthening the validity of interpretations drawn from Wechsler test scores. *School Psychology Quarterly, 15*, 295–329.

Flanagan, D. P., Ortiz, S. O., & Alfonso, V. C. (2007). *Essentials of cross-battery assessment* (2nd ed.). Hoboken, NJ: Wiley.

Fleischman, S., & Heppen, J. (2009). Improving low-performing high schools: Searching for evidence of promise. *The Future of Children, 19*(1), 105–134.

Ford, D. Y. (2008). Intelligence testing and cultural diversity: The need for alternative instruments, policies, and procedures. In J. L. VanTassel-Baska (Ed.), *Alternative assessments with gifted and talented students* (pp. 107–128). Waco, TX: Prufrock Press.

Ford, D. Y., & Helms, J. E. (2012). Overview and introduction: Testing and assessing African Americans: "Unbiased" tests are still unfair. *The Journal of Negro Education, 81*, 186–189.

KIPP. (n.d.). *The promise of college completion: 2013 alumni update.* Retrieved from www.kipp.org/results/college-completion-report/2013-alumni-data-update

Kranzler, J. H., Flores, C. G., & Coady, M. (2010). Examination of the cross-battery approach for the cognitive assessment of children and youth from diverse linguistic and cultural backgrounds. *School Psychology Review, 39,* 431–436.

Leonhardt, D. (2015, September). California's upward-mobility machine. *New York Times.* Retrieved from www.nytimes.com/2015/09/17/upshot/californias-university-system-an-upward-mobility-machine.html?_r=0

McGrew, K. S., Flanagan, D. P., Keith, T. Z., & Vanderwood, M. (1997). Beyond *g:* The impact of Gf-Gc specific cognitive abilities research on the future use and interpretation of intelligence tests in schools. *School Psychology Review, 26,* 189–210.

National Alliance for Public Charter Schools. (2015). *Estimated number of public charter schools & students, 2014–2015.* Washington, DC: National Alliance for Public Charter Schools. Retrieved from www.publiccharters.org/wp-content/uploads/2015/02/open_closed_FINAL.pdf

Parkin, J. R., & Beaujean, A. A. (2012). The effects of Wechsler Intelligence Scale for Children –Fourth Edition cognitive abilities on math achievement. *Journal of School Psychology, 50,* 113–128.

Plucker, J. A., Burroughs, N., & Song, R. (2010). *Mind the (other) gap!* Bloomington, IN: Center for Evaluation and Education Policy, Indiana University.

Plucker, J. A., Hardesty, J., & Burroughs, N. (2013). *Talent on the sidelines: Excellence gaps and America's persistent talent underclass.* Storrs, CT: Center for Education Policy Analysis, Neag School of Education, University of Connecticut.

Powers, K. (2014, March). *Closing the academic achievement gap with Common Core.* Retrieved from www.aeaonline.org/blogs/closing-academic-achievement-gap-common-core

Rogers, J., Terriquez, V., Valladares, S., & Oakes, J. (2006). *California educational opportunity report 2006: Roadblocks to college.* Los Angeles, CA: UCLA IDEA. Retrieved from http:// idea.gseis.ucla.edu/publications/eor-06/EOR-2006.pdf

RTI International. (n.d.). *The 2013 Broad Prize for Public Charter Schools: Aspire Public Schools California.* Los Angeles, CA: The Eli and Edythe Broad Foundation. Retrieved from www. broadprize.org/pdfs/CA_Aspire_PDFTBP2013.pdf

University of California, Berkeley, Office of Undergraduate Admissions. (n.d.). *How Berkeley selects students.* Retrieved from http://admissions.berkeley.edu/selectsstudents

Warne, R. T., Yoon, M., & Price, C. J. (2014). Exploring the various interpretations of "test bias." *Cultural Diversity and Ethnic Minority Psychology, 20,* 570–582.

Weingarten, R. (2011, August). Are we testing too much? *The Huffington Post.* Retrieved from www.huffingtonpost.com/randi-weingarten/are-we-testing-too-much_b_876107.html

Wohlstetter, P., Smith, J., & Farrell, C. C. (2013). *Choices and challenges: Charter school performance in perspective.* Cambridge, MA: Harvard Education Press.

Worrell, F. C. (2003). Why are there so few African Americans in gifted programs? In C. C Yeakey & R. D. Henderson (Eds.), *Surmounting the odds: Education, opportunity, and society in the new millennium* (pp. 423–454). Greenwich, CT: Information Age.

Worrell, F. C. (2013, November). *Gifted education's focus on bias in identification: Misinformed and misdirected.* Distinguished Scholar Award address at the annual meeting of the National Association for Gifted Children, Indianapolis, IN.

Worrell, F. C., Brabeck, M. M., Dwyer, C. A., Geisinger, K. F., Marx, R. W., Noell, G. H., & Pianta, R. C. (2014). *Assessing and evaluating teacher education programs.* Washington, DC: American Psychological Association.

Worrell, F. C., & Roberson, C. C. B. (2016). 2014 Standards for educational and psychological testing: Implications for ethnic minority youth. In S. L. Graves, Jr. & J. J. Blake (Eds.), *Psychoeducational assessment and intervention for ethnic minority youth: Evidence-based approaches* (pp. 41–57). Washington, DC: American Psychological Association.

16 The Implications of Societal Changes for Fairness Assessment

Neil J. Dorans and Linda L. Cook[1]

On the evening of April 15, 1997, baseball and softball teams in stadiums throughout America commemorated the 50th anniversary of the breaking of the color barrier in professional baseball by Jackie Robinson. At Quarry Field, in Hopewell Township, New Jersey, a simple ceremony was held that brisk evening. One of the players in attendance was a descendent of Branch Rickey, the general manager of the Brooklyn Dodgers who knew that Robinson possessed both the athletic skill and the character to break the color barrier. She watched this ceremony from one of the two benches and then went on to play the game. On a grander scale at Shea Stadium in New York City, President Bill Clinton, Jackie's wife Rachel, and other family members were on hand to observe Major League Baseball retire Robinson's uniform number, 42. President Clinton's remarks at the occasion included:

> Today, I think every American should say a special word of thanks to Jackie Robinson and to Branch Rickey and to the members of the Dodger team who made him one of their own and proved that America is a bigger, stronger, richer country when we all work together and give everybody a chance. And today I think we should remember that Jackie Robinson's legacy did not end with baseball; for afterward, he spent the rest of his life trying to open other doors and keep them open for all kinds of people. He knew that education, not sports, was the key to success in life for nearly everyone. And he took that message to young people wherever he went.
>
> (Clinton, 1997, p. 444)

Robinson's number was retired 50 years after he broke the color barrier. Much had changed over those five decades, in professional sports and in society. Society lagged behind professional baseball, which was fully integrated by 1959. The Civil Rights legislation of the mid-1960s had eliminated much *de jure* segregation. Societal change came much slower. By 2016, however, as the first Black man elected President of the United States neared the end of his second term in office, much *de facto* change had occurred.

Since its inception, the United States has undergone broad societal changes over long periods of time with quite different rates of change in different regions of the country affecting different members of society. Any attempt to contrast two time periods is likely to be an oversimplification. Having stated that caveat, it is instructive to consider social changes that occurred during the 1960s (Patterson, 2012). Compared to today, American society in the 1950s was characterized by conformity and an adherence to expectations. An individual tended to know his or her "proper place" and those places were in part determined by race, creed, sex, and ethnic background. Stability in society was much more important than the rights of the individual, especially those of color. In the mid-1960s, the various rights movements gained traction, led by advocates of the civil rights for what was regarded as the most downtrodden group, the Black community. Soon society was segmented into many hyphenated-American subgroups.

The changes that occurred in the mid-1960s were rather dramatic, as noted by Patterson (2012), and eventually affected the measurement profession, which started to focus on subgroups of test takers. The fairness procedures that evolved during the 1970s and 1980s reflected this emphasis on the rights of subgroups of Americans—whether the subgroup was defined as African American, Hispanic American, or Asian American—and the rights of other groups, such as females and individuals with disabilities.

Part I of this volume includes two chapters that examine existing strategies for designing, developing, and administering fair assessments. It also includes chapters that describe techniques to detect unfairness in scoring assessments and in the fair use of scores. Sinharay (this volume, Chapter 6) summarizes the contents of these four chapters and includes points that he believed should have been included in the chapters.

The classes of unfairness detection methods described in Part I were designed to be used where the conditions of measurement permit direct comparisons of test takers. As noted by Thissen (this volume, Chapter 11), Part II considers the fairness of assessments in a variety of distinct settings that are typically carried out by different groups of professionals who might not realize that they share something in common. Thissen stitches these different settings together such that they can be viewed as distinct manifestations of an underlying theme: linking scores in the absence of common measurement conditions.

Chapters in Part III of the volume considers derived scores, which could easily be viewed as a misuse of scores, the legal context surrounding assessment issues, and alternative philosophical perspectives on fairness as they pertain to fair assessment. Worrell (this volume, Chapter 15) notes the ongoing concern with the achievement gap, which in essence focuses on differences in test performance between hyphenated subgroups of Americans. He also notes that the existence of subgroup differences does not in itself mean that the use of the test is unfair.

The statistical approaches that have been in place for decades, as described by Penfield (this volume, Chapter 4) and Liu and Dorans (this volume, Chapter 5), focus on comparing groups that are believed to be comparable on the construct of interest. The procedures have been used primarily to examine fairness in subgroups defined by race/ethnicity and gender. These statistical approaches, as noted earlier, evolved from a sociopolitical milieu in which much emphasis was given to groups of Americans who were believed to have been discriminated against in the past. In addition, sorting individuals into subgroups was fairly straightforward back then.

Before the Civil Rights legislation of the 1960s began to take effect and transform the United States from a largely segregated to a more integrated society, race/ethnicity served as a convenient surrogate for a construct that might be called opportunity to succeed in society. Interracial marriage was illegal in some southern states prior to 1965. Housing discrimination was legal. Today, intermarriage is not uncommon, and many neighborhoods are far more integrated than they were in the mid-1960s. This integration of groups that had been kept apart by social convention and legal sanctions until the latter decades of the 20th century has had consequences for the practice of detecting unfairness in items and tests.

Census data collection, for example, has become more complex. To address concerns about a rising share of "some other race" selections in earlier census, a consideration is being given to revising this question for the 2020 census. Respondents may be offered all the race and Hispanic options in one place. They could check a box to identify as White, Black, Hispanic/Latino/Spanish origin, American Indian/Alaska Native, Asian, Native Hawaiian/Other Pacific Islander, or some other race or origin. They would be offered a line under each category to supply more detail about their origin, tribe, or race. Examples of this include: German, African American, Mexican, Navajo, Asian Indian, and Samoan. The implications for DIF and other fairness analyses are profound. The surrogate, race/ethnicity, is no longer easy to measure, which impacts its efficacy as a surrogate.

A surrogate for what? Novick and Ellis (1977) examined the social and legal foundations of the group-parity concept in which the focus of fairness is on groups of people. They rejected group parity as socially undesirable, and questioned its consistency with fundamental constitutional principles. They suggested what they perceived as a socially desirable and constitutionally acceptable selection strategy based on formal statistical decision theory. Rather than defining groups on the basis of race, sex, or ethnicity, they preferred to use the relative advantage or disadvantage experienced by a person and to measure the utility of the contribution to society that can be expected from that person as a result of any particular allocation of resources or comparative advantage. They noted that a major implication for the field of educational and psychological measurement was the need to include the measurement of individual disadvantage and individual utilities. It remains a major need. The integration that has occurred since the mid-1960s that has seriously diminished the value of using race/ethnicity as a readily available surrogate. It has had another consequence, as well. Perhaps the time has come to shift the focus from groups to individuals by placing an emphasis on the individual's advantage or disadvantage, an individual attribute that is more malleable than race, ethnicity, gender, or disability.

Note

1. The views expressed are those of the author and not necessarily those of the Educational Testing Service.

References

Clinton, W. R. (1997). Remarks in Queens celebrating the 50th anniversary of Jackie Robinson's integration of Major League Baseball April 15, 1997. *Public Papers of the Presidents of the United States: William J. Clinton, 1997.* Retrieved from www.gpo.gov/fdsys/pkg/PPP-1997-book1/pdf/PPP-1997-book1-doc-pg444.pdf

Novick, M. R., & Ellis, D. D. (1977). Equal opportunity in educational and employment selection. *American Psychologist, 32,* 306–320.

Patterson, J. T. (2012). *The eve of destruction: How 1965 transformed America.* New York: Basic Books.

Author Index[1]

Abedi, J. 160, 176
Ackerman, T. A. 104
Agresti, A. 68
Alfonso, V. C. 285
Algina, J 68, 103
Allalouf, A. 190, 191–194, 196, 206, 210
Almond, R. G. 14, 98
Amrein-Beardsley, A. 44, 232
Angoff, W. H. 57, 59, 117, 190, 212
Ariely, G. 193
Aristotle 272, 277, 279
Audard, C. 274
Aud, S. 283
Ayotte, K. 182

Baer, J. 182
Baker, E. L. 232, 283, 285
Baker, F. B. 68
Baldi, S. 182
Ballou, D. 143, 231
Bandeira de Mello, V. 233
Barton, P. E. 283
Bartram, D. 120
Baumer, M. 122
Baydoun, R. B. 114
Beaujean, A. A. 285
Beimers, J. N. 227
Bejar, I. I. 69
Bell, C. A. 153
Beller, M. 191
Ben-Dov, N. 39
Benitez, I. 196
Bennett, R.E. 122–123
Bentham, J. 278
Berberoglu, G. 189
Berger, K. 42
Bergstrom, B. A. 120

Berliner, D. C. 44
Bertenthal, M. W. 111, 203, 233
Betebenner, D. W. 145–146
Billeaud, K. 203
Blazer, C. 119
Bleistein, C. A. 104
Bock, R. D. 204
Bohle, B. 208
Boldt, R. F. 189
Borsboom, D. 143
Bowers, M. J. 255
Bowles, M. 183
Braddy, P. W. 193
Branch, T. 4
Brandt, D. 142
Braun, H. 232
Breland, R. L. 116
Brennan, R. L. 80, 117, 125, 127, 142, 188,
    191, 205, 209, 247–250
Breyer, F. J. 62
Bridgeman, B. 62, 122
Briggs, D. C. 143, 146, 208
Brigham, C. 2–3
Brooks, T. 119–120
Bryden, P. 14
Buckendahl, C. W. 192
Bugbee, A. C. 114
Bunkley, N. 255
Burroughs, N. 283
Buzick, H. M. 135, 153, 172, 176
Byrne, B. M. 193

Cahalan-Laitusis, C. 174
Cahn, M. F. 78–79, 127
Camara, W. J. 57, 174, 227
Camilli, G. 29, 57, 59–61, 111–112, 116
Caro, R. 4

1 Index commissioned and approved by Routledge

Subject Index[1]

National Governors Association 142
National Merit Scholarship Corporation
(NMSC) 271, 277–278
National Research Council 224–226
Newsweek 208
New York 257
New York Standardized Testing Act 1980
(STA) 256
Nixon, President Richard 4
No Child Left Behind Act 2002 (NCLB) 159,
217, 227, 239
Nozick, Robert 272–273, 275, 277–279

odds ratio 60, 68–69
opportunity to learn 144, 170, 240, 244,
268–270
Organization for Economic Co-operation
and Development (OECD) 182

paper-and-pencil scores (P&P) 113, 115,
118
parents 171, 221, 243, 254, 256–257, 259,
287, 288
Parks, Rosa 3–4
Partnership for Assessment of Readiness
for College and Careers 142, 227, 228,
260
performance levels 149–152
Phoenix Newspapers Inc. v. Keegan (2001)
257
prediction invariance 77–78, 87–88, 94,
104–105
predictive equivalence: establishing 128;
fairness properties, as 118, 205;
interchangeable scores 207; meaning 116,
188
principles for fairness: application 16; design
106; difference 274–275; fair equal
opportunity 275; general 24; Guidelines
for Fair Tests and Communications
16–17; justice, on 273–274; philosophical
perspectives on 267; universal design (UD)
161–162, 287
privacy 43, 246, 256–257, 259
proctoring 7, 34–35, 38, 43, 45–46
proxy test takers 37–39
PSAT/NMSQT 270–271, 277–278
Psychometric Committee (2001) 250
Psychometric Entrance Test (PET, Israel)
190

quadratic-weighted Kappa 64, 73
quality control 84, 97, 105, 209

R Core Team 146
rater consistency 62–64, 67, 103
Rawls, John 215, 272–280, 288–290
Reagan, President Ronald 4
Reform Support Network 230
Rehabilitation Act (1973) 159, 239
Rene v. Reid (2001) 243
Robinson, Jackie 3, 295
Robinson, Rachel 295
reviewers 17, 24–26, 99, 139
Roosevelt, President Franklin 3
Roosevelt, President Theodore 2
RTI International 288

Sanger, Margaret 2
Saxe, John Godfrey 163
Sch. Dist. of Grand Rapids v. Ball (1985)
259
Scholastic Aptitude Tests (SAT) 2–3, 125;
see also ACT-SAT concordances
score comparability: fairness, and 111, 116;
individualized determinations 247–248
languages, different 185–188, 190, 209;
mode of administration, and 122–124;
population size 211; proving 251; threats
to 120–121, 245–246
score equating 78, 83–84, 113–114, 188;
requirements 79, 86
Score Equity Assessment (SEA) 77–84, 93,
104–105, 127, 207
score interpretation: aim 99; comparability
110; fairness in 104–106; subpopulations
92–93, 97; test administration 33, 35, 100;
threats to 52; *see also* differential
prediction; factorial invariance
score linking 77–79, 92–93, 112, 219
scoring: automated 55–56, 69–73; averaging
222; bias 227; human scorers 26–29, 99,
102–104, 106; interpretation/use
arguments 219–221, 225; multiple–choice
56; pattern 258; quality control 97; rater
consistency 62–63; rubrics 55, 217;
standardization 100, 284; unfairness,
detecting 7; value added estimates 231;
vendor 51
Shaw, George Bernard 2
Smarter Balanced Assessment Consortium
16, 142, 227, 228
staffing 37–41, 101
standard setting: college and career readiness
226–229; due process 241; faulty 226;
judgmental 217–218, 221–222, 224–225,
227; parallel 192, 211; process 150–151